DIPLOMATS IN

SMITHSONIAN INSTITUTION PRESS

BUCKSKINS

A History of Indian Delegations in Washington City

HERMAN J. VIOLA

Washington, D.C. 1981

Library of Congress Cataloging in Publication Data
Viola, Herman J
   Diplomats in buckskins.

  Bibliography: p.
  Includes index.
  1.   Indians of North America—Government
relations. I. Title.
E93.V784   323.1′197′073   80-607804
ISBN 0-87474-944-1

To John C. Ewers, friend and mentor

CONTENTS

PREFACE

Perhaps no aspect of American history has captured the popular imagination more than the image of Indians in war paint and feathers lashing out in desperate attempts to keep the white man at bay. The Indians fought hard and well to protect their traditional way of life, and their inspired resistance to white encroachment has made places like Tippecanoe and the Little Big Horn as much a part of our American heritage as the Alamo and Sutter's Mill. But the focus on warfare overlooks other important areas in this clash of cultures. One of these, perhaps less brutal but no less bitter, is the series of conferences that took place in the nation's capital when Indian leaders met with government officials and tried through diplomacy to defend tribal interests from national desires. The story of these delegations is fascinating, filled with humor and sadness, color and drama, promises made and treaties broken.

Delegations have been a major component of Indian-white relations since the first Europeans reached the shores of North America. The officials of Jamestown colony invited neighboring chiefs to a conference to negotiate a peace; then they poisoned the entire delegation. Later delegations may have faced less dire personal perils, but they endured their share of political and cultural pressures. The French, Spanish, and English escorted Indian leaders to their respective capitals both to overawe them and to acquire their friendship for religious, economic, and military purposes. The United States, following its successful struggle for independence, continued this practice of inviting Indian delegations to visit large cities. The new republic could ill afford a prolonged war with the powerful tribes arrayed along its borders, and the policy of hosting important chiefs and warriors at the national capital proved a relatively inexpensive yet effective means of convincing them of the folly of resisting the hegemony and territorial designs of the United States. After meeting the president, being showered with gifts and attention, and then inspecting battleships and forts, even the most militant chieftains could not fail to be impressed by the power and wealth of the new nation.

No doubt many of the Indians never suspected the true purpose behind the reception they received. For most of them being a delegate was a valued opportunity to convey personally the wishes and needs of their people to the president of the United States, and they believed their conversations with him and other officials were being conducted in an atmosphere of mutual trust and respect. "I am a man, and you are another," declared Black Hawk, the Sac leader, upon meeting President Andrew Jackson in 1833. A similar pride was expressed by Flat Mouth of the Chippewas when, in an audience with Franklin Pierce some twenty years later, he said: "Two great men have met."[1]

Unfortunately, this sense of brotherhood and equality was not always felt by the government officials in Washington. For the most part, they were patronizing and insincere in their dealings with the Indian visitors. They humored, cajoled, and tolerated the delegates, whose culture they viewed with a mixture of contempt and curiosity. Few Washingtonians were as blatant in their racism as the southern congressmen who generated a minor tempest in 1827 because the commissioner of Indian affairs had addressed the members of a Cherokee delegation as "gentlemen."[2] However, even whites supposedly friendly to the Indians regarded them more as objects of pity and philanthropy than as a proud people with a rich cultural heritage of their own.

Although I have tried to make this history as objective and comprehensive as possible, I have faced certain insurmountable problems. One is the dearth of Indian source material. Efforts to use Indian oral history were not entirely successful because of the prevailing suspicion and mistrust of non-Indians, but I did obtain some valuable insights from Indian informants. For the most part, however, I have had to rely on printed and manuscript sources for the Indian side of the story. Such sources are at best a poor substitute; the events that whites chose to record are often anecdotal, and observers stressed outrageous or humorous incidents that portray the Indian delegates as either fools or scoundrels. Equally suspect are the many interviews with Indian delegates that were printed in the newspapers. Since almost all the statements purporting to be direct quotations were obtained through interpreters, one has to question whether the accounts were the product of the delegates, the interpreters, or the reporters. A few of the early delegates were literate enough to record their own versions of what transpired in Washington, but these individuals were usually mixed-bloods well on the road to assimilation into white society; their experiences were by no means typical.

Another problem is the result of nineteenth-century racial attitudes. Most whites regarded Indians as inferior, uncivilized peoples who could be uplifted only to the extent that they adopted white values and habits. This attitude permeates almost everything they wrote about Indians, including those who visited the East. Because I relied heavily on white sources and because I have tried to let the participants tell the story in their own words, the narrative is colored by terminology some readers may find offensive. This I regret. Nevertheless, I have not attempted to lay blame on any person or group or to soften accounts of excesses by whites or Indians. I do ask the reader to bring an open mind to this book and to avoid imposing twentieth-century values on nineteenth-century events: it is difficult to understand the present without a thorough knowledge of the past, warts and all.

The delegation story is not always pretty. Many of the whites who were involved with the delegations were not individuals of the best moral character. The exploitation and manipulation of the delegates was unconscionable, and the swindlers' harvest attracted participants from all walks of life. The Indians had their weaknesses as well, and women was one of them. Prostitutes did a flourishing business with some of the delegations. The extent of this traffic is unknown, but there is enough evidence to suggest that it was more widespread than government officers cared to admit. Alcohol was another temptation to which many of the delegates succumbed. A few delegations consumed so much liquor that one has to wonder if the members had a sober moment. In fact, this liberal use of alcohol by Indian visitors to Washington should raise questions about the validity of several important treaties negotiated with them.

Even if alcohol were not a factor, one has to question the legitimacy of treaties arranged in Washington between government officials and Indians on their first visit to a large urban area. The culture shock alone could have impaired judgments without the additional confusion caused by the limitations of the interpreters, the desire of the Indians to please hosts seemingly so generous and hospitable, and the probable inability of the delegates to comprehend fully, under the best of circumstances, the ultimate significance of the agreements. Black Hawk spoke for all Indians when he declared in his remarkable autobiography: "What do we know of the manner of the laws and customs of the white people? They might buy our bodies for dissection, and we would touch the goose quill to confirm it, without knowing what we are doing."[3]

Bleak as the record may be, Indians did benefit from their eastern visits. Going to Washington was seldom a once-in-a-lifetime experience. A number of Indian leaders were frequent visitors. Red Cloud, for instance, made a dozen trips to the capital. With each visit, the Indians became more adept at dealing with the government. Most of the tribes eventually developed a cadre of leaders who could deal effectively with the white community. Admittedly, the learning experience was painful and left many of the tribes bereft of land, culture, and language. Nonetheless, the bewildered "savages" who had to be led by the hand about the capital and its environs have since become some of the most sophisticated lobbyists on the Washington scene. Indians are perhaps second only to the environmentalists in their ability to have favorable legislation introduced and enacted. As one Indian spokesman so aptly put it, "Before the white man came the Indians had the buffalo and the buffalo gave them everything they needed—food, shelter, clothing. The white man came and took the buffalo away, but he gave the Indians the government and now . . . that is their buffalo."[4]

The focus of this book is the delegation story in the nineteenth century. In part this focus is accidental, in part deliberate. Since delegations were official government undertakings, the essential documentation is to be found in the federal records in the National Archives, primarily the records of the Office of the Secretary of War and the Bureau of Indians Affairs. Those records, however, date only from 1800 because of a fire that year in the War Department building. In the second place, the nature and purpose of delegations had largely changed by 1900. No longer were Indians being paraded about eastern cities to gape in wonder at the marvels of the white man's world. Indeed, most of the tribes by 1900 were adapting, with varying degrees of success, to a new way of life determined by the firm and heavy hand of the Bureau of Indian Affairs.

This book would have been impossible without the assistance and encouragement of many people. John C. Ewers, senior scientist in the Department of Anthropology at the Smithsonian Institution, took time from his own work to read and comment on each chapter. His generous criticisms combined candor and humor while offering leads to obscure but important publications discovered over a lifetime of research in western history. I owe much to his advice and support.

The assistance of Robert M. Kvasnicka, colleague and friend on the staff of the National Archives, has also been invaluable. Whenever I needed a citation, an essential document, or the verification of a fact, it was Bob who always willingly came to my rescue. His thorough knowledge of federal Indian policy and the records that document it strengthened all the many drafts of the manuscript and saved me from numerous errors.

Special thanks are due to the staff of the National Anthropological Archives at the Smithsonian Institution. Michele Albert, Nigel Elmore, Paula Richardson Fleming, James R. Glenn, Carolyn James, Elaine Mills, and Vyrtis Thomas listened patiently to my delegation stories and always kept a sharp eye for any information that might be useful to my research. I am especially grateful to Michele Albert, who accepted without

12

complaint the challenge of typing the manuscript.

The welcome assistance of F. P. Prucha, S. J., and Jan Shelton Danis (who prepared the index) must also be acknowledged. They read the manuscript and offered their usual perceptive comments and editorial advice.

I owe a large debt of gratitude to my library science students at Catholic University who researched specific delegations. Their efforts made the story more comprehensive than otherwise would have been possible. Among those who deserve recognition are Devereux Clarke, Martha Crawley, Joanne Elliot, Kent R. Giffiths, Elizabeth Elaine Hartman, Rebecca A. Heller, Signe Larson, Robert L. MacKnight, Calista Moon, Barbara T. Newcombe, Vanessa J. Piala, and Erika E. Stokes.

Several research assistants helped me comb Washington newspapers and the extensive records of the Bureau of Indian Affairs at the National Archives. These include Theodore Bleeker, Kathleen Collier, Deborah A. Harsch, Karen Holman, Marilyn Harsch Jackson, and Joyce Park Rhodes. I am especially grateful to Ann J. Brickfield, who performed a multitude of important, time-consuming chores that enabled me to complete the manuscript before doomsday.

I am also grateful to those members of the Indian community who shared ideas and delegation experiences with me. These include Billie Burke, George Horse Capture, Henry Old Coyote, Joseph Medicine Crow, Dixie Davis, Frank Ducheneaux, Gerald Red Elk, Michael Her Many Horses, and Reeves and Clydia Nahwooksy.

The staff of the Branch of Tribal Services at the Bureau of Indian Affairs took particular interest in this book. I would especially like to acknowledge the assistance and support of Robert Pennington, the branch chief. Others who deserve special mention for sharing their knowledge of present-day delegations are Arlene Brown, Mitchell L. Bush, Jr., Robert Farring, Jr., Leslie M. Gay, Dennis Petersen, Evelyn Pickett, John "Bud" Shapard, Michael Smith, James Thomas, and Chizu Toda.

The staffs and collections of numerous libraries and manuscript repositories have served me well. I wish to acknowledge my appreciation to the librarians of the Smithsonian Institution, especially Carolyn Hahn, Jack Marquardt, and Janette Saquet. At the National Archives so many individuals assisted me that it is impossible to list them all. Those who deserve special recognition are Samella Anderson, George Chalou, Jerry Clark, Richard Crawford, Robert Fowler, Edward E. Hill, Sara Dunlop Jackson, Renee Jaussaud, Marie Jones, Maria Joy, Frederick Pernell, George P. Perros, Jane Smith, Joe Thomas, Phil Ward, and Victoria Washington. Valuable assistance was also provided by the staffs of the Beinecke Library of Yale University, the British Museum, the Columbia Historical Society, the Indiana State Historical Society, the Library of Congress, the Martin Luther King Memorial Library, the Newberry Library, the Oklahoma Historical Society, the Public Archives of Canada, the Public Record Office of Great Britain, and the State Historical Society of Wisconsin.

I would also like to recognize the contributions of the following individuals: Allan J. Clark, R. David Edmonds, James Goode, Harry Kelsey, Margaret Klapthor, Frank L. Klement, Victor E. Krantz, Harold Moore, Floyd A. O'Neil, Gary Roberts, Carolyn Sung, and James Wallace.

I wish to extend my thanks to the staff of the Smithsonian Institution Press. In particular I would like to express my appreciation to Bess DeBeck, John Harris, Maureen Jacoby, Stephen Kraft, Felix Lowe, and Edward Rivinus.

I am especially grateful to S. Dillon Ripley, Secretary of the Smithsonian Institution, for the research grants that enabled me to employ research assistants and to visit archives in Canada and Great Britain.

Finally, I wish to acknowledge the understanding, loyalty, enthusiasm, and encouragement of my family—Susan, Joseph, Paul, and Peter.

1 PROLOGUE: DELEGATIONS IN
THE COLONIAL PERIOD

Delegations became an important component of Indian-white relations during the colonial wars of empire in the late seventeenth century. Indians had visited the royal courts of Europe before that time, of course. Columbus, in fact, returned to Spain with nine Indians after his first voyage to the New World. But these Indians were curiosities, living proof that a New World had indeed been found; they were not tribal ambassadors. In the century that followed, hundreds of Indians were carried overseas. Most were sold into slavery to recoup the expenses of the early voyages of discovery. Not until the colonial powers recognized the value of Indian friendship and support did delegations in the true sense become an established method of conducting business with the peoples of the New World. As France, Spain, and England carved their empires out of the North American wilderness, they came increasingly to view the Indians in economic, religious, and military terms. The tribes offered the Europeans wonderful opportunities for trade and religious conversion; their warriors could supply colonial armies with much-needed manpower.

Credit for initiating the practice of courting Indian friendship by bringing delegations to the mother country belongs to the French. According to John Nelson of Boston, who had been a French captive, the Bourbon rulers frequently invited to Versailles "a few of their most eminent and enterprising Indians." Nelson, writing in 1696, urged the British Board of Trade to counteract French influence among the Indians by bringing prominent chiefs to England. He predicted a few visits of this sort would "give counterpoise to the French reputation and greatness, which a sight of the City of London and of what else may be shewed them . . . will easily effect."[1]

Nelson's suggestion was not new. The British for some time had tried without success to persuade tribal leaders to visit London. The reluctance of the Indians to venture overseas may have been the product of long-standing mistrust of the British, for the history of Indian-white relations in the American colonies had not been one to inspire trust and confidence. In 1623, for instance, officials at Jamestown invited the "great Kinge Apochanzion" and his leading chiefs to meet with them to negotiate a peace agreement. "After a manye fayned speches," one of the colonists later reported, "the pease was . . . concluded in a helthe or tooe in sacke which was sente of porpose in the butte . . . to poysen them." The colonist did not know the exact death toll, "but yt is thought some tooe hundred weare poysned."[2]

13

Whatever the reason, the British did not succeed in bringing a delegation of Indian leaders to London until 1710. This delegation consisted of four Mohawk sachems, known as the "Four Kings," who were brought to England by Peter Schuyler, mayor of Albany. Schuyler hoped the Mohawks could help persuade Queen Anne to support colonial plans for the invasion and conquest of French Canada. England at the time was embroiled in the War of the Spanish Succession (known in America as Queen Anne's War), and the colonists feared the mother country had lost interest in their problems. The novelty of presenting the Mohawks at court, Schuyler believed, would raise flagging interest in the colonies. The delegates included Hendrick, one of the most influential leaders of the Iroquois Confederacy, and Brant, grandfather of the celebrated Joseph Brant who was such a valuable ally of the British during the American Revolution.[3] The treatment accorded the so-called kings established a pattern for hosting Indian delegations that was followed by British leaders until the American colonies gained their independence seventy-five years later. By then the precedents had become so firmly established that the fledgling United States had little choice but to continue practices which Indian leaders expected and demanded.

Before sending the delegation to London, colonial authorities arranged for five Mohawks to visit Boston, where they could get a correct impression of British military strength. They hoped the visit would reassure the Mohawks that they had selected the right side in the forthcoming struggle with the French. The report of Colonel Samuel Vetch, the grand strategist for the planned invasion of Canada and the person responsible for the subsequent visit to England, makes it obvious that no opportunity was lost to impress the Mohawks with British power and resources. The Indians, Vetch wrote, "have seen All our Regiments In Arms, Exercise & fire, which they performe Equally to most In the service; yesterday we shewed them the Castle, with fireing Bombs & great guns, and the five men of warr and All the transports In All their glory." As a special touch to the martial display, the Indians were placed in a small dinghy in the center of a great circle formed by the five battleships, whereupon "All of them fired, first from their topps & decks In platoons, and then with their great guns upon one an other untill we were all lost In Smoak." The demonstration had the desired effect. Vetch claimed the Mohawks urged him to launch the attack at once, "saying we have already too manie Men to take All Canada." Before the chiefs left Boston, each received an army uniform "lac'd with true gold & silver lace, made as ours."[4]

When Queen Anne failed to provide the anticipated military support, the colonial authorities decided to send a Mohawk delegation overseas. The purpose behind the visit was not to impress the Indians, however. That had been accomplished in Boston. This visit was to impress the crown with the urgency of supporting an attack on Canada.

The delegates reached London in April 1710 and secured lodgings at the Two Crowns and Cushions on King Street. Their host was Thomas Arne, an upholsterer as well as innkeeper, who so pleased the Indians with his attentions they gave him a name— Cadaroque, after the French fort—during a Mohawk christening ceremony. Among his kindnesses, Arne introduced the delegates to beds, something the Mohawks had never used.[5]

The Mohawks pursued a staggering schedule. Their most important appointment, of course, was the audience with Queen Anne on April 19. Speaking through their interpreter, a cousin of Peter Schuyler, the Mohawks made an impassioned plea for assistance. "We have undertaken a long and tedious Voyage, which none of our Predecessors could ever be prevail'd upon to undertake," they declared. "The Motive that induc'd us was, that we might see our *Great Queen*, and relate to Her those things we thought absolutely necessary for the Good of *Her* and us Her Allies." The chiefs, obviously well coached by their patrons, told Queen Anne that the capture of Canada would bring England important economic benefits, for the Mohawks would then be able to conduct "a great Trade with Our *Great Queen*'s Children." If the queen did not see the wisdom in this, they warned, "we must, with our Families, forsake our Country and seek other Habitations, or stand Neuter; either of which will be much against our Inclinations." The chiefs concluded their remarks with an appeal for missionaries, and then they presented Anne with several belts of wampum. She, in turn, ordered gifts for her American visitors and directed that their entertainment while in England be at her expense.[6]

Thanks to her generosity, the Mohawks enjoyed a round of social and diplomatic activities normally bestowed on foreign potentates. They paid a courtesy call on the Duke of Ormande and with him reviewed four troops of the Life Guard at Hyde Park; they appeared before the Commissioners for Trade and Plantations, and they were entertained by an association of New England and New York merchants; they rode the queen's barge to Greenwich, where they viewed the hospital and toured the yard and dock at Woolwich; they visited Bethlehem Hospital in Moor Fields and the Work-House at Bishopsgate; they had an audience with the Bishop of Norwich, and they heard a sermon at St. James's Chapel by the Lord Bishop of London; and they dined with William Penn at the Devil Tavern in Charing Cross.

No matter where the Mohawks went, however, they were besieged by crowds. Such popularity could not be left unexploited. The day after the Indians had their royal audience, a London theater informed the public that they would attend the April 24 performance of the play "The Old Bachelor." The play was later changed to "Macbeth," but this made no difference. It was the Indians the patrons came to see. When the throng in the gallery discovered they could not see the Mohawks, the performance had to be halted until the Indians took seats on the stage. The play must have been financially successful despite the uproar, for it inspired imitation by other entrepreneurs. According to advertisements in the London press heralding forthcoming events, the Mohawks attended several plays and operas, a cockfight, a Punch and Judy show, a display of swordsmanship, and a few theatricals of questionable taste.[7]

Somehow during their hectic schedule, the sachems found time to sit for their portraits, launching a tradition that continued until the twentieth century. The artist John Verelst received £100 plus "office ffees" from Queen Anne for executing full-length portraits of each delegate for display at Kensington Palace. These were the finest likenesses of the Mohawks. Numerous other likenesses were also produced, each purporting to be an authorized copy of the official portraits. These claims prompted Verelst to deny giving anyone permission to copy his portraits. "If he should," the artist announced, "he would take Care to have it correctly done by a skilful Hand, and inform the Publick thereof." The skillful hand he eventually selected belonged to John Simon, a Huguenot engraver, who produced a set of handsome, full-length mezzotints measuring approximately twenty by twelve inches. The sachems later received a set of the prints, framed in glass, for display in their "castle" in Onondaga, New York.[8]

The rage for Mohawk memorabilia was not confined to engravings. Londoners caught up in the excitement over the Indians purchased broadsides, pamphlets, ballads. Indeed, almost anything relating to the "Four Kings," no matter how trivial, found a market. The Mohawks did not impress everyone, however. Daniel Defoe, author of *Robinson Crusoe*, called the visit a "Fools Errand" and criticized his countrymen for making heroes of people "always esteem'd as the most Desperate, and most Cruel of the Natives of *North-America*."[9]

The Mohawks left England in early May, after a visit of about four weeks, and reached Boston harbor in mid-July. The fruits of the trip probably exceeded all expectations. Queen Anne sent a medal and twenty silver coins to each of the five tribes in the Iroquois Confederacy. The coins, forerunners of the "peace medals" of a later generation, bore the queen's likeness and the royal coat of arms. For the chapel at Onondaga named for her, she sent rich furnishings and a set of communion plates. More important, Anne pressed her colonial contest with France with renewed vigor, and she took greater notice of England's Indian allies. Nor were the spiritual needs of the Mohawks forgotten. In 1712 the Society for the Propagation of the Gospel in Foreign Parts resumed its missionary activity among the Mohawks, even though an earlier effort had produced less than dramatic results. These benefits may have been forthcoming without the Indian delegation, of course. Such considerations aside, the visit is important for the bond of friendship established between the Iroquois Confederacy and England. According to one British historian, "It is, on the whole, fair to think that the link formed by this long, strange journey of these foreign envoys became one, and not the weakest one, in the chain of loyalty of Indian to England."[10]

The treatment accorded the Mohawks was not unusual for Indians visiting European capitals in this era of intense colonial rivalry. The French, whose holdings in North America greatly depended upon native allegiance and support, lavished their Indian visitors with gifts and accolades. A well-documented example is the delegation of 1725, which was sponsored and organized by the French India Company in an effort to combat Spanish competition for Indian friendship and trade in the Mississippi Valley. It was hoped the visit would impress the delegates with French power and keep them loyal. A few of the delegates seem to have had their own reasons for undertaking the hazardous journey. The tribes of the Illinois Confederacy—Cahokia, Kaskaskia, Michigamea, Moingwena, Peoria, and Tamaroa—wanted the French to protect them from the Fox Indians, their aggressive neighbors to the north in present-day Wisconsin.[11]

Some two dozen Indians accepted the invitation to assemble at Mobile Bay in April 1725. Plans seemed to be progressing smoothly until the vessel selected to carry the delegation capsized during loading. Not only was there a two-month delay until another ship could be secured, but most of the delegates decided against ocean travel. Seven Indians eventually agreed to the trip: Chicagou, a young chief of the Illinois Confederacy; four representatives of the Oto, Missouri, and Osage tribes; a slave; and a woman who was the mistress of a French official.[12]

Like the Mohawks in London, the Indians were the toast of Paris and enjoyed a round of activities that would have exhausted the hardiest tourist. At the Hôtel des Invalides they marveled at the great copper vats and roasting spits in the kitchen. "Were there enough men in France to eat all that meat?" they inquired. The opera so delighted the delegates they asked to see it again. But it was the fountains at Versailles that pleased them most. According to a report in the *Mercure de France*, "their astonishment at the beauty of the things they had seen was inexpressible."[13]

The Indians were in France two months before meeting Louis XV, then a lad of fifteen. This made no difference to the artless delegates, who spoke as if they were in the presence of the Supreme Being. "You are like a beautiful rising star that sparkles in a lovely sky where there are absolutely no clouds," declared Chicagou. "I no longer regret having suffered so much and having left my wife, my children, and all my Nation, because today I see the Father of all the French in the midst of his Chiefs. I myself am a Chief and am well thought of in my Nation; but I now see that I am nothing in comparison to you, to whom so many Chiefs and as many people as there are trees in our forests give their obedience." The other chiefs, speaking in turn, asked for protection from their enemies and for "Black Robes" to instruct them. "Those whom you designate will be our leaders," avowed the Osage, Oto, and Missouri delegates. "Our lands have been yours for a long time; do not abandon them." Upon concluding their remarks, the Indians removed their headdresses and placed them and their pipes, clubs, and bows and arrows at the king's feet. "This act of homage, which could not have been more complete or submissive," declared an observer, "was accompanied by oaths in the name of all their Nations. Everyone found these acts to be in new and singular taste and spoke of them as showing great imagination and understanding."[14]

A bountiful supply of presents rounded out the delegation ritual. The India Company gave the delegates complete suits of clothes—blue dress coats with silver lace and buttons, red jackets trimmed with silver, red knee breeches, and plumed hats. The "savagesse" received a flame-colored dress with a gold flower design, a hoop petticoat, two corsets, six blouses, six pairs of puffed sleeves, "but no other ornaments because she always went bare-headed." Louis XV gave each chief a royal medallion on a gold chain, a rifle, sword, watch, and an engraving that depicted the delegation's royal audience. Upon reaching New Orleans, the Indians received additional presents from the India Company to distribute to their people.[15]

The delegation presumably had the desired effect, for the Illinois Confederacy and other midwestern tribes remained loyal to France and served it well in the colonial wars that soon engulfed North America. Individually, the delegates were less fortunate. One chief had died during the journey. The others, their wondrous gifts notwithstanding, found their veracity questioned upon their return. Chicagou's people discounted almost everything he said. Some thought the French had bribed him. Others insisted he had been bewitched, that "there must have been some charm which fascinated your eyes, for it is not possible that France can be such as you have painted it." His tribesmen refused to believe that buildings could be as high as the tallest trees, that people on the streets of Paris were as numerous as mosquitoes in the woods, or that the delegates had traveled about the countryside in cabins of leather pulled by horses. Chicagou's experiences were not unique. Thirty years later, the French traveler Jean-Bernard Bossu met an old Indian who had also been a member of that delegation. He told Bossu that no one would believe his descriptions of France. When told of the vast numbers of Frenchmen he had seen, his tribesmen claimed he had merely seen the same ones over and over again. Sadly, the old man now suspected that the French had in fact bewitched him and that what he had seen had only been imagined.[16]

The number of Indians who visited Europe in the eighteenth century as official tribal ambassadors was probably not large. Certainly the logistics for such undertakings were as prohibitive as the expense. Besides the "Four Kings," the British are known to have hosted a delegation of seven Cherokees from South Carolina who were taken to England in 1730 by Sir Alexander Cuming, and, four years later, a party of fourteen Creeks who were escorted by Governor James Ogelthorpe of Georgia. Joseph Brant, the staunch Mohawk ally of the British, was a frequent visitor to England during the American Revolution.[17]

But official tribal ambassadors were by no means the only Indians who visited England. As British authorities (and, presumably, the French and Spanish also) learned to their dismay, it was very difficult to keep the Indians at home once the precedent of dealing directly with the crown was established. Tribal leaders were reluctant to conduct business with lesser officials in the colonies. Furthermore, Indians who had been abroad enjoyed greater status with their people. As one colonial official noted in 1763, "Warriors who have been in England [have] a right to speak first" in council. This naturally inspired ambitious tribesmen to seek the same benefits. Even the ocean was no longer a barrier. Indians unable to arrange passage on their own could often count on the intercession of some obliging white man. These individuals expected to be handsomely rewarded for their services, of course, either from the Indians themselves or from the crown. At the very least, the Indians could be exhibited in taverns for room-and-board and pocket money once they reached Europe.[18]

The problems caused by unauthorized Indian visitors can be seen from two such groups that were in London at the same time in early 1765. Two Mohawks were being exhibited at a tavern by a man named Hyam Myers. When the Lords of Trade learned of this "scandalous" activity, they arranged to have the Indians and their patron returned to New York at public expense. The bill, including expenses for lodging, presents, and passage home, totaled £108. Myers had promised the Mohawks £100 apiece for cooperating with him, but efforts to collect the promised money were futile. According to the lieutenant governor of New York, Myers "would not Suffer us [even] to Speak to him, being afraid of being Arrested by his Creditors."[19]

Meanwhile, London authorities had to deal with another group of unauthorized Indian visitors, three Cherokees who had been brought to England by Henry Timberlake, a soldier of fortune from Hanover County, Virginia. Lieutenant Timberlake was no stranger to the delegation business. Three years earlier, "thinking he might be of service in giving them such Impressions of our wealth and power, as might hereafter produce the happiest Effects, and at the same time hoping his services might meet with some recompense," Timberlake had escorted another group of Cherokees to England under less than official circumstances. The young lieutenant fared rather well on that occasion, despite some awkward moments. His major problem had been the death at sea of the interpreter, a loss which deprived the Indians of their principal means of benefiting from the trip. The Cherokees nonetheless enjoyed the usual round of activities and received a goodly supply of clothes and presents. Timberlake not only recovered his expenses; he was awarded an additional £100 for his "trouble" in bringing the Indians to London and was promised the first vacant commission in His Majesty's forces in North America.[20]

Perhaps the success of the previous adventure, coupled with his failure to receive the promised commission, encouraged Timberlake to conduct a second group of Cherokees to England. It was not a wise decision in light of the governor of Virginia's previous refusal to give the Cherokees permission to make the trip. As it was, the only way the Indians could afford the visit was through the generosity of Timberlake's business partner, a Mr. Truehart, who bore all the expenses on the promise of reimbursement when the party reached England.[21]

The enterprise was ill-fated from the start. One of the Indians died before leaving Virginia. Another died at sea. Shortly after the party reached England, in November 1764, Truehart died, leaving Timberlake responsible for everyone's welfare. He appealed to the Lords of Trade for financial assistance, but they rejected his petitions. Complicating matters for Timberlake were the Mohawks with Myers. Their plight colored the opinion of the Lords of Trade as to his true motives. The Lords of Trade, Timberlake claimed, regarded the Cherokees as either imposters or "Indians brought over for a shew." Ironically, only when the desperate adventurer threatened to exhibit the Cherokees to meet expenses did the Lords of Trade agree to finance their return to Virginia.[22]

This news was conveyed to the governor of Virginia in March 1765. Although the Cherokees had been brought over "in a very improper manner," they were now "in danger of being deserted and exposed to the greatest distress." Therefore, the Lords of

The Three Cherokees, came over from the head of the River Savanna to London 1762.
Their Interpreter that was Poisoned.

2 Ostacite or Man killer, who sets up the War Whoop, as (Wanch Woach la la hoch Waoch) with his Wampum.

3 Austenaco or King a great Warrior who has his tulamut or Pipe, by taking a Whiff of which, is their most sacred emblem of Peace.

4 Uschesees & Great Hunter or Scalper, as the Character of a Warrior depends on the Number of Scalps he has them without Number.

An engraving depicting the three Cherokees who accompanied Lt. Henry Timberlake to England in 1762. The Cherokees are, left to right: Outacity, Austenaco, and Uschesees.

Trade decided to give the Indians some presents and send them home. They asked the governor to give the Cherokees such attentions upon their arrival "as may fix in them proper Impressions, & induce them to make just reports in their Nation, of his Majesty's Goodness to them, in relieving them from a Situation of so much danger and distress."[23]

Timberlake was not so fortunate. The experience left him spiritually and financially broken. "What in cloaths, paint, trinkets, coach-hire, and other expences, including the bill from their late lodgings (for which I was arrested, and put to considerable expence) and the time they lived with me, I had expended near seventy pounds, which I must enevitably lose," Timberlake complained after the Cherokees left for Virginia. To recover some of his money, he began writing his memoirs, but he died before completing them.[24]

Meanwhile, the House of Lords, hoping to prevent such embarrassing episodes in the future, issued a resolution condemning unauthorized delegations. Dated March 6, 1765, it declared: "That the bringing from America any of the Indians who are under his Majesty's Protection, without proper authority for so doing, may tend to give great Dissatisfaction to the Indian Nations, & be of dangerous Consequence to His Majesty's subjects in the Colonies [and] That the making of a public shew of Indians, Ignorant of such Proceedings is Unbecoming & Inhuman."[25]

This decree may have been the earliest official effort to address a problem that was never resolved. Neither edicts nor threats could keep at home Indians determined to visit the Queen Mother or Great Father. Moreover, instead of punishment for violating regulations on the subject, the uninvited visitors often received the same treatment accorded authorized delegates, a reaction that only served to reinforce the problem.

By the close of the eighteenth century, delegations had become an accepted method of conducting business with the North American Indians. The various delegations generally underwent the same experiences—sightseeing, a round of social and diplomatic appointments, and interviews with high state officials. No opportunity was lost to stress the power and resources of the host nation. As Lieutenant Timberlake noted following his visit to England in 1762, "During our voyage the Indians conceived very advantageous ideas of our naval force; the Captain having chased and brought too about sixteen sail, found them all to be English or neutral vessels, on which the Cherokees concluded the French and Spaniards were certainly afraid to put to sea."[26] Great emphasis was also placed on the benevolence, authority, and protective qualities of the crown, which asked nothing of the Indians but their loyalty and allegiance. Terms like the Queen Mother, Great Father, and Great Captain were used to denote the paternal relationship between the tribes and the European monarchs. To confirm this personal relationship, the Indians were often given pictures of the ruling monarch and special gifts bearing the royal seal.

The gifts were probably the most important aspect of the delegation experience. In aboriginal eyes the exchange of gifts held special significance, and the failure to give Indian leaders a generous supply of presents would have foredoomed these diplomatic missions. Gifts were the political cement that bound the two races in friendship. The Indians gave the Europeans land, furs, and, in time of war, men. They expected in return metal tools, weapons, clothes, and food. These the delegates received in abundance, but what they most appreciated were certain ceremonial gifts that denoted authority. In this category were medals, flags, commissions, uniforms, and canes. These gifts not only confirmed the recipient's status within a tribe, but they were also a visible sign that the conferring European nation recognized and accepted that leadership.[27]

Medals were the most important ceremonial gift. Made of solid silver and bearing the likeness of the reigning monarch, they usually came in two sizes. A large one went to the principal chief of a tribe or band, and the other size went to chiefs of lesser rank. The medals, which usually came with a large, colorful ribbon, were to be worn around the neck and were often presented with great pomp and ceremony. Silver gorgets bearing the royal seal were sometimes given to leading warriors who did not qualify for medals.

Flags were less durable than medals, but the Indians appreciated them nonetheless. The English, French, and Spanish are known to have given flags to Indian leaders. Very few of these flags have survived, however, because the chiefs would often keep them on display in their villages until they disintegrated. A Spanish official residing at St. Louis in 1779 claimed that most of the neighboring Indian villages could boast only a flagpole adorned with "some rags full of holes and patches."[28]

Commissions were printed or hand-lettered certificates. These colorful documents confirmed the recipient's chiefly status and might include a description of the circumstances for which it was awarded. The inability of illiterate Indians to read them did not diminish their importance. According to a British officer who attended a conference of Cherokee leaders in 1763, a chief showed him a "testimonial" he had received while in England from "the Great King George." The testimonial was "a Certificate of his having been at the Peace of Williamsburg in Virginia and obtained leave to go home to England in a Man of War, was graciously received there and sent back again in a Ship of War." The chief vowed that "he hath and always will take care of the same."[29]

Uniforms were also popular with the chiefs, who were delighted with the bright colors and gilt decoration. The medals and uniforms together were a combination that few impressionable natives could resist. Chief Iron Shirt of the Comanches probably strutted like a peacock after receiving his medal from Don Juan Bautista de Anza, governor of New Mexico. "I presented him [also] with a complete uniform and another suit of color in order that this insignia might be displayed with the greatest propriety and luster," Anza later reported.[30]

The Spanish also gave their loyal Indian leaders a gift that was not adopted by the other colonial powers—the cane or *bastón* (staff of office). The *bastón* was a uniquely Spanish symbol of authority used in Spanish-Indian relations in the New World as early as 1690. That year General Alonso de León gave the head chief of a Nebedache village "a staff with a cross, giving him the title of governor of all his people." The chief accepted the staff "with much pleasure, promising to do all that was desired of him."[31]

These diplomatic gifts were more than mere secular symbols of allegiance and authority. Among some of the tribes they took on religious qualities. Jean-Baptiste Truteau, a St. Louis fur trader who visited an Arikara village in 1795, noticed the head chief hung a Spanish flag at the entrance to his earth lodge and wore a medal around his neck. Inside his lodge, the chief had a Spanish commission lying on a mat and burned incense before it. "They hold such things as medals, flags, and letters in such deep veneration," Truteau explained, "that whenever these are taken from their wrappings, they are smoked [sic] and hold the most important place at their feasts."[32]

A Spanish official in New Mexico observed similar reactions among the warlike Comanche. "We would never have believed the benefit that has accrued to this province from this practice [of giving diplomatic gifts to the chiefs] if we had not seen it," he wrote in 1812. Because of the gifts, the Comanches "were placed under great obligation to us; their gratefulness continued to increase, and their esteem for the King of Spain, whom they call the general chief, has likewise increased." To get an idea of this esteem, the official continued, "one needs only to note that any appointments they receive from their [tribal] government are ignored unless they are confirmed . . . [by] our officers in the name of the general chief."[33]

By 1789 the pattern of Indian-white diplomacy had become so firmly established that the United States had to conform to colonial practices or risk offending the powerful tribes arrayed along its frontiers. No one knew this better than the first leaders of the new republic. "In the administration of the Indians," declared Henry Knox, secretary of war in the first administration, "every proper expedient that can be devised to gain their affections, and attach them to the interest of the Union, should be adopted." One expedient that had been very successsful for the British was "the practice of making the Indians presents of silver medals and gorgets, uniform clothing, and a sort of military commission." Since the Indians were now "exceedingly desirous of receiving similar gifts from the United States, for which they would willingly resign those received from the British officers," it was important for the new government to make them available. Obviously, Knox pointed out in a report to Congress, "the policy of gratifying them cannot be doubted."[34]

Confronted with the problem of establishing cordial relations with the neighboring tribes, many of which were former allies of the British, the United States adopted all the "expedients" at its disposal. The federal government issued its own medals, commissions, and uniforms. It also encouraged delegations of Indian leaders to visit the capital of the new nation, where, following a script now more than a century old, they met their new Great Father and learned firsthand about the strength and resources of the United States.

11 INVITATION TO WASHINGTON

Although delegations have been basic to the administration of Indian affairs in the United States from 1789 to the present, the reasons for them have changed greatly in that time. Traditionally, as seen in the preceding chapter, the European states used delegations to maintain the friendship and loyalty of the tribes within their spheres of influence. The United States, however, did not have to view tribal friendship in international terms. For the most part, the new republic had little to fear from foreign intervention in the conduct of its internal affairs. Its most serious crisis had occurred during the American Revolution, but even then the native peoples were not a major factor in the balance of power. Never was their loyalty or support the key to winning or losing the war with England. Although the British made extensive use of Indian auxiliaries, American policy was aimed at keeping the Indians friendly and neutral. Indians were frequent visitors to General George Washington's headquarters during the war, and he accorded them every courtesy, including parading his troops for their inspection. These attentions irritated Washington's staff, who considered the business humiliating, but the officers had to suffer in silence because, as one noted in his diary, "his Excellency deems it good policy . . . to convince them of the strength and discipline of our army, that they may be encouraged, if disposed to be friendly, or deterred from aggression, if they should become hostile to our country."[1]

The only other time in which Native American allegiance concerned the United States came during the War of 1812. This was the last real opportunity Indians had to ally themselves with a foreign power against the United States, and several tribes took advantage of it. Support for England focused in the Old Northwest and in the South, where some bands of Creeks were influenced by British overtures. Neither the British nor the Americans, however, viewed the Indians as the critical factor in the conflict. Nevertheless, the United States could not ignore threats like the following by an Iowa chief: "The time is drawing nigh when the murder is to begin, and all the Indians who will not join are to die with the Whites."[2]

Heeding the warning of William Clark, superintendent of Indian affairs at St. Louis, that a crisis was "fast approaching," the secretary of war authorized him to gather a delegation of representative chiefs and warriors for a visit to Washington. By early May 1812, Clark had assembled a massive delegation of thirty-three chiefs and warriors, four women, three boys, and eight agents and interpreters representing the tribes along the American frontier from the Great Lakes to the Arkansas River, including the Osage, Sac and Fox, Shawnee, Sioux, Iowa, and Winnebago. The party had been on the road a few weeks when Clark received word that war with England had become a reality. "Your vigilence and attention are rendered peculiarly necessary . . . at this time," the secretary of war wrote, "and no exertions or reasonable expenses will be spared to keep the Indians quiet and friendly."[3]

Although the delegation took two months to reach Washington, the Indians had little time to relax and recuperate after their arrival. Where delegations of similar size and importance might easily have spent months in the city, this one was on its way home in a matter of days. The problems of preparing the nation for war gave government officials little opportunity to do more than extend the basic courtesies to the visitors. Of highest priority was an audience with the Great Father, James Madison.[4]

The Indians received a warm welcome at the White House, where they dined with the president and his wife before hearing a stern message about the war with England. "Your father loves justice," Madison told them. "He extends it to all the red tribes. When they keep the chain of friendship with the eighteen fires bright, he will protect them, and do them good. If any make the chain bloody, it must be broken on their heads." Already Indians had murdered some of the Great Father's white children; they would be punished.

The troubles with England were the result of an old grudge, Madison explained. The British had been unhappy ever since the Americans won their freedom from the king's tyranny. Now the king wanted to retake the United States, and he hoped the Indians would help him. The British, who were weak and anxious "to decoy the red people into the war on their own side," were sending "bad birds" from Canada "with bloody belts in their beaks to drop among the red people, who would otherwise remain at peace." The red children must avoid this ruin. "Sit still on your seats," Madison urged the delegates. "Be witnesses that we are able to beat our enemies and protect our red friends."

Several chiefs accepted the invitation to speak. Their remarks must have comforted Madison and the other officials in the room, for the Indians generally expressed their support for the United States. The Blue, head chief of the Sac and Fox, agreed that the Great Father's advice was wise and good, but he could not promise all his people would heed it. "You have found it wrong that we have communication with the English," he said. "We have been in the habit of receiving presents from the English—we cannot leave them all at once—I will do my best." Clermont of the Arkansas Osages also promised neutrality: "I know the bad road from the good and know how to take the best." Dekaury of the Winnebagos admitted that some of his people joined the British at Mackinac. "You know," he said as he handed a calumet to Madison, "that among all nations some will go astray—that is the case with my nation—it has gone astray but my heart is good."

The Indians left Washington with more than the words of the Great Father to sustain them. They also had new rifles and an array of presents. The six principal chiefs, for example, each received a blue coat laced with silver, two silver epaulets, a fur-trimmed hat with a red plume, ruffled shirts, pants, socks, boots, silk and cotton handkerchiefs, a blanket, pipe, sword, and a presidential peace medal. Even the interpreters were remembered; each one got a silver pocket watch. As the Indians passed through Pittsburgh, their new clothes and weapons drew sharp criticism from the editor of the *Gazette*. He was especially disturbed about the "*first-rate Rifles*" the warriors brandished. "This information will, no doubt, be highly gratifying to the frontier people who have had their relatives & friends butchered by the tomahawk and scalping knife of the ferocious savage," he informed his readers.[5]

The delegates were evidently ineffective in keeping the midwestern tribes neutral, for the British enjoyed considerable native support in their second conflict with the United States. Even after the Treaty of Ghent, whereby the British callously abandoned their former allies, a number of the Indians continued to look to England for support and advice. In March 1816, *Niles' Weekly Register* reported that "an ambassador from the Creek Indians is . . . in London," and "the question is asked—has the late hostile dispositions of the Creeks any connection with this agency?" Three years later, the same paper reported the arrival in England of another Creek chief, "in order to lay before the British ministers the details of the sufferings of his tribe." In 1817 an American official warned of the need to counteract the impressions Indians had received from visits to Canadian cities. "I think it of the highest importance," declared Benjamin O'Fallon, agent for the tribes of the Upper Missouri, "that a few . . . [chiefs] should visit the President together with some of the most populous States and Citys to enable them to see the wealth and Population [of the United States] which they can not be induced to believe is equal to what they have seen in Canada."[6]

Although the War of 1812 had, in fact, ended any real hope the tribes may have entertained of escaping United States hegemony, the question of Indian loyalty became an issue during two other conflicts, the war with Mexico and the Civil War. The fear that Mexico would try to enlist the support of the southwestern tribes in its conflict with the United States was one of the justifications for a delegation from the Southern Plains, which included representatives from thirteen tribes, that was brought to Washington in 1846. The threat had been more imagined than real, however. Much more effective were the Confederate overtures to the Five Civilized Tribes, many of whose leaders were slaveholders and sympathetic to the Southern cause. As a result, the South enjoyed considerable success in its efforts to bring those tribes into the Confederate fold. Not only did the five tribes supply the Southern armies with large numbers of troops, they also signed treaties with the new nation that incorporated some long-sought rights, including the privilege of sending delegates to the Confederate congress. The Lincoln administration evidently at first did not regard the five tribes as a serious military threat and so did little to counter the Confederate efforts until too late.

Although the allegiance of the Indians through the nineteenth century was never much of a concern to the United States, Indian belligerency was. Warfare with Indians took an enormous toll in lives and money. It impeded the westward expansion of the United States. It caused political problems at home and abroad. Delegations were often found to be a deterrent when dealing with potentially militant Indians. Bringing tribal leaders to large eastern cities was a relatively inexpensive and effective method of introducing the Indian leadership to the resources and power of the United States. As the commissioner of Indian affairs reasoned when justifying the Winnebago delegation of 1828: "This mode of conquering these people is merciful, and it is cheap, in comparison to what a war with them would cost, to say nothing of the loss of Human life."[7]

Accordingly, when encountering a tribe not formerly under its control, the United States would attempt to bring a delegation of leaders to the capital, where they could meet the president and learn firsthand about the nation's economic and military strength. Meriwether Lewis and William Clark during their bold trek across the continent sent back delegates from perhaps a dozen tribes, including the Pawnee, Mandan, Osage, and Arikara. Before returning home, the Indians visited several eastern cities and met with President Thomas Jefferson, who told them that the Americans had taken the place of the French and Spanish as their white neighbors. This was as it should be, he said, because both the Indians and the Americans were "natives" of this country. Jefferson assured them that the United States had no designs other than to develop a useful commerce with the western tribes and to ensure that everyone stayed at peace. "On your return tell your people that I take them all by the hand, that I become their father hereafter, [and] that they shall know our nation only as friends and benefactors."[8]

In 1821 several tribes of the Upper Missouri region received a similar introduction to the power of the United States. Secretary of War John C. Calhoun, following the War of 1812, had conceived a grand plan to overawe the Upper Missouri tribes and cut off their intercourse with British traders operating out of Canada. Essentially, he planned to establish one military post on the Missouri River at its confluence with the Yellowstone and another at the mouth of the Minnesota on the Mississippi, thereby securing the vast area of the two river valleys for American interests. The depression of 1819 and an economy-minded Congress shattered Calhoun's plans for western expansion, leaving Fort Atkinson and the Upper Missouri Indian Agency, established at Council Bluffs, as exposed vanguards of the United States.

The Indian agent Benjamin O'Fallon was sitting on a powder keg. The region was occupied by bands of some fourteen tribes, including the militant Blackfeet, Sioux, Assiniboin, and Pawnee. The obvious inadequacy of the American military presence along the Missouri River had emboldened the Indians, while the encroachment of American traders and trappers had aroused their fear and anger. O'Fallon, anxious to forestall hostilities, requested permission to visit Washington with fifteen chiefs from the more militant tribes. As he explained to Calhoun in April 1821, the troops at Fort Atkinson had inspired respect and the steamboats on the Missouri "additional astonishment," but the Indians for the most part were "still disposed to underrate our strength, to believe that the detachment of troops on the Missouri is not a part, but the whole of our Army." Because of the expense, Calhoun asked O'Fallon to delay a year before bringing the delegation.[9]

But O'Fallon could not wait. Shortly after he made his request, a Pawnee war party attacked nine fur traders near the Arkansas River. The raiders killed several of them and escaped with about a thousand dollars'-worth of plunder—trade goods, guns, and ammunition—and two American flags, which they flagrantly displayed at their village. O'Fallon wanted the army to punish the culprits. Calhoun agreed that such temerity could not be ignored, but he thought it more prudent and economical to invite tribal leaders to Washington, where they could be cautioned about their reckless behavior. Within a month, O'Fallon was on his way east, accompanied by two interpreters and seventeen Kansa, Missouri, Omaha, Oto, and Pawnee Indians.[10]

Although the O'Fallon delegation cost the federal government $6,085, it was considered money well spent, as this editorial from the *Washington Gazette* indicates. "The object of their interesting mission, we believe, has been fully accomplished: these aborigines are deeply impressed with the power of the *long-knives*, that for the future the *tomahawk* will not be *raised* with their consent, against their white brethren." And the tribes from which the delegates came did remain remarkably peaceful as the inexorable tide of white settlement swept across the headwaters of the Missouri.[11]

The Indians did not always cooperate so easily. The Comanches and Kiowas, warlords of the Southern Plains, resented government efforts to relocate eastern Indian tribes onto their traditional hunting grounds, and in 1834 these magnificent warriors began a campaign to drive out their unwelcome brethren. Again, the United States resorted to diplomacy instead of force. Colonel Henry Dodge, who was sent out with eight companies of dragoons to locate the hostile bands, found the main camp of the Kiowas near the

Wichita Mountains in western Oklahoma.

Dodge's journal documents his strenuous efforts to convince the militant tribesmen to send a delegation to Washington. "I wish to show you the road that leads to the great American captain, and make you acquainted with the Indians that live on the way thither," Dodge declared during a conference with the Kiowas. "You shall be well treated; presents shall be made to you, and you shall be sent back in safety." Their visit would make the president so happy he would give the delegates guns, uniform coats, and medals in appreciation. But these wonderful gifts could not be given unless the Indians went east. "I am not the great captain," Dodge stressed, "*he only* can make peace with you, and other red men." A few days later, Dodge made a similar appeal during a conference with the Comanches. "The great American captain has sent me to view this country, and to offer the hand of friendship to all the red men who are here." Dodge told the Comanches that the president wanted to see all the Indians at peace with each other. "He desires you to come and see him, that he may fix a permanent peace with your tribes: he will make you presents, and he will send traders among you, who will serve you with a great many things that you want to make you happy."[12]

Dodge eventually persuaded fifteen Kiowa chiefs to accompany him. The Comanches, who did not want any part of the delegation, reluctantly assigned eight leaders to join the group. All went well until the party reached the Cross Timbers, a thirty-mile belt of trees and brush between the Arkansas and Colorado Rivers. The Comanches claimed that "it will be hard for our horses to pass through the thick timber," and refused to go any further. Dodge accepted the ultimatum and arranged to conclude the peace at Camp Holmes, a headquarters he established on the Arkansas River. Although the Comanches and Kiowas eventually signed peace treaties with the intruding eastern tribes—Cherokees, Choctaws, Creeks, and Osages—the agreements were meaningless. All that prevented the wholesale slaughter of the eastern Indians was their wisdom in staying east of the Cross Timbers, where they were safe from the Comanches and Kiowas.[13] Not until 1846 did the Comanche and Kiowa leaders deign to visit Washington.

The efficacy of delegations as a means of controlling warlike Indians was espoused by government policymakers time and again during the nineteenth century and was the most frequently used reason to justify the cost of bringing Indian leaders to Washington. Even the Board of Indian Commissioners, appointed during Grant's presidency to oversee the administration of Indian affairs in an effort to curb waste and inefficiency, strongly endorsed the delegation policy on this ground. "It would cost less to carry every warrior of the untamed tribes on a tour through the States than [to incur] the expense of one campaign against a single tribe," the commissioners declared in their annual report for 1872. The commissioners maintained that the visits destroyed the belief of the Indians in their own strength and impressed them "with permanent convictions of their inferiority to the whites in knowledge and power," thus restraining their warlike propensities. "In this respect," the commissioners concluded, "inviting these Indian delegations to Washington has already been found to be one of the most effective peace measures which the government has ever adopted." As late as 1888, the commissioner of Indian affairs approved a Shoshone and Bannock delegation for this reason. "The Bannocks especially are a turbulent lot," he informed the secretary of the interior, and "a visit east will be of benefit to them and open their eyes to the power of the Government; in short, it would 'knock the fight out of them.' "[14]

In this instance, the policymakers were correct. Indians who had been east were generally less likely to wage war against whites. Until the middle of the nineteenth century, government officials liked to boast that no Indian visitor to Washington had ever

TWO. MOONS   AMERICAN HORSE

JULES SEMINOLE.

Northern Cheyenne delegates Two Moons, American Horse, and Jules Seminole, a half-blood interpreter, with Benjamin F. Beveridge, the Indians' innkeeper. The Northern Cheyenne Indian agent authorized the visit so that the delegates could be "impressed fully with their comparative insignificance and the overwhelming power of the Government." The delegates were in Washington from March 21 to April 9, 1888, when this photograph was taken.

taken a white life after his return home. Whether true or not, the theory collapsed in August 1862 when Little Crow of the Santee Sioux led the uprising that resulted in the death of some eight hundred white Minnesotans. Little Crow had been to Washington only four years earlier and knew that the war would be hopeless, but hunger, despair, and pressure from his people drove him into the conflict for which he paid with his life.[15]

Little Crow was only the first of several delegates who later turned belligerent. Satanta and Lone Wolf of the Kiowas were certainly not intimidated by their visit to Washington in 1863. They became inveterate hostiles and were eventually imprisoned for their raids on the Southern Plains. Little Raven of the Arapahos had been in Washington only the year before he led an attack on a wagon train near Fort Lyon, Kansas, that left fifteen teamsters dead or wounded. Critics of delegations used this incident as evidence to denounce the practice as a waste of money that did little more than give Indians the impression that the government was afraid of them.[16]

Despite such exceptions, the preponderance of evidence supports the conclusion that delegations were effective in keeping the Indians peaceful—if not friendly—until the last decades of the nineteenth century, when a number of the far western tribes lashed out in desperate attempts to maintain their traditional way of life. Had not so many Indian leaders already been to Washington, however, the post-Civil War years probably would have witnessed even greater hostility and bloodshed. Each tribe probably had chiefs like Black Eagle of the Yankton Sioux, who had been east in 1867. When challenged by the pro-war faction of his tribe for serving as a scout for the U.S. Army, he called the militants "a set of fools" who did not know what they were doing. "Do not think because you kill a few white men . . . that this will end the war," he told them. "You can strike white men until your arms are tired out and can kill no more and then there will be enough left to come and sweep every Indian in this country from the face of the earth as a mighty river sweeps when the waters break over the banks in a great freshet."[17]

Intimidation was by no means the only purpose of delegations. Delegations were also meant to expose the Indians to the benefits of white civilization. Actually, the two reasons were used to complement each other. While being impressed with the power of the whites, the untutored delegates were also expected to see the superiority of civilized life compared to theirs. The whites presumed that the delegates would want to see their children educated, that they would want to till the soil and foresake the hunt, and that they would embrace the white man's religion at the expense of their own.

This aspect of delegation policy was a signal failure. Few Indians returned home with a desire to trade places with their white brothers. The evident failure of the Indians to appreciate the benefits of civilized life never ceased to puzzle their benefactors. This consternation was well expressed by a member of the Board of Indian Commissioners who had accompanied several delegations on a tour of New York City in 1872. "It is a curious, and almost a painful fact," he later wrote, "that nearly all these Indians— including the squaws—were often so home-sick that they would urge the agents to move on, as fast as possible, toward their wild homes in the remote West. They seemed, at times, to long to get away from the most attractive sights which the large cities could afford them." The only explanation he could offer was that "to an Indian, as to a civilized man, 'there is no place like home.' "[18]

The Indian attitude toward these efforts is well summarized by the famous (and probably apocryphal) response of the Six Nations to the Commissioners of Virginia in 1774, who invited the tribesmen to send six young men to Williamsburg College to be educated at state expense. The Indians graciously declined the invitation in this way:

You, who are wise, must know that different nations have different conceptions of things; and you will therefore not take it amiss, if our ideas of this kind of education happen not to be the same with yours. We have had some experience of it; several of our young people were formerly brought up at the colleges of the northern provinces; they were instructed in all your sciences; but when they came back to us they were . . . unable to bear cold or hunger, knew neither how to build a cabin, take a deer, nor kill an enemy, spoke our language imperfectly, were therefore neither fit for hunters, warriors, nor counsellors; they were totally good for nothing. We are however not the less obliged by your kind offer, though we decline accepting it; and, to show our grateful sense of it, if the gentlemen of Virginia will send us a dozen of their sons, we will take great care of their education, instruct them in all we know, and make *men* of them.[19]

The negotiation of treaties or other agreements was another important reason for bringing Indian leaders to Washington. In negotiating formal treaties with the Indians, the United States was following a procedure established by Great Britain and other colonial powers and continued by the Continental Congress. By 1789 the concept that the tribes were independent sovereign nations had become so firmly accepted that, despite the many complications the assumption caused, the federal government entered into formal compacts with the Indians. These agreements covered not only all aspects of intercourse between white and red Americans but also the internal affairs of the tribes. The first treaties were primarily pacts of friendship whereby the tribes acknowledged American sovereignty and protection, but following the War of 1812 their main purpose was the acquisition of Indian land. These Indian treaties were considered to have the same force and status as agreements with foreign nations and as such required the consent of the Senate and ratification by the president. The fiction of regarding the tribes as independent nations continued until 1871, when an act of Congress ended it.

In its negotiations with the tribes, the federal government followed traditional principles of international protocol. Amid much pomp and ceremony, plenipotentiary commissioners of the United States would formally meet tribal leaders at some convenient location where, after considerable discussion, they would sign a solemn document detailing compensations, guarantees, and grants. The parties often exchanged gifts affirming continued friendship and loyalty. Altogether, some 370 treaties the United States negotiated with Indian tribes were formally ratified, perfected, or proclaimed as part of the law of the land.

Surprisingly few of the treaties were negotiated in the nation's capital. Two were negotiated in New York City, two in Philadelphia, and sixty-five in Washington, D.C. Mostly, these involved either important land cessions or significant controversies. Because of unproductive negotiations in the field, government officials would summon tribal leaders to Washington where, under pressure, even the most sophisticated Indians would eventually come to terms. Only the Choctaw delegation of 1824 left the capital confident that it had skinned the government.

The difficulties with the Choctaws dated from 1820 and the Treaty of Doak's Stand. Pressured by southern planters, the government had persuaded the tribe—with threats of the loss of American friendship on one hand and nearly $5,000 in "donations" to Choctaw leaders on the other—to exchange a large section of ancestral land in southwestern Mississippi for a tract of wild country in Arkansas Territory. Elation in Washington over the successful negotiations was immediately tempered by a howl of protest from the five thousand white settlers who occupied much of the tribe's newly acquired land; they insisted the Choctaws move further west. The Choctaws then not only refused to accept another location, they refused to leave Mississippi.[20]

After wrestling with the problem for three years, Secretary of War Calhoun became convinced the only solution lay in renegotiating the 1820 agreement. In 1823 he appointed two commissioners to meet the Choctaws at the agency in Mississippi. The Choctaws, however, cannily refused to talk with anyone except the "President and heads of Departments." They asked their agent, William Ward, for permission to visit "the City Washington, and hold a talk with the President about the Land, beyond the Mississippi. In preference to make a Treaty with any Commissionours that may be sent." When Calhoun ignored the initial request from Ward, tribal leaders met in general council at the agency and formally asked to visit Washington. Not only did the Choctaws agree to pay their own expenses, they also assured the officials "whatever Treaty or other Acts that may be done by us or any negotiation between the U States and this nation shall be considered as Obligatory on this nation." When four more months passed without response, Ward wrote Calhoun again. "I have heard nothing recently from you in relation to the Contemplated Treaty with the Choctaws. The Chiefs are extemely anxious to visit Washington and negotiate the Treaty." Moreover, Ward pointed out, "the expence attending their journey would be much less than a general assemblage of the whole nation." Calhoun finally agreed to hear the chiefs plead the case but warned Ward to observe "the strictest economy" in preparing for the trip east. Ward promptly reported that the delighted Choctaws planned to arrive in Washington by mid-June "so as to be at the Seat of Government at a time when the heds of Department were not crouded with business and Congress had adjourned."[21]

Although the Choctaws were willing to pay their own expenses, federal officials had no intention of allowing them to do so. Henry Conway, the Arkansas territorial delegate to Congress, explained to Calhoun, "I have thought that the views of the Government would probably be defeated unless a sufficient sum was retained to pay the expenses incidental to the Treaty," and he asked the secretary of war what he thought adequate. Ten thousand dollars, Calhoun replied. Four days later Congress appropriated $10,000 "to defray the expenses of negotiating with the Choctaw Indians."[22]

Now came the first in a series of frustrations. A week after the delegation's expected arrival, the bureau heard from Ward that the Choctaws had not yet left home. Deaths in the families of several of the delegates would prevent their departure until autumn. The most likely reason for the delay was disagreement over the composition of the delegation and the issues to be discussed in Washington. In addition to settling the boundary dispute in Arkansas, Ward warned, the Indians were anxious to press additional claims—a $6,000 annuity promised at Doak's Stand and payments to the warriors who had aided General Andrew Jackson in his Pensacola campaign of 1817. Thomas L. McKenney, first head of the Bureau of Indian Affairs, grudgingly accepted the explanation. "A good deal of inconvenience is experienced in delays of this sort," he replied. "It is now distinctly understood that the Delegation do come on in the fall, with full powers as stated, to act in the business of their Mission."[23]

When, on September 23, 1824, the ten-member delegation finally left Mississippi, it represented the finest talent the Choctaws could command, including Pushmataha, Puckshenubbe, and Mushulatubbee, the first elected chiefs of the three political districts through which the nation was democratically governed. Each of them was a proven administrator and a tested warrior.

Perhaps the most articulate delegate was James L. McDonald, a half-blood lawyer practicing in Jackson, Mississippi. The young Choctaw was no stranger to Washington or the bureaucracy: he had boarded at McKenney's home while attending school in Georgetown. McKenney had hoped the young man would emerge as the Tallyrand of his people and serve as an example to doubting whites of what the assimilated Indian could achieve. McDonald, whose entire education was financed by the federal government, went from Washington to Lebanon, Ohio, where he studied law under Judge John McLean, later a justice on the U.S. Supreme Court. Had the young man been able to cope with the pressures imposed upon him by his white benefactors, he might well have fulfilled the role they envisioned, but by 1824 he was already an alcoholic. He committed suicide a few years later. Nevertheless, his handling of the negotiations in this instance—the first occasion on which an Indian delegation was represented by a lawyer in its dealings with the government—is a clear demonstration of his abilities and weaknesses. [24]

The delegates arrived the last week of October. The group had been delayed even more by the accidental death en route of the eighty-five-year-old Puckshenubbe. Despite the bad omen, his companions continued on to Washington, where they took lodgings at Joshua Tennison's hotel on the south side of Pennsylvania Avenue between Twelfth and Thirteenth streets, a short, refreshing walk from the War Department Building, the site of most of the negotiations.

As expected, the negotiations were protracted and difficult. Calhoun opened discussions by asking the Choctaws to cede additional land in Mississippi as well as their holdings in Arkansas, promising in return an enlarged area west of Arkansas Territory that would be theirs permanently. The delegates refused to discuss Mississippi, and they would consider selling only that part of their Arkansas holdings most thickly populated with white settlers.

"Do you want us to give up farming and become hunters?" Pushmataha asked. "Take us to the western boundary of Arkansas Territory, and you will take all our valuable land."

"Good chief," Calhoun replied, "you are contradicting yourself. When we were trying to sell you those lands in 1820 you insisted they were all rocks and hills, and that the waters were only fit to overflow the crops, put out fires, and float canoes. What is the meaning of this great change?"

"I can only say, good father, that I am imitating the white man. In 1820 we wanted to buy; now we are anxious to sell." [25]

After conferring with the president, Calhoun accepted the Choctaw limitations, asking only that the delegates agree to sell a slightly larger portion of their Arkansas holdings. McDonald responded for the delegation. "In that spirit of accommodation and compromise which brought them to your city," he informed the secretary of war, the delegates "have determined to accede to the request of the Government. The next consideration, and perhaps the most important one, is," McDonald continued, "what compensation are the Choctaws to receive?" [26]

That all depends, McKenney replied. How did the Choctaws wish to be paid—"in one payment, in limited annuities, or in annuities forever?" How would the money be spent? "For myself," he told them, "I should be much gratified to find the Choctaw Delegation so much alive to the interests of their Children, as to lay such a deep foundation for their future prosperity, as to make an appropriation of a permanent kind for their improvement in agriculture and knowledge. The act itself would be honorable to the Delegation, in the eyes of all reflecting and good men, in every part of the world." McDonald would not give a "decisive answer." First tell us what you are willing to pay, the young man responded, then the delegation "with the less hesitation" can tell you how it will be applied. [27] Three days were lost in this fruitless exchange.

On November 19, Calhoun sent the delegation the government's offer—$5,000 in cash and $6,000 annually for ten years, in other words, $65,000. The delegation found the proposal *"entirely inadequate."* Unless the government made "a far more liberal offer," they would terminate the negotiations. The delegates, McDonald wrote, would frame their own terms of what they considered "just and liberal."[28]

The promised reply, signed by the entire delegation, must have jolted the secretary of war. It was lengthy, logical, and outrageous. The delegates reminded Calhoun that the proposed cession totaled five million valuable acres drained by the Arkansas and Red rivers, which provided ready access to New Orleans. Even if only a third of the land were arable, at the minimum price for public lands the government would realize $2,000,000. "Is it not just and right we should receive, in annuities, a reasonable portion of that sum?" they asked. By "a reasonable portion" they meant $450,000, not including the Pensacola claims and the unpaid annuities from the Treaty of Doak's Stand. A promise to use the bulk of the money for educational purposes must have been of small comfort to the government.[29]

Again Calhoun conferred with the president. The terms are "wholly inadmissible," he replied four days later. The government would not realize $2,000,000 even if the entire tract were sold. Unless the Choctaws were prepared to make a very great reduction in their demands, "it would be useless to attempt to conclude a treaty," Calhoun declared. With Calhoun's official letter McKenney sent a note of his own addressed to McDonald. "You know me well, and my feelings towards your people, I am their friend," he wrote. The Choctaw delegates must realize the price they asked was simply beyond anything ever heard of before. Reconsider the government's original offer, McKenney pleaded. The money would be incalculably more valuable to them than the land would ever be, even if they held it forever. "You are to consider this not as an official, but private note," he cautioned.[30]

The delegates deliberated for three days. "Our determination is made: we cannot depart essentially from our original position," they answered. Perhaps they did ask too high a price, but they also had a great responsibility to their people, who expected an advantageous treaty or none at all. "The negotiation, therefore, comes to a close, and we shall prepare to return to our homes." Before leaving, however, they would like to settle claims unrelated to the Arkansas business; they listed them in a letter to Calhoun the following day.[31]

The hard line adopted by the delegation perplexed the federal officials, who then adopted a strategy of patient waiting. A week went by before McKenney wrote the delegates, excusing the delay on the grounds that the president was too busy to consider their grievances. The Indians heard nothing more until the end of December, a month later. There are two versions of Calhoun's letter to the delegation. One, dated December 28, remains in the Indian Office letterbook but evidently was not sent. In strong words Calhoun declares that the two parties are so far apart that the president "deems it unnecessary further to continue the negotiation." In the second version, dated three days later and printed in the *American State Papers*, he writes that the president "is desirous, both on your account and that of the United States, to conclude a treaty of cession" and trusts the delegation will reconsider its position "and agree on one more reasonable."[32]

The Choctaws responded to Calhoun's conciliatory letter. Although they had "believed the negotiation terminated," they remained anxious to make an amicable adjustment of the difficulties between the tribe and the United States. Rather than waste time in a further exchange of notes, they asked Calhoun to make an offer that he considered "more reasonable." "Tell us, at once, the highest price you can give—the utmost extent to which you can go; and we can immediately determine whether to accept or reject your offer." The secretary of war promptly replied: $90,000, payable over ten years. Still too low, the delegation declared after a week's deliberation. The tribe would, however, accept a package deal for cash, annuities, and claims settlements totaling $216,000. After a hasty conference with President Monroe, Calhoun agreed to the Choctaw terms the following day, and the treaty was signed in his office on January 22, 1825, almost three months after the delegation's arrival in the city.[33]

If settling the boundary dispute cost more than anticipated, so did the delegation's living expenses, which amounted to $7,463. Only about $2,000 went for room and board; the rest went for clothing, $1,771; liquor, $2,149; transportation, $960; oysters and brandy, $394.75; and such incidentals as bootblacking, $75; barbering, $58; and laundry, $25. McKenney was outraged by the bill, particularly by the incredible sum spent for liquor. He insisted that the delegation pay half the bar and refectory bill, or $1,469, leaving the government share at $6,000, not including medical expenses.[34]

Few Indian delegations returned to their homes without some illness or injury, but the Choctaws were especially unfortunate. Puckshenubbe's death was followed by that of Pushmataha, who died of the croup midway through the negotiations. Still another delegate, Robert Cole, had become so ill that he was unable to return home when the time came for the delegation to leave. Dismayed at the prospect of remaining behind alone, he asked McDonald and Daniel McCurtain, another delegate, to stay with him until he could travel. Although unhappy at the additional expense this entailed, Calhoun and McKenney approved the arrangement. They quickly came to regret the decision, for the delegates had no intention of leaving for Mississippi as long as money remained in the federal treasury. As the days passed into weeks and the weeks into months, McKenney's patience finally wore thin. "Do not delay this matter any longer," he snapped at McDonald on June 16. "Cole is now well enough, and wishes to be off, any further delay is an expense which it is desireable to avoid." He closed the curt note with "I wish Mr. Tennison's bill also."[35]

The innkeeper's bill, delivered the following day, showed the other delegates had been models of sobriety compared to the boon companions who remained behind. Tennison's bill for the three was $1,502.23, including $935 for liquor. McKenney was enraged. "I cannot recommend it for payment," he promptly wrote Tennison. How could the trio average $8.40 a day for liquor, he wanted to know, particularly since McDonald and McCurtain must have done most of the drinking, Cole "having been during the whole time, in the hands of the Doctor." He had warned Tennison about allowing extravagance when he received the earlier bill for the entire delegation. McKenney did concede one point: "Enormous as the bar bill is, I am quite sure . . . that you have charged no more than you actually furnished."[36]

McKenney sent a similar letter to the chiefs of the Choctaw Nation. The government would pay the trio's bill for room and board, McKenney explained, but would allow them only $3 a day for liquor. The tribe would have to make up the difference from its annuity. The Indian Office would pay $1,340.25, the tribe $622.75. "Robert Cole has not been extravagant—He could not be so," McKenney lectured. "He was too sick. But the others have been. A liberal allowance has been made. Enough for the President of the United States, to each of them—for we wished them to live like Gentlemen. But . . . if men will be so extravagant, and act so injuriously to themselves, they must pay for it themselves."[37] No doubt a righteously indignant McKenney escorted the wayward trio to their stagecoach and personally witnessed their departure.

The boundary dispute with the Choctaws had finally been settled, but the price had been enormous. Besides the treaty commitments, the government eventually paid an additional $8,000 in expenses; the tribe absorbed another $2,000. The cost to the Choctaws was even greater, for two of the tribe's most important leaders were dead.

The difficulties experienced in concluding this treaty were atypical. Normally, especially when negotiations were conducted in the Indian country, the bargaining was far less sophisticated and was completed in relatively short order. Treaty commissioners seldom did more than explain the needs of the federal government and the payments that would be made; the assembled Indians, interested more in the presents and food than in deliberations, would usually agree to the terms with little or no comment.

Washingtonians witnessed drama of a different variety whenever the government tried to establish peace between warring tribes, another common reason for delegations. Federal concern about intertribal warfare was at once humanitarian and pragmatic. Not only were innocent women and children often the victims, but there was also the constant danger that the fighting would engulf unsuspecting whites. This occurred in 1824 when a Chippewa war party looking for a Sioux village found four white men instead. The frustrated Indians did not want to return empty-handed, so they killed and scalped the white men.[38] To prevent incidents of this sort, the government on several occasions brought leaders of warring tribes to Washington in the hope of arranging a permanent peace. Such efforts were not very fruitful. It was one thing for tribal leaders to shake hands under the stern eye of the Great Father; it was quite another for them to persuade their young men to honor that pledge in the wilderness.

One of the most ambitious mediation efforts to take place in Washington occurred in 1837 when the government tried to establish peace between the Sac and Fox and their traditional enemies, the Santee or Minnesota Sioux. The hatred between them was so intense, one Indian agent declared, that the Sac and Fox would agree to anything "expect to *love a Sioux*, or spare his life if they met him in the wild prairies and have opportunity to scalp him."[39] An uneasy peace had prevailed until the spring of 1837, when a Sioux war party collected twenty Sac and Fox scalps. The outraged Sac and Fox immediately sent war belts to their Winnebago, Iowa, Oto, Pawnee, and Omaha neighbors in an attempt to enlist their help against the powerful Sioux. To blunt the full-scale war that threatened, the secretary of war invited the contending tribes to a general peace council in Washington that fall.

The Santee Sioux were the first to arrive, reaching the city in mid-September. Accompanied by their agent, Lawrence Taliaferro, the twenty-six chiefs and warriors created a mild sensation as they marched from the train station to Jimmy Maher's Globe Hotel at 13½ Street and Pennsylvania Avenue near the Treasury Building. "They are fierce-looking, stout, and able-bodied men," noted a reporter from the *Washington National Intelligencer*, who observed their arrival from a safe distance. "Carrying about with them in the streets their bows and arrows, tomahawks, and pikes [they] appear to be a very warlike people. With due deference to 'the powers that be,' we doubt the propriety of these Indians being encouraged to walk about our streets armed 'cap-a-pied,' *without their attendants.*"[40]

No less imposing were the other delegations. The eighteen Yankton Sioux, Sac and Fox of the Missouri, and Iowa representatives arrived September 27. Hard on their heels came the Sac and Fox of the Mississippi who were led by Keokuk, their forceful and progressive leader.

With the Sac and Fox delegation were Black Hawk and his son, Whirling Thunder, who were making their second eastern visit. Their first visit had been in 1833 as a result of the so-called Black Hawk War. After their capture, they had been imprisoned for a time in Fortress Monroe in Norfolk, Virginia, and then returned home by way of

Plaster frieze made by the German sculptor Ferdinand Pettrich, who was residing in Washington
in October 1837 when the government brought several large delegations to the capital in an effort
to establish peace between the Santee Sioux and Sac and Fox tribes. The frieze depicts the
warring factions during one of the negotiating sessions on the platform at the Reverend James
Laurie's Presbyterian church. Secretary of War Joel Poinsett is the seated, central figure.

Baltimore, Philadelphia, and New York so they could see firsthand the power of the
"long knives" and appreciate the folly of their abortive uprising. Black Hawk and Whirling
Thunder were not official delegates on this occasion either. According to the *Washington
Globe*, the two warriors had wished "to visit the great towns and villages of their white
brethren as freemen having been taken through the country as prisoners."[41] Whatever
the status of the father and son, it was the notorious Black Hawk the public wished to
see. As soon as word swept through the community that his party had arrived, the streets
swelled with onlookers. The delegation did not disappoint its admirers. Marching proudly
to the music of their drums and flutes, the thirty-four men, women, and children paraded
up Pennsylvania Avenue to their quarters at the Virginia Coffee House, just a few doors
away from the Globe Hotel.

Unfortunately, the vagaries of the weather, transportation, and mail service made it
impossible to coordinate the arrivals of so many far-flung delegations. As a result, the
twenty-two Winnebagos who reached Washington on October 12 missed much of the
congress. The twenty-five-member Pawnee, Omaha, Oto, and Missouri delegation fared
even worse. These Indians did not arrive until mid-November, more than a week after
the others had left the city.

No matter. By most standards the intertribal congress was a great success, although it
did stretch the city's convention capabilities. Indeed, the only suitable place for holding
the sessions proved to be the Reverend James Laurie's Presbyterian church on F Street,
which the government rented for four hundred dollars. A raised and carpeted platform,
extending from the pulpit over the first few rows of pews, became the dais upon which
the Indians and government officials conducted their business. Secretary of War Joel
Poinsett usually presided over the sessions. He occupied center stage, flanked by an
assortment of government bureaucrats and a continually changing cluster of dignitaries,
who included at times the vice president, secretary of the treasury, commissioner of
Indian affairs, and ambassadors from several foreign countries. The Indians, grouped by
tribe, sat on chairs in a semicircle facing Poinsett and the audience. The Sac and Fox
were on the right, the Sioux on the left. In between were the Iowas and, when they
finally arrived, the Winnebagos.[42]

The sessions, which were held several times a week for more than a month, proved
to be the highlight of the social season, attracting enormous crowds and receiving

extensive press coverage. "An interesting talk took place between the Secretary of War and the Sioux chiefs, in Dr. Laurie's church yesterday. Keokuk also had his talk with the secretary," the *Intelligencer* informed its readers on October 6. Four days later, the newspaper reported "a very numerous company of ladies and gentlemen arose at an early hour yesterday . . . to witness the interesting spectacle of an Indian council holding a talk, through their interpreters. All the seats in the church, both on the floor and in the galleries, were occupied, and many gentlemen remained standing in the aisles during the entire proceedings."

At times, the theatrical aspects of the affair distorted the true purpose of the congress. One churchgoer, disappointed at his inability to hear the deliberations, complained to the editor of the *Intelligencer:* "In common with the large audiences present," he wrote, "I have had reason to regret that the Interpreters speak so low as to be utterly inaudible. Now, it would add greatly to the gratification of the Public, whose wishes and accomodations have been provided for, if it should be made the duty of the Interpreters to speak so loud as to be heard."[43]

Despite the carnival atmosphere and distractions, the congress, at least from the government's point of view, accomplished much. Five treaties were negotiated and signed in Washington; a sixth was signed by the Iowa delegates before they reached home. The treaties, in theory, ironed out boundary disputes between the various tribes, thereby lessening opportunities for warfare. In reality, the treaties were a thinly disguised attempt to appropriate Indian land. Essentially, the Sioux and Winnebago delegates ceded all their holdings east of the Mississippi, including several islands they claimed in the river. The Sac and Fox sold more than a million acres of prime Iowa farm land.[44]

These major cessions frightened the Iowas, who knew they would soon be pressured by their dispossessed yet powerful neighbors. In fact, the Iowa chief No Heart tried to explain this to Poinsett. He presented a remarkably accurate map of the Mississippi River valley, drawn by one of his delegates, pointing out the territory his small and peaceful tribe had already lost to Sac and Fox encroachment. Keokuk, when Poinsett questioned him about this, responded: "It is true we have fought with the Iowas and taken a part of their land. If they want it back again, let them come and try to take it again."[45]

Keokuk's belligerence in this instance reflected the spirit of the entire council. Whatever its other accomplishments, the congress did not bring peace to the Indian country. The tone of the meetings was firmly established when, at one of the early sessions, a Fox warrior taunted the Sioux delegation by waving a buffalo-horn headdress he had taken from a Santee corpse. When Poinsett tried to discuss a permanent peace between the two tribes, he failed completely. "My Father," an old Sioux chief told him, "you cannot make those people hear any good words, unless you bore their ears with sticks." Another speaker agreed: "We have often made peace with them, but they would never observe any treaty. I would as soon think of making a treaty with that child," pointing to Keokuk's nine-year-old son, who sat on the floor between his legs, "as with a Sauk."

Such remarks could not go unanswered. Keokuk stepped forward and addressed Poinsett. "They tell you," he said, "that our ears must be bored with sticks; but, my Father, you could not penetrate their thick skulls in that way—it would require hot iron. They say they would as soon think of making peace with this child as with us—but they know better; for when they made war with us they found men."[46] If anything, the visiting tribesmen returned home with their hatred for each other intensified by their contact in Washington.

Another abortive peace effort, between the Arapahos and Utes, took place in 1873.

The agent of peace was to have been the son of the Ute Chief Ouray, whom the Arapahos had captured twelve years earlier. The young man, named Friday, was now an Arapaho warrior with only faint memories of his Ute childhood. Although he agreed to meet his father in Washington, he discouraged any hopes for his return to the Utes. The promising venture came to an abrupt end because Friday fell ill while in Washington and died two weeks later.

The government also arranged for the Arapahos to meet a Crow delegation that happened to be in the city at the same time. Although they too were traditional enemies, they agreed to meet in the lounge of the Washington House where, as one newspaper reported, they smoked pipes with each other. The Crow and Arapaho delegates were unable to converse except through sign language, but they appeared "quite cordial and friendly."[47]

The list of reasons offered to justify delegations is endless. Practically any excuse could be used to bring Indians to Washington if it served the interest of someone in the government. By the turn of the twentieth century, most of the traditional reasons were archaic. Intertribal warfare was a thing of the past; the Indians were no longer a military threat; even the practice of negotiating treaties had long since been discontinued. Now delegations, like the Osages who visited Washington in 1887, were often brought for little more reason than to give the tribesmen a pat on the back. As the commissioner of Indian affairs explained to the secretary of the interior, the Osages were "in that transition state, in which they need good advice, and encouragement, and I believe that the presence here of a small delegation of their representative men, might result beneficially to the whole tribe."[48]

One of the more unusual justifications concerned the Devil's Lake delegation of 1899. The government paid the expenses of three Sioux men to come to Washington to examine a copy of an agreement held by one of the delegates, Suna Wanata. The document was supposedly a boundary agreement that had once been worked out between the Sioux and their Chippewa neighbors. The agreement had never been formalized or made into law, and apparently Wanata now owned the only extant copy. Since the tribes were in the midst of a boundary dispute, bureau officials hoped the document might form the basis for a new agreement. Wanata, however, jealously guarded the document and would let no one read it, much less copy it. The bureau had no recourse but to pay his way to Washington to examine the agreement.[49]

The Indians had their own reasons for wanting to visit Washington, of course. An important one was tribal pride. When a delegation returned from Washington laden with presents and promises, the news often stirred feelings of envy and indignation among neighboring tribes. The agents in charge of those tribes would receive no rest until their people received identical treatment and benefits, even if more imagined than real. This certainly was the experience of the governor of the Dakota Territory, who also served as ex offico superintendent of Indian affairs for the region. As he explained the situation to the commissioner of Indian affairs in March 1866, the Yankton Sioux had been pestering him for some time for permission to send a delegation to Washington. He had thus far rejected those requests because the "great desire" stemmed from a Ponca visit the year before. The Yankton Sioux claimed that since then "the Poncas have been comfortably cared & provided for." The governor did not credit the delegation for the present prosperity of the Poncas, however. He thought they were simply better managers than the Sioux.[50]

By 1867, Yankton Sioux leaders had been to Washington many times. The resentment harbored by tribes whose leaders had never been east can easily be imagined. Alchesay

Ponca delegation of 1877. Front row, left to right: Black Crow, Big Elk, Standing Bear, Standing Buffalo Bull, White Swan, Smoke Maker. Back row, left to right: Big Snake, Baptiste Barnaby, White Eagle, Charles Le Clair, The Chief. Reclining in front: Hairy Grizzly Bear. When the commissioner of Indian affairs refused to authorize the delegation, the Poncas came anyway. Interestingly, Big Snake appears to be giving the Red Power salute some one hundred years before it became a familiar protest symbol. The photograph was taken on November 14, 1877, by William H. Jackson, who was working at the time for the United States Geological Survey of the Territories as a staff photographer.

of the White Mountain Apaches was personally offended by the oversight. The Apaches had heard much about the great cities and beautiful farms of the white man, he told his agent in 1887, but the Great Father had not seen fit to honor his tribe with the opportunity to learn about them firsthand. To Alchesay the explanation was obvious: he and his people had been friendly and peaceful, whereas the troublesome Indians received all the favors from the Great Father. Alchesay was in Washington within the year.[51]

Alchesay was not alone in his belief. Many Indians suspected that delegation trips were a privilege reserved for the militant tribes. When their request to visit Washington was rejected, the Pillager Chippewas of Minnesota complained that the Sioux, who were always "making war and trouble," received better treatment from the Great Father than did they, a people who had never fought against the United States. A similar complaint was expressed by the Poncas in 1877. Their request to visit Washington had also been turned down, yet at that very moment the Great Father was hosting a delegation of their Sioux enemies. The Ponca agent advised the commissioner of Indian affairs to approve the request, noting the "good opportunity for the Department to place a premium upon loyalty & good behavior." Approval would also help refute the expression, frequently repeated among the tribes, that "the Government usually does the most for those Indians who behave the worst."[52]

Perhaps no tribe campaigned harder for a trip to the capital than the Navajos. In January 1874 tribal leaders sent the commissioner a petition expressing their "unanimous" wish to send a delegation to Washington because they had "very important business to submit to their great father." The real reason, however, appears to have been the fact that no representatives from the tribe had ever been east. The Navajos could see no logic for this omission, they informed the commissioner, because their tribe was twice the size of any other in the United States. If it was a question of money, the Navajos would pay their own expenses from the next annuity due them. "We are as good as the Utes and Apaches, and the government has taken them to Washington," they declared.

With the request, their agent, William F. M. Arny, enclosed a private note urging approval. The Navajos had never been out of the mountains of New Mexico, he claimed, and they were "ignorant of our country and its resources." Arny believed "a visit at this time would tend to their advancement while it would also give to the government for settlement some of the best land in New Mexico, and would aid much in the settlement of the Utes and Jicarilla Apaches on reserves."[53]

The commissioner was not impressed. Delegations were not brought to Washington merely because the Indians wanted to take the tour. There had to be sufficient justification to warrant the time and expense involved. Nevertheless, if the Navajos were truly willing to pay their own way, he would consider their request after July 1, when their annuity money would be available. But the Navajos did not want to wait that long. A few weeks later the commissioner received another request from the tribe. The Navajos now wanted to change the boundaries of their reservation, and they wished to send a delegation to discuss the matter in person. The commissioner again refused. Correspondence could easily handle matters of this sort, he pointed out. The Navajos had only to send him a certified agreement of cession detailing the boundary changes they proposed. He would then send it to the Congress for ratification. As for a delegation, the commissioner again stressed the necessity of waiting until funds were available. "No definite encouragement should be given them on the subject," he warned Arny.[54]

The Navajos were not easily discouraged. They countered with a third request. The tribe had signed a treaty with the United States in 1868. This had never been fully explained to the Navajos. Could they discuss its provisions with the Great Father? The treaty, Arny explained, was intended to educate the Navajos and place them on individual land allotments. Although the treaty was to expire in 1878, no Navajo could yet read a page from any book and only one could sign his name. Perhaps a delegation might be the proper incentive to get things moving in the right direction. "There should be a mutual understanding and an exchange of views between the Indian Department, the Agent, and the principal Chiefs which can only be effected by a visit to Washington," Arny declared.[55]

By now the commissioner must have realized he would have no peace until the Navajos came. It was up to the agent, he informed Arny, to decide how best to spend the meager funds coming to the tribe. The "earnest desire" of the Navajos to become civilized was gratifying, but too much importance should not be placed on the anticipated benefits of a visit to Washington. The Navajos could only expect to hear a repetition of what they had heard before. Nor could they anticipate additional funds or support. "These," the commissioner noted, "are only obtained by appropriation, of which Congress is getting more and more chary." If the Navajos really wanted to become farmers, they needed suitable land. Why had the tribe failed to send the agreement for an exchange of lands as the commissioner had previously suggested? Congress could have had ample time to act and then, "at the visit of the Indians in the summer we might have had something to talk about which would have been of immediate benefit."[56]

With Arny's next letter the commissioner received the agreement and an apology. The document would have been sent sooner, the agent explained, but the commissioner's request had been received much later than was usual for correspondence from Washington, going by way of San Francisco and Tucson instead of Santa Fe and Fort Wingate. As for the delegation, Arny claimed he had continually tried to discourage the idea but tribal leaders were determined to go east.[57]

When further efforts to dissuade the Navajos were futile, the commissioner authorized Arny to bring twelve delegates and two interpreters to Washington. Arny conveyed the "grateful thanks" of the chiefs, who immediately began preparations for the trip, which proved to be little more than the sightseeing excursion the commissioner expected. Nevertheless, the Navajos were delighted with their adventure. As Arny reported in February 1875 upon the delegation's return, "the whole party are in good health and the Indians well pleased with the visit to the 'Great Father.' "[58]

The persistence of the Navajos was not at all unusual. Indians seeking a visit to Washington would hound the agent; they would enlist the support of anyone who might have influence with government officials; they would appeal directly to the commissioner, the secretary of the interior, and even the president himself. More than one field officer shared the plight of the Gros Ventre agent who admitted to the commissioner: "I will have no rest until . . . [the Indians] are allowed to go, and I would suggest that they be allowed to come if only for the sake of seeing Washington."[59] As a result of tenacity, many delegations journeyed east for less than significant reasons, and a few for no other purpose than to be humored.

The government's liberality could only go so far, however. Blue Teeth, an elderly Brulé Sioux warrior, was very anxious to get east, and on learning that a large delegation from his reservation was about to leave for Washington, he asked to be included. His reason? To buy a set of false teeth. "What difference does it make," he asked his agent, "if part of the travelling expenses for the benefit of those people is consumed by me?" Since the old man had his heart set upon obtaining dentures, the agent forwarded his request to the commissioner. Blue Teeth made a good try, but he was not a member of the 1881 delegation from the Rosebud Agency.[60]

Quite often tribal anxiety to send a delegation to Washington stemmed from an injustice or disagreement with the bureau regarding a regulation or new policy. Since the Indians mistrusted most white men, including their agents, tribal leaders frequently would not accept adverse decisions until they had discussed them personally with the commissioner or the president. Indeed, the Indians had so much faith in the wisdom and justice of the Great Father that they generally accepted his word without question. The bureau accepted this fact of life and approved delegations in many instances where the difficulties could have easily been resolved through correspondence. One reason for the Sac and Fox delegation of 1837, for instance, was to rectify a clerical error. The 1836 annuity due the Missouri Sac and Fox had been given by mistake to their Mississippi relatives. When inquiries about the problem directed to the governor of Wisconsin and the War Department went unanswered, the leaders of the Missouri Sac and Fox feared that the Great Father had decided "to throw them behind his other red children." The only way to correct this problem, the chiefs believed, was to speak personally with the president. "In my opinion," the agent declared, "they never will be Satisfied until they do so."[61]

As we have seen, there were enough valid reasons for delegations to keep government officials busy. But this was only one side of the delegation story. For every legitimate delegation, there was probably at least one that came without authority either from the tribe or the bureau. Unofficial delegations were a problem the government never solved.

III UNAUTHORIZED DELEGATIONS

Unauthorized Indian delegations were a problem that existed from the establishment of the federal government and grew worse as methods of transportation improved. The difficulty was compounded by the fact that Indians who reached the capital could count on receiving food and lodging, perhaps a present or two, and assistance in returning home. The problem of unauthorized delegations defied solution until well into the twentieth century when, thanks to a combination of factors, it seems to have resolved itself. By then the federal government had become so large and impersonal that uninvited Indians had less success in finding a sympathetic or patient ear to hear their complaints, and they were equally unlikely to obtain funds from the Bureau of Indian Affairs to support their stay in the city. At the same time, the expanding social welfare agencies of the federal and Washington city governments could be relied upon to assist frustrated bureau officials in sending home destitute and stranded Indians.

How different things were in the early years of the republic. In those informal times when the bureaucracy was small, access to the president was relatively easy, and the fledgling United States could ill afford to offend any of its native peoples. Indians wishing to confer with the Great Father merely had to set out for the nation's capital, whether it was New York, Philadelphia, or Washington. In time, with luck and with the assistance of strangers met along the way, they would be at the door of the President's House. They would be hungry, dirty, weary. Often no one in the party could speak English. They might not even be able to explain the reason for their visit. Still, the president would give them an audience and then see that they received clothes, presents, and assistance in returning home.

The experience of a young Chickasaw warrior named John Peter Brown was typical. He showed up in Washington in November 1800, alone, destitute, and completely unable to make himself understood. Brown evidently had started out from Tennessee with another Indian and a white man who was to have been their interpreter. Both of his companions fell ill along the way and returned to Tennessee, but Brown refused to turn back. At Hagerstown, Maryland, he stopped at a public house, where he got drunk and lost his identification papers. Local citizens gave him a letter testifying that they had seen documents of an official nature in his possession, and they then directed him to Washington. President John Adams interviewed Brown, but only the words "Captain Bowles" could be understood. Since William Augustus Bowles was a white adventurer who had caused the government some difficulties among the southern Indians, the president presumed the Indian had important information regarding him. What that information was, Adams never discovered. As for Brown, he returned to Tennessee with a new suit of clothes and a passport that read: "The Bearer John Peter Brown of the Chickasaw Nation of Indians is recommended to the Civility & Hospitality of all Officers Civil & Military and all other [of] the good People of the United States on his return to his own Country from the Seat of the Federal Government."[1]

Two other Chickasaws who appeared in Washington a year later had even less success than Brown in making known the nature of their business. Neither man could speak English very well, but both men obviously wanted to see the president. Secretary of War Henry Dearborn put them up at the public house in which he stayed and told them he would arrange a meeting with President Thomas Jefferson after they had recovered from their long journey. The Chickasaws evidently did not understand him and went to the President's House alone and unannounced. Jefferson was not home when they called, and they were turned away. Again, misunderstanding what had been said, they left Washington. When Dearborn discovered their absence, he promptly wrote to the Chickasaw agent asking him to explain to the tribal leaders that no rebuff had been intended. In fact, Dearborn wrote, "the President was much disappointed in not seeing them and [was] mortified at the manner of their going off. He has a great friendship for the Chickasaws and would have been happy in paying attention to these men, although it could not be discovered that they had any credentials from their Nation."[2]

On still another occasion, Dearborn found himself responsible for a party of eleven Chickasaws who had no identification papers and no interpreter except a little boy with a very poor grasp of English. Four of the men claimed to be chiefs, including one who had a captain's commission signed by General George Washington. Although, as Dearborn noted, these Chickasaws did not appear to be "the most respectable of their nation," they had an audience with Jefferson and received clothing, rifles and ammunition, and various trinkets. A covered wagon—courtesy of the government—took the Indians to the Tennessee River, where they obtained free boat passage home. Despite all this, the Chickasaws seemed very dissatisfied with their treatment, a fact that greatly irritated the secretary of war. He wasted no time in sharing his pique with the Chickasaw agent. The delegation caused the government "great embarrassment," he wrote. "It is an object of no small importance, to prevent the irregular manner in which Indians have been wont to visit the President of the U. States." Trouble and expense were not the only inconveniences. "The want of intelligent Interpreters may produce misunderstandings, that may lead to the most serious consequences." Dearborn hoped the agent would not only increase the vigilance in his own district but also work with other agents "to . . . adopt measures which shall be calculated to correct a practice which is at once, troublesome, expensive, and dangerous."[3]

About the only means of control available to the government in this period was the passport. Indians desiring to visit the president were to notify their agent, who in turn would obtain a passport from the secretary of war. This handwritten document bearing the seal of the United States and the signature of the secretary of war would authorize the Indians to draw assistance from state and federal officers while traveling to and from the capital. A typical passport would read as follows:

To all Persons to whom these present shall come,

Greeting.

It is hereby enjoined and required by order of the President of the United States of all Officers civil and military and all others the good people of these U. States to permit _____ Chiefs of the _____ Nation of Indians, to proceed from the place of their residence, to the City of Washington the Seat of the Government of the said U. States, freely and without molestation and to aid and assist them on the way as friends to the said United States.

Upon receiving the passport, the agent would fill in the names of the delegates and send them on their way.[4]

To make the system work, the War Department asked state and federal officers to intercept Indians traveling without passports. Most Indians going to Washington passed through Pittsburgh, and it was the duty of the army quartermaster stationed there to check the passports of any Indians seeking assistance. Those without passports were to be "explicitly informed" not to proceed, and the quartermaster could give them provisions and assistance in returning to their communities. If they appeared again without passports they were to receive no help whatsoever.[5]

Dearborn also tried to enlist the support of the governors of nearby states in the effort. As he pointed out, unauthorized delegations usually traveled without interpreters and therefore needed assistance to find Washington. It would be a great service to the government if state officers and magistrates encouraged such straggling parties to return home. The Indians should be told that the Great Father would not be pleased with their visit unless they had obeyed the regulations.[6]

Since the passport system could work only if the Indians cooperated, Dearborn tried to get their support as well. Writing to his agents in January 1802, he stressed the importance of controlling the traffic, since the large number of Indians arriving at the seat of government without warning greatly inconvenienced the president. The agents were to tell the chiefs that regulating the visits would benefit both them and the president. If the Great Father's red children had important business their agents could not handle, they must notify him in good season of their wishes and the number in their party; then he could make the proper arrangements. "Their journey will be rendered much easier; and many inconveniences which might otherwise happen will be avoided." For instance, the Indians had to realize that the president was not always in Washington. Only if the Indians warned him in advance could they be sure he would be there to receive them.[7]

Passports proved to be ineffective, and the practice of issuing them disappeared by the 1820s. Far more reliable was the agency system, which assigned resident agents to the tribes. A tribe with its own agent nearby presumably had no reason to make the time-consuming and expensive trips to the capital to conduct business with the Great Father. As the secretary of war explained to the chairman of the House Committee on Ways and Means in April 1800, "Resident agents . . . bring [the Indians] . . . into a narrower compass and place them more perfectly under the management and control of the United States."[8]

Agencies were at first established very casually. In 1792 the president appointed four special agents who were given specific assignments. The following year Congress authorized the president to appoint temporary agents to live among the Indians. Eventually, the word "temporary" was dropped from the title, and agents were permanently assigned to particular tribes or areas. The agents normally were responsible to a superintendent who had general jurisdiction over Indian affairs in a geographical area, usually a territory.[9]

The superintendency system is considered to have originated with the "Ordinance for the Regulation of Indian Affairs," enacted by the Continental Congress on August 7, 1786. This ordinance established Northern and Southern Indian Departments divided by the Ohio River. A superintendent was placed in charge of each department. These positions were continued when the new government was organized under the Constitution. In 1789 Congress appropriated funds for the governor of the Northwest Territory to act as superintendent of the Northern Department. Because of the precedent thus established, the territorial governor commonly served ex officio as superintendent of Indian affairs, particularly in newly organized territories. Where the duties were especially heavy, a full-time superintendent might be appointed. The practice of assigning agencies to a superintendent was discontinued in the decade following the Civil War, and by 1878 the last superintendency had been abolished. Thereafter all agents reported directly to the Bureau of Indian Affairs.[10]

The government had great hopes that the rapidly expanding network of superintendencies and agencies would prevent unauthorized delegations. Newly appointed agents were admonished to keep their Indians at home, and they were periodically reminded of the problem through circulars and directives. "The visits of Indians to the Seat of Government must be discouraged as they are expensive & burthensome & generally eventuate in nothing," the secretary of war instructed a newly appointed agent in November 1800. Allowing Indians to deal directly with the government, he warned, could only result in a lack of confidence in their agents. "They must be taught that the Agents are the immediate Representatives of the Government [and] that they are maintained among them at a serious annual expence for beneficent purposes [and] that they will be always willing to listen to the hopes & fears & to redress the injuries complained of by the Indians." To another agent, the secretary stressed the idea of urging the Indians to put their requests in writing. Letters traveled with more speed and less expense and received the same attention as requests made in person. When all other means failed, the agents were to "hint" that the government might not be willing to pay the costs of journeys undertaken without prior approval.[11]

The suggestions were repeated in 1824, a few months after the Bureau of Indian Affairs opened for business. "These visits are very expensive . . . [and] should not be encouraged," the commissioner wrote when rejecting a request by the Wyandots to send a delegation to Washington. Correspondence was preferred "in all cases like the present, as being less expensive and more convenient both to the Government and the Indians."[12]

The government may have preferred the mails to visits, but the Indians did not readily accept the concept. Until relatively late in the nineteenth century, few Indians had enough facility with the English language to write well. This meant that the tribes had to find a reliable white person who would take down their ideas and then communicate them to Washington. The most convenient person, of course, was the Indian agent, and he was the person most Indians called upon for their letter writing. But this arrangement was not always satisfactory, especially if a tribe wished to complain about the agent. Furthermore, there was the understandable mistrust Indians felt for most white people regardless of their official position. The only alternative was for the tribes to send delegations to Washington despite all threats and penalties.

When the problem of unauthorized delegations did not improve with the creation of the Bureau of Indian Affairs, the government attempted to prohibit all visits. The prohibition went into effect with passage of the Indian Intercourse Act of 1834, the milestone legislation that reorganized the Indian Department and governed the administration of Indian affairs for much of the nineteenth century. "You are requested to give special instructions to the Agents, to announce distinctly to the Tribes . . . that the visits of individuals or of Delegations to the Seat of Government will not be permitted," Commissioner Elbert Herring informed his superintendents when announcing the new policy. "The prohibition must be stated strongly," he warned. "The Government will not only not pay a dollar towards their expenses, but will refuse to transact any business with them." To enforce the prohibition, Congress stopped appropriating the general funds that had been used to finance delegations. Thereafter, a specific appropriation was passed before each authorized delegation could come to Washington.[13]

The tremendous cost of delegations was the primary reason for the prohibition, but there were other considerations as well. According to Charles E. Mix, who served the bureau for more than fifty years as both clerk and commissioner of Indian affairs, the delegations had become less effective as instruments of Indian policy. "Ample experience has shewn," he wrote in 1853, "that, except possibly in cases of remote tribes, who have scarcely been brought into contact with the Whites, and have had no opportunity of knowing our power and resources, but little if any good results from the visits of Indian delegations to our large Cities." The delegates generally fell prey to the vices and allurements to which they were inevitably exposed, and they often were adversely influenced by the attentions they received. Furthermore, when they returned home laden with presents and filled with tales about the wonderful things they had seen and experienced, they excited a desire in their tribesmen to enjoy the same privileges. Should the bureau refuse their requests to come east, the tribesmen generally came anyway and then the government, "as a matter of humanity," had to produce funds for their care and return home. Since Congress no longer provided money for delegations, the bills had to be paid from funds appropriated for other purposes. The inevitable results were embarrassment and difficulty. "For these and other reasons," Mix explained, "it has been the uniform policy to discourage and endeavor to prevent all visits of Indian delegations, unless under very rare and Special circumstances, and Congress has made the necessary appropriations to meet the expense."[14]

Prohibited or not, unauthorized delegations continued to appear regularly in Washington, to the dismay of the officials who had to deal with them. Two men of the Kansa tribe who showed up at the Bureau of Indian Affairs in July 1844 caused more than their share of problems. The men had almost no comprehension of English. One of them, named Kebacoma, claimed to be a chief and even had a few letters in his possession, including one signed by Thomas Harvey, superintendent of Indian affairs at St. Louis. None of the letters, however, pertained to the Washington visit.[15]

Commissioner of Indian Affairs T. Hartley Crawford promptly reminded Harvey of the prohibition against Indians coming to Washington. Unauthorized delegations had cost the U.S. Treasury more than $4,000 in the past four months alone, he scolded. Now the department had to do something with these two men who obviously had no valid business to conduct. Even if they did, "they are actually incapable of transacting the smallest part of it." About the only thing that the commissioner had been able to determine from his conversations with them was that Kebacoma had lost some cattle in a flood and wanted the government to reimburse him. "I suppose the poor creature has traveled all the way to Washington for relief." The situation could have been avoided had it not been for Harvey's letter, which gave Kebacoma some sort of official status. "Hereafter," Crawford ordered, "you will please not only withhold the granting of any papers to . . . [your Indians], but forbid their coming to the Seat of government as displeasing to their great Father. Whatever they may have to say can both be communicated thro' their proper agents and yourself [better] than by themselves."[16]

To get the Indians home as inexpensively as possible, Crawford decided to send them to Wheeling, Virginia. There they could get passage aboard a steamboat to St. Louis, where they would become Harvey's responsibility. He was to send them home without delay "so that the Expenses [which are] worse than useless may be kept down as low as possible."[17]

The plan was good, but Kebacoma would not cooperate. He refused to leave Washington until he had received clothes and money and had met the president and the secretary of war, who were then at Old Point Comfort, a few miles below the city on the

Potomac River. Kebacoma had already left for his rendezvous with the president before Crawford learned of the complication. "This," the outraged commissioner informed Harvey, "shows the injudiciousness of allowing a wild man . . . to come to the Seat of government."[18]

The commissioner gave the one Indian now going home a letter asking the Wheeling postmaster to put him on the first steamboat to St. Louis. Passage would be paid by Harvey when the boat arrived. "I am very sorry to trouble you," Crawford apologized, "but really I do not know how to get the poor creature to his home on any other plan, unless by sending some one all the way to take care of him which would be too Expensive. Please drop me a line saying you have complied with my request, so as to put my mind at ease about him, so serve the cause of humanity and you will greatly oblige."[19]

Two days later the intrepid Kebacoma returned to Washington thanks to an escort provided by the secretary of war. He probably never got his meeting with the president. Regardless, he was soon on his way to St. Louis under the same arrangements as his companion. In relaying the welcome news to Harvey, Commissioner Crawford urged him to devise some means of preventing a reoccurrence. Such visits, he wrote with restraint, are "a source of great annoyance to the Government." Why not publish a notice in St. Louis newspapers warning boat captains not to give any Indians passage to Washington unless they could pay for it? "The thing must be put an end to," Crawford grumbled, "or all discipline in the Indian Department will be of no avail."[20]

Crawford's experience was typical of any number of officials who tried without success to keep uninvited Indians out of Washington. Whether it was the secretary of war, the commissioner of Indian affairs, or the secretary of the interior who issued the circulars, directives, warnings, and threats, the problem of unauthorized delegations remained virtually unchanged over a period of 150 years. The explanation was quite simple: the officials had no legal authority to prevent Indians from coming to Washington. Moreover, the Indians quickly learned that once they reached the city, the bureau could not ignore their presence or withhold the means of returning them home. Thus, for all the bluster and admonitions, the bureau had no way of keeping out of Washington Indians who were determined to come. The lesson was learned the hard way.

On October 16, 1868, Commissioner Nathaniel G. Taylor notified his field officers that Congress at its annual budget hearings had failed to provide the department with general funds which could be used to finance unauthorized delegations. Therefore no delegations could visit Washington unless specifically ordered to do so. "You will, therefore, take such steps to prevent any Indians coming here, as may be necessary to accomplish the object."[21]

Just what steps Taylor had in mind is not clear. Unfortunately, one agent took the directive literally. Albert Wiley had been agent for the Sac and Fox of Kansas for little more than a year, and his experience with instructions of this sort was limited. To make matters worse, an unauthorized delegation was preparing to leave the reservation for Washington when the circular arrived. Wiley summoned the Indians to his office and told them they could not leave the reservation. The delegation was headed by James Keokuk, son of the famous Keokuk and an experienced delegate in his own right. He was not intimidated. "We will go where we please, when we please, independent of the Commissioner or anybody else," he declared.[22]

Wiley immediately wired Central Superintendent Thomas Murphy for instructions. Stop the delegation, Murphy wired back. By this time the Indians were at the train station in Lawrence, Kansas. When they refused to turn back, Wiley filed a complaint with the U.S. marshal in Lawrence, who arrested them. The Indians spent the night in the hall of the Douglas County jail, but they were released the following morning through the efforts of two white men who had been traveling with the delegation and who obtained a writ of habeas corpus. The Indians were eventually tried in the district court at Topeka, but the decision went against Wiley and the bureau. The prohibition was unenforceable, the judge declared, because there was no law restricting the travel of Indians. The delighted delegation decided to proceed with their trip to Washington, but before leaving Kansas they charged Wiley, Murphy, the marshal, and the jailer with false arrest and sued them for damages.[23]

Wiley was stunned. Relaying the unwelcome news to Murphy, he asked for a copy of the law that the commissioner's order had been based upon. "Pleas inform me where it can be found. If there is no authority of law, for such issues, what are Agents to do, when such orders are received?" Murphy did not have an answer and handed the problem to Taylor. The delegation would soon reach Washington, warned Murphy, who wanted the Indians punished to the fullest possible extent. "I regard this whole matter in no small light, and I earnestly recommend and hope you will deem it proper to sustain and protect the agent in his action in the premises."[24]

Alas, there was no law, and the commissioner could do nothing to untangle the mess he had caused. Taylor was obviously embarrassed and perplexed when he explained the situation to the secretary of the interior. The principal reason for the delegation's visit was to complain about Wiley, it turned out. The Indians claimed they had to come in person because they could not trust their complaints to the mails; Wiley might have intercepted their letters. Taylor discounted this argument, noting that the Indians could have worked through the same white people who had been so helpful in getting them released from jail. Moreover, the delegation had not received the required approval of the tribal council before leaving. It was clearly an unauthorized delegation in every respect, and it had come to Washington in flagrant disregard of bureau instructions. To make matters worse, the Indians had submitted a bill for $1,164.75 to cover the expenses they had sustained thus far; additional funds would be needed to get them back to Kansas. The Indians wanted the money to come out of tribal funds held in trust by the bureau.[25]

Commissioner Taylor realized the situation called for delicate handling. If Keokuk and his companions were recognized as an official delegation and their claim for expenses allowed or even conceded to be just, the precedent would weaken the control superintendents and agents exercised over their tribes. Indians would then think they had "the right to come to this City or go to any other place if they desire, at any time they please, and that the government has no right to restrict their actions . . . and is bound to pay any expenses that may be incurred." The bureau had to stand behind its directive, Taylor insisted, otherwise Washington would be overwhelmed with delegations representing any few tribal members who had real or fancied grievances. His solution? Refuse to reimburse the delegation for the expenses already incurred. These had been paid—except for $40—and posed no problem to the delegates. Since the delegates did need money to get home, Taylor suggested advancing them $300 from tribal funds to be paid back from annuities they would receive in the spring. The solution proved acceptable to all parties and the delegation left Washington.[26]

This, however, did not end the affair. Keokuk and his companions pressed their complaint against the officials involved in their arrest, suing them for $40,000. The cases against everyone except Wiley were eventually dismissed; Wiley was convicted of false imprisonment and ordered to pay court costs and $1,900 in damages to the Indians. Liens were placed on his personal property to ensure compliance. To compound his troubles, the administration had changed in the interim. Ulysses S. Grant was now president, and as part of his reform program he overhauled the Indian service, placing army officers in charge of the superintendencies and agencies. Wiley was dismissed from office in the midst of the legal proceedings against him.[27]

Wiley pleaded with the new commissioner, Ely S. Parker, to reinstate him as agent for the Sac and Fox. He needed the job, at least until the litigation was over, otherwise he would have to bear the court and legal fees as a private citizen. As he pointed out, all this had been heaped "upon me for carrying out the Orders of my Superiors." Wiley offered to come to Washington to argue his case in person. "The Endian has been heard there, falshood upon falshood have been piled up against me there, may I not be heard?" Parker was sympathetic. It did seem unfair that Wiley should suffer personally for following instructions. Parker asked the new central superintendent to investigate the case. When the superintendent confirmed that Wiley was an innocent victim of circumstances, Parker approved his recommendation that the bureau furnish legal assistance to the ex-agent.[28]

The case eventually went to the Supreme Court of Kansas, which upheld the original verdict. "This is no ordinary case," Keokuk's attorney argued. "It involves the rights and liberty of more than a million of men. It involves a great constitutional question; an *exercise of arbitrary power*; a violation of our magna charta; an attempt to destroy the liberty of all the domestic dependent Indian nations, with whom we are connected by treaty stipulations." The basic issue of *Wiley* v. *Keokuk*, he claimed, "involves the question whether the orders of an inferior executive officer can have the force of law; in reality, whether the Commissioner of Indian Affairs can, in open violation of law, make slaves of free men because their skin is red, and order their imprisonment should they dare to disobey his orders." The justices of the Kansas Supreme Court agreed that the commissioner had overreached his authority. Keokuk was awarded $1,700 in damages. Wiley was also responsible for an additional $686 in legal fees and court costs.[29]

Wiley did not pursue the matter any further. The bureau paid his bills from the contingency fund, and so the case was closed. Nevertheless, *Wiley* v. *Keokuk* left the bureau an important legacy. Commissioners, superintendents, and agents would continue to cajole, threaten, and denounce Indians who had the temerity to ignore warnings about traveling to Washington, but no one ever again tried to jail a delegation to keep it home.

Perhaps unauthorized delegations would not have been so troublesome had the government followed a consistent delegation policy, but this it failed to do. The prohibition against delegations was rather loosely enforced until the Civil War, which completely disrupted normal relations with the tribes. By the end of the war, Indian affairs were in a chaotic state. To expedite the normalization of relations, the bureau lifted its prohibition indiscriminately. Delegations from a score of tribes were invited to Washington. "The year 1866 will be a memorable one," noted Commissioner Dennis N. Cooley in his annual report. "The labors of the office have been very much increased, while, for several months, the halls of the department building have been filled with delegates from the various tribes, comprising all classes [of Indians], from the educated and intelligent men representing the nations in the Indian country south of Kansas, to the Chippewas of the far north." Writing to one of his agents in February of that year, Cooley announced that the department was "so much engaged with Delegations of various Tribes now here, that I am not disposed, except in cases where it is clearly necessary, to permit any more to come."[30]

Once lifted, the prohibition against delegations appears to have been forgotten. The policy for the next fifteen years or so seems to have depended on the official in office.

Ely S. Parker, the first Indian to head the bureau, disliked delegations. He considered them degrading to the Indians, who were often paraded around like a traveling circus. As a result, he banned delegations. "The business they come upon can be properly attended to in their Nation or their Agency," he directed in December 1869.[31]

Parker's opinion was not shared by his successor, Francis A. Walker, who was commissioner from November 1871 to March 1873. To Walker, it was "at once cheaper and more humane to bring the savages to a realizing sense of their weakness and the impossibility of long contending with the Government, by giving a few chiefs and braves free rides on our railroads and Broadway omnibuses, than by surprising their camps on winter nights and shooting down men, women, and children together in the snow." He thought as many delegations as possible should be brought east until the cumulative effect had convinced the members of all tribes that it was better to accept the white man's way than to oppose it.[32]

Delegations again fell into disfavor after the Indian troubles of the mid-1870s. The large and expensive delegations that had characterized the Grant peace policy had obviously failed to prevent hostilities from erupting in the Dakotas. That fact, plus the request of President Rutherford B. Hayes to curtail the number of Indian visitors, combined to raise a "blanket curtain" around Washington. Very few delegations were authorized between 1877 and 1879. Not one was authorized in 1878, the only year without a delegation in the nineteenth century.[33]

The respite was short-lived, however. In 1879, at the urging of Lieutenant Richard H. Pratt, an army officer who devoted his life to Indian education and assimilation, the bureau opened its famous off-reservation boarding school at Carlisle, Pennsylvania. Although many members of the Indian community stoutly resisted the idea of sending their children so far from home, the persuasive Pratt managed to convince the Sioux chief Spotted Tail to enroll his children at Carlisle. Other Sioux parents at Rosebud and at Pine Ridge followed his example. As a result, eighty-two Sioux children still wearing their tribal dress made a dramatic entry into the abandoned army post on October 6, 1879. Eleven-year-old Luther Standing Bear was one of the students. "I was the first boy inside," he was proud to recall. "At that time I thought nothing of it, but now I realize that I was the first Indian boy to step inside the Carlisle Indian School grounds." The Sioux children were soon joined by fifty-five students from tribes in the Indian Territory. In time enrollment swelled to almost a thousand students.[34]

Pratt must have been remarkably sincere and persuasive, but the consent of so many Indian parents was not gained without some concessions. One was the promise to allow tribal leaders to inspect the school soon after it opened. The first group of inspectors, some forty Sioux chiefs representing nine Missouri River agencies, visited Carlisle in June 1880.[35] By the end of the year, delegations from the Lake Superior Chippewas, the Crows, the Shoshones and Bannocks of Idaho, and the Cheyennes and Arapahos had also visited Carlisle. Before these delegations returned home they usually spent a few days in Washington, where they received the plaudits of government officials for allowing their children to participate in the Carlisle experiment. Children of the delegates often served as interpreters on these occasions, thus reinforcing in the parents' eyes the apparent success of the off-reservation education program.

Throughout the time Carlisle and another off-reservation boarding school at Hampton, Virginia, were in operation, the bureau had to entertain a steady stream of concerned Indian parents who wanted to see their children and inspect the schools. The bureau tried to limit these visits because they were expensive, but it could not curtail them entirely, for this would antagonize the parents and jeopardize future recruiting efforts.

Brulé Sioux delegation at Carlisle Indian school, May 1880. Delegates, left to right: Black Crow, Two Strike, White Thunder, Spotted Tail, and Iron Wing. The white men behind the delegates are Louis Roubedeaux, interpreter, and Charles Tackett, Spotted Tail's brother-in-law.

Besides, how could bureau officials refuse requests like this one from Black Bear, an Oglala Sioux chief:

My friend I going write to you on fourth of July. You came and took head mans sons & you ask me my son & I say yes. So now I want see Paul. I want come there. . . . I am your friend and I want my son come [to Carlisle]. I am head man. I shake hand with you. I am Black Bear.

Pratt, when sending the letter to the commissioner of Indian affairs, noted simply: "Black Bear was the first Chief to bring his child for Carlisle when I visited Pine Ridge Agency in Sept. 1879."[36]

Meanwhile, the bureau was trying to enforce its rules against unauthorized delegations. The effort was an exercise in futility. Fifteen years of off-again, on-again restrictions regarding delegations left even the Indian agents confused. As for the Indians, they seem to have done as they pleased. For one thing, enforcing such prohibitions was becoming almost impossible. Commercial transportation had become relatively convenient and inexpensive. Most tribes now had funds of their own to finance delegations when they wished. They also had a pool of experienced delegates thanks to the tremendous number of Indians who had been east in the post-Civil War years. By the close of the nineteenth century, travel to Washington held few terrors for Indians bent on going.

The bureau certainly did its best to keep the Indians on the reservation. "The practice of Indians coming to this City, claiming either to be delegates of their bands or on business in their individual capacity, without first obtaining the authority of this Department . . . must be discontinued," the commissioner declared in May 1886. As before, the only punishment the commissioner could hold over those Indians who ignored the order was the threat to make them responsible for their own expenses. His circular evidently had little impact, because it was reissued in 1892 and again in 1897. The 1897 circular was actually released by Secretary of the Interior Cornelius N. Bliss, who referred to the problem of unauthorized delegations as a "reprehensible custom that has grown up in recent years." Bliss, who had been in office less than four months, obviously did not know that he was tackling a problem that had defied solution since the colonial era. Nevertheless, the commissioner of Indian affairs dutifully forwarded the circular to his field officers, admonishing them to see that the secretary's directions "are faithfully observed."[37]

Bliss had no more success than his predecessors in stemming the flow of Indian visitors. Indeed, as the Indians became increasingly sophisticated in the ways of the bureaucracy, they would often take a rejection of their request for a visit as an opportunity to apply extra political pressure. Then as now, harried bureaucrats did not appreciate the tactic. Congressman Robert A. Gamble of South Dakota learned this lesson in December 1899, when he suggested to Commissioner William A. Jones that a Sioux delegation from Crow Creek Reservation be authorized to visit Washington. The bureau was "intensely hostile" to the idea, Jones responded. To the famous author George Bird Grinnell, who on another occasion interceded on behalf of the Cheyennes at Tongue River, the beleagured Jones replied: "We cannot prevent an Indian from coming or going whenever and wherever he pleases as long as he pays his own way. He has as much right to do so as a white man." Nevertheless, most Indians visiting Washington were wasting both their time and money, and the Cheyennes would be no exception. "I can see no earthly good to be accomplished by the delegation coming on," Grinnell was told. "The Office is pestered with delegations all winter and they are usually left stranded and without means for returning."[38]

The major problem was not the petitioners; it was the Indians who came to Washington without seeking permission beforehand. As travel became easier and cheaper, especially after the advent of the automobile, the number of Indian visitors increased accordingly. Since most Indians now traveled on their own funds, the bureau tried to discourage these jaunts as a waste of money that should be used for more worthwhile purposes. The logic usually fell on deaf ears because the Indians knew that the bureau would find funds somewhere to assist them in getting home.

The last major effort to prohibit delegations from visiting Washington occurred during the First World War. Citing "the abnormal condition of the country" and the need to conserve limited tribal funds, Commissioner Cato Sells informed his field officers that he would no longer approve delegations except "in absolutely necessary cases." How Sells planned to enforce this order remains a mystery because the only penalty he offered was the old, ineffective threat to make the violators responsible for their own expenses. Sells had to reissue his circular in 1921 because it was "disregarded in many instances," an indication of the futility of such pronouncements.[39]

At the same time the bureau continued to try to enforce its regulations regarding unauthorized delegations, even though the effort often caused more trouble and embarrassment than it was worth. Certainly this was the experience of Commissioner John Collier, who was visited by four full-blood Sioux from Pine Ridge in April 1938. The men had come to protest the actions of the mixed-blood or progressive members of the Pine Ridge community who were trying to eradicate surviving cultural practices on the reservation. Because the full-bloods refused to participate in the political life of the reservation, they had not received permission from either the tribal council or the bureau for their trip to Washington. They were now in the city and destitute. Moreover, before they could return to South Dakota, they needed money to repair their car. It was a classic example of an unauthorized delegation.

Collier wanted to make an example of the men, but he was afraid of the consequences. As he explained the situation to Interior Secretary Harold Ickes, two of the men had been to Washington twice before under similar circumstances. Both times Collier had tried to enforce the regulations regarding the expenses of unauthorized delegations. Both times the men had gone to their congressman, who had urged the bureau to treat them as relief cases and use relief funds to cover their traveling expenses. "If we make the payment this time," Collier warned, "we may expect an instreaming of other Indians from the Sioux area and other areas. If we *do not* make the payment, we may expect that these unofficial delegates will work upon us through the members of Congress and will be hostile to us." Ickes urged Collier to enforce the regulations regardless of pressure.[40]

Even Collier was probably surprised, however, when the four Sioux showed up at the Bureau of Indian Affairs with the famous sculptor Gutzon Borglum in tow. The strategy did not work. Collier immediately issued a press release exposing the pressures to get him to pay the expenses of the delegation and justifying his position. Indians continually come to Washington on "private joy rides," Collier pointed out. When their money is gone, the Indians turn to the bureau for relief on the grounds they are destitute delegates from their tribes. If they get assistance, they merely repeat the performance, confident that the bureau will always bail them out. "There is an important principle involved," the commissioner declared. "Should we be able technically to use relief-of-destitution money for the travel expenses and Washington costs of individual Indians and groups of Indians who come here without proper authority from their tribes, there simply is no limit to the number who might throng in here."[41] Collier made his point and this delegation, at least, found some other means of returning home.

Collier then issued his own circular on the subject of delegations, one of the last in a series begun some 150 years earlier. The lengthy policy statement requested the cooperation of superintendents, tribal councils, and tribal organizations in helping to solve the problem of groups and individuals coming to Washington without sufficient funds to cover their expenses. As Collier pointed out, even tribes using their own money to finance delegations needed his approval before the funds could be released. "Congress, not the Commissioner, has made this rule." Collier would not do business with delegations until the necessary paperwork was completed. This could mean inconvenience and embarrassment for the waiting Indians. More serious was the problem of Indians who came to Washington without any authority whatsoever. No longer would the bureau assist them, as several recent groups had learned to their regret. "These groups underwent some hardships," Collier admitted, "but, again, the responsibility for these hardships was their own, not that of the Indian Service."[42]

Today Indians cannot easily manipulate the bureaucracy for relief. According to a directive issued in 1951, Indians stranded in Washington, whether delegates or otherwise, are referred either to the U.S. Employment Service for assistance in obtaining work or to the District of Columbia Welfare Department for shelter. The bureau assumes no responsibility for their stay in Washington or their return home.[43]

IV FINANCING THE DELEGATIONS

Each delegation, whether authorized or not, had to be paid for. The money at first came primarily from the annual appropriations for the administration of Indian affairs, but by the turn of the twentieth century the cost of the delegations had been shifted to the tribes, which paid for them through their own monies held in trust by the federal government. Regardless of source, however, enormous sums were spent on the delegations, making them a major business activity and inspiring intense competition for the delegation trade. The rivalry among innkeepers, merchants, and other entrepreneurs who wished to feed at the federal trough spawned a host of abuses that were difficult to control because many government officials participated in the profiteering.

Although the financial records are the best means of documenting the history of Indian delegations, they are an accountant's nightmare. Most of the records for the period before November 1800 were destroyed in a War Department fire. The financial records since 1800 are complete—indeed, they are voluminous. Even so, unraveling the financial story of the delegations is still difficult because funding could come from a number of appropriation categories, and government officers would often deliberately bury costs to thwart charges of extravagance and waste. These problems notwithstanding, the financial records reveal an important dimension of the delegation story.

Authorization to pay the expenses of Indian delegations dates from an act of May 13, 1800. This statute empowered the president "to cause to be defrayed, on the part of the United States, the reasonable expenses of such Indians as may from time to time visit the seat of government thereof, for their journeys to, stay at, and return from the same; and also to cause to be given to such Indians, during their stay . . . such presents as he shall judge necessary." To cover the anticipated costs for 1800, Congress provided $7,500. This sum was based on a report to the House Committee on Ways and Means by the secretary of war, who declared that delegations in 1798 and 1799 had cost the government $15,178.[1]

Although the act of 1800 remained in effect until 1834, Congress did not renew the separate appropriation. The money to finance delegations during this thirty-five-year period came primarily from two general funds—presents and contingencies—included in the annual appropriation for the Indian Department. The authority for giving presents to the Indians stemmed from the Indian Intercourse Act of 1802, which specified that $15,000 would be available each year to the president "to promote civilization among the friendly Indian tribes, and to secure the continuance of their friendship . . . [by causing] them to be furnished with useful domestic animals, and implements of husbandry, and with goods or money, as he shall judge proper."[2] The appropriation act of 1822 provided $75,000 "for the contingent expenses of the Indian department." Although this all-purpose fund was renewed each year for the next decade, the appropriation varied from a high of $95,000 in 1828 to a low of $20,000 in 1832.[3] How much of this money was spent on delegations is not known, but the sum was probably quite large. In 1833 Congress eliminated the contingency fund; and, with passage of the Indian Trade and Intercourse Act of 1834, it repealed the blanket authorization for delegations.[4] Thereafter, each delegation required a specific appropriation before the bureau could pay its expenses.

The 1834 act may have reduced but by no means did it abolish the delegation business. In 1838 alone, Congress provided $57,000 for delegation expenses, most for charges incurred the preceding year when some one hundred Indians from a dozen tribes visited Washington as part of a major peace-keeping effort. In 1846, $50,000 was appropriated for the expenses of a large delegation of the "wild tribes" of the Southwest, principally Comanches and Kiowas. Such large sums were exceptional, however. Funds were usually doled out in small amounts: $2,000 in 1839 for a Stockbridge-Munsee and Seneca delegation; $2,225 in 1844 for a Cherokee delegation; $5,000 in 1846 for a Winnebago delegation; $7,500 in 1852 for a Pueblo delegation.[5]

During the administration of Ulysses S. Grant, when numerous delegations were invited to Washington as part of his vaunted "peace policy," Congress again appropriated general delegation funds. In 1870, the secretary of the interior received $50,000 "to defray the expenses of delegations of Indians visiting Washington, and to purchase presents." In 1873 he received $15,000. In 1874, only $5,000 was appropriated, and Congress stipulated that the only other money that could be used for delegations must come from the contingency fund, which consisted of $30,000.[6] This was the last general appropriation for delegations.

Congress also readily appropriated delegation funds when treaty negotiations were involved. In 1838 Congress provided $9,500 for the expenses "of a delegation of Senecas, who visited Washington to urge the ratification of the late treaty with them and other New York Indians, and [for] the expenses of negotiating that Treaty . . . including all the [incidental] expenses." It appropriated $100,000 in 1851 for "holding treaties with the wild tribes of the prairie, and for bringing delegates" to Washington. Even the Civil War did not interrupt westward expansion. In 1864, thanks to an appropriation of $10,000, the Pembina and Red Lake Chippewas concluded a treaty in Washington whereby they surrendered their claims to land in Minnesota and Dakota. For signing an agreement to cede some of their Montana land holdings in 1891, the Crows received, among other things, $5,000 "or so much thereof as may be necessary . . . to pay expenses of twelve Crow chiefs and one interpreter to visit the President . . . in Washington, to consult with him" on tribal business.[7]

The promise of a free trip to Washington was not always a successful lure, however. When the Wyandots refused to sign a treaty in 1832 providing for their removal west of the Mississippi River, it was suggested that the chiefs visit Washington to discuss the subject. Lest there be any illusions about the expected result of the trip, the bureau made its position very clear to the treaty negotiators. "The tribe must be made to understand distinctly . . . that if they come, they must pay their own expenses. If a treaty should be concluded, then, but then only, will the Government pay the expenses of their visit."[8] The Wyandots turned down the invitation.

One would think that an examination of the annual appropriations for the Bureau of

Indian Affairs would be sufficient for determining the extent of at least the official delegation business. Unfortunately, such is not the case. First of all, not all authorized delegations were financed by the bureau. The War Department, "in the interest of peace, and restoration of good feeling between the Citizens and Indians of the [Washington] Territory," brought Chief Moses and several other Colville leaders to the capital in 1883. This delegation (and presumably others as well) was completely under the auspices and funding of the War Department.[9] Secondly, the bureau charged delegation expenses under any number of budget categories within each appropriation. For example, a bill for $1,682 submitted to the bureau in April 1867 by Dr. Alexander McWilliams for medical services rendered various Indian delegations was paid from four different funds: Negotiating Treaty with Sioux of Lake Traverse, $174.00; Negotiating Treaty with Chippewas of the Mississippi, $263.00; Presents to Indians, $654.00; Incidental Expenses of the Indian Service in Dakota, $591.00. The $5,494.50 hotel bill for the Red Cloud and Spotted Tail delegation of 1872 was charged to two funds: Fulfilling Treaty with Sioux of Different Tribes, including the Santee Sioux of Nebraska, $3,256.50; and Support and Civilization of the Teton Sioux, $2,238.00.[10]

The reason for this juggling of funds is unclear. Perhaps the bureaucrats wanted to mask the total costs of delegations or to ensure that all appropriated funds were spent each year so that parsimonious congressmen would have no excuse for reducing the Indian department budget. Whatever the reason, the manipulations were confusing, and they contributed to the complaints of waste, extravagance, and corruption that were so often voiced against the bureau in the nineteenth century. Even bureau employees were puzzled. "The derangements in the fiscal affairs of the Indian department are in the extreme," grumbled one official in 1828. "One would think that appropriations had been handled with a pitchfork. There is a screw loose in the public machinery somewhere."[11]

Despite their limitations, the appropriation acts do document some of the shifts in delegation policy. The transfer from federal to tribal financing of delegations was a major change. By the closing decades of the nineteenth century, most tribes paid their own delegation expenses. The money came primarily from income derived from land sales, grazing leases, and the like. The financial responsibility does not indicate Indian self-management, however, for the old rules still applied. The Indians may have footed the bills, but they still had to obtain prior authorization to send a delegation to Washington.

The normal procedure was to make a formal request through the Indian agent. As Sac and Fox Agent Augustus Brosius informed the commissioner in January 1882, "the Indian Territory fever" had become rampant among his Indians, and tribal leaders wanted to send a delegation to Washington to discuss the possibility of moving from Missouri. Since Brosius thought the commissioner could talk the Indians out of moving, he believed the delegation would be worthwhile. Cost was no problem, because the Sac and Fox had "plenty of money at their Command."[12]

Before the commissioner could approve the delegation, however, the Indians had to submit a petition signed by tribal leaders certifying that the expenses could be paid from money held in trust at the bureau. The required document arrived a few weeks later. Dated March 16, 1882, it read as follows:

We the undersigned head men of the Sac and Fox of Mo. Tribe of Indians hereby certify that we, and our tribe, are, willing that the necessary expenses, from their home to Washington, while in Washington, and from Washington to their home again of Moless Quash-qua-mee, Ko-sho-way, Sha-ko-pee, and William A. Margrave shall be paid from the fund realized from the sale of the ten western sections on our reserve, and known as "Proceeds of Land," and we hereby authorize said payment.

The petition bore eight signatures, plus the following statement signed by the interpreter: "I hereby certify that I have explained to the Sac & Fox of Mo Indians the nature of the above certificate that it was understood by them and signed in my presence." To this Brosius appended his own statement: "I hereby certify that the above certificates are correct and were signed in my presence."[13] Armed with this authorization, the commissioner approved the delegation.

Financing unauthorized delegations was another matter. Since few of the tribes had enough cash on hand to finance delegations, the standard recourse was to borrow the money, either from an obliging individual, perhaps a trader or merchant, or from a bank. The Stockbridge and Munsee Indians of Wisconsin found a benefactor in Samuel W. Beall. He loaned them some $3,000 between 1832 and 1856 during their endless litigation against the federal government. He bought clothes for the delegates, he gave money to their families, and he paid some of their traveling expenses. The Indians had promised him one-third of whatever indemnity they eventually obtained from the government, but Beall was no profiteer. Although the tribe received $78,650 in 1856, he only wanted the money he had loaned the Stockbridge and Munsees over the intervening years. Beall submitted an itemized statement to the secretary of the interior and left the determination of what he should receive to him. Of the $3,000 he claimed, Beall eventually received $2,740.26.[14]

Not all tribes could find philanthropists like Beall. More often than not they had to do their borrowing from lending institutions. The nine "Prairie Band" Potawatomis who visited Washington in early 1858 borrowed $200 at an annual interest rate of ten percent from the Kansas City, Missouri, firm of Northrup & Chilk. According to the note signed by thirty-four "Chiefs, Braves and young Men," the Potawatomis had determined to "create" a delegation, but they were destitute. They wanted only enough money to get them to Washington, however, because "there we expect to get enough money to defray our expenses back and pay what we get from this firm." The Potawatomis must have had a crystal ball. The delegation returned to Missouri four months later and repaid the loan, including the $6.66 for interest.[15]

The Otos who visited in Washington in 1899 were not so fortunate. They borrowed money from a bank in Oklahoma City using their homes as collateral. Only an appeal from the commissioner to the secretary of the interior saved the delegates from foreclosure. The secretary at first refused to pay the delegates' expenses because the men had come to Washington without authorization. He relented only after the commissioner had assured him that the men had learned a valuable lesson and would never again violate department regulations.[16]

Indians unable to borrow money would sell whatever valuables they possessed. The Menominees were so anxious to visit Washington in January 1868 that they planned to sell the hay they needed to winter their livestock. Upon learning this, the commissioner ordered the Menominee agent to endeavor "by all the means in your power to prevent the sale of their hay, or any other property, for the object contemplated." The commissioner insisted he would not recognize the Menominees or conduct any business with them if they succeeded in reaching Washington.[17]

Similar threats were needed in 1882 to prevent the Pawnees from selling their horses to finance a delegation. Because the bureau had failed to comply with several agreements, the Pawnees feared that the government had forgotten its promises to them and so requested permission to refresh the commissioner's memory in person. When he refused to authorize a visit, the Pawnees decided on the desperate strategem of selling their horses. The government farmer tried to convince them this was foolish, but they refused to listen. "If you have any instructions please forward [them]," he pleaded to the commissioner. "Tell them that their coming is not approved. Better stay at home and attend to their crops," the commissioner responded. The telegram evidently did the trick, for the delegation did not leave. The excitement, it appears, had been encouraged by a local trader who had enjoyed a brief but brisk trade in horses. He bought one herd of twenty for $300. "The pony trade is dull now," reported the farmer with good humor. "I think . . . [the trader] exhibits a strong disposition to make grist for his mill without regard for the welfare of the Pawnees."[18]

Not all unauthorized delegations were intercepted, of course. If the unwelcome visitors applied for financial assistance, the government then had to determine whether their expenses could be paid from tribal funds, whether the application should be rejected, or whether a special appropriation should be sought. Getting tribal approval for the expenses of an unauthorized delegation after the fact was not always easy, as two Peoria visitors learned to their regret in 1882. James Charley, Sr., and John Wadsworth had come to Washington without proper authorization, but they were certain their tribesmen would approve payment of their expenses if asked. They were wrong. By a small majority, the Peorias voted to refuse payment because, as they informed the commissioner, "these delegations to Washington accomplish nothing and . . . [we] are heartily sick of their going." The Columbia and Colville delegation of 1899 was also left to its own resources. Since the delegates had come east without obtaining either departmental or tribal authorization, the secretary of the interior flatly rejected their request for assistance. The resourceful delegates eventually borrowed the money from the Bureau of Catholic Indian Missions.[19]

Such rigidity was unusual. The philosophy expressed in 1895 by the commissioner of Indian affairs when weighing the merits of an unauthorized Sac and Fox delegation usually prevailed: "They are here . . . and must be cared for and sent to their reservation. If this is not done at once, they will be made to suffer from privation." The Sac and Fox expenses were paid from tribal funds, as were those of an unauthorized Ponca delegation that visited Washington in 1899. Six Poncas had come to protest a bureau decision to allot their reservation. Nevertheless, the commissioner paid their expenses from tribal funds. In explaining his decision to the secretary of the interior, he declared: "It was considered as a matter of policy in order to persuade them to agree to the [allotment] terms." The Poncas did, in fact, agree to "terms," prompting the commissioner to boast: "The treatment accorded them while here no doubt tended in a great measure to influence them in this direction."[20]

If all other efforts to obtain travel money failed, unauthorized delegates could seek congressional assistance. This must have been a very effective strategy, because the appropriation acts abound with entries of this sort: "To defray the expenses of a certain party of Omaha Indians who visited the City of Washington during the months of February and March 1852 . . . three thousand dollars" and "to defray the expenses of the chiefs of the Oneida Indians in Wisconsin, on a visit to Washington in 1851, in relation to their treaties with the United States, rendered necessary by the deranged condition of their affairs with the federal government, one thousand dollars."[21]

The success of the Oneidas in getting their expenses reimbursed probably encouraged the ones who came to Washington the following year. Elijah Schenandoah, Christian Beechtree, and Thomas Antone, representing the Christian Party of Oneidas, were obviously well versed in the art of Washington politics. Claiming to be on tribal business, they appeared at the bureau in March 1852 bearing a letter from Congressman Timothy Jenkins of New York requesting payment of their expenses. "I hope the government will give them means with which to pay their bills here and to go home," Jenkins wrote. "I believe them to be men of good habits. The sooner they are enabled to return the better it will be for all concerned." Commissioner Luke Lea rejected the appeal. He told the delegates they had violated department regulations in coming to Washington, and, furthermore, he had no money to give them. Undaunted, the delegates returned a week later with another and more forceful letter from the congressman. Jenkins realized Schenandoah had not received permission for the trip, but his expenses should be paid regardless. He advised Lea to discuss the matter with President Millard Fillmore, who had a special interest in the Oneidas, before again rejecting the application. Lea was no fool. Accepting the inevitable, he told the delegates they would be reimbursed from the next Indian department appropriation. The Oneidas, however, did not want to wait, so they asked President Fillmore to intercede on their behalf. Stressing the "magnaminity & generosity of the Great Father," they asked him to provide the needed funds. Fillmore referred their letter to Lea, who sent the Oneidas a brief, testy note: "I can only say to you, what I have already said to some of your friends, that if any one will advance the amount necessary to defray the expenses of your journey home, it will be refunded as soon as Congress shall make an appropriation applicable to the purpose." Like it or not, the Oneidas had to wait for their money until passage of a supplemental appropriation bill the following July.[22]

Even the government's attempt to chastise the Colville and Columbia delegation of 1899 had been fruitless. The appropriation act of 1900 provided $186.50 "to reimburse the Bureau of Catholic Indian Missions for expenses incurred on account of and in returning to their home . . . a delegation of Colville Indians."[23]

In 1934 Congress changed the method of authorizing expenditures for delegations. That year it placed a ceiling of $25,000 on the use of tribal money for "travelling expenses of tribal councils, business committees, or other tribal organizations . . . including visits to Washington . . . when duly authorized by the Commissioner of Indian Affairs." No tribe or band could spend more than $5,000 of this total. The following year the travel allotment was increased to $50,000, but Congress stipulated that no delegate could receive more than $6 per diem and no delegate could stay in Washington longer than thirty days without approval from the secretary of the interior. The travel allotment fluctuated greatly, ranging from a low of $10,000 in 1942 to a high of $65,000 in 1949. In 1937 the per diem was reduced to $5, but Indians for the first time were authorized to use automobiles at a rate of five cents a mile for travel to Washington. In 1941, visits to Washington were limited to fifteen days; the following year this limit was lowered to eight days.[24]

Since 1951, the language of the appropriation act has changed. Under the heading "Tribal Funds," there is a large appropriation, usually several million dollars, for various purposes including "pay, travel, and other expenses of tribal officers, councils, and committees thereof, or other tribal organizations, including mileage for use of privately owned automobiles and per diem . . . at rates established administratively but not to exceed those applicable to civilian employees of the Government."[25] No reference is made to travel to Washington, but such travel is presumed to be included in the authorization.

The nineteenth-century appropriation process may have been troublesome and unwieldy, but it was a model of efficiency compared to what was involved in spending and accounting for the money.[26] A score of officials and clerks, yards of red tape, and a blizzard of paperwork made fiscal matters so complicated and cumbersome it is amazing that any Indians ever got to Washington. At times the Treasury Department and Bureau of Indian Affairs appeared to be working at cross purposes. Endless hours were consumed in haggling over technicalities and minor points of interpretation. One such controversy occurred in December 1829 when Commissioner Thomas L. McKenney requisitioned $350 to cover the expenses of two Passamaquoddy visitors. Because the Indians had not received permission to make the trip, the Treasury Department rejected the requisition on the grounds that the appropriation act *"forbids advances."* McKenney retorted that the act had been passed "to enable the President to conduct a certain course of policy." The president had the right "to 'authorize' deputations of Indians to come to him in person," so how were the Indians to get to Washington without money? "If the construction given at the Treasury to this act be correct, and the law applying to *advances* is interpreted to apply in such a case, then the President is virtually *forbid* to bring on Deputations . . . no matter how *'necessary'* he may esteem it to be." The question was academic anyway. "The visit is made," McKenney pointed out. "The cost of it here is known. There is no *advance* . . . in the case." The Passamaquoddys got their money.[27]

A similar disagreement occurred over the appropriation act of 1870, which provided $50,000 for delegation expenses. Commissioner Ely S. Parker asked Interior Secretary John D. Cox whether the money could be used to defray the expenses of delegations that had not been approved before their arrival into Washington. Cox said no. His decision stood until March 1872 when a new commissioner and a new secretary were in office. According to Commissioner Francis A. Walker, the law stated that the money should be used for delegations visiting Washington "by authority of the United States." Walker interpreted this to mean that the money could be used to defray delegation costs if the business transacted was subsequently determined to have been of sufficient importance to have justified prior approval. "Did the law read 'by invitation' I should not deem the question an open one," he explained to Secretary of the Interior Columbus Delano, "but it appears to me a fair subject for consideration, whether the expression 'by authority' may not be construed to include a sanction subsequently given by the Department upon the objects and results of the visit being fully and finally determined." Delano agreed. Thereafter, the commissioner of Indian affairs was allowed to decide the propriety of a delegation's visit "after such Delegation have arrived."[28]

Still another dispute occurred in 1880 when the second comptroller tried to disallow the expenses of a Ute delegation by citing a statute that prohibited the use of appropriated funds by a tribe at war with the United States. The ruling shocked the commissioner, who could not "conceive" that the law was being applied against the Ute delegation. "The Utes as *a tribe*, have not been in hostility against the Government," he informed the comptroller. "A few *individuals* of said tribe undoubtedly have been, but it cannot reasonably be claimed that it was the intention of Congress . . . to punish the whole tribe for the hostile action of a few with whom the majority were not in sympathy."[29]

These disagreements were nothing compared to those that arose during the accountability process, which was designed to insure that federal funds were properly spent.[30] Normally, officials authorized to bring a delegation to Washington received a travel advance to cover most of the anticipated expenses. As soon as possible after returning home, the official had to "account" for the money he had received. This was done by submitting to the commissioner of Indian affairs an itemized list of expenses supported by signed receipts and vouchers. Accompanying the list would be a covering statement in the official's hand explaining unusual expenses, missing vouchers, and the like. Every penny charged to the government had to be accounted for; an expense lacking proper documentation or a satisfactory explanation would be charged to the official. As a result, delegation accounts are often detailed and replete, containing invaluable information that would otherwise be unobtainable. The statement Joseph M. Street submitted for the Sac and Fox delegation of 1837 is typical:

In going on to Washington with a deputation of Sac and Fox Indians, leaving Rock Island the 12 of September, and arriving in Washington the 1 of November 1837, I paid out for Apples & other fruits, Cakes and Small refreshments for the Indians of the deputation, at their request, during the trip, $38.25:—and in returning with them home, between the 4 and 24 of November 1837, I paid out for Similar Small refreshments, $21.12½; and for chickens to make soup for sick Indians & way marketing $12.50:—also, for purchase of [?], Kettles &c. for the Indians, $15.25; and during their stay at St. Louis $76; and I paid the Steam Boat Bar Keeper at Kee okucks desire $8.50 for a Bill, he (Kee okuck) had made for Spirits for himself & the rest of the deputation.

At Harrisburg on Examination the Indian trunks and Baggage, being 26 trunks and Several large Bundles, were missing. I could not stop with so many Indians, and I sent back for them to Columbia, which involved an expence of $40 as in the account. Doct. Crow who went in pursuit of the baggage, over took me at Pits burg where I had delayed for him with all the Baggage Safe.

When Kee okuck and the Sacs left me, and Started out for his village in the Indian Country at his request, I handed him $20 to buy provisions to take them home, being 60 or 70 miles by land.

I make the foregoing statement, to explain the items Numbered in my account, (No. 17. 27. 28. 29. 30. 31. 32. 33.) And I also have to remark as to (no. 13 & 15. being Rail Road fare) that the Agents declined giving me any thing but a ticket, which was taken by the attending Agent on the way, and I could not procure any other paper to exhibit the fact of our having passed on the Rail Road and paid the price demanded. I therefore furnish this for a voucher, for the items 17. 27. 28. 29. 30. 31. 32. 33. and 13 & 15.) From the nature of the services performed, and the consequent hurry, and attention to keep the Indians together & the people from crowding them almost to Suffocation, and having no help but Doct. Crow, I found it impossible in most cases to do more than to take a hasty note or memorandum of payments, and therefore have been compelled to furnish this statement, to accompany my account of money expended in Taking these Indians to Washington and conducting them home again.
November 24. 1837.   Jos. M. Street U.S. Indian Agent[31]

As procedures became even more formal later in the century, the bureau required its officers to submit the following affidavit as well:

I certify, on honor, that the foregoing account is correct and just; that the services were actually rendered as stated, and that the items of expenses, as embraced therein, were actually incurred and have been paid; that said expenses were necessary for the purpose of _____ that the journey was made by the shortest usually traveled routes; that there was no unnecessary delay; that said journey was made with all practicable dispatch; that no part of the same was made upon a free pass; that it was impracticable to obtain sub-vouchers for all the items embraced in said account; that the different charges in detail therein have been taken from, and verified by, my memorandum, kept throughout the whole trip; that no part of said account has been paid; that there is due thereon to _____ the sum of _____ dollars, and I have certified vouchers in duplicate.
                     Signed. _____
Dated. _____ [32]

Government regulations dictated an elaborate review procedure before the accounts were accepted or "settled." The commissioner of Indian affairs was the first examiner. If he approved the account, he sent it to the second auditor of the Treasury Department, who had responsibility for reviewing expenditures relating to Indian affairs. The second auditor in the course of his examination would make a statement of "differences" or "exceptions," which were questionable items that required further explanation before they could be approved. If an explanation was unsatisfactory the charge would be suspended, which meant the agent would have to bear the cost himself. The second auditor then sent the account and statement of "differences" (if any remained) to the second comptroller. The comptroller reviewed the work of the auditor and stated the final balance. This, in effect, "settled" the account. From the comptroller the account went back to the auditor, who made out a transcript for payment. The transcript went to the secretary of war (later the secretary of the interior), who submitted a requisition to the secretary of the treasury. He in turn issued a warrant on the treasurer to pay the account out of the appropriation designated in the auditor's transcript. Questions concerning the account could be raised at any point in the settlement process, which could take years to complete.

These cumbersome accountability procedures, which remained in effect until the General Accounting Office was established in 1921, were a source of continual confusion and aggravation.[33] Keeping track of vouchers and receipts while conducting an Indian delegation through the American wilderness to Washington proved a challenge to the official escorts. No less imposing was the task of the auditors, who had to sort the accounts and make sense of barely legible and awkwardly written notes. To compound problems, the auditors on occasion seemed determined to enforce the letter rather than the intent of the law.

The frustrations aroused by overzealous auditors often sparked heated exchanges between Treasury Department and bureau officials. A classic confrontation occurred in 1847 over accounts submitted by Governor Pierce M. Butler of South Carolina and M. G. Lewis of Tennessee, who had been appointed special commissioners to make peace with "the wild tribes" of the Southern Plains. Their accounts were so muddled and poorly prepared that the second comptroller charged the commissioner of Indian affairs with failing to give them the careful examination required by law. Only the commissioner, he declared, could say whether certain expenditures had been "reasonable and proper," especially the enormous sums spent on delegation presents. "If there has ever been a case where . . . the administrative examination of the Commissioner of Indian Affairs seemed to be indispensible to a correct understanding of its merits by the Accounting Officers, the case under consideration is the one." Nonsense, the commissioner retorted. He had no intention of making the bureau "an auditing or accounting office." Furthermore, the examination he had provided was all that was called for "by the spirit and intent of the regulation upon that subject."[34]

A similar exchange in 1884 over a bill submitted by the firm of Hamburger & Sons, a Washington clothier, well illustrates the way in which the accounting process was applied to the merchants, vendors, and other private citizens who furnished goods or services to delegations. To receive their money, they had to submit notarized bills signed by the agent, interpreter, and the delegates. (Illiterate Indians merely placed an *x* next to their names.) The bill from Hamburger & Sons was typical of the delegation trade. On February 6, 1884, a Chiricahua Apache delegation had purchased the following merchandise:

Chiricahua Charley—suit and shirt	$13
Antoine—coat, vest, and hat	$12
Chaquita—coat, vest, and hat	$12
Not—coat and vest	$10
Telma—shirt, collar, pair of socks	$ 1.70

The bill included the required signatures and this statement by the agent: "I hereby certify the above to be correct and that the goods above mentioned were purchased by me for the Indians above mentioned at the date above mentioned." Although the bill had not been notarized, the commissioner sent it to the auditor for payment. The auditor sent it back because of the missing notarization. The commissioner immediately returned it, insisting "that for a number of years up to the present time in settling claims of this character, the receipt of the Indians, witnessed by the Interpreter, and the certificate of the agent as to the correctness of the account have been considered amply sufficient evidence for the settlement of the claims, and in view of this I do not see the equity of the requirements of an affidavit of the claimant in the present case. If the affidavit is deemed absolutely necessary by you, I would suggest that you call on the claimant to furnish it."[35]

Most agents took the review procedures in stride. Since the justification process was an ordeal that had to be endured, they attempted to answer the sometimes ridiculous queries with patience and restraint. To the suggestion that the $30 he paid in November 1858 for hiring a wagon and driver for five days was "enormous," Pawnee agent William W. Dennison responded: "If $6. pr day is considered 'enormous' for the hire of a pair of horses, with wagon and driver, no explanation I can make will be satisfactory." The second auditor must have liked the reply. "Suspension removed," he jotted in the margin.[36]

Fellows D. Pease, who escorted the Crow delegation on 1873, faced a staggering list of "exceptions" to his accounts. Most concerned the absence of signed receipts. His explanations provide an insight into the problems agents encountered in carrying out their responsibilities. He could not get a receipt for the $12.75 he spent for meals at a stage station in Montana, Pease explained, because "there was neither ink nor paper at this locality." His explanation for the $28 spent on cabs and medicines in St. Louis was also accepted. "The expenses for hacks were incurred because it was difficult and almost impossible to get the Indians to the Hotel on account of the great crowd of people who surrounded the Indians when they walked on the street. The hacks were picked up promiscuously from those that stood by the theatre and the charges were the usual rates." In his efforts to get the Indians to their rooms, admitted Pease, "I neglected to get sub-vouchers." As for the medicines, these "were purchased as needed for the Indians and the interpreters neglected to furnish me with sub-vouchers."[37]

Not so patient was the response of the agent who was told he had paid an "exorbitant" price—$1.50 for each delegate—for the bathing and barbering services his Indians enjoyed while en route to Washington in 1875. "Probably it is dearer cleaning Indians than white men," he retorted.[38]

When a charge seemed especially suspicious, the accounting officers were not above questioning the supplier. This served a dual purpose. It enabled the Treasury Department to check the veracity of the agent, and it alerted merchants benefitting from the delegation trade that the government would not condone waste or extravagance. The Washington firm of Auerbach and Brother at 623 Pennsylvania Avenue enjoyed a lucrative business furnishing clothing to delegations in the 1870s and 1880s. When questioned by the second comptroller in February 1880, the brothers readily confirmed that the Ute agent had spent $32.25 at their store in outfitting Chief Ouray with a hat, shirts, and other incidentals. Perhaps concerned that they might lose future business, the Auerbach brothers were eloquent in their defense of the expensive goods. "We can only say that: *None but the best of Everything would answer his purpose.*" Ouray was so short and stocky, they explained, his shirts had to be specially ordered. True, the silk hat at $7 was expensive, but it was the top of the line. "We can prove, that no hatter in the Country can furnish, the same quality for a smaller price." The same was true of the collars, gloves, silk scarfs, gold-plated collar buttons, gold-plated stick-pin, and cashmere stockings they sold Ouray. He wanted the best, and he got it.[39]

Despite the scrutiny the accounts received, considerable fraud seems to have gone undetected. Both agents and merchants cheated. Shopkeepers charged the government inflated prices for inferior products, while agents and interpreters authorized payment for services and merchandise that had not been provided. Agents also received kickbacks in merchandise or money for patronizing certain hotels and businesses. Perhaps the agents padded their accounts to protect themselves against overzealous government auditors who would disapprove legitimate claims, but most of the manipulations seem to have been outright theft.

The temptations were certainly great. Agents and interpreters, with their low salaries and simple lives, were probably as dazzled as the Indians by the attractions and temptations of the East. It must have taken great strength of character to resist the money, clothes, liquor, and women offered by the drummers who hounded the delegations from the moment they reached a city. "It is no easy matter for an Agent to visit Washington and get off whole," admitted a government clerk in 1874. "The town is full of sharks who make Indian delegations and their Agents a summer prey." General O. O. Howard, who brought an Apache delegation to the city in 1872, claimed that drummers offered his Indians one hundred dollars each if they would insist on being entertained at a certain hotel. "Of course this was a bribe and a decoy to have them visit the lowest places in Washington and subject themselves to the vilest doings. I was told," Howard later reported, "that other Indian delegations had been dealt with successfully for the purposes of gain."[40]

Although the frauds were probably an accepted evil of the delegation business throughout the nineteenth century, they seem to have been at their worst during the Grant administration. Perhaps the great number of delegations invited to Washington during this period accounts for the high incidence of frauds and scandals. Whatever the reason, swindlers reaped their greatest harvests in the early 1870s.

One of the most notorious defrauders was Henry E. Alvord, a retired army officer from Fairfax County, Virginia, who served as a special commissioner with the Comanches and Kiowas in June 1872. The delegation Alvord brought to Washington later that summer cost the government some $30,000. A government clerk characterized the visit as "one of the biggest 'Jobs' " ever done on the bureau. Almost every purchase for the delegation resulted in larceny. The store that received the contract for clothing the delegation allegedly paid Alvord $900 for the privilege. The store, in turn, charged the government $4,876 for damaged and inferior goods. The bureau paid $42.25 for suits that should have cost $15 or $20; it paid $6 for $3 hats. The bill for drugs and medicines supposedly given the Indians was more than $1,200. Throughout the delegation's stay, Alvord and his wife were seen hauling wagonloads of clothing, cooking utensils, and other items intended for the Indians to their nearby farm. Alvord was so open about his activities that whenever anyone inquired about his whereabouts, the response would be: "Gone with another load." According to Treasury Department auditors, the accounts he eventually submitted were "the very worst ever received." Nevertheless, they were approved because it was not considered "advisable to open a conflict with the Interior Department, where supporting evidence would be so hard to get."[41]

Wanton pillaging of the treasury was checked at least temporarily the following year when the Board of Indian Commissioners exposed some of the most flagrant abuses. In an effort to stem the widespread and well-known frauds that were embarrassing the Grant administration, Congress had established the board in 1869 to oversee the disbursement of funds appropriated for the Indians. As part of their mandate, board members began examining the accounts submitted to the bureau for payment. Their examinations revealed frauds relating to the delegation business that only a blind accountant could have missed. The subsequent investigation uncovered a pattern of abuse that probably typified the frauds involving delegations. Although numerous individuals were implicated, only one person was held accountable for the scandal of 1873. This was Benjamin F. Beveridge, a saloon keeper whose family was sustained by the delegation business for more than fifty years.

At the time of the scandal, the Beveridges operated the Washington House, a fashionable hotel at the corner of Third Street and Pennsylvania Avenue that was favored by congressmen and their families. Its most important resident was Henry Wilson, senator from Ohio and later vice-president of the United States. Ben's mother, Amanda, ran the hotel; he operated a saloon and restaurant on the ground floor. With its favored location near the railroad station and the Capitol Building, the hotel also enjoyed a lively delegation trade. Amanda provided the Indians with lodging; Ben supplied them with "extras" like grapes, raisins, almonds, theater tickets, and outings to the nearby attractions of Mount Vernon, Arlington Cemetery, and Rock Creek Park.

This cozy arrangement collapsed in 1873 when the Board of Indian Commissioners closely examined bills that Ben had submitted to the bureau for payment. That autumn the Beveridges hosted some sixty Indians from three delegations—Crow, Ute, and Southern Cheyenne and Arapaho. Ben submitted a bill for $1,338.65 in "extras" furnished these delegations. The extras included tickets to the opera and theater, tickets and meals for outings to Mount Vernon aboard a Potomac River excursion boat, and such incidentals as cigars, lemonade, ginger ale, apples, dates, and figs. Although the bills had all been approved by the agents and Beveridge had testified to their accuracy, they had a decidedly suspicious character. A preliminary examination indicated certain discrepancies. Beveridge requested payment for twenty-four tickets and meals furnished the Ute delegation during its visit to Mount Vernon, but the entire delegation, including agents and interpreters, consisted of only fifteen people. How could fifteen people eat twenty-four lunches? A wit in the comptroller's office thought this demonstrated "the wonderfully bracing effect of a short voyage on the Potomac." Similar discrepancies were found in the totals for the theater and opera tickets. The Cheyennes and Arapahos supposedly attended the opera and theater a total of twenty-three times in two weeks, but an analysis of the schedule suggested that the delegation on several occasions had viewed three different performances at the same time. The second comptroller finally concluded that so many discrepancies made it "highly improbable that any large percentage of the articles was supplied."[42]

Further investigation seemed necessary. The secretary of the Board of Indian Commissioners informed the agents involved of the discrepancies and asked them once again to certify the accuracy of the accounts they had submitted. Their replies were not very reassuring. Charles Adams, the Ute agent, tried to excuse himself from culpability by claiming that Beveridge had gotten him to sign the vouchers just as his delegation was preparing to leave Washington. His time had been so taken up with last-minute business that he had not been able to examine them carefully. Nevertheless, upon reexamination, the vouchers still looked fairly accurate to him. He admitted that it might seem unusual for a delegation of ten Indians (including one boy) to consume 196 pounds of tobacco in two weeks, "but when it is taken into account that the most of this Tobacco in the shape of cigars was not only smoked by the Utes continually during the day, but also given by them in token of friendship to the Crows and in their company smoked often all night, to which I can certify from observation, I can well imagine that the amount as charged was actually expended by Mr. Beveridge." Interestingly, the Cheyenne and

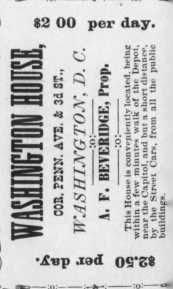

Above: The Washington House as it looked in the early twentieth century. Opened in 1846 by William Gadsby, it stood at the northwest corner of Pennsylvania Avenue and Third Street until 1933, when it was torn down to make room for a municipal building. It was known as the Hotel Vendôme from approximately 1880 until its demolition.

Right: Back of advertising card for the Washington House. Original in Columbia Historical Society.

Owing to the decline in the cost of many articles appertaining to our expenses, the rates of Board will be reduced to

$2.00 and $2.50
PER DAY.

Weekly Boarders
$10, $12, and $14, according to room.

Monthly Boarders
From $30 to $45.

☞ Parlors and Bed-Rooms suitable for Members and Families.

$2 00 per day.

WASHINGTON HOUSE,
COR. PENN. AVE. & 3d ST.,
WASHINGTON, D. C.
A. F. BEVERIDGE, Prop.

This House is conveniently located, being within a few minutes walk of the Depot, near the Capitol, and but a short distance, by the Street Cars, from all the public buildings.

$2.50 per day.

Arapaho agent in his reply denied that Beveridge had supplied cigars to his Indians, although they were charged for four boxes. "Indians don't smoke cigars," John D. Miles declared flatly. Nevertheless, Miles had signed the voucher for those cigars. Like Adams, he claimed that Beveridge gave him the bills to sign just as the delegation was leaving. "I told him," Miles admitted, "I was trusting entirely to his honesty." The agent tried to defend himself by blaming the bureau. "I had confidence to believe that . . . [Beveridge] had been selected by the Dept. officers to serve us on account of his integrity. I had no reason to believe other wise, and again as these bills were to all be settled in Washington, and rates were agreed upon, it was not so necessary that I should scrutinize so closely—not expecting any *advantage* would be taken." Fellows Pease, the Crow agent, offered the same excuse. "The Department made the arrangement for the Delegation and . . . I did not feel the responsibility that I should in other circumstances." Beveridge must be honest, Pease, concluded, otherwise the bureau "would not for the last 20 years or more [have] made similar arrangements with him."[43]

The ultimate shock for the high-minded members of the Board of Indian Commissioners was the discovery that the "extras" Beveridge furnished the Indians included more than opera tickets and cigars. Beveridge eventually admitted that some of the discrepancies in his accounts could be explained by hidden charges for prostitutes. The visits to the brothels had been ordered by agents Pease and Adams, he insisted. Beveridge, in an attempt to exonerate himself, claimed he had been providing this service for more than twelve years. "It has been the almost invariable custom of those in charge of visiting Indians, to sanction the expenditure of money for such purposes," he argued.[44]

Such revelations could not be ignored. Interior Secretary Columbus Delano ordered Commissioner Edward P. Smith to investigate "the circumstances connected with the claim and report whether any officer or employee of the Indian Office or of the Interior Department had any knowledge of the claim, or of the circumstances attending the contracting of the same prior to or at the time of this occurrence or prior to the auditing of the claim in your office, or of the method of entertaining the Indians as indicated by said account." Inspector William Vandever was assigned to the case. After a month's work, Vandever submitted a report that did little more than confirm what everyone already knew. No evidence could be found incriminating anyone other than Beveridge and the agents already implicated. Rumors that employees of the bureau and Interior Department regularly received discounts and merchandise from Saks and Company, one of the major suppliers of goods to visiting Indians, could not be confirmed. Vandever thought the rumors should be discounted, although he admitted "it would be difficult to establish the fact, even if such had been the practice." Certainly there were grounds for suspicion. The three delegations in question had purchased $8,225.40-worth of clothing at Saks. Included in the purchases were several suits for each delegate, numerous pairs of boots, liberal supplies of underclothing, several hats for each delegate, plus balmoral skirts, sleeve buttons, shirt studs, suspenders, ladies' kid gauntlets, pulse warmers, and a variety of other incidentals—"indicating quite a civilized taste on the part of the poor Indian."[45]

Since corruption appears to have pervaded all levels of the Indian department, it is probably safe to assume that Vandever did not probe too deeply into areas other than those that had already been exposed. Indeed, he seems to have focused his energies on the entertainment arranged for the Indians. To him, this was "the most deplorable feature" of the affair. Because agents Pease and Adams must have known the bills they had approved contained falsified entries to disguise the visits to houses of prostitution, the "perpetration of a deliberate fraud . . . [was] thus added to the revolting criminality of the act." Vandever felt the agents were as culpable as Beveridge in the sordid business. As government officers, they could offer no excuse for failing to ensure that the vouchers they approved were accurate and legitimate. Agent Miles was especially derelict. "It was his special duty," Vandever noted, "to inform himself fully of the correctness of the charges before appending his approval." That others were to examine the bills after they left his hands was no excuse for his delinquency. "It is much to be regretted that he did not take the necessary time to enable him to discharge a plain and imperative duty."

Other than the Indians, the only one who suffered from the scandal was Beveridge. No charges were placed against the agents and, as far as they were concerned, the unhappy business was settled. Beveridge was not so lucky. His entire claim for "extras" was disallowed. Secretary Delano realized Beveridge had actually provided some of the services in the account, but he felt "the entire transaction was [so] tainted with irregularities and immoralities, if not absolute fraud and dishonesty, as to justify the disallowance of the whole account." Commissioner Smith concurred. He admitted that "the evil practices" exposed by the scandal "have probably for a long time attended the visits of Indian delegations to Washington," but such "a surprising depth of low wickedness" could not go unpunished. Furthermore, Beveridge had often entertained delegations in the past, and he must have submitted and received payment for similar "unwarrantable and extravagant" accounts; so that "it may be entirely equitable to balance old accounts by disallowing the full amount of this bill."[46]

It was not a decision Beveridge readily accepted. He hired a lawyer to argue his case, and he tried to use congressional influence, including the assistance of Vice-President Wilson, to get the decision reversed. He spent more than five years in the effort, all to no avail. Meanwhile, the Washington House was declared off-limits to delegations, an edict that remained in effect for several years. Only after most of the bureau employees involved in the affair had gone to other jobs was the ban relaxed.[47]

In some respects Beveridge was a scapegoat. No doubt he was a rascal of the first order, but he was also offered up as an appeasement to the forces clamoring for the reform of the Indian service. Support for this opinion comes from Ute Agent Charles Adams, who wished to make a clean breast of things before leaving the Indian service in 1880. "I wish to address you upon a matter which has been many years before your Dept unsettled and which should be disposed of equitably and justly," he informed Commissioner Hiram Price. It was unfair to deny Beveridge his money since he had actually supplied most of the services listed in his accounts. "I saw the Indians from day to day feast upon the best the markets afforded, have fruit of all kinds in unlimited quantities in their rooms, smoke the best cigars, go to the theatres every night, be taken in carriages whenever and wherever they pleased, so that I myself was astonished at the extravagance and wondered what caused this seeming generosity on the part of the Indian office." Adams had tried to question these excesses at the time; he had also known there were errors in the accounts, which he signed only "in accordance with direct orders from the then Commissioner of Indian Affairs." It seems Beveridge had a close working relationship with the Indian Office. In fact, a bureau clerk, who had full knowledge of everything that went on, was at the hotel at all times. To blame everything on Beveridge, then, was an obvious miscarriage of justice. Give him his money, Adams declared. What difference did it make? The Indians enjoyed the "full benefit" of the money spent, which, after all, was theirs anyway.[48]

V   THE INDIAN DRAMATIS PERSONAE

The tribal status of the delegates, the ways they were chosen, and the impact the delegation experience had upon them are important questions about which relatively little is known and much is taken for granted. Since delegations often transacted important business concerning national and tribal policy and affecting the welfare of thousands of people, both white and red, the logical assumption is that only the most influential tribal leaders went to Washington. Another assumption is that serving as a delegate enhanced an individual's tribal status and ensured his continued leadership in the community. For the most part these assumptions are correct. The important leaders usually went east, and they usually retained the high regard of their people when they returned. But not always. Circumstance and desire as much as ability played a part in the selection of delegates. Quite frequently it was a matter of availability: who could leave for Washington on short notice? The status of returned delegates is another issue altogether. If a delegate's people felt betrayed by what had occurred in Washington, his very life might be in jeopardy. In 1855, the Pillager Chippewas of Minnesota, incited by unfounded reports that Chief Flat Mouth had sold their lands for a pittance, were so angry and frustrated that they killed and ate the carriage horse that had taken him to the agency on his way to Washington.[1]

Despite the popular impression, the Indian visitors to Washington, especially in the early years of the republic, were not necessarily the most influential leaders. Tribes just coming into contact with the United States government were understandably suspicious and mistrustful of invitations to visit the heartland of the whites. Therefore, the men who accepted these invitations were often the more daring and ambitious tribal members and were not necessarily the true tribal leaders. Who would know the difference? Certainly not the officials in Washington.

The failure of the government to discriminate between important chiefs and chiefly pretenders could seriously damage later relations with tribes. This occurred in 1806 when two young Pawnees with no tribal status joined the large delegation from the Plains that visited Washington as a result of the Lewis and Clark expedition. Unaware of their actual status, government officers accorded them the same treatment as the other delegates; each received one of the peace medals, uniform coats, and other diplomatic gifts. The mistake was not discovered until later that year when Lieutenant Zebulon Pike, the first official representative of the United States to visit the Pawnee villages, attempted to distribute peace medals to tribal leaders. One high-ranking chief refused to accept his medal because it was smaller than the ones the Pawnee delegates had received in Washington. "Of what use will it be to me!" he sneered. The hard feelings caused by the mistake were not readily forgotten. Even fifteen years later, the government had difficulty bringing Pawnee chiefs to Washington.[2]

The question of chiefly status did disrupt a delegation from the Upper Platte region that visited Washington in 1851. Led by the famous mountain man Thomas Fitzpatrick, it consisted of some twenty Indians representing five tribes—Sioux, Cheyenne, Arapaho, Oto, and Iowa. While traveling east the Indians began questioning the status of one of the delegates, a Blackfoot Sioux named Mahga. If Mahga was not a chief, the other delegates did not think it was right for him to represent his band before the Great Father. The discontent became so open and vocal that Commissioner Luke Lea finally had to intercede. He apologized to the Indians for including someone in the delegation who may not have been a qualified representative of his people. Nevertheless, nothing could be done about it now. "Here," he declared, "you will be considered equal, no matter what might be the difference of position you hold at home." He assured the delegates "the purposes of their mission" would not be affected. Neither he nor the president would inquire further into the matter. "You will all be considered as fully and fairly representing before the Government of the United States your respective tribes." Lea hoped his assurances would end the turmoil and no "jealousies" or "heartburnings" would linger to mar the good that was being accomplished by their visit.[3]

The agency system, which expanded rapidly during the first quarter of the nineteenth century, should have prevented mistakes of this sort. Agents who resided any length of time with a tribe soon learned the power structure. Yet, even when the true leaders were known, they were not always willing to accompany a delegation. There were many reasons for this. Some chiefs were too old to endure the rigors of cross-country travel. Others, like Tecumseh of the Shawnees, Cochise of the Apaches, and Crazy Horse of the Sioux, did not want to compromise their militancy by accepting the hospitality of the Great Father. Tarecawawaho, head chief of the Pawnees, scorned his invitation to visit Washington in 1821, viewing it as an act of submission. Confident that the president of the United States could not have as many wives and warriors as he had, the Pawnee chief refused to humble himself by visiting the Great Father.[4]

Superstition and fear kept still others at home, for going to Washington was no casual undertaking. It was akin to joining a war party and might be viewed in life-and-death terms. This attitude was reported as late as 1891 by a journalist observing a delegation of Sioux leaders preparing to leave Pine Ridge. While the men were in the agency headquarters receiving last-minute instructions, their wives and children were outside singing and chanting. "The singing," the reporter was told, "advised the men they were going into danger and they should be brave like their fathers."[5]

Unfortunately, officials in Washington seldom understood or appreciated psychological factors in dealing with Indians. When the Great Father beckoned, it was the duty of his red children to report. The burden of this task, of course, fell on the Indian agent. What was he to do if it proved impossible to bring a tribe's most important leaders as ordered? Most reacted exactly as did J. R. Hanson, agent for the Sioux of the Upper Missouri. When leaders of the Yankton, Santee, and Upper Missouri Sioux were summoned to Washington in January 1867 to discuss the subject of uniting these groups on one large reservation in Nebraska, Hanson brought the correct number of Indians, but his delegation was lacking some of the more prominent chiefs of his agency. No one would have been the wiser had not the commandant of Fort Rice, Dakota Territory, brought the omission to the commissioner's attention after the Indians left Washington. "It is evident that some one has been imposed upon," declared the commandant. "The Agent should know who the leading men of the several bands of Indians under his charge are, and the most prominent among them should have been brought."[6]

Hanson's response to this criticism provides useful and humorous insight into the difficulties of assembling a delegation. As he explained to the commissioner, he knew well enough the leaders of his Indians. He had done his best to include them in the delegation, but it had been impossible; he had been given only twelve days to assemble the group. Two feet of snow were already on the ground when he set out for Fort Rice. A blizzard caught him on the road, and he lost his way trying to find refuge at Crow Creek Agency. As a result, he had to spend a night in the storm with the temperature at sixteen degrees below zero. After seven days on the road, he finally reached Crow Creek, "alive & sound much to the surprise of every body here & [the] exquisite delight of myself." Since Fort Rice was still sixty miles away, Hanson hired two young Indians to complete the trip for him, instructing them to return with certain specified chiefs. The runners returned a few days later with several prominent leaders but not the ones Hanson had requested; they could not be found.

Fourteen days had now passed and Hanson was well behind schedule. To make matters worse, none of the Indians would agree to visit Washington. "The proposed journey was regarded by them as the greatest event of their lives," Hanson recalled, yet it caused them great anxiety. "Vague ideas of the many wonders they would see, the great distance they would travel and dangers they must encounter in the mystical land of the white man; together with a general fear that they would be forced to sell their lands before returning, seemed to confound their common sense." Hanson gave them one day to consider the problem among themselves. The next morning he returned with several wagons. Meeting once again with the Sioux leaders, he tried to overcome their fears and apprehensions. "The spirit began to move and one after another announced his readiness to accompany me, until I had obtained the required number." Just as he began loading his delegates aboard the wagons, however, the Indian camp erupted in a state of bedlam. "The Squaws struck up the death song and appraided me as a murderer of their chiefs & braves; the papposes yelled, and dogs barked and snapped at my heels. The prospect seemed fair that I would be, there and then, killed by squaws and devoured by dogs." Somehow Hanson escaped serious harm, and he managed to reach Washington with a delegation that, in his opinion, was fairly representative of the Upper Missouri Sioux. And for all this he had been criticized for dereliction of duty. "I neither controlled time nor storms," Hanson emphasized as he concluded his defense.[7]

For the most part, the government seems to have done its best to accommodate tribal interests, feelings, and prejudices in its handling of delegations. When a tribe or band was split into one or more factions or political parties, the government would try to obtain an equal number of delegates from each group. Its primary concern was that the delegates be authorized to conduct business binding on the entire tribe.

The ideal size for a delegation would be six Indians, an interpreter, and the agent, but this number was not always feasible, especially when dealing with large tribes like the Sioux. A subtribe such as the Oglalas might have a dozen bands, and even a dominant leader like Red Cloud could not pretend to speak for all of them. For the Oglalas alone, a delegation might require a score of chiefs and warriors.

Frequently, in the interests of economy and efficiency, the government would combine several small delegations from a region into one large group. The per-person rates for transportation and lodging would sometimes be cheaper than for small parties, while the combined delegations allowed busy government officials to reduce the number of meetings, interviews, and other official functions that would otherwise be required. This did not always sit well with the delegates. The thought of sharing their limited time in Washington with representatives from other tribes whose interests and needs might be far different from their own annoyed some Indian leaders. The Spokans, a small group of Salish-speaking Indians from Washington State, refused to be part of a larger delegation in 1886 for this very reason. "To hear them," grumbled their agent, "you would believe their national pride is not less than that of the old Romans."[8]

The government seldom forced the issue because jeopardizing important policy matters for the sake of a few dollars or a few minutes was foolish economy. Furthermore, traveling across the country with unhappy delegates was not a desirable prospect for the agent in charge. Even under the best of circumstances, supervising a large and diverse delegation could challenge an agent's abilities, as Benjamin O'Fallon discovered when he brought representatives of five Upper Missouri tribes to Washington in 1821. Simply communicating with the seventeen delegates was a problem since they spoke two distinct languages and none of them understood English. Consequently the interpreters had to translate all instructions and messages twice. More troublesome were the personalities and temperaments of the delegates themselves. Dominating the party were the haughty and militant Pawnees, whose behavior O'Fallon regarded as "insolent." The Kansa chiefs were not only "impudent," their tribe was at war with most of its neighbors, further adding to the tensions within the group. Only the Missouri, Omaha, and Oto delegates caused O'Fallon no trouble. Yet the twenty-six-year-old bachelor was more than willing to put up with whatever difficulties he encountered: having spent two years at his wilderness outpost, he viewed the delegation as a well-earned vacation and anticipated a lively winter in the East.[9]

Indeed, escorting delegations to Washington was probably one of the few "perks" Indian agents enjoyed. Any agent in the service for more than a few months could expect a trip east; several of them seem to have spent as much time in Washington as they did with their Indians, lending credence to the claim by one government official that "tramping Indians through the country as a special U.S. circus has long been a positive itch in the aspirations of Agents, and in a large majority of cases, if the truth could be reached, the visit East originated in the suggestions of the Agents rather than in the requests of the Indians." Certainly, the agents took full advantage of the opportunities offered them. Many brought their spouses and a few brought their entire families. Samuel G. Colley, the Upper Arkansas agent, who escorted the Cheyenne, Arapaho, Comanche, Caddo, and Kiowa delegation of 1863, not only brought his wife and son, but he also put the son on the payroll as a special assistant to help take care of the Indians. John Clum, an Apache agent, put together a delegation in 1876 just so he could justify going to Ohio at government expense to get married.[10]

The attitude of the Indians toward their white escorts is difficult to determine. Some tribes went to great lengths to avoid bringing the agent along to oversee their activities and conversations. Others were just as insistent that the agent come, for they placed great trust in his judgment and advice. The highest tribute to an agent was expressed by the Seminoles in 1868. Their request to send a delegation to Washington was turned down, so tribal leaders asked permission to send their agent instead. When the commissioner agreed to the unusual request, the council certified George A. Reynolds as a Seminole delegate with full power to act for the tribe.[11]

Even the irascible Red Cloud wanted his agent to accompany him when he was invited to Washington in 1881. "I went to Washington last summer without . . . [the agent] and we got into trouble," the old chief informed the commissioner. "When Indians

Oglala Sioux delegation. Delegates, left to right: Red Dog, Little Wound, Red Cloud, American Horse, and Red Shirt. The white man standing behind the Indians is John Bridgeman, an interpreter. Photograph taken in Washington in June 1880.

go to see the Great Father the agent should go with them to prevent trouble. There has been much woman's talk at Washington and here, and it makes trouble for our people. If we go to Washington, I want . . . our agent, to go with us and have this talk stopped."[12]

Such sentiments were a delight to the Bureau of Indian Affairs, which frowned on delegations coming east without an agent. In fact, until well into the twentieth century, the bureau insisted that an agent or some other competent person accompany each delegation. Only rarely was this requirement lifted. Baptiste Peoria, head chief of the Confederated Bands of Peoria, Kaskaskia, Piankeshaw, and Wea Indians, was one of the few leaders permitted to travel alone. As the secretary of the interior explained to the commissioner in 1868, when giving the chief permission to come east, "there seems to be no necessity for an Agent coming with him. I believe he is civilized and intelligent and capable of taking care of himself." On those occasions when a suitable attendant was unavailable, the bureau would issue instructions like the following, which went to the

Delaware agent in 1858: "Place the money in the charge of a sober and prudent delegate, who will make a proper use of the same."[13]

The bureau should have had more faith in the Indians, for they would rise to the occasion when given the opportunity. No one could have asked for better judgment than was demonstrated by the two Pueblo men who found themselves stuck in New York City with a drunken Indian agent. Ambrose Abeita and Alexander Padilla had been to Washington in 1868 to appeal a decision of the New Mexico courts to the United States Supreme Court. When the hearing ended, the bureau assigned Special Agent John Ward the task of returning the two men to New Mexico, giving him nine hundred dollars in cash for traveling expenses. Ward decided to go west by way of New York City, where he embarked on a classic alcoholic binge. The Indians were so disgusted with his behavior that they asked the New York City Police for assistance in returning to Washington. When Abeita and Padilla reached the bureau, the commissioner of Indian affairs immediately wired the New York police to send Ward back also, as soon as he was in the "proper condition." Ward, who had no desire to face his superiors, promptly left for New Mexico instead.[14]

Interpreters were essential delegation members because without them it was useless to attempt any business. They were usually tribal members of mixed Indian-white ancestry, although black interpreters were common among the southern tribes. The blacks were slaves or freedmen, many of whom were connected with the tribes through marriage. Interpreting was largely a male occupation, but an occasional female interpreter would show up with a delegation. Interpreters were paid for services: for much of the nineteenth century the rate was five dollars a day plus expenses, but because most of the interpreters were tribal members as well, they would often share in the gifts, clothes, and other presents the delegates received. Government auditors questioned this practice, which they viewed as paying the interpreters twice for their services, but bureau officials argued strongly in support of it. For one reason, the Indians often asked that their interpreters be given clothes and presents, claiming they were poorly paid and part of their people. It was also important to keep the interpreters satisfied, since so much depended on their efforts. "The object of making presents to a delegation . . . is not the supply of their necessities, but to gain their good will, so as to prevent the failure of pending negotiations," wrote Commissioner Edward P. Smith, when responding to an Interior Department auditor in 1875. "The interpreters share in these presents for the same reason; and . . . to have failed to observe the ordinary custom in this regard . . . would quite likely have defeated the whole object of the visit."[15]

Despite their importance, interpreters as a rule were barely literate and were often burdened by the vices of both races. John Richard, of Sioux and French ancestry, served as an interpreter to the Red Cloud delegation of 1870, yet just a few months before coming to Washington he had killed a soldier in a drunken shooting spree at Fort Fetterman. Richard later died at the hands of his Sioux relatives in a similar fracas. Alex Rencountre, interpreter at the Lower Brulé agency, was described by the Indian agent as "good and reliable." Perhaps he was. But when selected to accompany a delegation in 1889, two of the Brulé chiefs asked the commissioner to keep him home. "He is a bad man," they wrote. "2 time we went to Washington, every day he got drunk and takes the Indian to Bad houses where the women are at night."[16]

The government would have preferred using more dependable interpreters, but the Indians demanded people they trusted. The commissioner could not refuse requests like this one from the Sioux chief White Ghost: "My people agree with me to take our own agency interpreter to Washington . . . to counsel about my reservation as we trust him before we would any other interpreter . . . and with him we can do more satisfactory business before the great father." Red Cloud demanded that his brother-in-law, Todd Randall, serve as his personal interpreter in 1875, but he had such a poor grasp of the Sioux language that the chief was left visibly confused after the initial discussions.[17]

The bureau eventually developed a corps of its own interpreters. These included churchmen like the Reverend L. D. Hinman (an Episcopalian missionary who was an accomplished Lakota speaker) and bureau employees of Indian descent and students attending the nearby Carlisle Indian school. Joshua Given, son of the notorious Comanche raider Big Tree, served as an interpreter for several delegations. He stayed with the Indians while they were in Washington and then returned to Carlisle when they left. Evidently Given viewed himself as more than an interpreter, for he would also encourage the delegates "to go to work and improve their reservation." These efforts were probably not very successful. One chief told him he was "getting to be like a white man" and was talking "dangerously" to them.[18]

Employing local interpreters may have been efficient and economical, but the practice lost sight of larger issues. Without interpreters as traveling companions, the Indians could not benefit as much from their exposure to eastern life. Because of this, delegations served by two interpreters became increasingly common. One would be a bureau appointee; the other, a member of the delegation. By the end of the nineteenth century, this practice had become so accepted that the old chiefs would insist on two interpreters during their deliberations—one to check on the other.

The following dialogue between the secretary of the interior, the commissioner of Indian affairs, and the Red Cloud and Spotted Tail delegation of 1875 indicates the efforts that were made to achieve accurate interpreting.

Commissioner of Indian Affairs: You have with you three or four interpreters. I have sent for another man [Hinman] whom most of you know, who will be here to-morrow, so that we will make no mistake in what we say to one another. It is not an easy matter for two persons to talk together when they do not understand each other's language. I want no mistake made. I want those interpreters to keep their ears open, and if they do not exactly understand, say so on the spot.

Spotted Tail: I want to say that we brought our own interpreters at our own expense, and I want them to be in the council with the Great Father and hear what is said.

Commissioner: Your interpreters can come in whenever they like.

Secretary of the Interior: Before I say anything to the delegation of Indians here, I wish to say to all the interpreters, that if the interpretation made by the person who has been designated to translate, shall in their opinion be inaccurate at any time, I wish them to repeat the inaccuracy at once, and have the correction made, because my object is to obtain through the shorthand reporter that I have employed . . . an accurate account of all that is said.[19]

Such efforts notwithstanding, Indians continually complained about the interpreters. Blackfoot, a Crow chief, directed his complaints personally to President Ulysses S. Grant. After meeting Grant in 1873, Blackfoot dictated a letter thanking the president for his hospitality and for the presents given to him and his wife. In his letter the old chief claimed that he had been unable to tell Grant everything he wished during the interview because the interpreters refused to repeat what he said. "The interpreters were scared," Blackfoot declared, "but *I was not*." A similar complaint was expressed by Joseph of the Nez Percé, who visited the East after his famous struggle with the United States Army. "When I was in Washington I had an Interpreter with me who was a white man whom

Ute Chief Ouray and his wife Chipeta. Photograph taken by J. N. Choate during their visit to Carlisle Indian school in February 1880.

I find now, misrepresented everything what was said while we there. Had I understood what transpired between us then, we would have been better contented."[20] Such complaints were so common that they must have been more valid than government officials dared admit.

The use of interpreters has diminished considerably; now there is probably no real need for them at anytime. When interpreters are employed today, it is likely for dramatic effect or for attention from the image-hungry news media. The experience of John C. Ewers, the prominent Smithsonian anthropologist who worked among the Blackfeet in the 1930s, suggests another reason. He reports that the members of a Blackfoot delegation about to leave for Washington agreed among themselves as to who would and who would not be able to speak English when they met with government officials. All were bilingual, but they wanted the opportunity to hear questions and discussions twice, thereby giving themselves more time before replying.

Although participation in delegations was generally a male prerogative, women and children were included on occasion. The government may not have welcomed the additional expense, but no objections were raised when family members unexpectedly appeared with a delegation. The number of women who came east was not large—only a few each year. This remained true until the closing decades of the nineteenth century, when Richard H. Pratt, founder of the Indian school at Carlisle, asked the bureau to encourage women to accompany their husbands to Washington. He believed that he would have more success recruiting girls for Carlisle if Indian women saw the school and returned home with favorable reports about the East.[21]

Since relatively few Indian women came east, those who did would often be singled out for special attention. One of the most popular was Eagle of Delight of the Otos. The only woman in the O'Fallon delegation of 1821, the attractive fourteen-year-old who accompanied her husband, Shaumonekusse, became the darling of Washington society that winter. Laura Wirt, daughter of the attorney general, met her at the home of the French ambassador. "She was dressed in a scarlet stuff robe, trimmed very fine with gold lace; and presented by the President." The gossipy Miss Wirt grudgingly admitted Eagle of Delight was quite pretty. "At least, she is, no doubt considered so in her own nation, and even with us, her modest, goodnatured countenance would pass here for comely, notwithstanding her broad face and high cheek bones. She is not more than fifteen they say, tho' I should think her two or three years older. She is the favorite wife of one of the Chiefs, and for that reason accompanied him." The French ambassador had promised to lead off the first cotillion with "Madame Le Squa," but he could not coax the reluctant debutante into dancing. Needless to say, Laura Wirt confided to a friend, "there has been nothing else talked of since these Indians have been here, and a vast many more anecdotes are related of them than I shall undertake to tell you." Like so many of the Indian delegates, Eagle of Delight did not have long to cherish her memories of Washington. She died of measles soon after leaving the city. [22]

Little is known about most of the women and children who came to Washington. Even their names were often unrecorded. Lacking status, they had little opportunity to participate in the official activities, although they generally enjoyed the tours and other amusements. The experience of the two Kiowa women who accompanied the Comanche, Kiowa, Arapaho, Caddo, and Cheyenne delegation of 1863 was typical. At the audience with President Abraham Lincoln, the fourteen men were introduced, but not the women. At the conclusion of the brief ceremony, however, Lincoln made a point of shaking hands and chatting with them. They were so startled at this recognition that they shook his hand very vigorously and with every expression of delight. "Those girls," commented one observer, "will go home highly elated by the honor thus unexpectedly conferred upon them, and will probably boast all their days that they shook hands with the great Chief of the Pale faces." [23]

Only a few women were themselves delegates. One was Cynthia Farmer, an Onondaga woman of the Six Nations Confederacy from New York who served as a delegate in January 1884. She was chosen by her tribe to look after its interests before Congress "and particularly to urge that steps be taken to oppose the division of their lands in severalty." [24]

Children were seen even less frequently in the East. Those who came were usually in their early teens, the sons of important leaders and soon to be leaders in their own right. Spotted Tail of the Brulé Sioux brought a son in 1873. President Grant, anxious to make a good impression on the proud father, offered to have the boy educated at government expense. Spotted Tail graciously declined the offer, noting that his son had just killed his first enemy and appeared to be well on the way toward the warrior life expected of him. [25]

Besides the official members, delegations could include assemblages of attendants and hangers-on that today defy enumeration. In the early period when delegations required months of travel, the typical entourage could include a great many paid assistants such as cooks, drivers, guards, and the like. The O'Fallon delegation, which was away from home about one year, included two blacks: one was a wagon driver who also prepared the meals en route to Washington; the other was a slave, the agent's body servant, who drowned while crossing a rain-swollen river. There were also two interpreters, one of whom served as a clerk and handled all business matters. [26]

The hangers-on were delegation followers. Generally they had some vested interest in the delegation. Some were traders who had money coming and expected to collect their debts in Washington. Others might be mixed-blood relatives of the delegates who hoped to share in the presents and other largess the government might bestow on their more fortunate relatives. Most were shadowy figures the bureau preferred to ignore. Lawrence Taliaferro, who brought a Sioux delegation to Washington in 1837, gave the commissioner of Indian affairs a list of the persons "not on the Delegation but followers of it." A seasoned veteran of the Indian service, Taliaferro probably considered it important to alert the bureau to their presence.

Persons who have business with the Sioux & connected, & unconnected by ties of blood—
1. Francis Labarthe—half Sioux employ of Am[erican] F[ur] Cpy
2. Oliver Farribault—no business[,] expenses paid by others—these persons are for the present with the Indians.—
3. H. H. Sibley Agt Am F Cpy—not yet located in this City but hourly expected—He will find Quarters at some Hotel in Washington—
4. Benj. F. Baker—now in Washington—both himself & Sibley have claims against the Indians Mr. B—never intrudes himself, but Keeps *constantly aloof* from the Indians—

Taliaferro also brought a physician with his delegation. As he explained to the commissioner, the doctor had two reasons for accompanying the delegation from Minnesota: "to see Society and to visit with the Delegation."[27]

The entourage accompanying the Red Cloud and Spotted Tail delegation of 1875 included six men of mixed Indian-white ancestry, all of them claiming to be interpreters. The bureau had agreed to employ only three of them; the others came hoping to share somehow in the government bounty. When asked why these men had permission to join the delegation, one of the chiefs said they wanted to ensure harmony when the party returned home. If all of them had not been allowed to come, those left behind would have disputed everything the delegates might have accomplished.

The mixed-bloods were a constant source of trouble. None of the six was very good at interpreting, but they were all expert at drinking and patronizing prostitutes. One of the three paid interpreters had to be dismissed for being continually drunk during the negotiations, and the deliberations had to be suspended until a suitable replacement could arrive from Dakota Territory. Imagine the commissioner's pique when the three hangers-on also insisted on being paid for their services. "They are not interpreters at all," the outraged commissioner informed Red Cloud, who had made the request on their behalf. "They have not come by the wish of any body but themselves, so far as I know, and they have been sources of mischief and trouble, ever since they came here. They have taken you . . . at night into bad places; and now they have the impudence to come and ask me to pay them for that sort of service." Needless to say, they did not get paid.[28]

The bureau normally paid scant heed to the delegation followers if they did not cause trouble or interfere in the business at hand. The one uninvited member of a delegation the bureau could not tolerate, however, was a lawyer. Early on, Indians learned the benefit of having legal counsel in their deliberations with the government, and some delegations tried to employ attorneys at their own expense. Such efforts were roundly criticized as a waste of money. Why would Indians need an attorney when their agent was employed to provide all the assistance they needed for dealing with the government? The standard government philosophy was well expressed by the commissioner in January 1866: "It is not only unnecessary but unwise and improper for these Indians to spend their means in employing an Attorney when no such Attorney will be recognized and their Agent is the proper and only medium through which negotiations will be carried on for a treaty, if a Treaty is desired."[29]

Generalizations about delegates and delegations are difficult to make because of the great variation between tribes. Much depended on such factors as the degree of acculturation and political sophistication. The so-called civilized tribes like the Cherokees, Choctaws, and Creeks already had a highly developed political system at the close of the colonial era. The Cherokees, especially, were blessed with a large group of bilingual, educated leaders—literally an aristocracy—who were capable of dealing with the federal government on even terms and traveled freely between their homes and Washington.

The Cherokees developed these leaders as a matter of self-preservation, for they had the misfortune to occupy vast tracts of rich plantation lands that were the envy of their white neighbors. As a result, southern planters were continually pressuring the federal government to remove the Cherokees (and the Creeks, Choctaws, and Chickasaws as well) to less-populated areas west of the Mississippi River. The Cherokees, surrounded as they were by hostile whites and suspicious of the government officals from whom they sought protection, had no choice but to educate themselves in statecraft. During the 1820s and 1830s Cherokee delegates were virtual residents of Washington as they monitored and fought legislation designed to evict them from their ancestral homes. The result is well known. Although ably assisted by many eastern humanitarians and church groups, the Cherokees were able to delay, but they could not prevent, enactment of the program that culminated in their forced removal to present-day Oklahoma.

The Cherokees were undone by the United States legal system, not their delegates, most of whom were talented and dedicated individuals like Richard Taylor, William Shorey Coody, and John Ridge, who came to the capital in November 1830. Their liberal education, polished manners, and dignified demeanor made them welcome and comfortable in any circle. The senior delegate was Taylor, a congenial and stout man who enjoyed smoking a silver pipe that George Washington had presented to a Cherokee chief a half-century before. During their stay, the Cherokees befriended Calvin Colton, a correspondent for the *New York Observer*. He described them as "well-dressed gentlemen of good manners—themselves good society for any sensible man—sitting at the publick tables throughout the City—undistinguished from the common mass except it be in superior delicacy of feeling."[30] Taylor impressed the journalist as "a plain, practical, common-sense man, of good manners, of unbending integrity, . . . [who] speaks English with purity, and but for the cast of his countenance, might be taken any where, as a branch of the English lineage." Although Coody and Ridge were both less than thirty years of age, they surprised Colton with their knowledge of affairs of state. "They actually know more of the institutions, laws, and government of the United States," he believed, "than a large fraction of those, who occupy a seat in the House of Representatives."[31]

The foremost Cherokee delegate in the pre-Civil War era was John Ross, who held the office of chief for thirty-eight years. He boasted only about one-eighth Indian blood; he had difficulty with the Cherokee language; and he was more comfortable rubbing elbows with the eastern elite than sharing the life of the Cherokee full-bloods who were his devoted followers. Nevertheless, he was an ardent nationalist who struggled to maintain the delicate balance between the needs of his people and the demands of white Americans. Ross died in Washington during the protracted and bitter post-Civil War negotiations between the federal government and the Cherokee nation.

After the war, the dean of the Cherokee diplomatic corps in Washington was William P. Adair. Like Ross, he had a deep commitment to his people. Not only did Adair serve as a delegate on twelve occasions, but he also held various tribal offices, including that of assistant principal chief and senator to the Cherokee National Council. He too died in Washington, on October 21, 1889.[32]

John Ross, chief of the Cherokees, from a photograph taken
in 1858.

The Cherokees, obviously, were in a class by themselves. Still, by the middle of the nineteenth century, eastern and midwestern tribes like the Six Nations of New York, the Miamis, and the Stockbridge-Munsees appointed their own delegates and were on the road to self-government. Other tribes, primarily those of the Northern Plains and the Southwest, were considerably behind their eastern brethren in regard to their working relations with the federal government. As late as 1935, the commissioner of Indian affairs was admonishing the Pine Ridge superintendent to let the Sioux pick their own tribal delegates: "While you may, of course, make suggestions and advise the Indians, the actual selection of the delegates should remain with the Indians."[33]

Another factor in the process of selecting delegates was tribal factionalism. Intratribal disputes are still a fact of Indian life, and nowhere were these disputes more evident than in the assembling of delegations. This anguished plea from a Sioux agent in 1891 is typical: "Indians quarreling as to who shall go to Washington. Can I come without them?" The agent who succeeded in assembling a delegation might provoke a letter to the commissioner like the following, signed by seventy Winnebagos in 1881:

We wish to talk to our Great Father & tell him the truth he has asked us to send to Washington three of our best men to council with other tribes about the best way to do our business, but the Agent . . . will not let us have anything to say, he has picked out three of his friends & when in council we chosen our three men, but the Agent tells us he has picked out his own men & we are not allowed to have any voice in our own affairs, so the men of our tribe whose names are signed to this paper Desire to say that they do not approve of the men which the Agent has chosen, & are not willing to be bound by anything that they may say or do nor are we willing that their expenses should be paid out of our money.

Unauthorized delegations were just as likely to raise tribal hackles, and when that happened the commissioner was sure to receive an urgent message like the following from Chief Cup Paw Hee of the Sac and Fox: "I let you notify Them Sac and Fox Delegates he make Delegation Themselves. He never Tell The Peoples. And People he don't know anything about it. Them delegates and nobody Senting Them."[34]

Because of such squabbling, the bureau required delegates to present credentials certifying that they were fully empowered to transact tribal busines. Credentials began appearing in the 1830s and were fairly common by the Civil War. The early ones were sometimes several pages long, consisting essentially of lists of names marked with an *x* indicating that each person had actually signed. The following credentials, signed by forty-eight tribal members, were presented by an Ottawa delegation in 1856:

The Chiefs and head men of the Ottawa Nation desirous of effecting a Treaty with the proper officers of the United States Government in regard to the lands, in Kansas Territory on which they now live, commuting their anuity &c. met in open council on the 19th [?] of April, AD 1856 and after free consultation it was unanimously agreed that a delegation be appointed, and sent to Washington, by the council, to transact business for the Nation. And it was also agreed that Komchaw, Shawpunda, Pah tee and John T. Jones be that delegation. Whatever business or treaty they may conclude is consented to, and will be considered the unanimous act of the Ottawa Nation.[35]

By the end of the nineteenth century, the accrediting of delegates had become so routine that many tribes used printed forms, which required only a signature or two for validation.

Credentials of Overton Love, dated January 16, 1890, appointing him official delegate to Washington for the Chickasaw Nation.

Credentials may have saved the bureau from many problems, but they were no panacea. It was not uncommon for the credentials submitted by a delegate to be challenged by other tribal members. When this occurred, long and tedious investigation was required. Invariably, the challenges were the results of tribal politics. Few tribes caused the commissioner more headaches than the Stockbridge-Munsees of Shawano County, Wisconsin. Descended from eastern Algonquians, mostly Mahicans and Munsees, their name derives from a Mahican mission community that was established in Stockbridge, Massachusetts, in 1734. The Stockbridge-Munsees were never very numerous, perhaps five hundred enrolled members at most. Nonetheless, they endured almost a century of internal stress because of the conflict between two political factions: the Indian Party and the Citizen Party.[36]

The split occurred because of the act of 1843 by which the Stockbridge-Munsees were granted citizenship and their lands were allotted in severalty. The tribal members who accepted citizenship and the allotments became known as the Citizen Party. The adherents of the Indian Party opposed the act of 1843 and did not want their federal status terminated. The Indian Party was not interested in reviving aboriginal culture, however. Its members were concerned primarily with maintaining a distinct Stockbridge community as opposed to being absorbed by the surrounding white community, the inevitable result of the course of the Citizen Party. The Indian Party, in fact, adopted a tribal constitution patterned after the U.S. Constitution and was governed by elected officers, a sheriff, and a three-member court. Besides the question of citizenship, the parties argued over tribal claims and enrollment and hurled accusations of fraud and misappropriation of tribal monies at each other.

The federal government made repeated efforts to resolve the intratribal differences, but the solutions offered would fail to please one faction or the other. As a result, both groups year after year sent delegates to Washington. Each party hoped to resolve the conflict through government intervention in its favor. Each side claimed its delegate was the one authorized to speak for the tribe as a whole. Solomon himself could not have determined which faction to do business with.

A crisis developed in 1883 when Albert Miller of the Citizen Party attempted to charge his expenses as the Stockbridge-Munsee delegate to tribal monies held in trust by the bureau. Miller had been in Washington from February 17 to August 1, and his expenses totaled $277. As proof that he was entitled to the money, he submitted a power of attorney dated January 17, 1883, and signed by the tribal sachem and four councillors who declared Miller "to be our *true* and *lawful attorney*, for *us* and our tribe" and authorized to prosecute all claims arising out of various treaties "as fully and in every respect as we *ourselves* could do were we personally present." The commissioner, meanwhile, had received a letter signed by sixteen members of the Indian Party asking him not to recognize Miller as a delegate and not to use tribal funds to pay his expenses. The petitioners claimed Miller had no authority to be a delegate. "If he holds any Document purporting to come from the tribe and confirming such authority," they wrote, "it has not been signed by any Officers Competent to Constitute him the Agent of said tribe." Miller responded with an eighteen-page rebuttal affirming his status as a delegate and demanding payment.[37]

A special investigating agent visited the Stockbridge-Munsee reservation and called a meeting to resolve the issue. Forty people—thirty-three men and seven women, all heads of families—attended. When asked to decide the question of paying Miller's expenses, they voted seventeen to sixteen in his favor. The vote was a farce, however. The women, although widowed heads of families, had not been allowed to vote because of their sex.

Had they voted, six would have opposed paying Miller's expenses. Of the votes Miller did receive, eight came from people with the surname Miller, including a mentally incompetent brother. Several of the others who voted for him were also relatives. In a private conversation with the agent, the sachem admitted Miller was "wholly unreliable" and that "he has time and again defrauded his people." Despite this background, the sachem had voted in his favor because, having sent Miller to Washington in the first place, he did not want to appear inconsistent. The agent had little difficulty in reaching a decision. He recommended against paying Miller's expenses. To do so, he said, would be tantamount to taxing needy widows without their consent and forcing them "to pay for services not rendered and to meet expenses wholly unnecessary."[38]

Miller received his money anyway. Perhaps the commissioner could think of no other way to get him out of the city. Nevertheless, it was a decision that even the secretary of the interior questioned. "I am not of my own mind assured of either of the competence or necessity of the services alleged on the part of Mr. Miller," the secretary remarked, "and would suggest that in future the incurring of such large expenses be discouraged, and, if possible, avoided."[39]

Except for the Five Civilized Tribes from Indian Territory, little is known of the process by which other Indians selected delegates. Few tribes were concerned about recording their deliberations; even fewer cared to make that information public. Nevertheless, such data occasionally is found among the records of the Bureau of Indian Affairs at the National Archives. Usually, it consists of transcripts of tribal council meetings submitted as part of the documentation needed to certify that a delegation was duly authorized to represent the tribe.

One such transcript was furnished in 1932 by the tribal council for the Southern Cheyennes and Arapahos, whose headquarters are at Concho, Oklahoma. Twenty-nine of the thirty-six members, who represented the agency's twelve administrative districts, were present on January 27 of that year when the council decided to send a delegation to promote passage of Senate Bill 6236 authorizing "the Arapahoe and Cheyenne Indians to submit claims to the Court of Claims, and for other purposes." As Chief Turkey Leg pointed out, "You all know the Bill we are now talking about is what we all want. We should send our best men to attend to it. Young men that are experienced should be considered." He suggested that Jesse Rowlodge, the tribal secretary, be the principal delegate. "I know that he is experienced and acquainted with matters in Washington, as I have been with him. We should send him as our main delegate. We, the Cheyennes and Arapahoes, should unite and try our best to bring results for the good of our people."[40]

The council concerned itself first with the number of delegates that would be needed to accomplish the assignment. Councilman George Frass suggested sending four men. "We want men who are active and understand all the turns of the business," he declared. Henry Rowlodge thought the entire discussion was premature. "I suggest that we consider the nature of the duties of the delegates before we can tell what number to elect. If they are required to do heavy work, we should consider the best and most intelligent and the number necessary." When his suggestion was ignored, Rowlodge supported the recommendation of Councilman Crooked Nose, who urged his colleagues to send six delegates. "It seems," Rowlodge said, "that six delegates that will be represented by a mixed element is a good way to represent the mixed classes of our tribes." The motion for six delegates passed unanimously.

The council next turned its attention to the delegates themselves. Rowlodge recommended the delegation consist of three men from each tribe, each one representing a different class within the tribe. "We should elect one well informed educated young man that is also a good interpreter, one old chief and the third man [should be] a middle age[d] headman or leader who can understand both Cheyenne and Arapaho and some English, like John Otterby or Arnold Woolworth. Making three and three of each tribe." Crooked Nose disagreed. "We should elect two old chiefs from each tribe and one interpreter each. The old men know our treaties and our dealings of the past." Councilman Frass did not think a delegation of old chiefs would adequately serve the council's needs in this instance. "I suggest," he said, "we elect one live-wire young man to act as main delegate. One that will get right in with our Senators and Congressmen."

Henry Rowlodge's recommendation was accepted, and the nominations began. The Cheyenne delegates were selected first. Alfred Wilson was elected the Cheyenne "educated young man" by a vote of twenty-seven to two. John Otterby, who agreed to be the middle-aged English-speaking delegate, received a vote of twenty to zero. There were three nominees for the "Cheyenne old chief": Jacob All Runner, Kias, and Little Face. Sixty-five year old Kias won with fifteen votes. For the Arapahos, White Shirt was elected the "old chief" delegate, and Jesse Rowlodge the "live-wire young man." The balloting was completed when seventy-year-old Arnold Woolworth—"a man active and well-informed"—agreed to serve as the Arapaho delegate who could speak English.

The question of the delegates' per diem was the final item on the agenda. Each delegate normally received $5 a day for expenses, but Jesse Rowlodge said that was insufficient to cover the costs of the delegation secretary. On his last trip to Washington he had spent $28 for out-of-pocket expenses like taxis, telegrams, and postage. He hoped the council could figure out some way to cover these expenses. Henry Rowlodge agreed that something had to be done. It was unfair for someone so conscientious and hardworking to suffer financially while working for the tribe. "What he does for us and can very competently perform for us, no other young man of our tribe that I know of can do." Henry Rowlodge suggested raising the secretary's per diem to $7.50. Crooked Nose supported the recommendation, noting that he had been to Washington with Jesse six years before and could testify to his energy and activity on the tribe's behalf. Crooked Nose thought *all* delegates should have a per diem of $6, because "we should consider the delegates' families while they are away." Accordingly, the council resolved:

that the delegates selected by this council and authorized to proceed to Washington, D.C. to represent the Southern Arapaho and Cheyenne tribes be and they are hereby authorized as delegates, agents and attorneys in fact for the tribe to appear before the committees of Congress and the Department of the Interior to advocate and urge the passage of such legislation and departmental action as they may deem for the best interest of the tribes; that they have authority from this council to incur such necessary expenses in connection with their work at Washington as may be proper, reasonable and just, subject to the approval of the Commissioner of Indian Affairs; and that the necessary expenses of the delegation including their transportation, subsistence, and a per diem of $6.00 a day be allowed and paid out of tribal funds by the Department of the Interior, and that the Secretary, Jesse Rowlodge, as managing delegate be allowed $7.50.

The meeting was closed by Chief Little Face, a new council member. "We have selected good men as I know all of them personally," he said. "I can see the good order all through this council. It is not good to pull apart or away. We are all poor, think of our children who are depending on us. Let us not fool them. Let us depend on the Almighty to help us. He will pity us if we ask him for His mercy. So before closing," Little Face continued, "I ask the delegates to Washington to try hard and think of the people who will stay awake in their homes at night listening for good news. That's all."

Although the majority of Indian delegates made relatively brief visits to the capital,

John Quinney, Stockbridge delegate, whose portrait was painted by Charles Bird King in 1842. Quinney, appropriately, is holding a rolled sheet of paper that reads: "Memorial to Congress, 1842."

some remained for considerable lengths of time and could be described as resident delegates. Usually literate and bilingual, of mixed Indian-white or Indian-black parentage, these delegates were actually lobbyists who were wise in the ways of the bureaucracy and knew how to get legislation enacted as well as introduced. They would be employed by their tribes to promote passage of special-interest legislation or to pursue claims against the government. Their residence in the city would coincide with the sessions of Congress, although they might interrupt their stay with trips home to attend to tribal business or family matters. Indian lobbyists appeared on the Washington scene as early as the 1820s, with most of them coming from acculturated tribes like the Cherokees, Creeks, Six Nations, and Stockbridge-Munsees.

The most prominent of the Stockbridge-Munsee delegates was John W. Quinney, who first came to Washington in 1828 and eventually made ten trips before he died in 1855. A slender, almost gaunt man with Lincolnesque features, Quinney was an ordained Presbyterian minister, mild in manner, and articulate. His greatest success as a lobbyist occurred in 1846 when he almost single-handedly managed to get the act of 1843 repealed, thereby restoring the Stockbridge-Munsees to federal status and making them, once again, wards of the government.[41]

Thanks to a brief diary that Quinney kept during his 1846 stay, we can follow his activities as a lobbyist. He arrived from Wisconsin shortly before New Year's Day 1846, and he remained in Washington until August. Most of his time was spent explaining the plight of the Stockbridge-Munsees to members of Congress and other government officials. On January 19, he met with Jacob Thompson, chairman of the House Committee on Indian Affairs, who told him to see the commissioner of Indian affairs because his committee needed certain key reports before it could discuss the Stockbridge-Munsee question. Quinney visited the bureau the next day and was allowed to read some of the pertinent correspondence, including a letter the commissioner had drafted for the House committee. When Quinney raised some objections about the letter, the commissioner promised to revise it. Quinney returned the following day to approve the new draft and was pleased to find that the Stockbridge-Munsee business was now "better understood."[42]

As the weeks passed, Quinney kept the House committee supplied with relevant documents and chatted with any congressmen willing to hear him. He appeared before the committee on March 5 and then went to Albany, New York. There he conferred with sympathizers who had sought support for the Stockbridge-Munsee cause in the New York legislature. Quinney returned two weeks later to find his bill reported out of committee. He now worked even harder to get it on the House calendar. Among the congressmen who promised support was John Quincy Adams, now almost eighty years old. Quinney found Adams gracious and encouraging. "Kind words do me good," he noted in his diary after meeting the former president.[43]

When the bill moved from the House to the Senate, Quinney repeated his pattern of activities. Both Thomas Hart Benton and Dixon Lewis, chairman of the Senate Committee on Indian Affairs, promised their assistance. They evidently kept their promise, because the bill passed the Senate unanimously and was signed into law on August 6. "Good, good, I can now return home gladly," a delighted Quinney exclaimed upon learning the news. "We Stockbridges are now Indians again."[44]

Unfortunately, the success of the bill did not occur in time to benefit Quinney's youngest son, who died while his father was in Washington. Nor did it ease the bitter political strife among the Stockbridge-Munsees. If anything, passage of the bill intensified the conflict between the Indian and Citizen parties, a conflict that continued until well into the twentieth century. As a result, Quinney was only the first in a succession of Stockbridge-Munsee lobbyists. Men like Albert Miller, John Chickey, Moses Ladd, Jacob Jacobs, and John C. Adams became familiar faces to government officials. Quite often delegates of both parties would be in Washington at the same time. Then each delegate would work as hard to keep the other from accomplishing objectives as he would to attain his own. Since federal funds were almost unobtainable for the Stockbridge-Munsees, the delegates depended on funds furnished by their supporters at home, who mortgaged their farms, sold livestock, sponsored benefit dances, and cut firewood to keep their delegates working for the cause. For a party to keep its delegate in Washington was as much a matter of pride and accomplishment as to attain legislative victories, which were few and far between.

One of the more able lobbyists for the Citizen Party was John C. Adams, son of a Stockbridge-Munsee Indian and missionary's daughter, who was active in the last quarter of the nineteenth century. A zealous and tireless advocate of the Citizen cause, Adams for more than twenty years divided his time between his Wisconsin farm and the boardinghouses of Washington. His was a precarious existence at best, because he was almost completely dependent on the contributions of tribal supporters.[45]

One of Adams's most faithful benefactors was Sara Slingerhand, who regularly furnished him with funds, and gossip. "We have all (our party I mean) made Every Effort we could to send you money," she wrote on April 17, 1888, when forwarding twelve dollars. "I know how disappointed you must have felt in not getting the 10, in the promised time but that is nothing. you will be thankful I know that it is 12 instead of a poor 10." More money would soon be on its way. One man was selling his oxen,

John C. Adams, the tireless lobbyist for the Citizen Party of the Stockbridge Munsee Indians of Wisconsin. Photograph taken during his 1876 visit to Washington.

which would fetch at least fifty dollars. "I think you may rest assured that the money will be raised at some rate, none of them want you to come home before the business is finished." In the meantime, Slingerhand hoped Adams would not "suffer for money or loose credit, or have to go through with any Scenes of discomfort both mortifying and disgraceful for a *Delegate* to Washington to bear." On another occasion, she informed Adams that members of the Indian Party were boasting that they supported their delegate in better style. They were saying that the Citizen Party "cant get money Enough to keep their man therc, they can only send him a little at a time, but when we undertake to raise money we get for our man two or three hundred dollars so that he can live good there [in Washington]."[46]

No matter how difficult it was for Adams, his sponsors preferred he remain in Washington rather than return to Wisconsin. "They are very anxious that you should stay to see the business through," Slingerhand reported, "and I feel that you must not come away until it is accomplished as it might be necessary for you to go back which would double the cost. The cheapest as well as wisest thing you can do is to stay, as long as it is necessary." And Adams did stay, living a hand-to-mouth existence, eagerly awaiting the next mail and the money needed to survive another week, another month. Funds were so meager that he would write his letters on the blank space of incoming letters, and he would ask correspondents to enclose the postage if they wished a reply. Adams eventually had to sell his farm to support his lobbying efforts. Despite his years of dedicated service, however, he was not rewarded by the tribe. Adams died penniless in 1895.[47]

How many of these resident delegates were there at any one time? The number, though difficult to determine, is far greater than one would imagine. The commissioner of Indian affairs, in response to a congressional inquiry on the subject, compiled the following list of resident delegates in 1876:

Cherokees
L. H. Ross, W. P. Adair, John L. Adair, Rufus Q. Ross, Delegates

Old Settler Cherokees
Joel M. Bryan and J. L. McCoy, Commissioners

Creeks
D. N. McIntosh and David M. Hodge, Delegates

Choctaws
P. P. Pitchlynn, Representative

The commissioner also listed the following individuals as being in the city "upon business appertaining to themselves as individuals or as bands":

Wyandottes
Mathew Mudeater, John Sarrahass, and Nicholas Cotter

Stockbridges
Moses Ladd and Jacob Jacobs

North Carolina Cherokees
Lloyd R. Welch and C. H. Taylor

The commissioner never recognized Welch and Taylor as delegates, even though they claimed to have been appointed by a general council of the Eastern Cherokees. Although the commissioner had been asked about the salary of all these resident delegates as well as their names, he was unable to answer because, he replied, they "are appointed, and paid, if at all, by their respective tribes."[48]

The bureau seemingly had no general policy toward the Indian lobbyists, for they became subject to official action only when they submitted claims for payment from federal or tribal funds. Usually such a claim was a fruitless exercise. Most of the lobbyists seem to have survived on odd jobs and commissions from claims they might collect from the federal government on behalf of other Indians. John C. Adams, for instance, drafted correspondence, bills, and other documents for less literate delegates from other tribes. Andrew John, a Seneca delegate who spent a good deal of time in the capital near the turn of the twentieth century, earned money by escorting Indians to the Bureau of American Ethnology and the Smithsonian Institution to be photographed.

Some Indian lobbyists hoped to achieve personal success in Washington while escaping for a time the drab existence of their home communities. These were persuasive individuals who relied on force of personality and guile to obtain their objectives. Their forte was convincing the less-sophisticated members of their tribes that they were doing great things in Washington that would eventually return significant benefits to their supporters. One of the more notorious of these individuals was J. I. Coffey, a Chippewa from Minnesota who was active in Washington in the early 1920s. He regularly submitted claims to the bureau requesting $125 monthly for his services as the Chippewa delegate.

These the commissioner just as regularly ignored, although Coffey successfully got several congressmen to intercede on his behalf. Coffey kept up a lively correspondence with the Minnesota Indian communities and claimed credit for any and all legislation in Congress that benefited them. As a result, the Chippewas were convinced he was doing important things for them, and they continually sponsored dances and collected money for his expenses. The commissioner was powerless to thwart Coffey and could only withhold official recognition of him as a Chippewa delegate.[49]

Serving as a delegate was not necessarily the key to continued tribal prominence. In many instances, the delegation experience seems to have had the opposite effect. It was a person of strong character who did not return home with a greatly inflated ego caused by all the attention and presents he had received in the East. Even the famous Red Jacket of the Senecas after his return would greatly magnify the importance and circumstances of his meetings with the Great Father. "I remember having seen him on one of these occasions," recalled one witness. "After having seated the Indians around him in a semicircle [and] taking the cocked-hat that had been presented to him . . . in his hand, he went round bowing to the Indians, as though they were the company at the President's house, and himself the President." Red Jacket "would then repeat to one and another all the compliments which he chose to suppose the President had bestowed upon him, and which his auditors and admiring people supposed had been thus bestowed."[50]

Under the best of conditions misunderstandings and distortions occurred. Perhaps these were caused by the typical human frailty of hearing what one wanted to hear; perhaps mistakes were more deliberate. Whatever the explanation, misrepresentation of what transpired in Washington was a serious problem. The members of a delegation from the Southern Plains who visited Washington during the Civil War returned home happy in the belief that the whites would soon kill one another and allow the Indians to retake the country. Lone Wolf of the Kiowas, one of the delegates, returned "impudent and insulting." Claiming the Great Father had authorized him to collect tolls from wagon trains crossing the Southern Plains, he would show the papers he had received in Washington to the teamsters and demand payment from their supplies. "From what I can learn he exercises his presumed rights without any conscientious scruples," marveled an army officer stationed in the area.[51]

Lone Wolf 's son was made from the same mold. In 1887 the Kiowa agent complained to the commissioner of Indian affairs about the younger Lone Wolf and a companion, Caddo Jake, following their visit to Washington. "They have been persistently advising their people and telling them exactly the contrary to what you told them or advised [them] while there," he declared. The two troublemakers used a letter signed by the commissioner to back up their claims. No Indian who could read was allowed to see it. Although the Indian agent had a copy, Lone Wolf insisted it was a fake. The only explanation the agent could offer for their mischief was the belief that the men had been "tampered with by parties outside of the Indian office."[52]

These were not isolated incidents. To the Winnebago agent, nothing so "demoralized" an Indian as "going to Washington." The Indian upon his return always distorted what was said to him and insisted that the agent was not following the Great Father's instructions. "We have more trouble from this source than any other," he affirmed. The underlying reason, the agent believed, was that reliable men seldom served as delegates. Instead, the "disturbers and miscontents" went to Washington, and when they returned, "their importance is so magnified that they are intolerable."[53]

Such sentiments were shared by the agent for the Standing Rock Sioux. "I find that the visits of Indian chiefs to Washington has this bad effect," he wrote in 1881. "When the chiefs come home, in order to cement their power as authority among their people, they state the number of heroic demands they have made on the 'Great Father,' and that he promised to fulfill them all." Tribesmen would eventually come to the agent and demand that the promises be kept. The agent, in turn, would inquire at the bureau for confirmation and discover that no such promises were ever made. The matter would then become one of veracity, pitting the agent against the delegates. "I have had to shoulder that trouble, and speak only from bitter experience."[54]

The agent for the Southern Cheyennes and Arapahos also regarded the delegation experience as counterproductive. "I had hoped their visit to Washington, and the advice and instruction which it was expected you would give them, would go a long way towards making my work less difficult in the effort to advance them in civilized habits," he wrote the commissioner in January 1899. Instead, the returned delegates caused him nothing but trouble. They claimed they had been told they could use their own discretion in obeying the agent's orders about compulsory school attendance for their children, travel restrictions, and similar touchy issues. "By their manner, [they] have exhibited a marked disposition to ignore the rules and regulations heretofore imposed." Even worse, some of the Indians—primarily those from the "least progressive" areas of the agency—insisted they would obey no orders not given personally by the commissioner of Indian affairs. "I can only point to the evil consequences which may result if they continue to be imbued with such ideas. Their influence exerted over the Indians who have not visited Washington cannot be otherwise than deleterious."[55]

The returned delegates had their own problems, of course. Many found their fellow tribesmen unwilling to believe what they said about their experiences. Big White, a Mandan visitor to Washington in 1805, found himself totally discredited for his incredible tales. A fellow tribesman described him as "a bag of lies." A traveler who met the unhappy man a few years after his eastern visit described Big White "as a fat man, extremely talkative, and no great warrior."[56]

Other delegates returned to discover that their standing within the tribe had been undermined because of their extended absence. One Assiniboin visitor lost more than his tribal status. The Light was one of four delegates who visited Washington in 1832 representing the Assiniboin, Cree, Plains Ojibway, and Yanktonai Sioux from the present North Dakota-Montana border area. The first of their tribes to visit the East, the four young men received the usual whirlwind tour, complete with an audience with the Great Father. When The Light returned, he sported new clothes and an umbrella that he proudly carried as a symbol of his exalted status. His fellow tribesmen were not impressed. They were annoyed not only at his arrogance but also at his fantastic tales about the strange and marvelous things he had seen in the East. All that saved him from instant disaster was the belief that he had special powers protecting him from ordinary lead bullets. This tolerance, however, ended the night he described the Baltimore shot tower to a group of disbelieving companions, who openly hooted at the story of a building so tall. Angry and disgusted, The Light broke his prized umbrella over the back of one particulary obnoxious heckler and stalked off into the darkness. The heckler, in turn, fashioned a bullet from iron—just in case The Light did have magical powers—and went looking for him. He found the former delegate sulking in his tent before the fire and shot off the top of his head.[57]

The Light's misfortunes may have been unique. Still, the loss of credibility on the part of returned delegates appears to have been a widespread hazard until the end of the nineteenth century, when even the most remote tribes had been exposed to the wonders of the white man's world. One army officer, writing in 1872, declared flatly that "when

The Light, the Assinniboin chief who visited Washington in January 1832 and then met an untimely fate because of his delegation experience. This well-known portrait by George Catlin depicts the chief going to and returning from his eastern visit. Catlin's dismay at the change that occurred in the noble warrior is obvious. The Light for his return home is wearing an army uniform and sporting a fan, umbrella, and white gloves; a pair of ill-concealed whiskey bottles peek from beneath the tails of his military greatcoat.

a chief returns from Washington to his tribe his Indians do not follow him. They declare that he has been bewitched, or had 'bad medicine,' and they do not believe anything he tells them." This opinion was shared by another officer, who wrote: "For a long time those [Indians] who remained at home were disbelievers, and said those who had gone East were bewitched by the whites who had escorted them, and that they were great liars." Even the renowned Sitting Bull, who had not accompanied a delegation before the Battle of the Little Big Horn, discounted the fabulous tales of other Sioux delegates as figments of their imagination, induced by the powerful "medicine" of the white man.[58]

The officials in Washington were aware of the credibility problem. The commissioner in his report for 1872 noted that even trusted delegates were not always believed when they reported seeing whites as numerous as the sands on the seashore and houses piled on top of houses and stretching miles in every direction. Such tales were dismissed by their people, who claimed that the whites had put "bad medicine" in their eyes so they would see things that did not exist. "It has only been the concurrent testimony of many chiefs and braves, out of many bands and tribes, that has dissipated this happy conceit of the Indian of the plains, and made him appreciate, as he is beginning to do, the power and resources of the whites."[59]

The credibility problem was not confined to the people at home. Even the delegates could scarcely believe the things they saw. An agent accompanying the Red Cloud and Spotted Tail delegation of 1870 overheard several of the Indians discussing the great numbers of whites they were seeing. The astonished warriors could only reason that they were seeing the same people in each city. The people in Chicago had somehow followed them to Washington, Philadelphia, and then New York. The delegates were certain that the white men, with their superior technology, had developed the means of moving whole cities, much like the Sioux themselves, who could move their teepee villages from one site to another.[60]

An interpreter with another delegation overheard a similar conversation. The Indians wondered where the knowledge came from that enabled the white people to make such amazing devices as guns, steamboats, trains, and the telegraph. After considerable discussion among themselves, they concluded that wise spirits visited white men during their sleep and told them how to make these things. Indians did not receive the same nocturnal visits, they believed, because their ancestors had somehow offended the spirits who now favored whites.[61]

Some of the things the Indians saw and heard seemed so incomprehensible that they shut their minds to them. This is how the Apaches escorted to Washington in 1870 by General O. O. Howard reacted to his explanation of the rotation of the earth. They insisted he stop talking about it or risk losing their friendship. He had never before lied to them, they admitted, but nothing he could say would make them believe the earth revolved on an axis. "Indians do not think that way" was their only comment.[62]

The failure to accomplish intended objectives also caused delegates to lose prestige. Indians expected to return with valuable gifts—a uniform, a medal, perhaps a horse—as tangible evidence of their importance and the great things they had achieved in Washington. By the close of the nineteenth century, the old rules no longer applied, and delegates were lucky to go home with a new suit of clothes and a pat on the back. The dissatisfaction with such treatment was well expressed by Young Man Afraid of His Horses, an Oglala chief who visited Washington in 1891. When asked by a Chicago reporter what his delegation had accomplished, the Sioux militant retorted: "We had some promises, but they are like all other promises of the Great Father. We are not fooled and we go home with heavy hearts. . . . We shall tell our people that we have got more promises. Then they will laugh at us and call us old men."[63]

Undue stress should not be placed on the negative aspects of the delegation experience. Despite all the problems, frustrations, and misunderstandings, most Indians seem to have returned home delighted with their adventure and embued with a sense of pride and accomplishment. A Winnebago woman who accompanied her husband to Washington in 1828 was pleased to be known thereafter as "The Washington Woman." The Omaha Chief Big Elk, who came east with O'Fallon in 1821, commemorated that experience by painting two large steamboats on the cover of his teepee so that everyone who saw it would know the honor bestowed upon him. For doubting congressmen, the officials of the Indian service had a bulging file of correspondence with delegates who

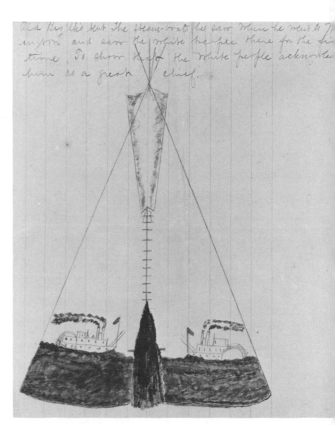

Left: Big Elk (Onpatonga), an Omaha chief who visited Washington in 1821 as a member of the Benjamin O'Fallon delegation. Portrait by Charles Bird King.

Right: Big Elk was so pleased with his visit to Washington that he commemorated the experience by painting steamboats on the cover of his teepee. The above pencil-and-watercolor drawing was done by George Miller in 1889.

were gratified at their treatment and eager to implement whatever suggestions had been given them for the advancement and betterment of their people. Two such delegates were Andrew Saltise and Pierre Wildshoe. "We went to Washington & saw with our own eyes that our Chiefs at Washington were our Friends," they wrote after returning to the Coeur D'Alène Reservation in 1887. "We shook hands, & our meeting was held, and our hearts were cured . . . we came back and our Friends, the Indians and Chiefs here, after hearing what had been said & done at Washington were all satisfied. . . . We beg of you to shake hands, and say 'Goodday,' to the President, Secretary Lamar and ... [Commissioner] Atkins for all the Coeur D'Alènes."[64]

VI MEETING THE GREAT FATHER

The central figure in the delegation story is the president of the United States. He personified the majesty and strength of the United States to the Indians, who called him the Great Father in keeping with the seeming magical powers of the white man. He was never known as the Great White Father; Indians did not think in racial terms. Although the expression is commonly used today, not a single instance has been found in which Indians in the nineteenth century or earlier referred to the president as the Great White Father. The expression probably entered the popular lexicon sometime early in the twentieth century, perhaps as a contribution of the dime-novel industry.

It was, in fact, the Great Father who inspired the delegation pageantry. The Indians proudly wore medallions, known as peace medals, which bore his likeness. Many of the gifts they received carried his seal. He was a symbol of power and rectitude who aroused unquestioning loyalty in his red children. No matter how unwelcome might be the Great Father's ruling on an issue, it would be respected.

The Great Father image is difficult for us to understand today. We wonder how Indians could accept and submit to the explicit paternalism the title conveys. Actually, it may have been a diplomatic tactic by the Indians. The father-child relationship is an important one among Indians. Since the Indian father tries to be as generous as possible to his children, tribal leaders probably used the father-child metaphor in their discussions with government officials in order to strengthen their requests for gifts and favors. Thus, at least on the part of the Indians, the term Great Father was a diplomatic device rather than an expression of subordinance. Most government officials failed to grasp the metaphor, however. They thought the Indians were merely acknowledging their subordinate status to the president and, through him, to whites in general.[1]

Whatever the explanation, Indians meeting the president for the first time often reacted like children when confronted by an unyielding figure of authority. Delegates who had traveled enormous distances at great personal hardship to meet the Great Father would manifest fear and awe in his presence. The experience of the Southern Cheyenne and Arapaho delegation of 1851 is typical. The first of their tribe to meet the Great Father, they were apprehensive and depressed as they awaited their audience with President Millard Fillmore. According to an observer, "they were under such mental solicitude and constraint, lest in his august greatness . . . [the Great Father] might not be gracious unto them." After their meeting, the delegates reflected a marked change in disposition. "The depression they had before exhibited was seen to have left them, and was succeeded by a freedom and joyousness of manner much in contrast with their prior uneasy posture of mind." Lean Bear, spokesman for the Southern Plains delegation of 1863, was so nervous when meeting Abraham Lincoln that he could not speak until he was brought a chair to sit on. Hoowaneka, a Winnebago chief who met John Quincy Adams in 1828, thought he had entered another world. "So large and beautiful was the President's House, the carpets, the tables, the mirrors, the chairs, and every article in it, were so beautiful, that when I entered it," he recalled, "I thought I was in heaven, and the old man there, I thought was the Great Spirit." Even acculturated Indians like James N. Cusick, a Tuscarora delegate who met President James K. Polk in 1845, would be awestruck. "He appearance like as a Priest, and his countenance pleasant and tender voice most beautiful," Cusick later wrote. "[He] is not large but . . . smallest man. But his knowledge and his dignity most greatness in the world."[2]

This almost mystical veneration for the presidency survived among many of the tribes until at least the turn of the twentieth century. Indeed, the name Great Father was regularly used by Indians when speaking of the president until the 1890s, and some old chiefs used the term as late as the 1920s. "Tell my new Great father that I want to see him very much. I want to shake hand with him before any Indians will," wrote Spotted Tail in April 1881, following the inauguration of James Garfield. "I heard the new great father is good man and I want to see him. I always like to see a good Peaceable man like I am." A few months later, following Garfield's assassination, the White House received another letter from Dakota Territory. This one was signed by Rain in the Face and other Sioux leaders who had fled to Canada after the Battle of the Little Big Horn. Now back from their exile, they wished to visit Washington and reaffirm their loyalty to the United States. "Great Father, We are poor, we want your protection and help, we want to see your face. We have heard that the Great Father has been shot, we want to see him; if he is dead we want to go to his grave and mourn for him." Mandan and Gros Ventre leaders used the term in 1898 when requesting permission to send a delegation to Washington. "We have been true friends to the Great Father," they wrote, "and . . . we have no desire to mbarross [sic] the Department, by sending a delegation of discontented savages to Washington to have a big talk about small matters." Their business involved a major land dispute, and their lawyers felt the Fort Berthold Indians should press their claim. Thus, "we earnestly ask for the right to present our claims in person through our representatives, to the Great Father himself."[3]

Even today Indians hold the presidency in special regard, a regard that extends to the city of Washington itself. Perhaps this is due to the treaties housed at the National Archives that provide a link to their past and to their ancestors. Perhaps it is because Washington is the capital of their country, and Indians more than any other group in the United States are intensely patriotic. Perhaps it is simply because Washington is the headquarters for the Bureau of Indian Affairs, the agency that has controlled their destiny for 150 years. Whatever the explanation, Washington is special to the American Indians. Henry Old Coyote, a member of the Crow tribe working for the Senate as an adviser on Indian legislation, tried to explain this feeling in an interview in April 1978. "Indians love their country and this country is administered by the government so they tie the two of them together. They show the respect to the government." Washington symbolizes that government, he said. "It's the nation's capital, that's where the president resides. It's more like a shrine to the Indians . . . and they hold it as such and they feel that a certain reverence should be extended to the place."[4]

This emphasis on the presidency sometimes complicates the administration of Indian affairs even today. "Many tribes, particularly the Onondagas and some of the New York

Iroquois, still feel to meet with anybody less than the president is impossible because they are a nation equal to the United States," explained Leslie Gay, a tribal operations officer at the bureau. "When they have problems the only person they want to deal with is their respective leader who is the president, not the secretary of the interior and not the commissioner of Indian affairs." Actually, Gay asserted, "every Indian delegation would like to meet with the president, but many of them realize now that they just aren't going to do it. They're wasting their time." Despite the odds, Indian delegations continue to make the effort. A common pretext, Gay reports, is the desire to present the president with a peace pipe. The president realizes, however, that if he met privately with members from one tribe, he would be doing nothing but meeting with Indian delegations: all of the tribes would want the same privilege. "The logical thing to do under these circumstances is to not meet with any of them or else only meet with them when they all come in at once like Jerry Ford did when he appeared before a conference of Indian leaders in 1976. He whipped in, said hello, and suddenly the lights went out. When the lights came back on Ford was gone." That is how President Ford escaped without having to answer any real questions, Gay said. Group meetings are also impractical because the delegates would naturally seek to address problems of unique significance to their tribes. "Let's face it, 260 tribal representatives would not really be interested in listening to discussions, for example, of the Blackfoot water problem." Most Indians today realize that their problems are handled at much lower levels of government. Seldom do Indian affairs merit the attention of cabinet officers. "That does not mean that Indians all over who want to meet with the White House have given up the idea," Gay declared. "I think if any of them had the opportunity they would jump at it. They don't have that opportunity, and they realize now that they are not going to get the opportunity."[5]

In the nineteenth century, meetings between the Great Father and delegations varied little from administration to administration. Seldom was serious business transacted. Such discussions were held with officials who administered Indian affairs at the cabinet level. Audiences with the president were ceremonial interviews, courtesies of state. As a result, they would often be large gatherings, consisting of the presidential family, congressmen, Supreme Court justices, high-ranking military officers, and ambassadors from foreign countries and their families. These highly orchestrated affairs included the pomp and pagentry accorded visiting heads of state.

The meeting between President James Monroe and the O'Fallon delegation of 1821 excited considerable interest and was well-publicized in the local press. For this important occasion, the Indians were wearing new clothes, which consisted of military uniforms complete with silver epaulets, hats, and black boots. Followed by O'Fallon and the interpreters, the seventeen Indians were ushered into the president's antechamber, where they nervously awaited his arrival. They were not completely at ease in their strange clothes. "Their coats seemed to pinch them about the shoulders," one bystander noticed; "now and then they would take off their uneasy headdresses, and one sought a temporary relief by pulling off his boots." Monroe's entrance brought the assembly to attention.[6]

Speaking from prepared notes held in one hand, the president addressed the delegates, thanking them for coming such a great distance to see him and the wonders of the white man's world. Now he hoped the Indians would want the comforts of civilized life for themselves. If so, he was prepared to send missionaries to teach their people agriculture and the lessons of Christianity. The president was also pleased that the Indians had visited forts, arsenals, and navy yards; but, he warned, they had seen only a fraction of American military strength. Few fighting men were needed at the capital; in time of war all citizens took up arms and became warriors. Thus, he urged the Indians to remain at peace with each other and not to listen to those who advised them to mistrust or fight with the United States. As Monroe spoke, the interpreters translated his speech sentence by sentence; the Indians in return nodded gravely, indicating that they understood what had been said.

When the president finished, the delegates were invited to respond. Sharitarish, spokesman for the Pawnees, stepped forward, solemnly shook hands with Monroe, and slowly delivered a long speech. "My Great Father," he said, "I have traveled a great distance to see you—I have seen you and my heart rejoices. I have heard your words . . . and I will carry them to my people as pure as they came from your mouth . . . [I] have seen your people, your homes, your vessels on the big lake, and a great many wonderful things far beyond my comprehension, which appears to have been made by the Great Spirit and placed in your hands." But, wonderful as it was, he would not trade his way of life for that of the white man. There were still plenty of buffalo to hunt and beaver to trap. "It is too soon," Sharitarish continued, "to send those good men [the missionaries] among us—we are not starving yet—we wish you to permit us to enjoy the chase until the game of our country is exhausted—until the wild animals become extinct. . . . I have grown up, and lived this long without work," he declared; "I am in hopes you will suffer me to die without it. We have everything we want—we have plenty of land, if you will keep your people off it."

The other chiefs then spoke in turn, each stressing his love for the Indian way of life. The first speakers were noticeably nervous, but each succeeding orator became less reserved until the last—claimed a witness—spoke "as loud as you ever heard a lawyer at a county court bar."

As each speaker finished, he laid a present at the president's feet. Monroe was sitting behind a mound of buffalo robes, calumets, moccasins, and feathered headdresses when the lengthy ceremony ended.

Everyone adjourned to the drawing room for cake and wine. The Indians capped the festivities by lighting their pipes and passing them to the president, Chief Justice John Marshall, and other dignitaries, who took token whiffs. By this time the visitors had endured their unfamiliar and uncomfortable clothing long enough. As a dismayed observer reported, "one of them, unable longer to bear the pressure of his boots, sat down and deliberately pulled them off. Another his coat, until the whole might have brought themselves back to a comfortable state of nature had they not been led out."

President John Quincy Adams presided over a similar ceremony when he met with a Winnebago delegation on November 29, 1828. The Winnebagos, a Siouan-speaking people from Wisconsin, were on the verge of a major uprising because of white encroachment on their lands. Only the year before there had been a brief flurry of hostilities when Red Bird, leader of a small Winnebago band residing about eighty miles above Prairie du Chien at La Crosse, had tried to retaliate against land speculators and miners who were continually trespassing on the rich mineral lands his people occupied. Provoked by a rumor that miners had killed two of his warriors, Red Bird sought revenge by killing two Prairie du Chien farmers and attacking two keelboats on the Mississippi River. The relatively mild outbreak ended when Red Bird and five of his warriors surrendered and were sent to Prairie du Chien for trial. The government, anxious to prevent another uprising, decided to bring the Winnebago leaders to Washington, where they could be persuaded to sell their coveted mineral lands.[7]

Adams was waiting for the Winnebagos when they reached the White House. The sixteen delegates were in full regalia as they entered the room in single file. One by one they shook the president's hand with brusque cordiality and then sat in their assigned seats. The first order of business was refreshments, consisting of madeira and macaroons, which the delegates seemed to relish. As the other guests continued to sip their wine, Nawkaw, an old and respected chief, stepped into the center of the room and faced the president. He held aloft a long-stemmed pipe, which he waved slowly over Adams's head. Then, extending the pipe before him, he delivered a short speech that required a double interpretation, first into French and then into English.[8]

"Father," Nawkaw said. "I am glad to see you. I hold out this pipe, and I take your hand in friendship. A cloud has been between us. It was thick and black. I thought once it would never be removed. But I now see your face. It looks upon me pleasantly." Nawkaw had been told that the path to the Great Father was blocked and red men could not pass it, but he was glad to learn this was not true. "Father," the old chief continued, "the Great Spirit gave to his children, the Winnebagos, a pleasant plant. It is good to smoke." Tapping the pipe bowl with his forefinger, he said, "I have it here. I give it to you in peace." A young man then came forward and lit the pipe using flint and steel. After Adams had taken a few puffs, it was passed to each of the spectators. When everyone in the room, including the other delegates, had smoked the pipe, Nawkaw returned it to Adams and asked him to keep it.

Adams accepted the pipe, but he told Nawkaw to keep one hand on it while he addressed the group. "Say this to the chief," Adams instructed the interpreter. "I rejoice to see him. He and his brethren are welcome to me and to my children." The president then expressed his sorrow at the thought of a black cloud between the Great Father and his red children. Surely it was no longer there. Like the smoke from the pipe, the cloud had dispersed. "May it never close down upon us any more." Adams thanked Nawkaw for the pipe and assured him that he would continue to look at it with satisfaction when the Winnebagos returned home. Should anyone ever tell him the tribe was again at war, Adams would not believe it, "for I have the word of a Winnebago, which must be true, that his people pledge their amity with mine, and have left this pipe in token of sincerity."

When Nawkaw sat down, another Winnebago came forward. Adams had been forewarned that this man would ask for the release of Red Bird and the Winnebago prisoners. "Father," the warrior said in a firm voice, "my heart is heavy. Indulge me with a request. When I and your Red Children go from you, permit us to bear a paper from your hands, that shall give light to the poor Winnebagos imprisoned at Prairie du Chien."

"I have indeed been vested by the people of these United States to remit at discretion, the punishment of death," Adams replied, adding that he had never used this power on behalf of his white children. Furthermore, the Great Spirit had ordained the death penalty for crimes like those committed at Prairie du Chien. "But," Adams continued after a dramatic pause, "to manifest the conciliatory dispositions wherewith my heart is filled, and to prove the sincerity of my pacific professions communicated this day, I will grant your tribe a favor withheld from individuals of my own nation." The president then drafted a letter commuting the death sentences of the imprisoned Winnebagos and handed it to Nawkaw.

The Great Father immediately tempered the joy of the Winnebagos by making a request of his own. He asked the delegation to consider selling to the United States the lands in Wisconsin that had been the source of the recent troubles. The tract was of little value to them, he argued, whereas in the hands of the whites, "it would prove of imminent utility." A fair price would be paid for the land, he assured the delegation.

The request stunned the Indians. After discussing it among themselves for a few minutes, one of the chiefs told Adams that none of their lands could be alienated without the consent of all the warriors in open council. Nevertheless, in light of the spirit of amity and indulgence the Great Father had just shown them, the delegates promised to return home and use their influence to permit the white settlers to have "a *small portion*" of the land in question. This, the delegates hoped, would be the only request for land that would ever be made of them, "as they felt themselves bound to hold in perpetuity the soil which the Great Spirit had given them."

Adams thanked the delegates for their generosity, whereupon a second calumet was presented and passed around as before. This one was also given to Adams. After another round of refreshments and the distribution of presents, the Winnebagos left the White House; but, as one observer wryly commented, they left not so rich as they had come. "They had forfeited," he later wrote, " '*the pound of flesh*,' and it will unyieldingly be exacted of them. Yes, Winnebagos, the *heel* of the white man is already upon your land, and ere long, the whole will be pressed down and made to cover it." Ironically, the presidential pardon came too late to save Red Bird, who had already died in prison.

Ceremonies such as this were repeated countless times during the nineteenth century. Even Abraham Lincoln during the darkest moments of the Civil War had to find time to enact his role as the Great Father. Although he met with several delegations and had private audiences with prominent Indian leaders like John Ross, chief of the Cherokees, almost nothing is known of these conversations except for a few meager records. Lincoln's secretary, John Hay, jotted a few notes during a meeting with three Potawatomi Indians from Iowa. Hay's account indicates that Lincoln, like most of the Great Fathers, had little conception of Indian culture. Apparently assuming all Indians spoke the same language, he greeted his visitors with the two or three Indian words he knew. Then, despite the fact that the leader of the delegation spoke fluent English, Lincoln switched to the broken English he thought the Indians would understand—"Where live now? When go back Iowa?" Hay thought Lincoln's awkward efforts were amusing; what the Indians thought was not recorded.[9]

One meeting between Lincoln and an Indian delegation was thoroughly documented. This was a delegation of sixteen Indians—fourteen men and two women—representing six tribes from the Southern Plains—Comanche, Kiowa, Cheyenne, Arapaho, Caddo, and Apache. A large crowd that included the families of the ministers of England, France, Prussia, and Brazil and the secretaries of state, treasury, navy, and interior, was already waiting in the East Room of the White House when the Indians arrived on the morning of March 27, 1863. Moving to one end of the long room, the Indians sat in a semicircle facing the unusually restless and noisy crowd that quickly surged around them; not everyone could get a good view, which resulted in a considerable amount of pushing and shoving. As one reporter commented, "There unfortunately seems to be an incurable habit among the good people of our country in the house of the Chief Magistrate to press forward and not give an inch to those behind." According to another observer, "Everybody seemed to find someone's bonnet or shoulder in the way, and to think himself or herself entitled to the best and most conspicuous place. . . . Still everything went off very well. These Indians are fine-looking men," he wrote. "They have all the hard and cruel lines in their faces which we might expect in savages; but they are evidently men of intelligence and force of character. They were both dignified and cordial in their manner, and listened to everything with great interest."[10]

The Indians had been waiting about fifteen minutes when Lincoln entered the room. The interpreter introduced each of the chiefs, who came forward and gave the president a quick, vigorous handshake. Lincoln then turned to the interpreter and said: "Say to them I am very glad to see them, and if they have anything to say, it will afford me great pleasure to hear them."

Cheyenne members of the Southern Plains delegation. Left to right: Agent Samuel G. Colley,
War Bonnet, Standing in the Water, and Lean Bear. Photograph taken in Leavenworth, Kansas,
by Alfred S. Addis on March 12 or 13, 1863.

At this, Lean Bear of the Cheyennes rose and stepped forward. The chief was so
nervous, however, that he asked for a chair so he could sit while speaking to the Great
Father. A comfortable armchair was quickly brought forward, but the unusual request
from this powerful and vigorous warrior surprised everyone. Nevertheless, despite his
nervousness, Lean Bear was soon recognized as a gifted orator, with a fluent and animate
style of speaking.

"The President is the Great Chief of the White People," he said; "I am the Great
Chief of the Indians. Our wigwams are not so fine as this; they are small and poor. I hope
the Great Chief will look upon his people with favor, and say in his wisdom what would
be best for them to do. We are here to listen to his advice and carry it in our hearts.

. . . I will hear all the Great Chief has to say; and when I go away I will not carry
. . . [his words] in my pocket, but in my heart, where they will not be lost." Lean Bear
then spoke about the many white people moving into his country. The Indians wished
to live in peace, he said, but he feared the white people were not so inclined. Nevertheless,
he would keep his warriors from the warpath unless the white men provoked a fight.
Lean Bear also spoke of the Civil War, promising to keep his people neutral.

Spotted Wolf, another Cheyenne, was the only other delegate who chose to speak.
Spotted Wolf said he was surprised to see how friendly the white people were. Everywhere
he went he found only brothers. He was also amazed at all the wonderful things the
delegates had seen. "When I look about me and see all these fine things, it seems like
some kind of magic. I do not even know how I got here, so far away from home. It seems
to me that I must have come on wings—like a bird through the air."

When no one else came forward, Lincoln addressed the delegation. "You have all
spoken of the strange sights you see here, among your pale-faced brethren," he said.
"But you have seen but a very small part of the pale-faced people—There are people in
this wigwam, now looking at you, who have come from other countries a great deal
farther off than you have come." Lincoln then launched into a geography lesson. He told
the Indians that the world was a great ball, and that visitors to Washington came from
all parts of that ball. As he spoke, an attendant carried a large globe into the circle.
Lincoln then introduced Joseph Henry, the first secretary of the Smithsonian Institution,
who gave the delegates a detailed explanation of the formation of the earth. Henry
pointed out the oceans, the various countries represented by the visitors in the room, and
the location of Washington in relation to the homeland of the Indians. When Henry
finished speaking, Lincoln resumed his remarks. He told the Indians they would have
to change their way of life if they wished to become as prosperous as the white man. In
his opinion there were two primary differences in their ways of life: whites cultivated the
soil and relied on bread rather than game for subsistence; whites were also a peaceful

Photograph of the Southern Plains
delegation, taken in the White
House Conservatory on March
27, 1863. The interpreter William Simpson Smith and the
agent Samuel G. Colley are
standing at the left of the group;
the white woman standing at
the far right is often identified as
Mary Todd Lincoln. The Indians in the front row are, left to
right: War Bonnet, Standing in
the Water, and Lean Bear of
the Cheyennes, and Yellow
Wolf of the Kiowas. Yellow
Wolf is wearing the Thomas
Jefferson peace medal that
aroused such interest. The
identities of the Indians in the
second row are unknown.
Within eighteen months from
the date of this sitting, all four
of the men in the front row
were dead. Yellow Wolf died of
pneumonia a few days after the
picture was taken; War Bonnet
and Standing in the Water died
in the Sand Creek Massacre;
and Lean Bear was killed by
troops from Colorado Territory
who mistook him for a hostile.

President Andrew Johnson and members of various Indian delegations at the White House in February 1867. Included in this photograph are representatives of the Yankton, Santee, and Upper Missouri Sioux; Sac and Fox; Chippewa; Ottawa; Kickapoo; and Miami Indians. Upwards of one hundred Indians were in Washington at one time in the early months of 1867. The picture was probably taken on February 23 by Alexander Gardner, who is credited with the photograph used for the engraving that appeared in *Harper's Weekly* on March 16, 1867 *(see opposite)*.

people. Despite the Civil War, Lincoln declared, "we are not, as a race, so much disposed to fight and kill one another as our red brethren."

Lincoln throughout his speech spoke slowly and paused frequently, allowing ample time for interpretation. The Indians must have liked the speech because, according to one reporter, they received it "with frequent marks of applause and approbation . . . and their countenances gave evident tokens of satisfaction."

As soon as Lincoln left the room, the crowd pressed close to the Indians and, like typical tourists, gawked at their costumes and plagued them with questions, which the interpreter had to translate. The most popular of the delegates was Yellow Wolf of the Kiowas. His obvious warmth appealed to the spectators, who were overheard saying such things as: "He is a good fellow," and "There now, I like that one." Yellow Wolf was especially interesting to the crowd because he was wearing a Thomas Jefferson peace medal. The Kiowa chief explained that it had been given to one of his ancestors and was now one of his tribe's most prized possessions.

Not all meetings between the president and Indian delegations were formal affairs of state. Indians were always welcome at White House receptions and parties. One of the more popular gatherings was the annual New Year's Day reception, an event that survived

President Andrew Johnson meets members of the Yankton, Santee, and Upper Missouri Sioux tribes at a reception in the East Room of the White House on February 23, 1867. The photograph on the left was probably taken on the same day.

until the Civil War. "In conformity to the good old Republican custom, the President and his family on New Year's day received and exchanged civilities with his fellow-citizens, of whom an unusually great number thronged the Halls of the President's House," the *National Intelligencer* informed its readers on January 2, 1822. "The band of Music of the Marine Corps gave animation to the scene, and the presence of the deputations from the Western Indians added novelty to its other charms." Novelty indeed. The Pawnee, Omaha, Missouri, Kansa, and Oto delegation stole the show from the fashionably dressed ladies of Washington. The reception was about to end when the Indians, arrayed in their finest ceremonial garb, stalked into the East Room. Three were wrapped in brightly painted buffalo robes and one wore an eagle-feather war bonnet, the first ever seen in the East. Vermilion on their faces made them seem even more awesome. Jonathan Elliot, editor of the *Gazette*, thought they looked "cadaverous, but the music and festivity put them at ease and soon, in place of pensive gravity, a heartfelt joy beamed in the sullen eye of the Indian warrior."[11]

Indians may have been welcome at these affairs, but they did not always take advantage of the invitation. John Quinney, in Washington on New Year's Day 1853, felt he would be embarrassed. "Presidents House open to day from 12 to 2 o clock for visitors," he confided in his diary that evening. "But my pride suffered me not to go—My old clothes, were not fit, (I thought)."[12]

The exchange of gifts was an integral part of the delegation pageantry, for Indians placed great emphasis on the quality and nature of the gifts they received. They viewed the gifts as a measure of the sincerity of the government in its deliberations with them. This feeling was well expressed by Little Wound of the Oglala Sioux as his delegation was about to leave Washington in 1875. The warrior was angry because his delegation had not received rifles. "We came here at the invitation of the President," he declared, "and we expected to go home with horses, equipment, and guns so that our people would receive us gladly; if we go home without anything of this kind, when we arrive there, the people will all laugh at us."[13]

Presentation gifts included flags, medals, pipe tomahawks, gorgets, silver arm and wrist bands, and weapons such as swords and guns. Specially made for presentation to the Indians, the gifts would usually carry the United States eagle and be engraved with various symbols and phrases. A popular design was two hands clasped in a handshake. The words "peace and friendship" might also appear.[14]

The most important gifts were medals and flags. These carried the full weight of national allegiance and conferred upon the recipients added status and rank within their tribes. As noted in Chapter I, the practice of giving medals to Indian leaders originated with the earliest explorers of this country. By 1789 the custom had become so fixed that the federal government had no choice but to issue its own medals if it wished to have satisfactory relations with the Indian tribes. The head of the Indian Office reaffirmed this point in 1829. "So important is its continuance esteemed to be," he informed the secretary of war, "that without medals, any plan of operations among the Indians, be it what it may, is essentially enfeebled. This comes of the high value which the Indians set upon these tokens of Friendship. They are, besides this indication of the Government Friendship, badges of power to them, and trophies of renown. They will not consent to part from this ancient *right*, as they esteem it; and according to the value they set upon medals is the importance to the Government in having them to bestow."[15]

The writer did not exaggerate. Indians at one time regarded a medal as a prized possession, to be buried with the owner when he died or to be handed down from generation to generation. Possession of a medal was such an important status symbol that leading warriors were very much offended if they did not receive one. The ceremonial presentation of these medals remained an integral part of the delegation drama until the time of the Civil War. By then the tribes had become much more sophisticated, and their relationship with the government had changed to such an extent that the traditional meanings associated with the medals had greatly diminished. No longer did they serve as hallmarks of allegiance and friendship. Instead, they were viewed as rewards for meritorious service or good behavior. This decline is evidenced by the Pawnee chiefs who were offered but refused medals in 1878. "A suit of clothes would do them much more good," they informed the commissioner of Indian affairs.[16]

Known as "peace medals" from the clasped hands of friendship embossed on the reverse side, the American medals were solid silver and bore the likeness of the president. With the exception of John Adams, each president from George Washington to Benjamin Harrison issued an Indian peace medal. Medals for the early administrations were issued in three sizes. The largest, about three inches in diameter, were presented to the most important chiefs; the smaller medals went to chiefs and warriors of correspondingly lesser rank. As the importance of the medals as instruments of Indian policy diminished, production was reduced accordingly. Beginning with the Millard Fillmore medal in 1850, only two sizes were issued; with the Ulysses Grant and subsequent peace medals, only one size appeared. Whereas the needs of the Indian service required as many as

Obverse *(left)* and reverse of James Monroe peace medal.

three hundred medals during the Monroe and John Quincy Adams administrations, the government issued fewer than fifty medals during the Grover Cleveland and Benjamin Harrison administrations.[17]

Another gift of great symbolic value was a gold chain representing the close ties of friendship between the United States and a tribe. The gold chain was presented to chiefs in the early federal period, usually when a treaty was negotiated. The practice ended in the first decade of the nineteenth century, although references to the gold chain appear much later. A delegation of Six Nations Indians from New York came to Washington in 1810 bearing the gold chain they had been given in 1795 at the Treaty of Canadaugqua. The delegation came to tell the Great Father that the permanent peace that had been effected fifteen years before was in danger of rupture. The delegation reminded the Great Father that he had appointed an agent for the tribe to "keep bright this chain of friendship." He had also told them that if the agent was unable to keep it bright, the tribe should send a delegation to Washington and they could make known their complaints to the president. "On our part we have to this day complied with the treaty, and still wish to hold fast to it—But Brother, let us remind you, that your part has become rusty." The Cherokee delegation of 1841 also chose this means of dramatizing the failure of the United States to honor treaty obligations. The Cherokees brought with them not only the "endless chain of gold" that President Thomas Jefferson had attached to one of their treaties, but also a silver-bound book President George Washington had presented to the tribe "as the record of the mutual obligations then existing between this Government and the Cherokee Nation." Unfortunately for the Indians, such symbolic protests made little impact on cynical congressmen.[18]

In the early years of the republic, American flags were often presented along with the medals. These flags were custom-made for the Indian service by Philadelphia merchants. The stripes resembled those of the official American flag, but the fields carried as a device an eagle or stars, or both in the case of the larger flags. The device was handpainted on both sides of the fabric, usually rough bunting that looked crude but was durable. The large flags measured seven feet six inches by four feet eight inches and cost twelve dollars, including tassels and cord.[19]

The government stopped giving flags to the Indians in the mid-1830s. Thereafter, even chiefs who specifically wanted flags to display at their villages had difficulty obtaining them. Chief Gabrielle Renville of the Wahpeton and Sisseton Sioux, for instance, waited more than five years for the flag he had been promised "as a mark of esteem for his services and kind acts to the settlers in Minnesota, during the Indian troubles in that state in 1862, and also for the friendly disposition he has at all times manifested toward the whites." Commissioner Ely S. Parker finally appealed to the War Department in hopes a used flag could be obtained for the chief from a military installation.[20]

The medals and flags were symbols of American allegiance, and Indians who accepted them were expected to be loyal to the United States. This was a matter of importance when the United States was competing with the British for tribal friendship. Thus, Indian agents and other government officials made concerted efforts to get Indians possessing British medals and flags to exchange them for American medals and flags. Usually, Indians confronted with such a request would readily make the exchange, but one delegate refused. This occurred in 1852 when five Indians from Tesuque Pueblo were in Washington. One of the men had a British medal bearing the likeness of King George III, but no inducement could make him part with it.[21]

Perhaps the most unique presentation gift was the cane given to each of the nineteen governors of the Rio Grande Pueblo Indians in 1864. Although these peaceful and hospitable peoples had come under United States jurisdiction in 1848 as a result of the war with Mexico, they were not officially recognized by the federal government until the Lincoln administration. It was Michael Steck, superintendent of Indian affairs for New Mexico, who suggested that canes would be more meaningful symbols of United States suzerainty than the peace medals that would otherwise have been given. As noted earlier, canes or *bastóns* had been used by Spain as symbols of authority when dealing with the Indians of the Southwest. Mexico, upon gaining its independence from Spain in 1820, reinforced this tradition by presenting its own canes to the pueblo governors. Lincoln wisely continued the tradition, thereby confirming in the eyes of the United States a line of succession that is now some 350 years old.[22]

Interestingly, the canes were not presented in Washington. Instead, they were given in Lincoln's name during special ceremonies at the Pueblo Agency at Pena Blanca, New Mexico, in September and October 1864. The canes had been purchased by Superintendent Steck from John Dold of Philadelphia at a cost of $5.50 each. Engraved on the silver head of each one was the name of the pueblo, the year, and "A. Lincoln."[23] The canes are still cherished possessions of the respective pueblos, and many of the governors have brought these staffs of office with them when conducting business with the government.

Less symbolic but highly prized nonetheless as gifts from the Great Father were weapons, especially firearms, which appealed to the warrior heritage of the delegates. The government, with its fixed policy of civilizing the Indians and keeping them peaceful, would have preferred giving less martial gifts, but it was almost impossible to do so without causing offense. Thus, despite criticism from church groups and westerners, presidents gave tomahawks, swords, and guns to prominent delegates until well into the nineteenth century. President John Quincy Adams, for instance, distributed a virtual arsenal to the Winnebagos who visited him in 1828. Each of the dozen or so warriors received a musket and either a cutlass or brace of pistols, according to his preference. The weapons so pleased the delegates that they immediately began snapping the gun locks and swinging the swords, much to the discomfort of the observers. As one later commented, "It was a curious spectacle to witness in such an apartment these destructive

Antonio al Churleta (Tse-wa-án-ye), governor of San Juan Pueblo, holding a Lincoln cane. Photographer and date not recorded.

weapons, bristling as in a fight, and tossed from hand to hand by men of such powerful frame with the lightness and sport of children's gewgaws."[24]

Later delegations may not have been so liberally supplied, but the traffic in firearms continued. Andrew Jackson presented each of the four delegates from the Upper Missouri who visited Washington in 1832 with a brace of pistols. In 1846 Polk gave a Winnebago chief a powder flask, shotbag, and doublebarreled gun "with silver plate and engraving." Even more formidable was the Henry repeating rifle that Grant gave to a Sioux visitor in 1872. The rifle, which today is in the Museum of the American Indian in New York City, bears the inscription, "from the President for Bravery & True Friendship."[25]

Whether medals, flags, or weapons, these state gifts had one purpose—to attach the Indians to the United States. A clear and explicit statement of this purpose is found in the letter accompanying the assortment of gifts sent in 1828 to The Little Prince, head chief of the Creeks, who was too elderly to visit Washington:

Brother—The Secretary of War sends you by the Presidents directions a Cloak bound with silver lace, and a sword and twelve silver Medals, and twelve Flags. He sends them to you. The Cloak is to keep you warm and dry, and make you live long; and the sword as a badge of honor, and the Medals are sent to you to be put, by your own hands around the necks of your faithful and true Chiefs—and with the Medal you will give also a flag—keeping a Medal, and flag for yourself.

Brother—This will show you what you are—and what the great men at Washington think of you. You will consider these things as fastening one of your hands in the hand of your Great Father, and the hand of the Secretary of War.[26]

Besides the formal presentation items, the Indians sometimes received personal gifts from the president and his family. Sarah Polk sent Cusick's wife "a handsome shawl" as a remembrance, and the Tuscarora delegate regarded the gift as "a token of friendship." Mrs. Polk must have been an open-hearted person who enjoyed her role as First Lady, because the Comanche delegation in 1846 called her the "great Mother."[27] She is the only First Lady known to have been so honored.

The favorite gifts of President Grant and his wife, Julia, were pipes and shawls. These would often be accompanied by a personal note. "Appreciating the good feeling between the Utes and the white people," the president wrote the Ute delegation in November 1873, " . . . I wish to send as a present from myself, a few things for the Chiefs, and from Mrs. Grant for the squaws, who called upon me a few days ago." Blackfoot, spokesman for the Crow delegation which also visited Washington that year, was so delighted with his presents he dictated a thank-you note. "I can't smoke Larb in the Pipe you sent me but its nice and I will keep it all the same," he responded. "Tell *your* squaw that our squaws are pleased with the shawls and their little girls will wear them in the first dance, they are nice and warm."[28]

The Indians, in return, showered the Great Father with items of their own manufacture—painted buffalo robes, calumets, moccasins, war shirts, and feathered headdresses. These were often personal possessions of the donors and the most significant gifts they could give. Medicine Bear, a Teton Sioux chief, literally took the shirt off his back when he met President Grant at an evening reception at the White House. The chief, who was in full regalia, had been asked to speak on behalf of his delegation. Before doing so, however, he took the large calumet he was holding and set it on the mantle of a nearby fireplace. After deliberately removing and setting aside his eagle-feather headdress, he removed his leather shirt and, holding it aloft, was about to slip it over Grant's head when one of the president's military aides intervened. Taking the shirt away from Medicine Bear and laying it on a chair, he told the delegation that Grant would not wear it that evening, "but would accept it as proof of Medicine Bear's good will." The garment was the chief's war shirt, his most valued possession, adorned with the scalp locks of his fallen enemies. Medicine Bear wanted the Great Father to have it "in token of the estimation in which he held him."[29]

The gift most often presented to the president was the calumet or peace pipe. As a gift, it had deep meaning and implications that the officials in Washington probably never fully appreciated. To the Indian tribes from the Great Lakes to the Rocky Mountains, the calumet possessed special powers when used ceremonially to confirm agreements, honor guests, and reinforce friendships. The Northern Arapahos in 1881 went so far as to send pipes to a number of high government officers, including President James Garfield, as a reminder of a promise that they could send a delegation to Washington and visit their children at Carlisle. Although the Arapahos got their trip, approval was due not to the pipes but to their agent, who urged the bureau to honor the commitment, "in order to keep faith with the Indians, whose memory never fails in cases where promises are made."[30]

The Indians must have realized their gifts were of little consequence to the Great Father. Most of them, however, probably shared the wish of Sharitarish, spokesman for the Pawnee delegation of 1821. As he told President Monroe, the Indians hoped he would deposit and preserve their gifts "in some conspicuous part of your lodge, so that when we are gone . . . [and] our children should visit this place, as we do now, they may see and recognize with pleasure the deposits of their fathers, and reflect on the times that are past."[31]

For the most part, Indians seem to have retained a high regard for the president, even when, as in the late nineteenth century, they all knew that the Great Father was an ordinary human and no deity. Grant, for one, was especially well liked. The fact that he was a warrior in his own right may account for this. Or perhaps it was his well-known fondness for tobacco. Chief Iron Bull of the Crows claimed he was looking forward to meeting Grant for that very reason. Since Grant smoked "a good deal," Iron Bull knew the smoke from his own pipe "would not get into the eyes" of the Great Father's assistants. According to a *New York Times* reporter, Spotted Tail of the Brulé Sioux was so delighted by his interview with Grant that he expressed the wish that Indians could vote so he could be reelected.[32]

Grover Cleveland also received Indian endorsement. When Andrew Saltise, head chief of the Coeur D'Alènes, learned that Cleveland had lost the election of 1888, he immediately sent him a letter of consolation. "We are all sorry you will not be our next President, for we feel that in losing you, the Indians lose their best friend."[33]

Not every delegate was so impressed by the Great Father. A Klamath Indian who met Grant in 1875 was disappointed by his interview. "I went to see the President," he said. "He looks just like any other man. I was not afraid of him. I intended to tell him what my people wanted, but his ear was too small, he could not hear me, [so] I brought all the things in my heart away." Sarah Winnemucca, the Paiute woman who spent several years in the 1880s trying to arouse humanitarian support for her people by lecturing in Boston and other eastern cities, was singularly unimpressed with President Rutherford B. Hayes, whom she met in January 1881. Serving as the interpreter for a Paiute delegation, Sarah accompanied the Indians when they called on Hayes at the White House. The meeting lasted all of five minutes. Hayes walked into the room, asked Sarah if the Paiutes were receiving what they needed, expressed a few platitudes about the progress the Indians were making in the arts and civilization, and then left. "That is all we saw of him," she later admitted in amazement. "That was President Hayes."[34]

President Calvin Coolidge with Osage delegation on White House grounds. Chief Bacon Rind is standing third from the right.

What Sarah Winnemucca had discovered, perhaps without realizing it, was the end of the era of the Great Father. Indeed, the last president to fill that role was Ulysses S. Grant, who seems to have enjoyed meeting his "red children" and participating in the centuries-old delegation pageantry. His administration hosted numerous large and important delegations, led by Red Cloud, Spotted Tail, and other prominent Indian leaders, which were brought to Washington as part of the government's effort to win the friendship of the militant tribes of the Northern Plains. In reality, these expensive and gaudy affairs marked the zenith of the old tradition of the Indian delegation. Their failure to prevent the hostilities that erupted in the mid-1870s, when the militants from the Northern Plains attempted to fight for a way of life that was already extinct, seems to have been largely responsible for the closing of this colorful chapter of American history.

The accelerated growth of industry and government in the post-Civil War years also played a part in eroding the Great Father image. The United States was emerging as a world power, and the demands on the president and his advisers were too pressing to permit the luxury of personal meetings with the many Indians who continued to visit the national capital. As a result, the role of the Great Father, when required, was gradually being taken over by the secretary of the interior. President Hayes hastened the transition. Early in his administration, he specifically asked the secretary of the interior to curtail the number of Indians who visited Washington.[35] His request was taken as an edict, and not a single delegation was authorized to visit Washington for more than a year.

This is not to suggest that presidents after Grant no longer met with Indian leaders: to this day, presidents deal with them on a variety of issues, but under vastly different circumstances. It has usually been considered good politics to be sympathetic to Indians. President Calvin Coolidge posed with visiting delegations for the White House photographer, and he even donned a warbonnet on occasion. But ever since the Grant administration, there has been a substantial difference in the relationship between the White House and Indians. After the bloody 1870s, Indian affairs seldom merited presidential attention. True, the exciting chase of Geronimo in the 1880s and the Ghost Dance outbreak that culminated in the massacre at Wounded Knee in 1890 briefly captured national attention. But in general Indian affairs were no longer matters of executive importance. As a result, presidents since Grant have had little time for Indians.

Above: Delegation of Indian chiefs prior to their participation in the Theodore Roosevelt Inaugural Parade of 1905. Left to right: Little Plume, Piegan Blackfoot; Buckskin Charley, Ute; Geronimo, Chiricahua Apache; Quanah Parker, Comanche; Hollow Horn Bear, Brulé Sioux; and American Horse, Oglala Sioux. The photograph was taken at Carlisle before the trip to Washington, where the chiefs led a contingent of Carlisle Indian students in the parade.

Left: Geronimo and Quanah Parker leading the Indian contingent in the Theodore Roosevelt Inaugural Parade.

This low state of affairs is confirmed by the Leech Lake Chippewas who visited Washington in 1907. Led by Chief Flatmouth, the delegation very much wished to meet President Theodore Roosevelt. Probably they never got their wish, although the commissioner of Indian affairs did send this note to Roosevelt's administrative assistant: "[The Indians] leave this afternoon for home and are very anxious to shake hands with the President before going. They promise that they will not introduce any speech-making."[36]

Despite Theodore Roosevelt's romantic regard for the West, his attitude toward Indians does not seem to have been particularly enlightened. Like most of his contemporaries Roosevelt believed the Indians were "vanishing Americans"—noble savages who had acquitted themselves well in their struggles against the white man and were now fulfilling their destiny by fading quietly into the sunset. In 1903 he permitted Chief Joseph of the Nez Percé to visit Washington and authorized the bureau to pay his expenses because he felt that in the past "Chief Joseph . . . had some genuine ground of serious complaint against our Government and people." Two years later Roosevelt requested the presence of some of the old chiefs "as a picturesque touch of color" for his second inaugural parade. The bureau supplied six: Geronimo of the Apaches, American Horse and Hollow Horn Bear of the Sioux, Quanah Parker of the Comanches, Little Plume of the Blackfeet, and Buckskin Charley of the Utes. The old men were in full regalia, riding painted ponies as they led a troop of marching Carlisle Indian students up Pennsylvania Avenue. War whoops and similar derisive shouts from the crowd accompanied them the length of the parade route. As soon as the parade was over they were whisked back to their quarters at Carlisle. When later asked why he had included the old chiefs in his parade, Roosevelt quipped: "I wanted to give the people a good show."[37]

VII INDIAN LIFE IN THE CAPITAL CITY

Serving as a delegate to Washington could be an overwhelming experience for an Indian making his first trip to the East. He traveled in first-class accommodations, he received the latest clothes, and he stayed at the best hotels. In fact, the government spared little effort or expense in the campaign to convince Indian visitors that the white man's way of life was superior to theirs in all respects. The government, of course, did not always have to go to such lengths to impress the Indians. For many, everything they saw and did was new and exciting. Things the average white citizen took for granted—mechanized travel, multistory buildings, processed foods—were objects of marvel and wonder to unsophisticated delegates.

Imagine confronting a train or steamboat for the first time. It was the rare individual who boarded these chugging, snorting monsters without some fear or hesitation. More than one delegate remained behind rather than trust his life to such a fantastic machine. An Apache delegation in 1872 was persuaded to enter a narrow-gauge railroad car at Santa Fe, but the men refused to sit on the seats. Instead, they sat on the floor and covered their faces with their hands. Their fear was relatively short-lived, and after traveling a few miles in this position they took to their seats. Before long they were seasoned travelers, although one of the men admitted he would have to trust his agent to get him home because he had lost count of the mountains. The Hopi delegates of 1890 had a similar experience. According to their agent, "the swift motion of the railway train whirling them through an everchanging scenery overpowered them with amazement, and almost completely stunned their every sense. But after a little this dazed condition subsided, and their faculties again reviving, they maintained a constant flow of inquiries, and began slowly to understand something of the great life beyond the solitudes of their table-lands."[1]

Trains were bad enough; tunnels were worse. In 1880 an east-bound passenger found himself on the same coach with a Crow delegation that boasted six of the tribe's most important war chiefs, including Plenty Coups and Medicine Crow. The delegates seemed at ease until the train plunged into a tunnel. When it emerged from the darkness a few minutes later, two of the delegates were found crouched under their seats. Once the nature of the tunnel was explained, the two men became the subject of much good-natured ribbing from their companions.[2]

The names the Indians gave these strange machines indicate the extent of their bewilderment. Steamboats were "fire boats." Railroad tracks were the "iron road."

Crow delegation. Delegates, left to right: Old Crow, Medicine Crow, Two Belly, Long Elk, Plenty Coups, and Pretty Eagle. The three white men are, left to right: A. M. Quivly, interpreter; Augustus R. Keller, Crow agent; and Tom Stewart, interpreter. Photograph taken April or May 1880 by C. M. Bell.

Engines were "fast wagons," "iron horses," "fire wagons," "fire horses," and "puffing wagons." Plenty Coups, when preparing for his first visit to Washington in 1880, was told by some Bannock friends that the train was a "fast wagon" pulled by a big black horse whose belly almost touched the ground. The horse carried a large bell, and whenever he stopped to rest he would be puffing so hard that his bell would ring. Plenty Coups soon discovered the Bannocks were wrong. "I realized . . . that it was not a horse that pulled it, and I wondered what made it go so fast. Birds would fly along outside our windows. They were swift, but before long we outdistanced them." Trains were probably most often characterized as "puffing wagons" because the depiction in Plains Indian sign-language for Washington, D.C., was "the home of our father, where we go on the puffing wagon to council."[3]

To the Indians the trains were merely a typical example of the white man's magic; to the railroad companies, the delegations meant publicity, prestige, and patronage. Cut rates and special accommodations were offered to attract the delegation trade. Railroads with direct routes (to avoid making the Indians change cars en route) would normally receive the government contracts, although competing railroads sometimes had to bid for the privilege of conveying the Indians. The Baltimore and Ohio Railroad, for instance, offered the Teton Sioux delegation of 1877 first-class transportation from Council Bluffs to Washington for $35.75 per person; for second-class the price was $26.50. The contract went to the Pennsylvania Railroad with a bid of $20 per person for first-class coaches with one change of cars. When the delegation was about to return home, the B and O passenger agent offered the Indians "emigrant tickets" at $20.50 apiece. "We ought to receive a *share at least* of the patronage," he carped. Learning that the Pennsylvania Railroad was about to get the contract for the return trip, the B and O agent promptly lowered his bid to $18 a ticket for first-class transportation, adding: "As our opponents brought the party In, we trust you . . . will let us have the party *Returning*."[4]

Thanks to the intense railroad rivalry, delegations often received very favorable rates. They even traveled free of charge on occasion, especially if the companies had a vested interest in the outcome. In the contest for favorable routes, the railroads were continually lobbying for rights-of-way across Indian lands. These required Indian approval, hence a delegation. Should the government or the tribe involved declare it could not afford the trip, the railroad would graciously offer free passage.

The government usually tried to book first-class coaches, reasoning that money was well spent if the trips were as comfortable and pleasant as possible. Yet there seems to have been some resistance to this practice on the part of the railroads. Only one delegation, however, is known to have been denied first-class seats. This occurred in 1866 when a delegation of Creeks and Seminoles from Indian Territory were brought to Washington as part of the effort to restore normal relations with the Five Civilized Tribes after the Civil War. The Indians, who were accompanied by two blacks who were tribal members as well as interpreters, traveled in first-class cars without incident until they crossed the Ohio River. When the delegation changed trains at Bellaire, West Virginia, the conductor would not allow the party into the first-class cars. The agent, whose outrage did not extend to riding with his delegation in the smoking car, filed a complaint with the commissioner of Indian affairs when he reached Washington. "No person can feel more keenly than an Indian any slight or indignity offered," he wrote. "These Indians and interpreters, were sober well dressed in citizens clothes, well behaved and orderly individuals." The president of the B and O Railroad eventually confirmed the agent's story, but he offered no apologies. In fact, he considered the entire affair a tempest in a teapot. "I say this," he informed the commissioner, "because the parties seemed, from our reports, to be getting along comfortably and satisfactorily." He hoped the commissioner would understand that conductors did not always comprehend "the nice questions" that arose in their work, "especially in this quarter, where there has been so long recognized such a marked distinction between colors."[5]

The discrimination was usually more subtle. For example, when one railroad official in 1881 was asked to quote the rates for first-class coaches, he furnished the bureau with the rates for second-class as well. Indians preferred riding in smoking cars, he pointed out. Furthermore, second-class cars traveled the same routes at the same speeds as first-class cars, "for the reason that . . . [both are] attached to the same train."[6]

The Indians, however, actually preferred private coaches, which enabled them to escape the almost insatiable desire of curious easterners to stare and gawk at them as though they were animals on display in a zoo. Private cars also shielded them from unruly westerners who often harbored hard feelings against their Indian neighbors and resented the special treatment accorded the delegates. Most of the Indians may not have been conversant in English, but the delegates fully understood the meaning of curses and glares coupled with statements such as "I'd like to put a bullet in that red devil" or "I'd like to stick a knife in that brute."[7] In private coaches the delegates could relax and enjoy the marvels of the white man's world flashing by on the iron road to Washington.

Even private coaches were not the whole solution. The Indians could ensure complete privacy only by posting guards at the doors to keep zealous reporters and curious onlookers from their midst at the various stops en route. Depending on the temper of the crowds that would gather at the railroad stations, the Indians might open the windows and shake hands or otherwise communicate with the spectators. A newspaperman who managed to enter the coach that was carrying the Sioux delegation of 1891 noted that the men were lounging about their "very ordinary" car in every conceivable position. A few were lying on the floor on improvised beds made from seat cushions. Each of the delegates was picturesquely attired in a combination of buckskins, blankets, and citizens' dress "more or less trimmed with beads and bits of gewgogs." One man, with "Big Road" painted on his slouch hat, had a pipe that would have raised the envy of any collector. This he was passing around so everyone could enjoy a puff or two.[8]

Crowds were such a problem that the bureau was forced to hire cabs and omnibuses so the delegates could get around the cities they visited. Indeed, delegates often complained about the boorish behavior of the public. The Indians especially resented the ill-mannered and unthinking individuals who would touch their garments and finger their ornaments. "It is like the smelling of a dog," an outraged Keokuk remarked during his 1837 visit. "If an Indian boy were to do such a thing to an American General, he would be hissed out of all the lodges." The Indians would be jostled, touched, and teased to such an extent that some delegations would only venture from their hotels in cabs or carriages. Agent William W. Dennison reported that the Pawnees he led to the capital in 1858 "could not pass through the streets without being molested by the boys & rowdies whenever invited by Gentlemen of Washington (as they often were) to visit their families of an evening." The Pawnees complained about this so much, he said, that he had to hire hacks for them. His experience was shared by Fellows Pease, the Crow agent, who declared in 1873 that "it was difficult and almost impossible to get the Indians to the Hotel, on account of the great crowd of people who surrounded the Indians when[ever] they walked on the street."[9]

Cabs were required for other reasons as well. Commissioner Edward P. Smith, writing in 1874, suggested that the delegations were provided with carriages and omnibuses "as a sanitary measure." This was especially necessary, he declared, "with wild Indians . . . as a preservation of health."[10] Just whose health Smith was concerned about is uncertain. Possibly the bureau feared the Indians would contract diseases by mingling with the crowds, but it is more likely government officers had in mind the lice that accompanied some of the delegates, as well as the Indians' lack of familiarity with indoor plumbing: many of the Indian visitors were unacquainted with the niceties of urban life.

Whatever the reason, private cabs and buses were available when needed. The Pawnees with Dennison, for instance, used the vehicles for more than avoiding rowdies. They made four excursions into the Virginia countryside to replenish their supply of smoking material made from willow and sumac bark. But this was unusual. Most delegations followed the itinerary of the Apaches who visited Washington in 1888. According to William S. Kelly, who submitted an itemized bill to the bureau for $22, the delegates used his hack for the following trips:[11]

March	3	Indian Office and store	$2.00
	5	Patent Office and return	2.50
	6	Smithsonian Museum and return	2.50
	7	President's House and return	2.50

7	(Evening) to 1825 O street and return	2.00
8	Agriculture Building, Bureau of Engraving	2.50
9	Hoe Building and return	2.00
10	Navy Yard and return	2.00
19	Arsenal and return	2.00
21	To Depot	1.00

One of the first stops for Indians visiting Washington would be a store, since a liberal supply of presents was essential to the success of any delegation. The government followed the maxim that "a present [was] the readiest door to an Indian's heart." One agent, when questioned about the large sums spent on gifts for his delegation, retorted: "Without presents Indians have no ears."[12] Accordingly, the government lavished its Indian visitors with gifts worth thousands of dollars. Not only was this in keeping with the imagery of the generous father who took special care of his obedient children; it also was meant to impress the Indians with the material and technical superiority of the whites. Even at the end of the nineteenth century, when most of the tribesmen were secured on reservations and the work of assimilation and acculturation was well under way, delegates to Washington could expect to receive at least a suit of clothes and pocket money.

The flow of presents would begin before the Indians left home and continue until their return. Several factors dictated this steady stream of gifts. Many of the leaders invited to Washington were reluctant to make the trip for one reason or another, and presents were often required to gain their cooperation. The Winnebagos who visited Washington in 1846, for instance, at first refused to go because "they had no suitable clothing . . . [and] they should be ashamed to appear in the presence of their Great Father, in their old blankets." The agent had no alternative but to buy them new outfits en route to the capital. To gather a representative delegation from the Red Cloud Agency, J. J. Saville first had to hold several conferences with tribal leaders, whom he plied with food and trade goods "to keep them in good humor." Then he had to give presents to the families of the chiefs selected for the delegation. "Without this course had been pursued in giving them the articles at the feasts, and to their families," declared Saville when explaining his expenses to the commissioner, "I am positive that there would have been much more trouble in securing a good delegation in accordance with the wishes of your office, which was that the delegation should consist of the best men at the agency . . . erespective [*sic*] of whether he was a good man or not." Still another reason was the need to prevent hard feelings among the Indians who were not invited to Washington. No-ko-wat, an ambitious young man of the Missouri Sac and Fox, for example, could be dissuaded from accompanying the 1866 delegation only by the promise of a suit of clothes worth fifty dollars.[13]

An indication of the enormous sums spent on delegation presents is provided by the Santee Sioux who visited Washington in 1837. The twenty-six chiefs shared $3,900-worth of presents; they received $1,200 in presents before they would even agree to leave the St. Peters Agency. Upon reaching Washington, they received the following gifts, which were worth $1,700:

26 Hair Trunks 2½ feet
26 Chiefs Coats, & Epaulets, laced, frock
26 Hats, Silver bands & feathers
26 pr Scarlet Legings
26 Jefferson Blue Buck Skin *bootees*
52 Calico Shirts
26 Black Silk Hdkfs

26 Britch Cloths
26 pr Buck Skin Gloves
26 fine tooth Combs
26 Com[mon] Horn Combs
26 Clothes Brushes
26 Worsted Sashes in place of body Belts

When the delegation reached St. Louis on its way home, the chiefs received another $1,000 in presents—guns, ammunition, and various types of cloth.[14]

The principal delegation gift was clothing. Since government policy was to turn the Indians into white men, it was presumed that making them look like white men was a giant stride in that direction. Thus, almost as soon as the bewildered visitors reached the city, they would be given complete wardrobes. They would be poked and measured by a corps of cobblers and tailors who scurried in and out of their quarters bringing samples of cloth and leather and fitting them with suits and shoes. The Indians would also make the rounds of the assorted mercantile establishments that lined Pennsylvania Avenue.

Chief Red Cloud of the Oglala Sioux, wearing the latest in fashionable clothes. Although the photograph is undated, J. N. Choate, a Carlisle photographer, probably took it during Red Cloud's visit to the Carlisle Indian school in May 1880.

Hamburger and Sons, Hable Brothers, Lansburghs, and A. Saks and Company, which claimed to be "the largest clothing house in the District," enjoyed a brisk trade from the many delegations that visited the capital. Large crowds would gather on the sidewalks outside these establishments trying to catch a glimpse of the Indians as they tested their first boots and tried on the latest fashions in hats. The delegates generally seem to have been pleased with their new clothes, but most observers shared the opinion of the journalist who thought that Indians in suits "looked about as comfortable as bears in moccasins."[15]

Unhappily for government policymakers, the new outfits would also fail to impress the families of the returned delegates. The shock at seeing one's father or husband decked out in top hat and tails can well be imagined. Luther Standing Bear recalled the first time his father returned from Washington. The children thought a white man had come to visit when they saw someone enter their teepee wearing a silk hat, starched shirt, and Prince Albert coat. Upon investigation they discovered it was their father. "He looked so funny to us—more like a real curiosity. He even had kid gloves and a cane, but with all this white man's stylish make-up, he still wore his hair long." Chief Standing Bear was so pleased with his outfit that he wore the starched shirt to bed that night. The next day

Southern Plains delegation shown wearing new outfits purchased from A. Saks and Company on August 2, 1880. Each man received one suit, one valise, one hat, two shirts, one box of collars, one pair of socks, one pair of trousers, a tie, shoes, and underwear. Total cost per person was $23.50. Delegates, left to right: Tosdiáko, Wichita; White Man, Kiowa-Apache; Stumbling Bear, Kiowa; and Wild Horse (Kobi), Comanche. The white men are Philemon B. Hunt, agent, and Edward L. Clark, interpreter.

he wore the clothes to a council meeting. The only change was an eagle feather tucked in the hatband. "Whenever a man returned from Washington and attended a council, he was expected to come dressed up," Luther Standing Bear recalled. "This was a sort of 'badge,' to prove that he had really been to Washington. I think Father satisfied them that he had been there!" Within a few days, however, the old man lost interest in his new wardrobe. The top hat received its coup de grâce from Standing Bear's little daughters, who used it as a water bucket.[16]

Instead of the so-called citizen's clothing, which became standard issue after the Civil War, the chiefs much preferred military uniforms. Giving uniforms to Indian leaders was, like the distribution of peace medals, a carry-over from the colonial era. Although the practice was at variance with efforts to civilize and christianize Indians, the delegates with their warrior tradition so prized the uniforms and military trappings that pragmatists in government continued the custom until well into the nineteenth century. When distributing military insignia and equipment, government officers generally made some attempt to distinguish the chiefs according to their tribal status. For instance, the coats of full chiefs would carry two epaulets, half chiefs one, and warriors none. These distinctions were maintained until the latter half of the nineteenth century, when the government decided to eradicate the traditional patterns of leadership.[17]

There can be no doubt of the esteem in which the uniforms were held. These, like the peace medals, served as visible symbols of the owner's status and importance. Bits and pieces of the uniform might become lost or discarded—trousers were especially subject to attrition—but not the coats. Most of the recipients were like Shaumonekusse of the Otos, who was still wearing his uniform coat twenty years after his visit to Washington in 1822. According to the informant, the coat was "adorned with red facings and enormously large brass buttons, and garnished upon each shoulder with a pair of tarnished, sickly-looking silver epaulettes." The rest of the uniform had evidently long since been discarded, because "from beneath the skirts of the coat appeared two bare legs; and . . . a pair of coarse moccasins of buffalo hide."[18]

The need for Indians to adopt citizen's dress was a constant government theme throughout the nineteenth century. The idea was reinforced at all levels of the bureaucracy. Even the president participated in the effort. When a Sioux delegation wearing traditional dress visited Rutherford B. Hayes, the Indians were informed of the Great Father's disappointment. He hoped that they would be in white man's clothing for their next visit "as a pledge that all other things needed for civilization will also be given." The stress on clothing succeeded to such an extent that Indian delegates were self-conscious and embarrassed by their traditional dress. For instance, the Poncas who visited Washington in 1880 refused to enter the city until they received citizen's dress. By the end of the century, few Indians even attempted to do business with the bureau unless they were similarly attired.[19]

Clothes were the most common presents, but they were by no means the only personal gifts the Indians received. Ornaments like earrings, crosses, and arm-and-wrist bands were popular, especially with the early delegations. Later delegations would receive new clothes and cash, perhaps thirty to fifty dollars, so they could buy their own presents. To carry their newly acquired treasures, the Indians would also receive suitcases and trunks.

A horse was probably the most useful present. In giving horses to the delegates, the government was accomplishing two objectives: it pleased the Indians and it simplified returning them home, since most of the delegates still had to travel considerable distances once they left commercial transportation. Agents who faced two or three hundred miles of cross-country travel before they could get their delegations home were usually

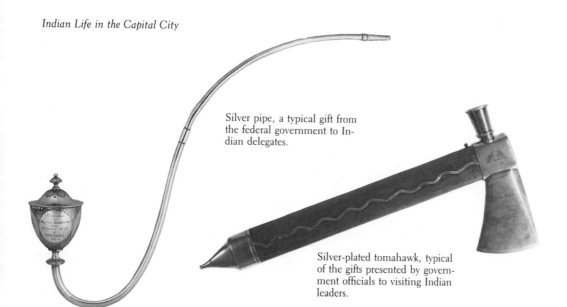

Silver pipe, a typical gift from the federal government to Indian delegates.

Silver-plated tomahawk, typical of the gifts presented by government officials to visiting Indian leaders.

authorized to buy a horse for each delegate, but this was not always easy to arrange. John D. Miles, the Arapaho and Cheyenne agent, had to distribute handbills advertising his need for twenty-five "good horses" when he reached Atchison, Kansas, in December 1873. The government, in keeping with its efforts to "civilize" the Indians, sometimes gave delegates work horses and wagons instead of saddle horses. Prominent chiefs might even receive carriages. Such generosity did not please everyone, however. When Red Cloud asked about a carriage that had been promised him during a recent visit, the Pine Ridge agent could not conceal his jealousy. "Red Cloud now has a better wagon than the agent given him by the 'Great Father' in 1880," he grumbled when relaying the chief's inquiry to the commissioner of Indian affairs.[20]

Accommodations for the Indians matched their fine clothes. Since Washington offered little in the way of hotels until after the War of 1812, most early visitors, including congressmen, national leaders, and the Indians, had to lodge in boardinghouses. These were clustered along Pennsylvania Avenue near the foot of Capitol Hill, offering convenient access to the legislative halls and other government buildings. There were still sixteen boardinghouses on Pennsylvania Avenue between First and Seventh streets as late as 1865.[21]

The boardinghouses were especially popular with resident Indian delegates because they were cheap and the atmosphere was family-like. A camaraderie would develop among the various delegates, who would help each other with advice, loans, and letter-writing. Joy's, at Eighth and Pennsylvania, which was the residence for several months for the "Loyal" Cherokee delegation of 1866, was probably typical. Chief John Ross described Joy's as "a *Yankee* Boarding House—Conducted systematically—economically—orderly and quietly." The table fare was plain but wholesome. At mealtimes the fifty boarders, who included four members of Congress and several government clerks, sat in designated seats at two long tables. Dinner was served at 4:00 P.M. to accomodate the congressmen and clerks. "This is later than we preferred," Ross admitted, "but we submit to the regulations of the house." Otherwise Ross found little to complain about. The linen was clean and the beds comfortable. Four servants tended tables, kept the fires lit, and emptied the slop pots. The cost for all this was fifty dollars a month, one-third what a hotel would charge.[22]

Jesse Brown's Indian Queen Hotel, located on the north side of Pennsylvania Avenue about midway between the Capitol Building and the White House, a few doors east of the Center Market. According to Brown, the Indian Queen was "a large and spacious building . . . with large back buildings attached: the front is an imitation of freestone. The proprietor having recently purchased this establishment, and fitted it up at great expense, having made many changes with large additions, adding many fine rooms thereto, renders it much more comfortable than it formerly was;—it is not surpassed by any Hotel in the District of Columbia, every attention will be paid to the comfort of those who may please to give a call. Gentlemen travelling with their families will at all times be accommodated with private parlours, and chambers attached thereto. A private entrance distinct from the public one, has recently been made which renders it much more pleasing than formerly. The general Stage & Steamboat Office is immediately east of the principal entrance."

Boardinghouses were fine for acculturated Indians, but they were not suitable for most delegations. In selecting hotels for Indian delegations, the government was guided by economy and convenience; hotels near the government buildings minimized the need for carriages and cabs. At the time the Bureau of Indian Affairs was established in 1824, three hotels competed for the delegation trade. These were operated by Joshua Tennison, Jesse Brown, and Basil Williamson. All were first-rate hotels and all were located on Pennsylvania Avenue within easy walking distance of the buildings the Indians would be expected to visit.

Tennison's Hotel, also known as the Washington Hotel, was located just east of the White House. It was "among the most commodious and convenient houses in the Metropolis," boasted an advertisement in 1821. "Its proximity to the Public Offices, President's House, the residence of all the Foreign Ministers and officers of government, added to the healthy situation on which it stands, (there not having been one case of indisposition, during the whole of the last sickly season, in the neighborhood) render it well adapted for strangers visiting the seat of government either for business or pleasure."[23·] Jesse Brown's Indian Queen Hotel was Washington's finest hotel until the late 1830s.

Situated midway between the Capitol Building and the White House, it offered many fine rooms and a private entrance for the comfort of gentlemen traveling with their families. The location was favored by being next door to the stage and steamboat office.[24]

The Indian Queen offered typical service for hotels of the era. Brown would greet newly arrived guests at the curb and then usher them inside under a large swinging sign adorned with a brightly painted Pocahontas. At mealtimes, Brown met his guests at the dining-room door, carved the main dishes, and helped with the serving. Room service was summoned by cords connected to rows of bells hanging behind the bar. The bartender also served as desk clerk, saw that the bells were answered, received and delivered messages, and dispensed information. He was said to know everybody of importance in Washington, where they lived, and at what hour they could be seen.[25]

The choice of hotel was left to the Indian agent. As the head of the Indian Office explained to an agent on the eve of a visit to Washington with a delegation, "The location of the Indians in your charge is left to your discretion—whether at Browns, Tennisons, or Williamsons. With the two first, rates are established, with the last if you select it, the terms must be distinctly understood, and agreed to." The allowable rate was $1.25 a day for each person. For this, the Indians were to receive "good accommodations at Table, in rooms, attendance, &c, and the usual supply of liquor, at table." Hotels could charge extra for laundry and barbering services, but nothing else.[26]

From 1837 until the outbreak of the Civil War, delegations favored the Union Hotel, operated by Jimmy and Bridget Maher. Known as the "Indian Headquarters," it stood near the present United States Treasury Department Building at 13½ Street and Pennsylvania Avenue. Jimmy Maher had quite a reputation as an innkeeper who could "talk to the Indians in their native language with his Irish brogue flavoring the whole conversation." Jimmy offered "to accommodate every delegation, however large, with the most convenient quarters, where every attention will be paid to their comfort and convenience." This was evidently no idle boast, for Agent Thomas Boyd was certainly pleased with the hotel. "I deem it a duty incumbent to State that Mr. Maher, at whose house, I have the pleasure to Stay with the Winnebago Delegation has in all things, and under all Circumstances, been Obliging and attentive," he informed the commissioner of Indian affairs in October 1837. The Comanches who stayed at the house in 1846 were so pleased with the warm and hospitable attention they received that they dubbed Bridget their "good mother." The Union Hotel remained the "Indian Headquarters" until 1859, when both the Mahers died within six months.[27]

Following the Civil War, the delegation trade was taken over by the Beveridge family. The Beveridges—Amanda, her son Benjamin, and his daughter Louise—were in the hotel business from 1854 until 1909. During this half-century, they hosted almost every prominent Indian leader who visited Washington, including Red Cloud, Spotted Tail, Satanta, Joseph, Geronimo, and Quanah Parker. Amanda Beveridge began with a small boardinghouse on Pennsylvania Avenue. Within four years she had become proprietress of Gadsby's Hotel at the northwest corner of Third Street and the Avenue. She changed its name to the Washington House and quickly established a fine reputation among the congressional corps for good food and service. James Buchanan and Henry Wilson, vice-president under Grant, were regular patrons. Indian delegations began staying at the hotel in 1863, and within a few years they formed a major portion of its clientele. The Washington House began a rapid decline after the scandal of 1873 when Benjamin, who operated the hotel saloon, admitted submitting fraudulent delegation bills that concealed payments to prostitutes. The bureau for a time tried to keep delegations from the Washington House, but the embargo was never completely effective. Even so, the hotel

124

never fully recovered from the scandal. Ill-health forced Amanda to give up the Washington House in 1881, and she died the following year.[28]

While operating the Washington House, the Beveridges lived in a three-story rowhouse a few doors north at 224 Third Street. Here the family had boarded patrons on those occasions when the hotel was filled. When Amanda died, Benjamin converted the family home into a boardinghouse that catered exclusively to Indian delegations. Known as the "Indian House," it was operated primarily by Ben's daughter Louise until her death in 1900. Ben then took over the business until his own death nine years later. Benjamin was a likable rogue who was always in trouble yet managed to stay out of jail. A large, burly man, some six feet tall, Ben seems to have enjoyed the respect and friendship of his Indian patrons even though he was known to keep order with his fists. (This friendship, in fact, thwarted the bureau's attempt to force him out of the delegation business.) Beveridge relished his unique role. "I have met Indians, more of them and of different tribes, I reckon, than any man in the United States," he boasted in 1906, "and I've never been a hundred miles from Washington."[29]

Two of his most loyal friends were Red Cloud and Spotted Tail. During the 1870s these prominent chiefs were regular visitors to Washington, and they usually stayed with

Comanche and Kiowa delegation of 1897 outside Beveridge House. Front row, left to right:
Quanah Parker, his wife Tonarcy, Apiatan, Apache John, and Big Looking Glass. William Tivis,
the Comanche interpreter, is standing in the middle row at the far right. Ben Beveridge is
lounging at the rear, and his daughter Louise is standing on the stairs. The photograph was taken
sometime during April 1897.

the Beveridges. They were quite surprised, therefore, when they reached Washington in
the spring of 1875 and were told they would have to stay at the Tremont House. After
one night there, Red Cloud and Spotted Tail went to the commissioner of Indian affairs
and demanded a change of lodgings. The rooms at the Tremont House were too small,
they claimed. Commissioner Ezra Hayt refused to consider their demands. If they did
not like their accommodations, they could sleep on the Mall, and he would gladly
furnish the tents and food. Red Cloud was enraged. He wanted his old headquarters or
none at all. [30]

Spotted Tail supported Red Cloud. He told the commissioner that Beveridge was his
friend. "I want to go there today." "Sometimes it is well to make new friends," the
commissioner replied. "I think when you have tried the Tremont House you will like

it as well as the Washington House. Regardless, I have made all the arrangements, and I cannot change them now."[31]

The Sioux were not intimidated. They moved to the Washington House anyway. When the commissioner told Beveridge that he would not pay their expenses, most of the Indians returned to the Tremont House. Several refused to move. At the final meeting with the commissioner before leaving Washington, Red Cloud asked the government to pay Beveridge's bill. "Six of my young men have remained four days at the Washington House, and one all the while. Wherever white men eat, they always expect to pay for it, and the bills there will amount to less than $100."[32]

The request fell on deaf ears. "[Beveridge] knew very well that I did not want you to go there," Hayt responded. "Yet he has tried from the day you came, to get you there. Some of you he has actually forced to go; and others of you who did go there, and some of you who remained at the Tremont, he has taken out himself at midnight, to some of the worst places in this city. I do not think he will have the face, and I give him credit for a great deal of cheek, but I do not think he will have the face to present me any bill for the board of Indians this year; and he has got you to do it, because he is ashamed to present it himself."

"I am not a relative of that man you speak of," Red Cloud replied. "I have never spoken evil against any white man; I think you are prejudiced against the man."

"Well," the hard-hearted commissioner admitted, "I am slightly."

Beveridge received a measure of satisfaction when Red Cloud and Spotted Tail returned to Washington in 1877. Although the bureau arranged for the delegation to stay at the Continental Hotel, the Indians spent only one night there. The next morning Red Cloud and Spotted Tail demanded an immediate transfer to the Washington House, which the commissioner reluctantly arranged. The Indians were so anxious to leave that most of them did not even eat breakfast. As the commissioner explained to the secretary of the interior, "It was not deemed good policy to use force to compel them to stay." The fact that the Continental Hotel did not allow liquor on its premises may have been a factor in the delegates' dissatisfaction. Another and more likely explanation is the covert encouragement of Beveridge. The commissioner certainly thought he was responsible, because when Red Cloud and Spotted Tail returned to Washington in 1880, he sent Beveridge the following note: "You are advised that if . . . [they] or any other Indians at present in this City, are at your house, that any indebtedness incurred by them, for any purpose whatever, will not be recognized by this office; and no bills of any kind contracted by them, need be presented for settlement."[33]

Only once did the government fail to provide hotel accommodations for a delegation. This was in January 1867, when delegations almost overran the city. Because of the crush, the commissioner received permission from the secretary of war to house Indians in unused army barracks. Some of the Indians stayed in barracks at Nineteenth and E streets; others were housed in barracks near Campbell Hospital at Seventh and E streets. The commissioner claimed he made the change to "avoid the close and unhealthy air of hotels or boarding houses, which has heretofore proved fatal to Indians in several cases." The commissioner was evidently referring to the pneumonia and smallpox that had afflicted several delegations the winter before. More likely, economy was the major factor. The barracks were free, and the meals were prepared at relatively little cost in the military mess halls. Whatever the reason, the delegates themselves were not pleased about the decision. The agents for three delegations sent a joint letter to the commissioner stating the desire of their Indians to stay "near their Agents & friends & near the [Interior] Department Building." They especially did not want to be "interfered with or molested by other delegations of Indians now in the city."[34]

The Indians may have stayed at first-class hotels, but they did not always receive first-class treatment. Indians were segregated from other guests, often eating at separate tables and in separate dining rooms. An entire delegation—men and women alike—would sometimes share a single room. Furniture would be sparse or nonexistent, with pallets on the floor or cots for beds. Accommodations given delegations were sometimes so bad there would be a public outcry. Among the worst were the quarters assigned the Sac and Fox delegation of 1837. The thirty-four men, women, and children, including the famous Black Hawk and Keokuk, occupied garret rooms on the third floor of the Virginia Coffee House on Pennsylvania Avenue. Their rooms were so cramped and dismal that several Washingtonians voiced complaints in the local press. According to "Humanitas," fifteen Sac and Fox shared a room less than fourteen feet square and aired by a small dormer window. "What does this mean?" he asked. "The Indians told me they would prefer the open commons if it were not that they would be dogged by the crowd which continually besets and torments them." "Humanitas" was echoed the next day by "Philanthropy," who declared: "There can be no economy in providing such quarters." The Indians may not care "for beds or sofas, but they want *decent accommodations* and *room* in some quiet place, and not in common taverns and grog shops." "Philanthropy" called on the people of Washington to implore the proper high officials to correct this evil, for "it must also be borne in mind that these Indians are *invited guests.*"[35]

Similar complaints were heard as late as the 1870s. According to Thomas Cree, secretary of the Board of Indian Commissioners, the fifteen members of the Crow delegation—twelve men and three women—shared a single room at the Washington House. The only furniture was tumble-down cots with straw-tick mattresses and "very dirty" sheets. The Indians had to sit either on the floor or their cots. Meals, consisting of food of the commonest sort, were served in a short, narrow hallway barely large enough for a table and two benches. The Crows claimed they ate better in Montana, where they had "good grub and a napkin to wipe their mouths with."[36]

The Tremont House, which hosted the Navajo delegation that visited Washington a year later, was evidently no more generous with its services. According to a visitor, the eleven Navajos shared "a small basement room, mattress on the floor, [and] no covering save what they furnish themselves." The visitor thought "some friendly voice" ought to intercede on their behalf. "Were I the agent," he declared, "I think matters would be different or there would be a row somewhere."[37]

Not all Indians accepted such treatment patiently. A Ute delegation refused to stay at the Washington House after seeing the accommodations given the Crows. "If this is the best that can be done for us," said Chief Ouray, "I am going to a good place and will pay my own bill." Another outraged delegate was Little Crow of the Santee Sioux, leader of the Sioux uprising of 1862. He resented being treated like an uncivilized aborigine. "We thought we would come here and live like white men, and sleep in beds," he informed Commissioner Charles E. Mix in June 1858, "but we had to sleep on the floor."[38]

In all, however, few delegates complained about their accommodations. Many of them probably never thought about the possibility of better facilities. Furthermore, the innkeepers soon learned that a liberal supply of liquor was more important to many of their Indian patrons than clean linen and soft beds. Table liquors were part of the standard hotel fare in the early nineteenth century, and Indians were allowed to indulge as freely as they wished. The reason this practice was permitted remains a mystery, especially since it was a crime to serve liquor to Indians in their own country. Despite this law, most Indians, until at least midcentury, were able to order as much liquor as they wanted. Some delegations consumed so much alcohol it is remarkable any business was transacted. This factor alone should cast doubt on the validity of at least a few of the treaties and agreements negotiated in Washington.

Cherokees who negotiated the treaty of 1828 are a case in point. Early in their stay, the Western Cherokee agent had warned Basil Williamson not to furnish the delegates more than a "sufficient" amount of whiskey. "I would not withhold from them any thing necessary to their comfort," Williamson was told, "but I am an enemy to excesses & debaucheries. I pray you to say to your barkeeper what may appear to you needful on this subject." Nevertheless, the twelve-member delegation, which included Black Fox and Sequoyah, ran up a liquor bill of $838 in ninety-four days, a remarkable sum considering a gallon of whiskey could be purchased for $1.25. When the head of the Indian Office suggested the Cherokees would have to pay their own liquor bill, the delegates were outraged. The secretary of war had told them that if they signed the treaty—which they did—the government would pay all their expenses while in Washington. The secretary of war was reminded of this by the clerk who gave him both the liquor bill for approval and a copy of the treaty, "by which the importance of the arrangements thereby effected may be seen."[39]

Aside from moral considerations, there was real danger in allowing the Indians to drink to excess. Most of the delegates, especially in the early period, were aggressive and militant by nature. Many of them carried tomahawks, knives, and pistols. Excessive drinking heightened their aggressive tendencies until some became a danger not only to themselves but to others. The Winnebagos who visited Washington were especially obstreperous. According to a fellow resident at Tennison's Hotel, the Winnebagos would become "ferocious & ungovernable" when drunk. They would invariably "commence fighting with whatever they got in their hands & it required incessant attention to prevent them from destroying each other" or from "rushing into the street & committing violence on the peaceful & passing citizens." Street gangs turned the intemperance of the Winnebagos into a cruel sport. They would wait outside the hotel for the inebriated Indians to stray their way and then "beat them severly & [were] even disposed to kill them." The Winnebagos were frequently saved from catastrophe by Jilson Dove, a street vendor who took a samaritan-like interest in their welfare. Described as "a very powerful & resolute man," Dove would rescue the Winnebagos from the hooligans and return them to their quarters. The Indian Office gave Dove eighty dollars in appreciation for this valuable service after the Winnebagos left Washington.[40]

The problem was not confined to the Winnebagos. The Indian Office hired bodyguards or policemen to remain with several other delegations "to preserve order during the day and especially at meal time." The Pawnees who visited in 1858 and the Ute delegations of 1880 and 1882 were furnished with security guards. The Ute delegation of 1882, in fact, had to stay an extra three days in the city to help prosecute a man caught selling whiskey to them.[41]

The drinking problem was so notorious that Washington newspapers would periodically remind their readers about the hazards. "No reflecting man, no one acquainted with the Indian temperament, no one who has any regard for the peace and safety of the community, will jeopardize it by pouring into the Indians a liquid poison that may produce the most mischievous and fatal consequences," the *National Intelligencer* editorialized in 1837. "As another body of Indians have arrived in this city, it appears to us not only desirable, but requisite, that we should give this public caution to our fellow-citizens, *to refrain from giving spirituous liquors, or strong drink of any kind, to the Indians during their sojourn among us.*" A similar appeal appeared in the *Washington*

Union twenty years later: "The Acting Commissioner of Indian Affairs desires us to request the keepers of hotels and restaurants not to furnish the Indians now in the city with liquor. The reasons for this request will readily suggest themselves to all thinking minds."[42]

One commissioner went so far as to persuade a delegation to take the temperance pledge. The document, dated April 12, 1858, and signed by twenty-eight delegates, read as follows: "We the undersigned Mdewakanton and Whpehute, and Sisiton and Wahpeteon Sioux, being at Washington on a visit to our Great Father, hereby pledge ourselves and sincerely promise that during twelve months from the date hereof we will not drink, or offer to others, any intoxicating liquor."[43]

Prostitution was another problem associated with the hotels. While drinking was condoned to a certain extent, sexual immorality was not. Hotels frequented by prostitutes were declared off limits to Indian delegations. As we saw in Chapter IV, prostitution led to the Beveridges' downfall. The hotel that benefited from the misfortunes of the Beveridges was the Tremont House, operated by Frank P. Hill. Ironically, this hotel came under fire for the same reason in 1880. When Hill learned of the rumors, he sent an angry protest to the commissioner denying that his establishment "was frequented by, and made a chosen place of resort of lewd and abandoned women." His denial was signed by fourteen boarders and accompanied by a note from still another patron, who claimed that "most of us have with us, our wives and little ones, whom we would rather see dead, than consorted with the vicious & depraved. We feel compelled to denounce the statement of the parties aforesaid as false, malicious, & damnable."[44]

The rumors may have been unfounded, but the bureau took no chances. A clerk was assigned to stay with a Ute delegation while it was at the Tremont House. "You will see that . . . [the Indians] get no intoxicating liquors while under charge and that they visit no immoral places and each night before retiring you will see that they are all in their rooms at the Hotel, and have matters so arranged that no person can intrude upon them, and that none of them attempt to leave the house without your knowledge."[45]

The innkeepers had their own complaints, of course. Hosting delegations, especially those composed of Indians on their first visit to the city, could be trying. Smashed furniture, broken windows and mirrors, and louse-infested bedding were just part of the price paid by uninitiated innkeepers who thought there would be a profit in welcoming Indians to their establishments. When Thomas McKenney, first head of the Indian Office, complained to Basil Williamson that his bill for boarding a party of six Osages was too high—$1.50 a day per person—the innkeeper vigorously protested. The bill was not only moderate, he avowed, "but really less than I could afford." Several of the Indians, who included two women and an infant, were sick and required extra attention. Furthermore, Williamson had to serve them at a private table. "I need only observe this to you, and you will at once perceive that it is not like having 15 or 20 in a mess, again there being females in [the] company, it must be evident for the character of the House that these persons should be provided for in a decent and respectable manner." Williamson, in fact, had tried to economize, but the Indians would not allow it. At every effort, their leader would immediately storm out of the inn, returning a few minutes later to say that the president and secretary of war had assured him the Osages could have anything they wanted. "I can assure you Sir, that they . . . gave [me] a great deal of trouble."[46]

McKenney understood. He authorized payment of the entire bill, noting that the Indians had eaten at a separate table. "Common boarding can be had at a Dollar a day, at a common table," he explained to the secretary of war, "but a separate table is always attended with additional cost—And Indians are troublesome, & in sickness especially so."[47]

Later commissioners were not so sympathetic. Mary Connor, who boarded five Potawatomis in 1841, was furious with the commissioner for reducing her bill by $58 without any explanation. She had charged $1.50 a day for room and board plus an extra $1 a day for light and heat. She had agreed to take the Indians as a special favor to a friend because the city was crowded to capacity, but she could have taken "double the number of *Gentlemen* in the same *rooms* who would not have been half the trouble at the rate of $2 per day which I was then charging all my trancient boarders without their grumbling at high charges, and I now think it very hard, after making *heavy deductions* myself, that the *Department* should still make greater."[48]

Her bitterness was shared by Amanda Beveridge when she found one of her bills reduced in a similar manner. Amanda had lodged the thirty-one members of the Red Cloud and Spotted Tail delegation of 1877 at the standard rate of $1.50 per day per person, but she had added extra charges of $25.40 for gas, $58.50 for washing, and $20 for the use of parlors. These the commissioner had disallowed. Even at $1.50 a day she had lost money, Amanda explained. "A strong healthy Indian will consume nearly that [amount] in meat each day." She could do nothing about that, she realized, because she had agreed to the rate by accepting the delegation. Nevertheless, she felt she had a legitimate complaint about the gas and the washing. Perhaps the commissioner did not realize that Indians "are in the habit of sleeping all day, and amusing themselves by singing and howling all night." The agents never made the Indians go to bed at a reasonable hour, so a full flow of gas was consumed every night for the ten days the Indians were at her house. She was even more incensed about the laundry. Never before had anyone questioned her charges for laundry service to Indians. "You must be aware," she said with no small amount of sarcasm, "that washing for 31 Indians under the best condition is no desirable task; but when the washing for Indians who had travelled a long distance on the cars is considered, imagination will hardly reach the true condition of their filth."[49]

Innkeepers had their greatest difficulties collecting bills from unauthorized delegations. As already seen in Chapter III, the government itself could hardly distinguish the authorized from unauthorized delegations. The problem was even worse for the owners of hotels and boardinghouses. Occasionally the bureau was able to warn local merchants with notices like the following that appeared in Washington newspapers in February 1838: "[A party of Sac and Fox] have come without the permission or the authority of the government, and contrary to the counsel and direction of its officers and agents at St. Louis. The person who has accompanied them is unknown to the department, and of course no engagements entered into, or purchases made, by him, will be recognized. Our citizens will see the propriety of being cautious in giving credits to any of the party."[50]

But what action was an innkeeper to take when a band of cold, hungry Indians appeared at his door late at night? Only on the following day could he determine whether the delegation was legitimate or not. If the Indians arrived before a weekend or holiday, it might be several days before a ruling could be had from the bureau. By then the Indians might have run up a considerable bill. Proprietors of boardinghouses were even more vulnerable, because the Indians who sought refuge in those establishments were usually articulate and persuasive. They would be carrying certificates from their tribes testifying that they were duly appointed delegates, and they might stay weeks or months at a time. The rub would come when it was time for them to leave and the promised

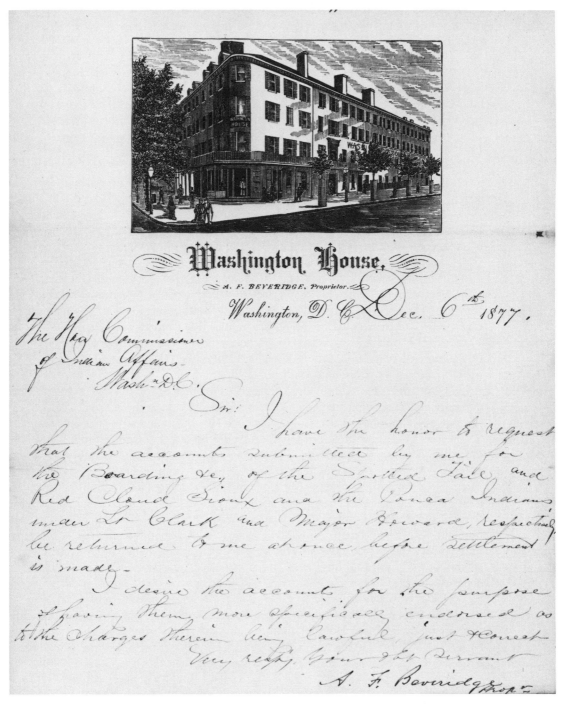

Letter from Amanda F. Beveridge to the commissioner of Indian affairs, December 6, 1877. "Sir: I have the honor to request that the accounts submitted by me for the Board &c., of the Spotted Tail and Red Cloud Sioux and the Ponca Indians under Lt. Clark and Major Howard, respectively, be returned to me at once, before settlement is made. I desire the accounts for the purpose of having them more specifically endorsed as to the charges therein being lawful, just & correct."

funds did not materialize. The only recourse was to hire a lawyer and try to collect from the bureau or the tribe. If the amount were large enough, an appeal to Congress for a special appropriation might produce the necessary funds, but this was a costly and lengthy process with no assurance that the effort would be rewarded.

T. J. Mesick waited seven years for the $391.50 owed him by George Bushyhead and his wife. The Cherokee couple had stayed with him in 1874 but were unable to pay their bill. The bureau gave Mesick $169 from the contingency fund, with a promise that the rest would follow. As the years passed, Mesick finally appealed to his representative in Congress, who interceded on his behalf. Mesick did receive the money, but not until 1881. By then he had lost his hotel and was living in Philadelphia.[51]

Marie Kolb, who operated a boardinghouse on E Street, was more fortunate. She was owed $664.50 by Nimrod Jarrett Smith, a Cherokee from North Carolina who spent the better part of five years in Washington pressing a claim against the Western Cherokees. When Smith could not pay his bill, Mrs. Kolb appealed to the bureau for assistance. She received $315 from the contingency fund, along with a reminder that "hotel and boarding house keepers who furnish board and lodging to Indians sojourning in this City, whether as delegates or otherwise, must look to the Indians themselves for payment of the bills . . . unless arrangements are previously made by some properly authorized representative of the Department." Mrs. Kolb collected the balance of the money thanks to Senator Henry L. Dawes, who informed her that Smith was about to receive payment on the claim. "You keep watch of the bill and as soon as it becomes a law be sure to go to the Treasury with him and have your share paid over to you when he gets his money," Dawes warned her. "Otherwise I am afraid he will get all the money and spend it, notwithstanding the agreement [with him.]"[52]

Even the Beveridges, with their years of experience with Indian delegations, had difficulty collecting their money on occasion, especially after the scandal of 1873. The Beveridges got in trouble because they tended to take in any Indians who wanted a room, for they believed their friends in Congress would be able to come to the rescue in any difficult situation with the bureau. For the most part they were right, but not always. In late 1875 they lodged several Warm Springs Indians from Oregon, escorted by A. B. Meacham, the former Oregon superintendent of Indian affairs. The Indians were members of a theatrical company that had been a box-office failure. The commissioner rejected the Beveridges' request for payment, and he was equally unmoved by requests from the legislative branch. To Congressman J. P. Kidder the commissioner declared: "The proprietress of the Washington House certainly ought by this time to be fully advised of the customs of this Office and of its repeated declaration to pay no bills of the board of Indians who stop at that hotel, without express order." The commissioner was equally adamant in his remarks to A. M. Scales, chairman of the House Committee on Indian Affairs. "If Mrs. Beveridge so desires the patronage of Indians visiting Washington, as to invite them to her Hotel, without the authority of and indeed against the known wish of this Office, she has hardly the right to complain, if the bills of such Indians are refused *in toto*." The bureau found it hard enough to pay legitimate bills, the commissioner explained, without having to pay bills "presented without authority, through the designing influence of professional runners for hotels."[53]

As administrations and personnel changed, the restrictions imposed on the Beveridges were relaxed and then forgotten. In time the bureau began referring delegations to the Beveridges once again. "Indian delegations, as a rule, stay at Mr. Beveridge's boarding house," the commissioner informed the Fort Peck agent in 1899. "I have no doubt your Indians will find satisfactory accommodation there." Indeed, the relationship between the bureau and the Beveridges became so cordial that the family worked out a system whereby they notified the commissioner whenever a delegation stopped at their house. If no one raised an objection, the Beveridges could assume the bill would be paid. Typical was the following note dated June 9, 1890: "There arrived at my house yesterday morning a Delegation of 2 Comanche Indians, Quanah Parker and Emmett Cox."[54]

Minor disagreements still arose, but now the parties worked from a basis of mutual trust. This cordiality is confirmed by the bill Beveridge submitted in 1903 for boarding a Blackfoot delegation. Of the fifteen delegates, only ten were in fact authorized. The bureau paid the entire bill nonetheless because, as the auditor explained, "the services were furnished in good faith and in accordance with a custom that has prevailed under like circumstances for a number of years—a custom which should be discontinued."[55]

With Ben Beveridge's death in 1909, the Indian House closed its doors. It was a sad day for Indian visitors and an even sadder one for the bureau, which had to educate another generation of hotel owners about the pitfalls of boarding delegations. "You are advised," the commissioner of Indian affairs informed the managers of five downtown hotels in 1914, "that the Indian Office will be not responsible for the board and lodging of Indian delegations visiting Washington from time to time, unless such expenses have been authorized previously by the Office."[56]

VIII EXCURSIONS AND DIVERSIONS

For many of the Indian visitors, their time in Washington was a bewildering kaleidoscope of meetings, conferences, and excursions. Each activity had its purpose—to assure the delegates of the friendship and good will of the whites; to demonstrate the advantages of white culture over the Indians'; and, of course, to convince the delegates of the superior strength and resources of the United States.

Meetings seem to have predominated. The Indians met not only with government officials but also with congressmen, vested-interest groups, and even other delegations. According to the interpreter for the Red Lake Chippewas who visited Washington in December 1883, his delegation alone met once with the president, twice with the commissioner of Indian affairs, and three times with the secretary of the interior.[1]

Considering the number of delegations that visited the capital each year, meetings must have imposed a tremendous strain on the staffs and resources of the government agencies, especially the Bureau of Indian Affairs. The commissioner of Indian affairs in December 1846 spent thirty-eight dollars to heat the meeting rooms used during protracted negotiations with delegations representing the Chippewa, Winnebago, Ottawa, and Potawatomi Indians. This sum included twelve dollars for two tons of coal and twenty-six dollars for the services of a messenger who was paid a dollar a day for tending the fires and running errands. As a bureau clerk explained when justifying the unusual charges, "The rooms occupied being large ones . . . and the weather extremely cold, the fires had to be made, and kept up during the nights as well as days: & the services of a messenger or laborer were therefore indispensible to enable us to carry on our consultations & negotiations, with any degree of comfort to ourselves or the large Deputation of Chiefs with whom we treated." Even finding space to meet with delegations became such a problem that in 1870 the commissioner of Indian affairs evicted the secretary of the Board of Indian Commissioners to appropriate a room at the bureau for meeting with the Red Cloud and Spotted Tail delegation.[2]

After the Civil War, the bureau began making complete transcriptions of negotiations with delegations, and the clerks who performed this service were called phonographers. One such clerk was C. M. Emerson, an Interior Department employee, who requested additional pay of $280 for phonographic service he performed on off-duty hours in 1866, 1867, and 1868. According to his sworn statement, Emerson furnished Commissioner Lewis Bogy with 1,120 pages of transcriptions he wrote out from shorthand notes taken during interviews with visiting delegations. "During the months of December, January,

February, and March of . . . [1866–67]," claimed Emerson, "I was constantly and almost daily summoned from my desk to attend the duties in the Indian Bureau." Once the clerk had to work two consecutive nights, "all the night through," because Commissioner Bogy insisted on having complete transcriptions each morning of the previous day's discussions. Despite this heavy demand on his time, Emerson declared when submitting his claim for compensation, "I wish it understood that while I was engaged in this work the duties of my desk were not neglected as I always found time to attend to them being always at my desk from 9 o'clock a.m. until 1 and 2 in the afternoon."[3]

The deliberate manner in which Indians conducted business was one reason so many meetings were required. According to Indian protocol, business transactions could not be hurried. An inevitable prelude to each meeting would be the lighting and passing around of a calumet or peace pipe. Blackfoot, the Crow chief, tried to explain this custom during a conference in 1873. "The reason we smoke [in council]," he told the commissioner of Indian affairs, "is because we want to tell the truth, and we are not going to lie to one another." Virtually every conference held in the capital with western delegations opened and closed with the ceremonial smoking of the calumet, often to the discomfiture of the government representatives, who found the practice distasteful. Although Commissioner Thomas L. McKenney, a nonsmoker, once remarked that he had a difficult time functioning "in a fog of this sort," most whites successfully hid their true feelings.[4] The Oglala Sioux, however, enjoy relating an anecdote about one government official who failed to do so. When he received the pipe during one of these ceremonies, the man pulled out his handkerchief and carefully wiped the stem before putting it to his lips. This so offended the owner of the pipe that when it was returned he took out a knife and cut the stem off.

This careful attention to formalities played havoc with the nerves of harried bureaucrats who were used to conducting business in a brisk and routine manner. One such bureaucrat was William Vilas, a career politician who served as secretary of the interior for eleven months during Grover Cleveland's first administration. Vilas, a nervous and bustling man, never had "a tenth part of a second to spare," but he soon learned otherwise in conducting business with Indians. In October 1888, a Sioux delegation paid him a courtesy call. The Indians had just arrived in the city and wanted to meet the secretary of the interior. As the Indians were ushered into his office, Vilas wheeled about in his chair and, in his usual brusque manner, said: "I am the Great Father's Secretary. What do you want to say?" Silence filled the room. Finally, one man spoke. He told Vilas the delegates did not wish to conduct any business; they were merely paying their respects. Having come a long distance on the train, their heads were still rocking and they needed to rest and gather their thoughts.

Vilas informed them he did not do business that way. "Speak up," he barked. "My time is limited. What is it you want?"

Nonplussed, another delegate spoke. "We are glad to see the Great Father's chief," he replied. "We are glad to hear his voice. We are his friends. We have come a long way in the Great Father's carriage . . . that rolls and bounces so! But we are tired and will see you another day."

Vilas had no intention of setting up another appointment. He was sorry they were so tired, but they had come to Washington for some reason and he wanted to know it. The Indians had to talk with him now or not at all. Try as he might, however, Vilas could not persuade the delegates to reveal the purpose of their visit. They merely repeated their intention to see him another day. At last the secretary surrendered. "Yes," he said, "another day will suit me just as well as today." With that the delegates rose, shook his hand, and left.[5]

By the close of the nineteenth century, government officials seemed to have less time to devote to their Indian constituents. Perhaps this change reflects the increased tempo of Washington life. More likely, it reflects a general lack of interest in Indian affairs. The Indians evidently came to accept this reality, because those visitors who wished to meet the president, the secretary of the interior, or the commissioner of Indian affairs often promised to keep their interviews short and to avoid any "speechmaking."[6] Francis E. Leupp, commissioner of Indian affairs for five years at the turn of the century, even developed a set of guidelines that he followed when dealing with visiting Indians. "I have only one general rule," Leupp declared when explaining his procedures, "and that is, that if I can spare the time I will always see them to say, 'How do you do?' and to hear briefly any statement they may have to make to me." Leupp did make one concession to his Indian visitors. "Although I tell all such Indians that I will see them on the same basis that I see other people who call, as a matter of fact I always give Indians the preference over the white man in any spare hours that I may have to place at anybody's disposal."[7] Apparently Indians were no longer a high priority even for the commissioner of Indian affairs.

The meetings may have been burdensome, even tiresome, for the government officials, but they were an essential part of the delegation experience. If nothing else, the meetings were the mechanism by which the Indian visitors received their intended indoctrination to the world of the white man. The Great Father, the secretary of the interior, the commissioner of Indian affairs, each in his turn would stress the overwhelming economic and military superiority of the United States and the need for the Indian to adopt the white man's ways or perish. "When you look around you, you will see that the white people are a great multitude which you cannot count," said Rutherford B. Hayes to the Red Cloud and Spotted Tail delegation of 1877. "Every year their number is increased by far more than the number of all the red men in this great land." The white man would eventually cover the western country. "If you live roaming about without homes they will sweep over you like a great flood of water. To sustain yourselves against that flood, you must have homes in which you and your families must permanently live and land on which you can raise that which is necessary to support you." Upon this firm ground the Indians would be safe. "I am a good friend to you and your people," Hayes assured them, "and as a good friend I give you this . . . advice."[8] This reasoning was the theme of most delegation activities.

Following a pattern the kings and queens of Europe had developed a century before, the delegates would inspect forts and battleships, visit arsenals, and watch parades and artillery demonstrations. Even the most diehard militant could not fail to be impressed by the awesome power of the white man.

The Winnebagos who visited Washington in 1828 probably had little notion of the real reason for the parade held in their honor. The Winnebagos had agreed to dance for the Great Father, and he sent a military escort to accompany them from their hotel to the White House. For the event, the First Brigade of the District of Columbia Militia assembled, fully equipped, in front of St. John's Church at 10:30 A.M. on Saturday, November 15. They were ostensibly needed to preserve order during the performance and to give "additional effect" to the exhibition, but the real reason, as the *National Intelligencer* informed its readers, was "to shew to the Winnebago warriors, here, as well as in other cities of the Union, which they have visited, the existence of Military Power; which they might not be properly impressed with, in seeing our People every where engaged only in their ordinary pursuits."[9]

Standard fare for the delegations was a visit to the Marine Barracks, the Washington Arsenal, and the Navy Yard. The marines always put on a good show, and one of the more spectacular was for the Pawnee, Ponca, Potawatomi, Sioux, and Sac and Fox delegations visiting Washington in January 1858. Four battalions in full dress accompanied by the Marine Band with fifes and drums executed their complex maneuvers in a mock battle complete with the firing of blank cartridges. It was a beautiful springlike day, and the sunshine reflected brilliantly from the polished bayonets and gold lace. According to one report, the marines "exhibited great proficiency in drill and manoeuvres, and the accomplished officer in command acquitted himself with his accustomed ability."[10]

An even greater display awaited Indians at the arsenal, where various weapons were demonstrated for their edification. Light field cannons that could destroy wooden targets with remarkable accuracy, huge shore guns that shook the ground and hurled thousand-pound projectiles at an unseen enemy miles away, and the Gatling guns with their seemingly inexhaustible supply of ammunition were weapons beyond the Indians' wildest imagination. Inside the arsenal were tens of thousands of muskets, stacked and ready for use. Few delegates were able to conceal their amazement at this "forest of guns," as they called the display. Most shared the opinion of the Cheyenne and Arapaho delegates who visited the arsenal in 1851. "We are now certain that nothing is impossible to the white people. They are next in power to the Great Spirit."[11]

The Navy Yard offered its own delights. Here the Indians moved through the machine shops where the weapons were manufactured. The throbbing and humming steam engines that operated the forges, lathes, and presses were almost as fascinating as the guns. What most impressed the delegates, however, were the metal shavings dropped by the lathes that shaped the cannon barrels. Few of the delegates could resist asking for samples to take home.[12]

Battleship tours were also part of a delegation's education. The Osage delegation of 1806 visited the frigate *Adams* accompanied by President Thomas Jefferson and the secretaries of navy and war. Although the tour ended with the traditional broadside, the chiefs displayed no emotion or surprise at the cannonade, much to everyone's disappointment. This restraint was not evident in the Sioux delegates who inspected a steam-driven monitor at the Navy Yard in 1870. They could not conceal their astonishment at the idea of an iron boat. Several of the men, in fact, tried to cut the deck with their knives. Finally convinced that the ship was indeed made of iron, they were reluctant to go aboard lest it sink under their weight. "None of the Indians wanted to stay long on board," the agent recalled, "and all were glad to step on shore when the inspection was over."[13]

The Indians much preferred the vessels that plied the waters between Washington and Mount Vernon. The secretary of the navy sometimes furnished gunboats for these visits to the home of the first Great Father, but usually the Indians had to settle for excursion steamers like the *Arrow*, which carried two Sioux delegations to Mount Vernon on September 24, 1872. "A more genial and joyous company it has rarely been our privilege to join," remarked a reporter for the *Washington Daily Chronicle*. The weather had been unusually hot, and the Sioux were delighted to get away from the crowded city. Exhilarated by the river breeze, the Indians began to sing; they kept time by tapping their tomahawks on the railing. Mount Vernon was reached at noon after a two-hour ride. George Washington's tomb was the first stop. As the Sioux filed past, several stuck their hands through the iron grating and waved them over the vault. When asked why they did this, they replied: "We are shaking hands with the Spirit of the Great Father." The delegates then enjoyed a hearty lunch under the trees, where they stretched out on the grass and, according to an observer, "exhibited more of satisfaction than they had done before for days."[14]

Yankton Sioux delegation in front of the United States Capitol Building, February or March 1905. The Indians are, left to right: Yellow Thunder, Black Thunder, Charging Bear, Hollow Horn, Eagle Track, and Shooting Hawk. The drivers are unidentified. Photograph by Karl H. Claudy.

A tour of the Capitol Building was also a requisite for the Indian visitors, but how much they benefited from the experience is open to conjecture. The Comanches who visited Washington in 1846 found the exhibits of paintings and statuary much more interesting than the speeches they heard on the House and Senate floors. They were especially delighted with the color prints by George Catlin which they saw in the library. "As they gazed upon Buffalo hunts, upon the groups of wild horses and wolves, and upon the various Indian warriors in their own costumes, and amid the scenes of their own distant homes, they could not restrain their emotions," noted one observer. "For the first time, men, women, and youths, fell into animated conversation, pointing out to each other what most interested them . . . and for the moment, seemed restored to the wild prairies or hills of Texas." The large paintings on display in the Rotunda also impressed the Comanches, who recognized President James K. Polk, whom they had just met, and Sam Houston, at whose portrait they "laughed heartily."[15]

According to Charles Eastman, a Santee Sioux physician who frequently visited Washington at the turn of the twentieth century, some of the old chiefs liked to sit in the House and Senate galleries and observe the congressmen at work. On one occasion Eastman accompanied several Oglala Sioux delegates to the Senate gallery. Instead of learning about the workings of government, however, the men spent their time characterizing the politicians. One they compared to a fish; another they thought was an actor and not a "true man" because he seemed to be striking a pose as he sat at his desk. Senator Orville Platt of Connecticut seemed cautious and diplomatic. They took Senator David Turpie of Indiana to be a preacher and were pleased with his "air of godliness and reverence." But Senator William Frye of Maine impressed them most because he was a rarity among white men—"honest to the core."[16]

Although the Indians much preferred outdoor activities to sitting in stuffy theaters watching the ballet or the latest comedy, all delegations had to endure some exposure to these cultural events. The Indians obviously were as much of an attraction as the performances themselves, and from the amount of advance publicity given their appearances, they were sometimes used to assure a full house. Two newspapers, for instance, advertised the forthcoming appearance of the Southern Plains delegation of 1863 at Grover's Theatre on Pennsylvania Avenue near the Willard Hotel. The newspapers even printed the seating assignments for the Indians, which assured theatergoers that they would be able to see "representatives of the influential tribes in the West—all great fighting nations—[in] their peculiar paints, [and] costumes." What the Indians thought of the entertainments is unknown, although it was unusual for a delegation to sit through an entire theatrical performance. The Winnebagos who attended a comedy in New York City did enjoy some hearty laughs, but at the wrong places. They found the love scenes especially amusing. Special effects were also lost on them. The stench of burning sulphur during a simulated earthquake caused the Indians to cover their faces with their blankets. By the end of the performance, only two of the twenty Winnebagos were still in their seats.[17]

One of the most stirring moments in Washington's theatrical history occurred in 1837 when visiting tribesmen attended a ballet at the National Theater. Because the theater was crowded, the Indians were seated on the stage, where they almost outshone the ballerina, a Miss Nelson, in her role as the Mountain Sylph. The Indians paid no heed to the audience, for the dancer's grace and beauty held them spellbound; a crown of ostrich plumes flashed and fluttered as the Mountain Sylph darted lightly and swiftly across the stage. Suddenly, one of the Sioux warriors stood up and tossed his warbonnet of eagle feathers at Miss Nelson's feet. A second bonnet soon followed, and the ballerina

This is believed to be the buffalo robe that the Sioux warrior Moukaushka gave to Miss Nelson, "the beauty of Washington," just one month before his death in Baltimore.

stopped dancing. Tokacou, a celebrated Yankton chief, then stepped forward and handed the startled dancer his splendid robe of white wolf skins. Not to be outdone, Moukaushka arose. This gallant young warrior would die within a month from one of the white man's dread diseases, but tonight his thoughts were only of the lovely Miss Nelson. He handed her his beautifully painted buffalo robe. He was offering this treasure, the interpreter explained to the audience, "to the beauty of Washington." The quick-thinking young woman acknowledged the gifts by plucking the ostrich plumes from her crown and giving one to each delegate. "The whole scene," the *Intelligencer* informed its readers, was "one of extraordinary and thrilling interest." The next day the Sioux delegation was seen striding along Pennsylvania Avenue toward the Capitol. Each warrior was proudly wearing a new military uniform, silver epaulets, and hat. Tucked in each hatband was one of Miss Nelson's ostrich plumes.[18]

When the Smithsonian Institution opened in 1850, it became a regular stop on the delegation itinerary. A gallery of Indian portraits by Charles Bird King and John Mix Stanley was especially popular, for the Indians often saw people whom they recognized. A Smithsonian clerk was present when the Pawnee delegation of 1858 visited the museum. The Indians went first to the art gallery, where they examined the portraits of Indian life with great interest. Although they seemed disappointed at not finding paintings related to their tribes, they were pleased with the gallery nonetheless. "A scene representing Indian warriors, dancing around a captive white woman and her child attracted much notice from them," the clerk recalled. "They gathered in groups in front of it and made many remarks about it in their own language."

From the gallery the Indians went into the apparatus room, where they were exposed to the latest scientific wonders. To explain the mysterious forces of electricity, one of the curators asked the Indians to form a circle and hold hands while they were connected to a galvanic machine. "As soon as it was set in motion," the clerk related, "they gave a simultaneous shout, started in amazement, and some of them seemed disposed to be angry." Good humor was soon restored and the Indians then formed their own circle again and again, but it always broke up with the participants yelling and rubbing their elbows amid shouts of laughter. Afterwards, the Indians one by one tried to test the machine. Grasping the wires firmly and defiantly, each in his turn surrendered to the mysterious force, exposing himself to the laughter of his companions. Following this they went into the Smithsonian tower and then into the lecture hall, where they put on an exhibition of their war songs and dances for tourists and staff.[19]

The spiritual needs of the Indians were not forgotten. As part of the christianizing effort, Indian leaders frequently attended church services and visited Sunday schools. Chief Iron Bull of the Crows delighted the students and mothers at the Bethany Sunday School by declaring he was a believer in religious instruction. Like all Crows, he said, he prayed to the same God as the whites, but in a different way. The attitude of most of the delegates toward these functions was probably best expressed by a cynical writer for the *Washington Star* when announcing that the Sioux delegation of 1891 would be at church the following Sunday. They go, he wrote, "not because they are piously inclined, but, like a great many of their white brethren, . . . to hear the music and see the people."[20]

Whatever the Indians' response, their presence in church made good press for government officials trying to convince the public that progress was being made in the civilization of the tribes. And in fact, the missionaries had not completely failed in their efforts. Most of the delegates from the acculturated tribes were professed Christians, and a few were ordained ministers. Jesse Bushyhead, a Baptist minister as well as an influential

Cherokee leader, regularly spoke to church groups while visiting Washington. John Quinney was a Presbyterian minister. When he was not lobbying on behalf of his people, he could be found in church seeking spiritual guidance. "I attended Dr. Lauries C[hurch]," he recorded in his diary on January 4, 1846. "Rev. Dr. L preached himself—with good Effect on myself, as I humbly thought." Although he regularly worshipped at Laurie's Presbyterian church on F Street, Quinney also visited other churches in the city. He spent most of one Sunday, including the evening, at St. Paul's Episcopal Church. "Very much satisfied as well as revived in my mind," Quinney noted in his diary upon returning to his boardinghouse. On another Sunday he attended services at the Capitol Building in the morning, and then went to a temperance meeting in the evening.[21]

A unique religious event took place in March 1831 after the defeat in Congress of an attempt to help the Cherokees prevent implementation of the Indian Removal Act. That evening various Indian deputations in Washington agreed to join the Cherokees in a day of fasting and prayer. Accordingly, the following morning, Sunday March 6, the delegations—Iroquois, Quapaw, Choctaw, Creek, as well as Cherokee—met at Brown's Hotel, where an Oneida minister led them in prayer. The Indians fasted the entire day and then met at Gadsby's Hotel that evening for another service, this one conducted by a Presbyterian minister, probably John Quinney. Only a few white people, known friends of the Indians, were present; most Washingtonians knew nothing about the observances. An Englishman visiting Washington at the time doubted "whether any set of men, in a day of adversity and public gloom, with nought but darkness overshadowing, and calamities heaped upon them, with great momentous interests at stake, ever felt more religiously, more keenly, or more weightily, their dependence on that High and Almighty Providence, which controls the destinies of nations."[22]

Many of the early delegations were asked to dance and sing while in Washington. The Indians, who believed they were honoring the Great Father and demonstrating their appreciation for his generosity, seldom refused. Usually held on White House grounds, the performances were well-publicized and festive affairs that attracted huge crowds. The Osage delegation of 1804 may have been the first to perform in this manner. According to the *National Intelligencer and Washington Advertiser*, a large concourse of ladies and gentlemen, including President Jefferson and members of his cabinet, watched the Osages perform a series of war dances to the music of the Italian band. The "king" of the Osages did not dance but sat with Jefferson and the other dignitaries.[23]

Thereafter, public dancing became routine for larger delegations like the seventeen Pawnee, Omaha, Oto, Missouri, and Kansa Indians who visited Washington in 1822. Favored with a crisp, sunny day, the midwinter spectacle attracted an enormous crowd that included many ladies and most of the congressmen, who had adjourned early for the show. The festivities opened with a mock council between the Indians and President James Monroe that afforded "a striking specimen of native oratory," according to one witness. "The gestures of the Indian speakers were violent, but energetic, and frequently graceful." When the conference ended, the warriors threw aside their blankets and, armed with tomahawks and clubs, performed dances described as "a rude kind of leaping, governed, in some measure, by the sullen sound of a sort of drum." Wearing nothing but paint and red flannel breechclouts, the Indians "uttered shocking yells, and writhed and twisted their bodies in frightful contortion." The three-hour theatrical was a tremendous success. "They were painted horribly, and exhibited the operation of scalping and tomahawking in fine style," a second observer claimed. Still another thought the exhibition one which "no person of liberal and philosophical curiosity would willingly have missed seeing, and which no one who viewed it . . . would choose to witness again."[24]

Not all dances were so successful. The one planned for the Santee Sioux and Sac and Fox delegations of 1837 bordered on the disastrous. The dance was held on the public square at the corner of Fourteenth Street near Franklin Row, but the ground was marshy and entirely unsuited for the purpose. Even worse was the disorderly conduct of the crowd, which pressed and jolted the Indians. The Sioux, who performed first, were so annoyed they stopped dancing and stalked from the grounds in disgust. The Sac and Fox, who had been waiting their turn, would not even attempt to perform because of the unruly crowd. More than five thousand Washingtonians had assembled for the affair, while thousands more never even got close, thanks to the colossal traffic jam of carriages, gigs, and vehicles of every description that clogged streets for blocks around. As one newsman wryly noted, "Public curiosity was, in a great measure, baffled."[25]

The Cherokee delegation of 1836 had even more reason to be angry. According to playbills distributed by the National Theater, the ten-member delegation had offered to perform a "real Indian War Dance exhibiting Hate, Triumph, Revenge, etc, and go through the ceremony of scalping on Thursday [evening], February 11." The *Washington Globe*, two days later, informed its readers that John Ross and his "merrie men" had performed as promised to the "great satisfaction" of the crowded house. But no such thing had occurred. Moreover, Ross, whose tribe was in the midst of a bitter and protracted fight with the government over the Indian removal program, was not amused by the effort to embarrass the Cherokees. "Neither I nor any of my associates of the Cherokee delegation have appeared on the stage," he sternly informed the *Globe's* editors on February 15. "We have been occupied with matters of graver import than to become allies of the white men forming the dramatis personae. We have too high a regard for ourselves—too deep an interest in the welfare of our people, to be merrymaking under our misfortunes." The *Globe*, in turn, claimed that the news about the Cherokee performance had been "thrust into our columns without our knowledge."[26]

It was one thing to dance in homage of the Great Father; it was quite another to dance in a theater for money. Commissioner Carey Harris was outraged to learn that Agent John Dougherty had allowed his Pawnee delegation to dance and sing on the stage in New York. "This proceeding is so directly at variance with the views of propriety entertained by the Department, and has been so repeatedly discountenanced here, that I have to request that it may not occur again." The commissioner also reminded Dougherty that it was improper for the Indians to receive money "for visiting public establishments, or the exhibitions of individuals." By midcentury, the official policy was to discourage dancing for any reason because of the conflict with the campaign to induce Indians to give up their traditional ways. "It is considered disreputable and demoralizing in the highest degree for respectable Indians to exhibit themselves in public under any circumstances and therefore the Department has heretofore and will continue to discountenance it," declared Commissioner Orlando Brown in April 1850.[27]

Nevertheless, government policy on this issue often seems to have been ambivalent. A Pawnee delegation danced with official sanction at the Marine Barracks in January 1858, even though the Indians tried to excuse themselves because of the inclement weather. Even more puzzling was the request by the commissioner for twenty Ute Indians to dance at the Denver Exposition of 1883. Instead of dancers, the commissioner received a sharply worded protest from the agent. "No Indian with any dignity or who has any prestige with his tribe will belittle himself . . . and make a fool of himself to amuse white people." Furthermore, the agent continued, "it is a mystery to them why Washington

Kiowa members of the Southern Plains delegation of 1863. Left to right: White Bear (Satanta), Little Heart, Lone Wolf, Yellow Buffalo, and Yellow Wolf. Seated on the floor are Coy, wife of White Bear, and Etla, wife of Lone Wolf. Photograph taken in Leavenworth, Kansas, by Alfred S. Addis on March 12 or 13, 1863.

wants them to stop the war and sun dance at home but is anxious to have them dance at Denver."[28]

Not all agents were so high-minded. John P. Clum, the young Apache agent at San Carlos, organized a touring company of Apaches so that he could finance his way east and marry the sweetheart waiting for him in Ohio. James McLaughlin, the Standing Rock agent, reputedly received half the proceeds for persuading the famous Sitting Bull to go on tour. The old Hunkpapa militant spent two seasons on the road, in 1884 and 1885, the second one with Buffalo Bill's Wild West Show. Sitting Bull drove a hard bargain. His contract with the Wild West Show called for a salary of $50 a week, a bonus of $125 for signing, and the sole right to sell his photographs and autographs.[29]

The most reprehensible episode of this sort occurred in April 1863 when a delegation was exhibited at the P. T. Barnum museum in New York City. Barnum claimed he accomplished this coup by bribing the agent, Samuel G. Colley, with "a pretty liberal outlay of money" and by promising the fifteen Cheyenne, Arapaho, Comanche, and

Kiowa Indians good food and many presents. That there was some sort of agreement is evident from a letter advising Barnum of the necessary arrangements for the Indians. "The Presents," Colley wrote," . . . will be most acceptable to them. [They] . . . will please them beyond my power to express. You are most likely aware that in this respect they resemble children. Indeed, their child-like simplicity combined with their prowess and their wisdom, offers a curious study to those not acquainted with Indian character." However, "as they [have] never slept on beds, I must trouble you to procure rooms where they can spread out their blankets and sleep on the floor. You will also please procure bread, raw beef and coffee, all of which they will cook in their own rude Indian style. They will also want some paint and some oil."[30]

Whatever the investment, Barnum got his money's worth, for he fully exploited the situation. His advertisements appeared daily in the New York newspapers, warning the public to "come now, or you're too late. Everybody is rushing to see . . . [the Indians]. It will be worth a quarter [just] to see the crowd." Between performances Barnum escorted the Indians to City Hall, Public School Number 14, and various tourist attractions. The Indians went everywhere in an omnibus drawn by six horses preceded by a circus wagon carrying a band. Although they appeared on stage with Barnum three times a day for more than a week, the guileless Indians did not know that the public paid to see them. They thought the crowds came in recognition of their importance and military accomplishments.[31]

The only difficulty Barnum had with the arrangement was the desire of the Indians for curiosities on display in the museum. A shirt of chain mail attracted particular attention. Barnum did not want to part with the armor because it had cost him one hundred dollars and was a popular attraction, but the Indians wanted it so badly that he finally traded it to a Kiowa chief for a suit of buckskins. (Interestingly, a decade later a Kiowa warrior wearing a shirt of chain mail was killed at the battle of Adobe Walls in eastern Texas. It is generally believed that this was Barnum's shirt.)[32]

The use of Indians for exhibition purposes was a problem that defied solution. As long as people were willing to pay for the privilege of seeing Indians dance, hucksters were eager to exploit the situation. The practice could not have been very profitable, however, considering the frequency with which the government had to rescue stranded Indian performers. The Indians would be penniless, hungry, and besieged by angry bill collectors. Because the bills were owed by Indians, they would inevitably find their way to the bureau for payment. Bureau officials would bluster at the bill collectors and reprimand the Indians, but the debts would be paid—from tribal monies if possible, or else from the contingency fund—and the Indians would be sent home.

Few theatrical troupes had the audacity of the Pawnees who presented themselves as an official delegation at the Bureau of Indian Affairs in August 1866. The nine Pawnees— seven men, one woman, and one child—were accompanied by two whites, one of whom claimed to be the delegation's interpreter. The Pawnees had come to collect money due them as army scouts, the interpreter said. An investigation revealed that the story had been fabricated by the so-called interpreter who had taken the Indians on tour. When this speculation fell through, the interpreter brought the Indians to Washington, where he hoped to leave them with the bureau. Having accomplished this much and fearing he would be arrested, the interpreter slipped out of town. His worries were unfounded, for he had broken no law in removing the Indians from their reservation. Furthermore, he had a letter from the Pawnee agent giving him permission to take the Indians on tour. The frustrated officials who had to feed and house the Pawnees before sending them home secured some satisfaction from the affair by dismissing the agent.[33]

Indians were generally on their best behavior while in Washington, but there were a few awkward episodes. The delegates frequently got disoriented, especially after indulging too liberally at the bar, and they would wander into the wrong hotel rooms and even into private homes. Catherine Akerly Cocks Mitchell, wife of Senator Samuel Latham Mitchell of New York, recalled the evening in December 1808 when a Passamaquoddy warrior entered their room while she and her husband were sitting before the fire. "Dressed in all his finery," the warrior shook hands with Mrs. Mitchell and asked for whiskey. "We soon discovered that he had had too much Whiskey before, for he was very much intoxicated, and it was with difficulty that we got him out of the room & shut the door upon him." Mrs. Mitchell was dismayed to learn the next day that several members of the delegation had consumed so much liquor they had been unable to reach their lodgings and had slept in the street. "They must have had a soaking time," she recalled, "for it rained violently during the night." Dolley Madison had a similar surprise one evening after entertaining a delegation at the White House. Upon retiring for the evening, she discovered in her chambers a warrior who had somehow gotten separated from the rest of his party as the delegation was leaving the White House. A quick tug on the bell cord summoned a servant who showed the bewildered Indian to the door.[34]

Although there is no known instance of a delegate harming any local residents while in the East, Washingtonians felt uneasy about the presence of Indians who, especially before the Civil War, were often armed with knives, tomahawks, and guns. More than one newspaper editorial questioned the wisdom of allowing Indians to walk the streets carrying weapons. This anxiety was not relieved by the rough behavior of some of the early visitors. One warrior leaving the White House after an interview with President James Madison in 1812 grabbed the long, blond hair of a little girl watching the delegation file past and pretended he was going to scalp her. Also unappreciated were the antics of the Winnebago delegation of 1828. According to Washington socialite Margaret Bayard Smith, "the ferocious Winebagoes" chased "several young ladies and others they have caught in their arms and kissed, till decent young women are nearly afraid to walk out." Proclaiming herself a representative of the women of Washington, she stormed into the secretary of war's office and demanded he do something about the Indians. Her mission was successful, but, as she later reported, "you have no idea what a general dread they inspired." The most dangerous episode occurred in 1837 when two rival Sac and Fox delegations met unexpectedly on Pennsylvania Avenue. As one witness later recalled, the Indians "enlightened the terrified citizens in the art of warfare by throwing tomahawks at each other for awhile."[35]

The Indians did not frighten everyone they met. At least two delegates—a Santee Sioux in 1858 and a Chippewa in 1867—married white women they met while in Washington. The exact circumstances are unclear. Some accounts claim the women were prostitutes; others claim they were employees of the hotels where the Indians stayed.[36] There were also many instances recorded of delegates being invited to private homes for tea or an evening by the fireside. The Oto Chief Shaumonekusse and his wife, Eagle of Delight, who visited Washington in 1822, were frequent guests of Jonathan Barber, a local physician. "She was a very good natured, mild woman," Barber wrote, whereas her husband "showed great readiness in acquiring our language, retaining anything that he was once informed, and imitating the tones of every word." The Indians also demonstrated a natural wit. On one occasion the doctor showed several members of the delegation a skeleton he kept in a closet, whereupon one of them grasped a bony hand and said, "How do you do?" In 1875 Congressman John S. Savage of Ohio held a reception at his Washington residence for a Chippewa delegation. The festivities got off to an awkward start. Everyone shook hands and stared at each other. Eventually, the Indians squatted on the floor and began to sing, keeping time by tapping their tomahawks on the floor. As one of the guests later remarked, "We made a show of them, and they made one of us. Which were the most civilized?"[37]

The craze to see the Indians would continue throughout their stay. Crowds of spectators would gather outside the hotel whenever a delegation arrived, with everyone hoping to catch a glimpse of an Indian at a window, or even better, to see the delegation parade out to some rendezvous. A reporter for the *Washington Daily Chronicle* was part of the throng outside the Washington House the day the Red Cloud and Spotted Tail delegation of 1872 arrived. Throughout the day, the boardwalk was lined with noisy urchins who shattered the Sabbath stillness with shouts of "You better get away," "Look, there's the Indians," or "They'll cut your head off." In this carnival atmosphere the crowd exchanged silly comments with passersby who inquired about the attraction. Occasionally, the sightseers would be rewarded by the appearance of one of the Indians peering down at them from a second-floor window, whereupon the entire mob would fall back in fright. The reporter thought the delegates looked "more like a caged set of human beings than an uncivilized set of men brought here to confer with their Great Father in regard to their own welfare."[38]

Even in their rooms the Indians could not escape the insatiable curiosity of the public. The Indians tended to oblige this interest by keeping their doors open, usually to get relief from summer heat and to ease the feeling of confinement. As a result, a stream of curiosity-seekers would peer into the rooms, perhaps expecting to catch the delegates eating raw meat or brandishing scalps. They were usually disappointed to find the Indians sleeping on pallets, smoking, or just chatting. According to a reporter for the *Daily Chronicle*, some of the female patrons of the Washington House—"with that curiosity peculiar to their sex"—joined the parade past the delegation rooms and saw more than they wanted. The chiefs were reclining "in an almost nude condition," oblivious to the onlookers whether male or female. "They strewed no blanket over themselves, nor covered their heads in pillows worth a cent, but, Indian like, moved not a muscle." It was not unusual for an Indian pestered this way to stroll carelessly to the door and slam it shut with a well-placed kick.[39]

Generally, the Indian visitors behaved much as they did at home. The women would sew and do beadwork; the men might draw or carve. They also enjoyed playing cards, gambling, and singing. A woman visiting Spotted Tail and Two Strike, Sioux delegates who were accompanied by their wives, noted that Mrs. Spotted Tail had some material of the "chaste Dolly Varden pattern," which she was trying to make into a garment of that design. Two Strike was sitting on the floor drawing "with red, blue and black pencils himself in various attitudes on horseback and killing Pawnees." The reporter thought the "effort was highly successful, considering the untutored hand of the artist."[40]

Unfortunately, very few examples of drawings done by Indian visitors have survived. Among the most interesting of those extant are twelve pencil drawings by the Crow chief Medicine Crow which were brought to the author's attention by Joseph Medicine Crow, his grandson. Now in the custody of the Library of Eastern Montana College in Billings, the drawings record Medicine Crow's impressions of his 1880 visit. The National Zoo seems to have especially excited the Crow artist: he drew many exotic birds and animals, naming them after creatures found in his own country. The elephant he called "long nose bull," the zebra "spotted mule," the camel "elk with a big back on him," the alligator "big snake with legs," the peacock "wonder tail comes from above," the hippopotamus "bull in the water." The monkey he characterized as a combination dog and man. Medicine Crow also drew trains, gunboats, steamboats, and even a picture of the Capitol Building complete with flags and the statue of the goddess of freedom on the dome which, because of her feathered helmet, he evidently mistook for an Indian.

The Indian visitors especially enjoyed singing and drumming. On warm summer evenings they often gathered on the front porch of the hotels, where their music was sure to gather a large and interested audience. To most Washingtonians, Indian singing was little more than "discordant sounds," but to the reporter for the *Washington Union*, who was part of the assembly listening to Pawnees singing in front of Jimmy Maher's boardinghouse in 1858, the people present "probably understood and enjoyed the chant as well, perhaps, as some of our fashionables will enjoy and understand the Italian opera week after next."[41]

Not all the singing and drumming was for entertainment; much of it had religious significance, for the delegates would often pray far into the night before important meetings with the Great Father or other government officials. Robert Yellowtail, today more than eighty years old, was the interpreter for the Crow delegation which visited Washington in April 1917 to protest an attempt to open the tribe's Montana reservation to homesteaders. The night before the final Senate hearing the old war chiefs with the delegation opened a sacred medicine bundle that they had brought to Washington. The medicine in the bundle was so powerful that it had made thirteen Crows into chiefs. In order to make the medicine work properly, however, the incense of buffalo chips was required. The chiefs asked Yellowtail and several other young men to visit the National Zoo and collect enough chips for a "medicine making" ceremony. Upon their return, the entire delegation assembled in a large dormitory room in their quarters at the National Hotel. The chiefs sat in a semicircle on the floor with the medicine bundle and their war regalia spread out before them. The other delegates watched silently as the chiefs burned the buffalo chips, sweet grass, and other ingredients over wood coals taken from the kitchen stove. "A real war party medicine making seance was in progress" Yellowtail recalls. "A smudge-like smoke filled the room. Chief Plenty Coups was master of ceremonies and each chief in turn prayed to the unseen Great Spirit to guide them through this last great conflict with . . . [the] whiteman government." The next day the attempted appropriation of their land was soundly defeated.[42]

To complete their introduction to white life, Indians visiting the East for the first time would usually be returned home by way of Baltimore, Philadelphia, and New York. The stay in these cities would be short, a day or two in each, for the Indians by now were impatient to get home. To them one American city was like another, and urban life held no magic. Most probably shared the opinion of Ten Bears of the Comanches, who said in 1863 that he had "a big disgust at the noise, confusion, and crowd of the city."[43]

Until 1838, Boston was on the typical delegation itinerary, but it was dropped that year because the mayor tried to bill the government for expenses the city incurred in hosting a delegation. The preceding fall, Secretary of War Joel Poinsett had summoned the leaders of some twenty tribes to Washington for a major conference designed to end intertribal warfare by defining tribal boundaries. As part of the effort to impress the Indians with American wealth and strength, bureau officials decided to send the Indians home by way of Baltimore, Philadelphia, New York, and Boston. Since no city could accommodate that many Indians at one time, the Indians went north in several large contingents, leaving a few days apart. The first group, consisting of thirty-four Sac and Fox men, women, and children led by chiefs Keokuk and Black Hawk, left in early November. A few days after the delegates left Washington, Commissioner Carey Harris received an acerbic note from an official in New York criticizing him for failing to alert

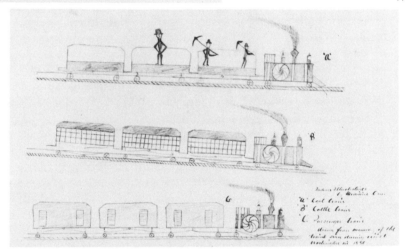

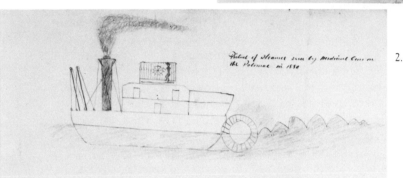

Series of pencil drawings by Chief Medicine Crow, a member of the Crow delegation of 1880. Captions by Charles H. Barstow, a clerk at the Crow agency, who encouraged the chief to make the drawings. The author is indebted to Joseph Medicine Crow, grandson of the artist, for bringing these drawings to his attention. Drawings reproduced through the courtesy of the Special Collections Division, Eastern Montana College, Billings, Montana.

1. Medicine Crow named the monitors "steam boats with wings" and the fishing boat "Bar shea Carty," which means "small boat" in the Crow language.

2. Medicine Crow's drawing of a steamer he saw on the Potomac River.

3. Different types of trains Medicine Crow saw during his eastern visit: (a) coal train, (b) cattle train, (c) passenger train.

4. Three animals Medicine Crow saw at the National Zoo. The one at top right is probably a llama. The "spotted mule" is obviously a giraffe, and the "Long nose Bull" is an elephant.

5. Medicine Crow's drawing of the U.S. Capitol Building. Note statue on the dome, which he evidently mistook for an Indian.

6. The birds are as follows: (a) sea gull that Medicine Crow called "Black spotted Bird," (b) parrot that he called "Big nose nice Red Bird," (c) peacock that he named "Wonder Tail Comes from above," (d) parrot that he named "Big nose nice green Bird," and (e) probably an ostrich or emu, which he named "The yellow Bird that runs."

7. Medicine Crow's drawing of a monkey, which he named "Dog and Man," and a "Big Head fish."

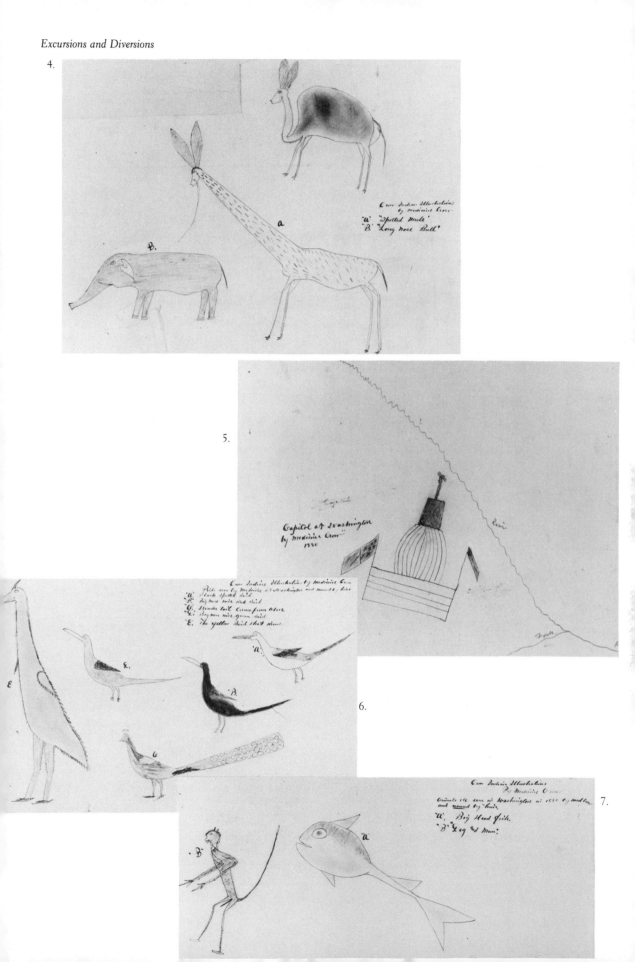

the city that the Indians were coming. "Had the character & merits of Keokuk, & the desire of him & his party to visit the north, been communicated to the Mayors of the different cities, their reception & departure would no doubt have been appropriate & gratifying; as it is they have left New York, & probably other cities, with unfavorable impressions."[44]

Harris learned by his mistake. Accordingly, as the next group was about to leave, he wrote to the mayors of the cities the Indians would visit and asked them to give the agent "such facilities as will as enable him more effectually to accomplish the objects of the Government, by giving the Indians under his charge, correct ideas of the power of the Government, the skill and resources of the people, and their benevolent disposition towards their red brethren."[45] Harris was probably ill prepared for the letter he received ten days later from Mayor Samuel A. Eliot of Boston. "I have paid such attention as was in my power, to the party of Indians under the conduct of Major Dougherty, who were recently in this City," the mayor wrote. "They seemed pleased by their reception, & I have no doubt that the effect was good upon their minds, & such as the government might desire." Eliot, however, was distressed to learn that other delegations were on their way. This had not been anticipated. "I beg of [you]," he wrote, "to reconsider the matter, as it cannot be expected that our citizens should be willing again to incur the trouble and expense which attend such visits. The curiosity which gave attraction to the first visitors is satisfied, & has almost entirely subsided; while the rapid succession of such ceremonious receptions will have a tendency to make the whole ridiculous, & then the effect upon the Indians themselves might be the reverse of what is desirable." Even more disconcerting was Eliot's intention to bill the government for the $1,507.52 in debts accumulated in serving as host to the first delegation. When Harris ignored the bill, Eliot asked Congressman Richard Fletcher of Massachusetts to pursue the matter. It was a fruitless exercise. Harris turned the problem over to Secretary of War Joel Poinsett for a ruling since nothing like this had ever occurred before. Poinsett simply refused to pay the bill. Never before had a city charged the federal government for entertaining an Indian delegation, he explained. For the government to allow payment in this instance, "would be a precedent which would cause it to be subjected to heavy charges from all the other cities."[46]

Presumably the citizens of these cities appreciated the opportunity to see the delegations, but this appreciation did not always extend to the civic fathers who had the hosts' responsibilities. They would be understandably annoyed when Indians arrived without warning, yet they were required to provide impromptu ceremonies and excursions. The bureau eventually learned to send clerks in advance of the delegations to arrange for accommodations and tours.

Obviously, the government spared no pains to impress the Indians with civilized life, but was it worth the effort? The experience of the Spotted Tail delegation of 1870 indicates it was not. Agent D. F. Poole was instructed to allow the Indians to see and do everything in which they appeared interested. "As far as could be ascertained," he recalled, "they did not desire to see anything, and so I selected such places as I thought might amuse and instruct them." After enduring visits to the theater, the Botanical Garden, the Patent Office, and the Smithsonian, the Indians began to get restless. They wanted to reach a quick understanding with the government so they could return home, but this was impossible because the government had planned an extensive itinerary that also included stops in Philadelphia and New York.[47]

The more the Indians saw, the less impressed they became. At the Treasury Department, the delegation was fascinated by the great numbers of young women sorting and counting money. Why did President Ulysses Grant have only one wife, Spotted Tail asked the agent, when he had so many beautiful women to choose from? Learning that whites allowed their men only one wife, he decided that, at least in this respect, the Indian way of life was better. Spotted Tail was even less impressed with the Philadelphia Mint. Gold and silver were nice to look at, he said, "but I would rather look at pretty squaws." By the time the Brulé delegation reached New York City, even pretty women failed to interest Spotted Tail. The chief slept during the carriage tour of Broadway and Central Park.[48]

In Agent Poole's opinion, this delegation had been a great waste of money. What had most impressed the Sioux during their eastern visit was a magician in Philadelphia. The bountiful supply of clothing they had worn so proudly while in the East was packed away upon reaching Sioux City. There the chiefs donned their traditional garb, claiming they wanted to save the citizen's clothes for a grand entry when they reached the agency. This plan was abandoned when they learned that Spotted Tail's favorite wife had died in his absence. Overwhelmed with grief, Spotted Tail immediately gave away all the presents he had received, including a fine horse and a trunkful of clothes. When the delegates reached the agency, each man quietly went his separate way. According to Poole, none of the chiefs and warriors ever appeared in public wearing the new clothes. "The predominance of Indian modes and customs had restored their ideas of dress to their normal condition," he said, "and they were all once more Indians among Indians."[49]

IX ACHES AND AILMENTS

The Indians cherished their visits to Washington, but they literally risked life and limb in making the trip. Cross-country travel, especially in the early years of the republic, was fraught with danger and discomfort. Fatigue and illness were constant companions. Delegations had to meet the challenges of rain-swollen rivers and winter storms, of intense heat and bone-chilling cold. Commercial transportation, when available, offered its own hazards, such as steamboat boiler explosions and overturned stagecoaches. The advent of the automobile made traveling easier if not safer. Four Sioux delegates from Pine Ridge, South Dakota, wrecked their car on the Pennsylvania Turnpike in 1940; one man died, the others were hospitalized.[1]

The Indians could cope with accidents and the caprices of nature; these they understood and expected. Far more menacing and mysterious were the diseases that claimed so many lives. Measles, smallpox, pneumonia, even the common cold, were serious threats to the Indians, many of whom were the elder statesmen of their tribes. Although the government tried to make the eastern visits as trouble-free as possible, few delegations returned home without incident or illness.

Medical care for the Indians, when it could be obtained, was no better and no worse than that available to Washington residents. Hospitals in the modern sense were unknown in the city until the second half of the nineteenth century; the first emergency room was not established until 1876. Until well into the twentieth century hospitals were generally viewed as places where people went to die and were avoided as much as possible. The first known instance of an Indian delegate being hospitalized occurred in 1859. The chief clerk of the bureau notified the commissioner of public buildings that a St. Regis Indian was lying "quite ill" at Robinson's boardinghouse on Pennsylvania Avenue. "It is considered important, with a view to his comfort and restoration to health, that he should be removed to the infirmary where he can receive proper treatment and attention." In 1884 the Flathead chief Charlot, and his interpreter Rivais, underwent surgery at Providence Hospital. The bureau paid Dr. W. V. Marmion five hundred dollars to improve the sight of both men, who were almost blind.[2]

In the first decades of the nineteenth century, the government tried to establish a standard procedure for providing medical care for Indian delegates by assigning the responsibility to the Office of the Surgeon General. One of the army physicians stationed in Washington would receive an increment in pay for the extra duty. Until 1824, the usual stipend was about $150 annually. With the creation of the Office of Indian Affairs in that year, the number of delegations increased to such an extent that the stipend was raised to $450, but this sum was also to include the cost of all medicines and drugs issued to the Indian patients.[3]

Immediately upon arriving in the capital with delegations, Indian agents received a letter from the bureau directing them to call on the army surgeon if anyone in the party needed medical care during their stay. His office was in the War Department Building adjacent to the President's House and his hours were nine to three daily except Sundays. After hours, he could be found at his residence with the garrison on Greenleaf Point.[4]

The practice of using army doctors to care for the delegates apparently did not work very well. Indian mistrust of the military and the reluctance of army doctors to make house calls seem to have been major problems. Whatever the reason, the order to use army doctors was often ignored. When the Iowa chief Mahaska broke his arm one July night in 1824, it was not anyone from the surgeon general's office but Dr. John B. Blake, a civilian physician, who went to the Indian Queen Hotel at 1:00 A.M. to set the fracture. Mahaska had indulged too freely at the hotel bar and then proceeded to beat his wife in their second floor room. Upon hearing the commotion, the Indian agent rushed into their room, causing the startled warrior, a stranger to the multistory buildings of the white man, to exit through the window. Fortunately, Mahaska's only injuries in the fall were the broken arm and a bruised ego. Setting the fracture cost twenty dollars. Blake charged an additional thirty-seven dollars for other services to the delegation, such as treating another Iowa chief for gonorrhea, and bleeding a Piankeshaw chief. The bureau deducted these bills from the agent's salary because he had violated the rule against employing civilian doctors.[5]

A Choctaw delegation that arrived in November of the same year also ignored the order, much to the dismay of economy-minded government officials. Indeed, the medical problems of this ten-member delegation were extraordinary. Before returning to Mississippi, two of the chiefs were to die. One, the eighty-five-year-old Puckshenubbe, did not even reach Washington. He fell while stretching his legs at a rest stop in Kentucky and fractured his skull. His death was followed two months later by that of Pushmataha, a victim of the croup. The sixty-year-old chief had arrived with a bad cold, which he failed to shake in the chilly, damp Washington weather. He collapsed on the morning of December 23 and died Christmas Eve despite the efforts of two physicians to save him. One of the physicians sent Commissioner of Indian Affairs Thomas L. McKenney a bill for twenty dollars for "attending Genl Push-a-ma-ta-ha preparing and administering four injections to him while on his Death Bed—together with all other necessary attentions until he was buried." McKenney considered the charge so excessive that he authorized payment of only half the bill.[6]

Meanwhile, still another delegate had taken ill; Robert Cole developed several large, open ulcers on his body. Ignoring the order to notify the surgeon general, his colleagues summoned James Wallace, a private physician. As the delegates explained, "It is Indispensible that a patient should have confidence in his physician; and Doctor Wallace has the confidence of Col. Cole & of the Delegation." Wallace visited Cole daily at Tennison's Hotel, dressing the open sores and attending to the needs of the other delegates as well. Sixty days of convalescence found Cole still unable to travel, and when the delegation finally left Washington in February 1825, he had to be left behind. Wallace continued to treat him until March 17, when Nathanial P. Causin, another private physician, took over the case. Not until mid-June was Cole well enough to leave the city.[7]

Although elated to see Cole depart, the commissioner still had to resolve the problem

154

of paying the bills. Wallace, who attended Cole for about three months, was authorized to receive two dollars for each visit. Wallace at first demanded a higher rate because he had brought a servant and two horses each time he visited Cole, but he finally accepted the payment. Dr. Causin, who submitted a bill for $300, was less cooperative. At the rate of two dollars a visit, Causin would have been entitled to $182, but he strongly objected that this amount was insufficient. "The chief never took a dose of medicine but from myself or [a] young Gentleman in my office," he claimed, "& during the whole of that time, the most abominable ulcers, almost that were ever seen, were cleansed & dressed twice a day with my own hands." Causin said he should have added another charge of one or two dollars a day for "nurse & dresser." The Choctaws should not even have called private physicians, the commissioner countered, but "a *gratification* of these unlettered people, being the object of the Department," he had complied with their "*notions.*" Only after Cole personally urged payment of the bill did the commissioner withdraw his objections and pass it to the auditors for settlement.[8]

Despite such difficulties, the Office of the Surgeon General was not relieved of its responsibility for the delegates until February 1832. At that time Commissioner of Indian Affairs Elbert Herring informed the surgeon general that the government had decided to stop bringing delegations to Washington because they were too expensive. "As very few are now permitted to come here," Herring wrote, "it is considered superfluous to employ a Physician to superintend and administer medical aid to such Indians as may from time to time visit the Seat of Government."[9]

Contrary to Herring's expectations, Indians continued to visit the capital, and they continued to need medical care. Now, however, it was permissible for them to summon physicians of their own choosing. For Indians in the city without agents or for members of unauthorized delegations the procedure was more complicated. More often than not the doctors had to apply directly to the commissioner for compensation. The bills eventually would be paid from monies held in trust for the tribe or from the contingency fund, but considerable time could elapse before a doctor collected his money.

When unusually large numbers of Indians were expected in the city at one time, the bureau sometimes arranged to have a physician on call. The doctors selected on these occasions had either asked for the assignment or were recommended to the bureau by interested parties, normally congressmen. Political clout rather than medical competence seems to have been the primary consideration. For instance, five Washingtonians petitioned the commissioner in October 1873 to allow "our esteemed fellow citizen Dr. J. L. Crouse whose established reputation in his profession is a sufficient guarantee that he is well qualified for the position" to be the physician for visiting Indians. The bureau apparently accepted the recommendation at face value, for the next day Crouse was informed that a Ute delegation would soon be at the Washington House, and he was authorized to attend to their medical needs, if any.[10]

An epidemic must have swept the delegation, because Crouse later submitted a bill for $768. He claimed he had charged only two dollars a visit, the minimum established by the District of Columbia Medical Society, for rendering "full and descriptive services" to the Utes. "They were mostly sick, many very ill," he assured the commissioner. "I was indefatigable in my efforts and attendance to do them full justice, and as the many efficient officers of the Bureau will attest." Admittedly, Crouse probably provided care to several other delegations which were at the Washington House at the same time, but the commissioner considered the charges exorbitant and allowed payment of only $498.[11] Crouse's appeal to the secretary of the interior for additional compensation was ignored.

The bureau had better luck with Dr. Alexander McWilliams, who served as the physician to Indian delegations for two years. He was initially hired in January 1867 on the recommendation of Congressman Charles Denison of Pennsylvania. The doctor's first responsibility was to vaccinate the more than one hundred Indians in the city, most of whom were quartered at the Army barracks at the intersection of Nineteenth and E streets. "You will leave your address at this office so that should there be occasion for your services, you may be readily found," McWilliams was instructed.[12]

The detailed records the doctor submitted to the bureau with his request for payment indicate that the Indians kept him very busy. He treated 134 delegates from thirteen tribes between January 28 and April 23, 1867, and he charged the government $1,682. His usual fee was two dollars a visit, but for special cases he charged more—for treating an Ottawa for gonorrhea, $15; for treating a Chippewa for syphilis, $25; for dressing the leg of a Chippewa, $5; for reducing the hernia and applying a truss to a Chippewa, $25. Only twenty-eight of the delegates did he visit once, presumably for their smallpox vaccinations; several required his attention more than a dozen times during their stay; a few, such as Lewis Davis, a Seneca from New York, were bedridden. McWilliams visited Davis ninety-two times, often two and three times in a day. So many of the delegates were ill that McWilliams asked the commissioner to issue an order to the agents that "no one will be allowed to visit any Sick Indian unless under an order from . . . [the] surgeon in charge."[13]

Alcohol abuse was part of the problem. McWilliams told the commissioner that many of the Indians were in a continual state "of beastly intoxication" thanks to the many taverns near the barracks. "Several of the Indians have been made sick and one is now on the verge of delirium from excessive intoxication," he claimed. "Medical treatment is of little avail while they are allowed free access to intoxicating drinks." His appeals to the tavernkeepers were ignored; they told him they would "sell to whom and when they please." McWilliams wanted the police to stop the sale of liquor to the Indians. The commissioner did, in fact, bring the matter to the attention of the superintendent of police, but probably not much was done.[14]

The bureau was so pleased with McWilliams that it reappointed him the following year. Although there were only half as many Indian visitors in 1868, they seemed to be far more sickly. Altogether between February 4 and July 24, McWilliams provided care to fifty-three delegates from five tribes—Sac and Fox, Shawnee, Nez Percé, Kaw, and Ute. One man, Blacktail Deer of the Utes, he visited seventy-two times. Of the four Nez Percé delegates, two became gravely ill: Lawyer recovered; Ute-Male-Sin-e-cum died. Perhaps aware that the doctor's bill of $1,030 would raise suspicions at the bureau, the Indian agents in charge of the delegations furnished the following testimonial: "Several of our Indians have been sick, off and on since their arrival here, several of them very sick, and . . . Dr. A. McWilliams has been in constant attendance upon them."[15]

Whereas alcohol-related illnesses had been the primary problem in 1867, venereal diseases caused the most difficulty in 1868. Of the 53 Indians McWilliams treated that year, 14 were suffering from either gonorrhea or syphilis. On the other hand, only 12 of the 134 Indians he treated the year before had had venereal disease. The problem must have been even more extensive than these figures indicate, because some of the Indians who contracted the diseases would not have developed symptoms until after their return home. The figures do confirm one fact: thanks to the appetites of the Indian agents and interpreters and the greed of hotelkeepers anxious to attract the delegation trade, the Indians were able to sample all the diversions of civilized life.

Although some of the delegates may have been themselves carriers of venereal disease, most of the cases were probably acquired in the East, if the experience of the Ponca delegation of 1877 is typical. Agent Albert G. Boone reported that "some of the chiefs were so badly afflicted [after their return from Washington] that it gave us much trouble." The chiefs claimed a clerk in the bureau, reputedly "a pet of the commissioner," had taken them to a brothel. After an investigation, the commissioner reported to the secretary of the interior that "several members of the [Ponca] delegation . . . which recently visited Washington are suffering from a loathsome disease contracted at a house of ill fame while here; and, contrary to explicit instructions, Mr. A. M. Bliss an employee of the Indian Bureau is amenable to the charge of having escorted these members to the house referred to." Pet or not, Bliss was promptly dismissed.[16]

Venereal disease, although endemic in the capital since its establishment, reached epidemic proportions in the decade or so following the Civil War. This doubtless reflects the growing pains Washington suffered because of the war, when the city almost overnight underwent the transition from a rural community to a large metropolis, with all its attendant urban ills.

Since there were no hospitals, the burden of caring for sick or injured Indians normally fell on their companions or the innkeepers. Mrs. E. A. Townely was paid $271 for caring for John Rogers, an elderly Cherokee delegate who had been "sick and entirely helpless" for some time before his death at her boardinghouse in 1846. It was also common to hire nurses to care for the delegates. Louise M. Beveridge, whose family catered to Indian delegations for more than fifty years, often accepted nursing jobs even when the patients were not boarding with her father. In 1887 she stayed six weeks with George Powers, a Sac and Fox interpreter, whose delegation was at Bell's boardinghouse on Pennsylvania Avenue just around the corner from the Beveridge house. The $60.25 she was paid covered both her professional services and the bill for her room and board.[17]

Compensation for treating Indians who were in Washington without authority was another matter. In 1876 Amanda Beveridge provided bed and board to a group of Warm Springs Indians from Oregon. The party included a seriously ill woman who remained with the Beveridges for more than a month. Because the Indians had come without authorization, the bureau refused to pay their hotel bill, although it did pay their medical expenses. "My claim is a just and honest one and should be entitled to compensation," Amanda declared when she appealed to the commissioner for her money. "For a long time . . . [the woman] laid at the point of death, and had it not been for the great attention paid her she would have surely died. The truth of this statement can be substantiated by the testimony of . . . the attending physician."[18] The decision may have been unfair, but it was not changed.

The Beveridges seem to have had more than their share of sick Indians. In 1866, an outbreak of smallpox and pneumonia almost put them out of business. At one time as many as ten Indians from four delegations were ill, including three Wisconsin Chippewas who died of smallpox on the same day. The era's standard practice of destroying all bedding and furnishings contaminated by smallpox was an unwelcome prospect for the proprietor of a hotel. Neither the bureau nor the Beveridges welcomed the expenses generated by this outbreak. For the Chippewas, the bureau paid the following expenses:

Chamber for sick	$1.25	Cash to Indian Widow	150.00
Paid Nurse for sick	$16.00	Suit Clothes for Interpreter on a/c	
Prescription and Medicines	8.95	destroyed his Small Pox	44.50
G. W. Sallay bill burying Chief	73.00	board & Room . . . [for other delegates]	
D. B. Clark's bill Medicines	20.00	on a/c Small Pox	30.00
Doc Homer's bill Medicines	35.00		

Louise Beveridge with a Cheyenne and Arapaho delegation outside the family boardinghouse. Front row, left to right: White Spoon, Black Coyote, He Bear, and Turkey Legs; back row: Cleaver Warden, Philip Cook, unidentified, Leonard Tyler. Photograph taken in January or February 1899.

The bureau evidently rejected Amanda's claim of $225 for bedding and furnishings, used by the Chippewas, that were destroyed on the doctor's orders.[19]

The Beveridges also submitted the following statement to cover the expenses of the other sick delegates:

To separate rooms, fire, lights, extra servant and attention for the following persons, delegates of the Choctaw, Chickasaw, and Cherokee nations, while sick at the Washington House, during the months of February, March, and April [1866], and the consequent loss of articles of bedding &c:

Colonel Adair, sick with small-pox about four weeks	$90
Mr. Mitchell, sick with small-pox about 20 days,	$60
Robert Love, sick with small-pox three weeks	$63
Governor Colbert, sick with pneumonia six weeks	$135
Governor Wade, sick with pneumonia five weeks,	$112
Governor Pickens, to separate rooms,	$30
2 large hair mattresses,	$70
1 small hair mattress,	$25
4 feather pilows, and 4 cases,	$10
5 sheets,	$10
2 blankets,	$20
2 comforts,	$15
6 towels,	$3

The Beveridges received $500 of the $673 they requested.[20]

Illnesses were to be expected, but fatalities were always a matter of deeper concern. Government officials worried about the adverse impact they might have on the people at home. This was especially important in the early years of the republic, when diplomatic relations with the western tribes were often precarious and the fledgling United States had to fear Indian alliances with foreign powers. The officials had much to worry about since delegation deaths were alarmingly frequent.

The first recorded death of an Indian delegate in Washington occurred in December 1805. The unnamed chief was a member of a large delegation of Osages, Pawnees, Sac and Fox, Sioux, Miami, Kansa, Kickapoo, and Iowa Indians—perhaps thirty in all—that was invited to Washington as a result of the Lewis and Clark expedition. Because the United States feared British and Spanish efforts to thwart American expansion into the newly acquired Louisiana Territory, it was considered politic to bring representatives of the western tribes to the East. The Indians seem to have suffered greatly from their adventure. Perhaps as many as five died during the trip. Only two of the deaths are documented, however. An Iowa chief died mysteriously while on the way to Washington. He owned a unique shell that he used as a tobacco pouch. While passing through Kentucky, a white man admired the shell and the Indian readily gave it to him. The chief later remarked to his companions: "I have given away my tobacco shell, and this circumstance puts me in mind that I shall die in a few days." Four days later he had a seizure and died.[21]

The other death occurred in Washington. Shortly after arriving, the delegation offered to dance at the only theater in the city, described by one observer as "a miserable little rope-dance theatre." The Indians, who received half the proceeds and all the rum they could drink as payment, performed a number of dances and executed a remarkable imitation of scalping using a wig. The festivities drew to a premature close when several of the performers became very intoxicated, throwing a scare into the audience. The following morning, an Osage chief who had participated in the dancing was found dead in his bed. His death was attributed to a combination of exhaustion and excessive drinking.[22]

An Arikara delegate was the next Indian visitor to die, passing away in April 1806. The Arikaras were also in the city because of Lewis and Clark. In fact, they would have accompanied the large delegation mentioned above, but several of the chiefs were too sick to travel when the main party left St. Louis for the East. Thomas Jefferson, when addressing the Arikara delegation before it left for home, spoke at length about the death of their "beloved chief," who had come east to visit his white brothers. "Wishing to see as much as he could of his new Brethren," Jefferson explained, "he consented to go on towards the sea as far as Baltimore and Philadelphia." The chief found nothing but kindness and good will wherever he went, but on his return to Washington he became ill. "Everything we could do to help him was done, but it pleased the great Spirit to take him from among us. We buried him among our own deceased friends and relations. We shed many tears over his grave." But, as Jefferson reminded the delegates, "death must happen to all Men, and his time was come."[23] The president's philosophy evidently did not impress the Arikaras: for the next twenty years they were notoriously hostile to white Americans. The death of their chief was likely one factor contributing to their belligerency.

Many ailments afflicted the delegates, but the two most mortal seem to have been smallpox and pneumonia. The bureau conducted massive smallpox vaccination programs in the first half of the nineteenth century, yet the dreaded disease continued to decimate Indian communities. An entire Santee Sioux delegation died of smallpox in 1838 while waiting for the Indian agent to take it to Washington. Mention has already been made of the smallpox deaths that occurred in Washington in 1866. The fear of a major epidemic prompted the bureau to keep other delegations out of the city that year until the crisis had passed. Thereafter, the bureau required all Indian delegates to be vaccinated as soon as they arrived.[24]

Medical technology solved the problem of smallpox, but it was helpless against pneumonia. Its victims included Taza of the Apaches, James McDaniel of the Cherokees, Yellow Wolf of the Kiowas, and Tuckalixtah of the Pawnees, whose delegation was particularly ill-fated. One of its nineteen delegates drowned while crossing a river in Nebraska. As two of his companions returned to his village with the body, the others proceeded to Washington, arriving in late December 1857. Despite their robust appearance, most of the delegates were sick throughout their stay. The Indian agent thought the illnesses were due to the change of diet and the confinements of city life; but, he admitted, "Indians are sometimes sick from other causes." The responsibility for medical care of the Indians he gave to the interpreter, who supposedly knew their "habits and constitution." The interpreter regularly supplied them with ointments, powders, pills, and oils, and he paid for injections and cuppings. Despite his efforts, or maybe because of them, the Indians were plagued with poor health. One newspaper reported that the delegates tried to excuse themselves from performing a war dance at the Marine Barracks because several were troubled with colds and hoarseness, but they finally relented. Certainly their health had not been improved by dancing half-naked in the January weather. Tuckalixtah, for one, took a turn for the worse. His severe cold persisted for seven weeks before he succumbed to pneumonia on March 28, 1858. According to the Washington press, "The poor little fellow had little faith in the medicine of the white man because it did not cure him instantly."[25]

The Indians who died in Washington probably represent but a small proportion of the total number of delegation deaths. The exact total will never be known. One reason is the lack of information about the Indians who died as a result of their visits to New York and Philadelphia before the establishment of Washington, D.C., as the national capital. The number of these deaths may be quite large. One delegation alone, consisting of sixteen chiefs and warriors from several Indiana and Illinois tribes, lost nine of their number to smallpox in 1793.[26] Another reason is the unreliability of Indian agents in reporting deaths of delegates, especially those that occurred en route. Perhaps the agents felt these deaths would reflect adversely upon themselves. More likely, their omissions indicate the general low regard whites of that era had for Indians as human beings. Such disregard surely contributed to the trauma experienced by the Indian who fell ill along the road. Schedules had to be met, and each extra day on the road meant wasted money. As a result, bedridden delegates were often left in the care of an innkeeper along the way.

Even seriously ill delegates, however, preferred to be jostled in coaches or exposed to the weather rather than be left behind to be tended by strangers in a foreign land. If die they must, they at least wanted the comfort of kinsmen in their last moments. This was

Passing Hail, Santee Sioux delegate who became ill with dropsy but refused to be left behind when his delegation departed from Washington in April 1867. He died the day after reaching home. Photograph by McClees Studio, January 1858.

the argument of Passing Hail, a Yankton Sioux chief who visited Washington in 1867. He was so ill with dropsy that his agent wanted to leave him behind when the delegation left for home. Passing Hail knew he was about to die, but he promised the commissioner he would remain alive until reaching home if permitted to leave. The old man pleaded so earnestly that the commissioner not only allowed him to leave but also authorized him to go by steamboat instead of making him travel overland with the rest of the delegation. True to his word, Passing Hail died the day after reaching the Nebraska reservation.[27]

Moukaushka, another Yankton Sioux delegate, was not so fortunate. He had been ill with fever for most of his stay in Washington; although his condition had improved he was not yet recovered when his companions prepared to leave. The delegation was to return home by way of Baltimore, Philadelphia, and New York. In 1837 this was a tiring journey even under the best of conditions, but the Sioux warrior would not be left behind. The delegation had been gone only a few days when the commissioner received the following message from Gadsby's Hotel in Baltimore: "Mon-ca-ush-ka is too low to go on with us . . . [and] we much fear that he will not recover." An interpreter was his only companion when he died.[28]

Fortunately, many agents were like Fellows D. Pease, who had charge of the Crow delegation of 1873. Rather than risk the lives of his delegates, several of whom were quite sick, he asked the commissioner to extend his stay in New York. "On our arrival here last night a couple of sick Indians were much worse and also Blackfoot and Thin Belly were taken very ill . . . [from] an attack of lung fever. All were a little better tonight but they are anxious to remain for a couple of days or so, or until they all partially recover and I *very much* dread leaving any of them behind." The fact that none of the Crows died so impressed Chief Blackfoot that he dictated a letter to President Grant relaying the good news. "I believe in the white man's medicine," Blackfoot declared. "It is stronger than ours for none of us died but all are now well and will soon be with our People again."[29]

Not all the Indians who died in the East were victims of disease. At least one took his own life, and several were murdered. The only confirmed suicide occurred in July 1824. According to agent Lawrence Taliaferro, his delegation was aboard a steamboat en route to Washington when the Sioux chief Marcpee jumped into the river and drowned. The night before the chief had been troubled by a nightmare in which he received a letter from a white man written "in characters of blood."[30]

Considering the tremendous culture shock the delegates experienced as well as the great pressures that were imposed on some of them during treaty negotiations, it is surprising there were not more suicides. Perhaps some of the delegates entertained the idea, but, as in the case of the Creek chief Opothele Yoholo, were prevented from killing themselves by their companions. Opothele Yoholo had brought a delegation to the capital in November 1825 to protest a fraudulent treaty that two citizens of Georgia, serving as commissioners for the United States, had negotiated with the Creeks the year before. According to the treaty, the tribe had agreed to sell its holdings in Georgia and move west of the Mississippi River. The commissioners claimed that representatives of the entire tribe had signed the treaty, although the signatory chiefs actually represented only a small faction. The Creeks were so enraged they killed three of the signatory chiefs; a fourth escaped the same fate only through the aid of a fast horse. Despite all this, the Senate ratified the treaty by a vote of thirty-eight to four, and President John Quincy Adams signed it into law, even though he knew the circumstances surrounding the treaty were not entirely honorable. By the time the delegation representing the dispossessed Creeks arrived, all Washington knew the treaty was a scandal.[31]

Garbed variously in citizen's and native dress, the Creeks and their interpreters called on Adams at the White House. Opothele Yoholo's appearance, like that of his eleven companions, was remarkable for its "dark and settled gloom," Adams thought. The president shook hands with each of the delegates.

"I am glad to see you," he said. "We should all meet in friendship."

"We are glad to be here," Opothele Yoholo responded. "Things have happened which frightened us. We hope now all will be well."

"That is my desire also," Adams replied reassuringly. "I also have heard of things which displeased me much, but I am sure the Secretary of War will be able to arrange matters to the satisfaction of all."

Adams authorized the secretary of war to renegotiate the controversial treaty, but only with the original terms: a complete cession of Creek lands in Georgia. This the delegation could not accept; they would consider ceding about two-thirds of the land in question. As the weeks dragged into months, the Creeks became desperate. The pressures became so intense that Opothele Yoholo, torn between the needs of his people and the demands of the white man's government, saw no solution but death. He tried to kill himself in his hotel room, but the other delegates restrained him. When Adams learned of the attempted suicide, he told the secretary of war to accept the Creek offer.[32]

Murder and violent crimes were also threats to the welfare of the delegates. Indeed, most of them somewhere during their travels had to endure abuse and even threats of bodily harm. In the turbulent post-Civil War years especially, Indian agents often took the precaution of boarding their delegations at remote railroad stations to avoid encounters with unruly whites in cities like Laramie, Bozeman, and Helena.[33] An even greater danger to delegations was posed by other Indians. Military escorts were sometimes needed to conduct delegations through the territory of neighboring Indian tribes. This was standard procedure for Ute delegations, which had to cross Cheyenne and Arapaho country to reach the nearest railroad.

Despite such precautions, confrontations took place. During the War of 1812, bushwackers shot at a large delegation under William Clark as the Indians traveled by flatboat on the Ohio River near Pittsburgh. Clark refused to proceed until a detachment of troops arrived to protect his delegation. In 1807, Arikaras attacked a small military force escorting a Mandan chief to his village. The party, which included fur traders and a dozen soldiers, was traveling by keelboat and had to pass an Arikara village on the Missouri River. The Arikaras, who were at war with the Mandans, stopped the keelboat and demanded the chief's surrender. When their order was refused, a brisk fight ensued in which several fur trappers were killed and three soldiers were wounded. The escort had to return to St. Louis, and it was another two years before Shahaka, or Big White, was returned to his people. Still another confrontation occurred during the Civil War when a Ute delegation escorted by three companies of cavalry met an overwhelming force of Cheyenne and Arapaho Indians near Julesburg, Kansas. Only the timely arrival of reinforcements allowed the party to continue unmolested.[34]

The number of delegates who were murdered while in the East is small. In fact, only two murders are confirmed, but there were probably some others, like the Crow subchief who, in 1851, deserted the delegation while it was passing through St. Louis on the way to Washington. Efforts to locate him were futile, and the party had to continue on its way. The man's body was found a few days later. Foul play was suspected, but hogs had so badly torn the corpse that the cause of death could not be determined. There was no doubt as to the cause of death in April 1867 of a Chippewa delegate from Minnesota. Because the ice had started to break up, the returning delegation had an unexpected one-day delay in crossing the Mississippi River at La Crosse, Wisconsin, and the Indian agent allowed the men to visit a nearby camp of Winnebagos. The next day one man was missing. A search revealed his body a few rods from the train station. He had been stabbed to death. His killer was never found.[35]

One delegate was even murdered while in Washington. Scarlet Crow, a Santee Sioux chief, disappeared on the evening of February 24, 1867. When efforts to locate him failed, the bureau ran the following notice in the lost-and-found section of the *Washington Chronicle:*

$100 REWARD.—ON SUNDAY NIGHT, February 24, one of the *Indians* belonging to the Sisseton and Warpeton Sioux delegation disappeared from the Barracks, corner of New York Avenue and Nineteenth Street, and has not since been heard from. Said Indian is about forty years old, and about five feet six inches high, and wears his hair cropped. He had on when he left satinet pants, laced shoes, striped flannel shirt, and wore a green three-point blanket. The above reward will be paid to any person returning said Indian to the aforesaid Barracks, or giving such information as will lead to his recovery, by applying to the Commissioner of Indian Affairs or to *Benjamin Thompson*, Special Agent, no. 64, Kirkwood House.[36]

Scarlet Crow, Santee Sioux delegate who died under mysterious circumstances while in Washington. Photograph by A. Zeno Shindler, February 1867.

Scarlet Crow had been missing about two weeks when two citizens of nearby Alexandria found his body in some woods near Arlington, Virginia. The Sioux chief appeared to have hanged himself, or at least that is what someone wanted the authorities to believe. As the Indian agent pointed out, however, the knots in the strip of blanket about his neck were never tied by an Indian; the branch from which he presumably hanged himself could not have supported his weight. Furthermore, the body had a blanket neatly tucked about it. Most important of all, the man had been dead a relatively short time, yet he appeared well fed. How could Scarlet Crow have been in the area for two weeks without someone noticing him? Had he been kept in a nearby house? The Indian agent hoped the government would not pay the reward; it would establish a precedent "under which other Indians would be kidnapped and hidden away until a reward was offered when he would be killed to prevent his making known the cause of his absence and the treatment he had received." Although the agent had no doubt that this is what had happened to Scarlet Crow, he did not wish "to be understood as charging either of the claimants [of the reward] to be perpetrators of so black and damnable a crime." With or without misgivings, the reward was paid. The government also compensated Scarlet Crow's family with five hundred dollars in trade goods. Not until 1916, however, was an appropriate tombstone provided for his grave. Congress authorized one hundred dollars for the headstone in recognition of the chief's "services and good work" as a scout for the United States during the Minnesota Sioux uprising of 1862.[37]

A delegate who came close to being murdered while in Washington was John Ross of the Cherokees. His assailant was another member of his delegation whom Ross had criticized for trying to arrange special considerations for himself during negotiations that culminated in the Cherokee treaty of February 27, 1819. Ross was working on correspondence in his hotel room the evening before the delegation was to return home, when the man entered and tried to stab him with a knife. Fortunately, another member of the delegation intervened and Ross suffered only a superficial shoulder wound.[38]

Except for concern about political complications, some officials responsible for the Indian visitors seem to have been unmoved by the mortalities. The culturally biased bureaucrats viewed it all as part of the Indians' learning experience. This opinion was expressed by the Indian agent who buried Taza, son of Cochise. "[His] . . . illness and death . . . were not devoid of beneficial results," the agent later wrote. "They afforded the Indians with our party an opportunity to observe the civilized methods and customs of caring for the sick and preparing the dead for burial, as well as our funeral rites and ceremonies."[39]

The benefit the Indians derived from observing this particular rite of passage is open to question. Nevertheless, it is true that the government took pains to share these moments with the Indians who were in the city when a delegate passed away. "Attended the funeral of Capt Rogers a Cherokee Chief whose mortal remains were put in the Congressional Burying ground," reads the entry for June 13, 1846, in the diary of John Quinney, the Stockbridge delegate. When James McDaniel, another prominent Cherokee, died in February 1868, several Indian delegations witnessed the funeral services conducted by the Reverend Dr. Gray at Joy's boardinghouse. Then they marched in the cortège, which included a company of soldiers and numerous carriages. At the grave, the spokesman for the Cherokees, Lewis Downing, eloquently thanked the citizens of Washington "for their kindness and sympathy upon the sad occasion."[40]

Such large attendance was not unusual, because the death and funeral of an Indian delegate often received extensive press coverage. Even his dying words would appear in the newspapers. Shortly before Tuckalixtah died in 1858, he expressed the regret that he had not fallen in battle. "I hope," the Pawnee warrior said, "that the Great Father will give my brother a horse as a memento of me." Tuckalixtah was laid to rest wearing white gloves and a citizen's black suit. His handsome mahogany coffin with silver fittings also contained a new blanket, flowers from the public greenhouse, and a small box with his pipe, tomahawk, and jewelry. Following a brief service at Maher's hotel, he was taken to the cemetery in a cortège that included twenty-seven carriages. The leader of the Pawnee delegation in his graveside eulogy thanked the Great Father for burying Tuckalixtah "like one of his own great chiefs."[41]

Yellow Wolf of the Kiowas came down with pneumonia in April 1863, a week after shaking hands with President Abraham Lincoln. While on his death-bed, the Kiowa warrior supposedly grasped his agent by the hand and said: "Tell my people that I entreat them with my last breath to live in peace with the pale faces. Tell them that I have seen their 'Great Father,' and that he has promised to take care of the red man. . . . I have ever been a friend to the pale face, and the inheritence I would leave my nation is that they conduct themselves so as to merit the smile of the Great Spirit, which watches over the red man and the pale face." When he died, Yellow Wolf was wearing his finest regalia and ceremonial paint. The rest of the delegation prepared him for burial by breaking his bow and arrows in half and placing them and all his other possessions, including his prized Thomas Jefferson peace medal, in his coffin. Government officials wanted the treasure for the Smithsonian Institution, but the other delegates insisted it remain with the chief.[42]

The most impressive funeral for an Indian delegate was held in December 1824, for Pushmataha, a general in the United States Army as a result of his services with Andrew Jackson at the Battle of New Orleans. Pushmataha's dying wish was for "the big guns to be fired over me." His request for a military funeral was fulfilled the day after Christmas by the Marine Corps under the direction of the secretary of the navy and two companies of the District of Columbia militia. Two thousand congressmen, government officials, and citizens followed the cortège to Congressional Cemetery. The minute guns that thundered on Capitol Hill were echoed by three crisp musket volleys at graveside as the United States paid tribute to a fallen ally.[43]

Few of the Indians received such elaborate funerals, of course. Most were more modest ceremonies attended by the rest of the delegation, a few officials, and the curious public. Taza did not even get a headstone after he died in 1876. The Indian agent was in a hurry to marry his fiancée waiting for him in Ohio, and he failed to make the necessary arrangements before leaving the city.[44] Taza's grave remained unmarked until a few years ago, when members of the American Indian Society of Washington provided a striking monument.

Most of the thirty or so delegates who died in Washington are buried in Congressional Cemetery, a picturesque yet little-known burial ground less than two miles from the Capitol Building. Only seven years younger than the city whose history it documents, the cemetery was established in 1807 by members of the vestry for Christ Church, then known as Washington Parish, who purchased the thirty acres of land on a gentle slope overlooking the Anacostia River. Five years later, title to the Washington Parish Burial Ground passed to Christ Church, which still owns the property.[45]

The graveyard is popularly known as Congressional Cemetery because for many years the members of Congress who died in Washington were buried there. Until well into the nineteenth century, it was not feasible to move the remains of deceased persons more than a short distance, hence a burial site for congressmen, visitors, and government officials who died in the capital was a necessity, and the vestry of Christ Church offered Congress the use of its cemetery.

Congressional Cemetery. Photographer and date unknown.

The first member of Congress to be buried there was Senator Urial Tracy of Connecticut, who died in April 1807. A major general in the Continental Army, he was honored by a special monument financed by a congressional appropriation. The precedent thus established lasted seventy years. The practice was formalized in 1815, when the noted architect Benjamin Latrobe was commissioned to design an appropriate cenotaph to honor deceased congressmen. His efforts produced a monument that may have proved profitable to stonecutters but was less than complimentary to the statesmen. Made from local sandstone (the same material used in constructing the Capitol Building), Latrobe's cenotaphs are squat and square and capped with a short, pointed column. Although some 180 of these memorials grace the grounds, probably as few as sixteen senators and sixty-eight members of the House of Representatives are buried in the cemetery; the last one known to be buried there died in 1835. Nevertheless, until 1876 Congress continued to appropriate funds to maintain the grounds and erect monuments. Senator George F. Hoar of Massachusetts brought the practice to an end when he remarked from the Senate floor that the thought of being interred beneath one of those atrocities added a new terror to the prospect of death.[46]

The tombstones for the Indian delegates are far less pretentious. Most are simple markers inscribed "American Indian" that show the name of the delegate and the date of death. Although records are incomplete, twenty-two delegates are known to be buried in the cemetery. The first one was Pushmataha; the last one was Efau Emarthla, a Creek who died in 1888. This total does not account for all the Indians who died in Washington. Two are known to have died before the cemetery was established, while several who died afterwards are buried elsewhere. One of them is John Ross, who died of natural causes in the capital in 1866; he is buried in Oklahoma. Two Chippewas of the Bois Fort band in Minnesota, who were asphyxiated in their hotel room by leaking gas in 1910, were returned home for burial.[47]

Today the cemetery suffers from obscurity and neglect. Many of the headstones and vaults have been vandalized, and the grounds now overgrown with weeds and vines are a haven for ticks and snakes. From time to time, proposals are put forward for Congress to assume the financial burden for preserving and restoring the cemetery, but thus far these efforts have had little success. In March 1976, a public-spirited group formed the Association for the Preservation of Historic Congressional Cemetery. The association has had some impact, but its task is only beginning.

The Indian delegates are not forgotten, however. Each Memorial Day, members of the American Indian Society of Washington, who represent tribes from all over the United States, visit the cemetery and decorate the graves of the delegates. Most of the members of the society are residents of Washington working for the federal government. In decorating the graves they are continuing a tradition that began more than one hundred years ago. In 1874 Peter Pitchlyn of the Choctaws honored the deceased delegates in this manner; ironically, before the year was out, he had joined them.[48]

For the delegates who died on the road to Washington or on the way home, the situation was vastly different. Most lie in unmarked graves and are remembered only in the oral traditions of their people. An appropriate tribute to those nameless travelers was composed in December 1802 by W. C. Larwill of Pittsburgh, a white man who buried a delegate on the banks of the Ohio River. The chief was one of ten Miami and Delaware Indians en route to Washington for a meeting with President Thomas Jefferson. After the funeral, Larwill led the unidentified man's companions the rest of the way to the new capital emerging from the inhospitable swamplands at the confluence of the Potomac and Anacostia rivers. The death of that unknown warrior must have greatly impressed Larwill, as this entry from his diary indicates:

Here the poor Chief of sage experience lies
Far from his country and his wigwam dies;
Yet infidels (for such are many whites)
Respect his virtues and his nation's rites,
Entomb him near Ohio's rapid wave,
Where strangers pensive sorrow o'er his grave.
His gun, and hatchet, clad in sables deep,

His bow and arrow—all beside him sleep
His beads and wampum—all his little store,
Thus in the warriors uniform well drest,
Of vension, tinder-box and steel possest,
He climbs on Eagle wings the ariel space,
Assumes new vigor, and a swift[er] chase![49]

X INDIAN DELEGATIONS AND THE ARTS AND SCIENCES

The Indian visitors were not the only ones being exposed to a new way of life. For most easterners, the Indians met through delegations were the only Native Americans with whom they would ever come in contact. Although the cultural exchange that occurred was admittedly minimal in an era when most whites were secure in the belief that their way of life was superior, the Indian visitors nonetheless made an impact on American arts and sciences.

In literature, an example is provided by James Fenimore Cooper, the popular novelist who contributed so much to the creation of the myth of the noble savage. After meeting a delegation from the Great Plains in 1822, Cooper wrote *The Prairie*, the only one of his Leatherstocking Tales to have a Great Plains setting. Cooper thought the chiefs from the Great Plains possessed a "loftiness of spirit, of noble bearing and of savage heroism . . . that might embarrass the fertility of the richest inventor to equal." The delegate who most excited Cooper was Petalesharro, a young Pawnee warrior who had saved a captive Comanche woman from being sacrificed in a tribal ceremony. Opposed to human sacrifice, he had freed the woman, thrown her across his horse, and carried her from the Pawnee village. Enhancing the chief's romantic image was his flowing bonnet of eagle feathers, the first ever seen in the East. Petalesharro had a profound effect on Cooper, who acknowledged years later that "the impression produced by his grave and haughty, though still courteous mien, the restless, but often steady, and bold glance of his dark, keen eye, and the quiet dignity of his air, are still present to my recollection."[1]

Petalesharro also left his mark on the fine arts. His dramatic rescue of the Comanche woman so fired the imagination of sentimental easterners that three artists are known to have painted his portrait—John Neagle, Charles Bird King, and Samuel F. B. Morse, who placed the dashing warrior in the visitor's gallery in his monumental painting "The Old House of Representatives," which he completed in 1822.

King, Neagle, and Morse were not the only white artists who viewed the Indian visitors as fitting subjects for their talents. George Catlin claimed the excitement of seeing a western delegation in Philadelphia inspired him to record in oils the Indians' vanishing way of life. Ferdinand Pettrich, a German sculptor living in Washington in 1837, was so fascinated by visiting Indians that he sketched and prepared busts of more than a score of them. Today these works are on display in the Missionary-Ethnological Museum of the Vatican.

Delegations touched many areas of eastern cultural life. The first museum in Washington, called the "Archives of the American Indian," was established largely because delegations offered a source of artifacts, portraits, and other ethnographic materials. The Indians were photographed, studied, and written about; their languages, stories, and songs were recorded and published. Until the early nineteenth century, however, efforts to collect information from and about Indians were sporadic and haphazard. Usually they were the result of individual curiosity and initiative.

The geographical knowledge possessed by the Indian visitors was particularly sought after, especially in the early years of the republic when reliable information about the interior of the American continent was almost nonexistent. Western delegates were always plied with questions about the natural history and physical geography of their homelands, and the Indians readily shared this information. Several delegations even prepared remarkably accurate and detailed maps, much to the surprise and delight of their eager questioners.

The cartographic skills of an Arikara chief who visited Washington in 1806 must have been especially outstanding. James Wilkinson, governor of Louisiana Territory, was so impressed he advised President Thomas Jefferson of the man's imminent arrival in the capital. "I think you may be able to derive a fund of correct information from this Chief, relative to the region Watered by the South Western Branches of the Missouri & its Inhabitants," Wilkinson wrote. "I understand Him to be a great traveller, a warrior & Geographer, and He is certainly a *learned* Savage, because he not only speaks Eleven different Languages, but is Master of the *Language* of Arms, Hands & Fingers." The painter William Dunlap, who met the chief during his eastern visit, recalled that the old man carried three sheets of paper which, when joined together, formed a map that described his own country, the course of the Missouri River, the locations of many Indian tribes, and the route he took to Washington. Among the "marvellous spots" on the map were a lake "in which a monstrous amphibious animal resides, with horns like a Cow," and Washington, D.C., which was depicted by "a rude figure" signifying the President's House, beyond which "he had drawn a gun, a sword, powder, ball & tobacco as the presents he expected."[2]

The skills of this Arikara chief were by no means unique. Senator Samuel Mitchell of New York invited several members of an Osage delegation to his boardinghouse one evening in 1806, and they drew a map of the Missouri country on the floor with chalk. "The proficiency made by our Red Men in Geography, I mean of their own Region," he wrote his wife, "is very remarkable." Even more amazing was an Indian map he saw at the President's House a few days later. Drawn on dressed buffalo hide, the map depicted the region between the Missouri and Platte rivers and included mountains, Indian villages, a volcano, and several copper and platina mines. "It is really a pleasing proof, of the Geographical knowledge of these self-educated People," Mitchell declared.[3]

Mitchell's interest in the Indians extended further than cartography. He transcribed two Osage songs that the delegates had sung during one of their visits to his quarters. The interpreter had translated the songs into French for Mitchell, who immediately copied the words and later translated them into English. The senator was so pleased with his efforts that he sent copies to his wife. "The leading sentiments are all Aboriginal. And the paraphrases are as few as the nature of the English composition would permit," he told her. "You may display this to the literati and the Critics, in vindication of the Character of our Native Americans, who, I am sure, have not had justice done them."[4] Mitchell also sent copies to the editor of the *Philadelphia Aurora and General Advertiser,* who published them on January 7, 1806. One was a war song; the other, which appears below, expressed the delight of the Osages with their visit to Washington and their interview with President Jefferson, their Great Father:

No Heart, Iowa chief who used the map reproduced opposite, during discussions in Washington in 1837. From a photographic copy of a daguerreotype by Thomas M. Easterly taken in 1846 or 1847.

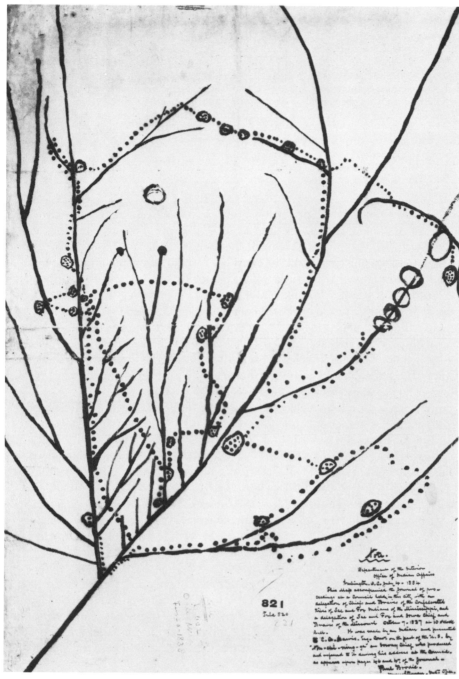

Map used by No Heart (Notchimine), the Iowa chief, during his confrontation with Keokuk in
Washington. Now in the National Archives, the manuscript map bears the following annotation,
dated July 4, 1884, by Paul Brodie, a draftsman in the Bureau of Indian Affairs: "This Map
accompanied the Journal of proceedings at a Council held in this city with a delegation of Chiefs
and Braves of the Confederated Tribes of the Sac and Fox Indians of the Mississippi, and a
delegation of Sac and Fox and Iowa Chiefs and Braves of the Missouri October 7, 1837 at 10
o'clock A.M. It was made by an Indian and presented to C. A. Harris, Esq. comr. on the part of
the U.S. by 'Non-chi-ning-ga' an Iowa Chief who produced and referred to it during his address
at the Council, as appears on pages 46 and 47 of the Journal."

172

My comrades brave, and friends of note!
You hither come from lands remote,
To see your grand exalted Sire
And his sagacious words admire.

The master of your life and breath
Averted accident and death,
That you might such a sight behold,
In spite of hunger, foes and cold.

Ye Red Men! since ye here have been,
Your Great White Father ye have seen,
Who cheered his children with his voice
And made their beating heart rejoice.

Thou chief Osage! fear not to come,
And leave a while thy sylvan home—
The path we passed is clear and free,
And wide and smoother grows for thee.

Whene'er to march thou feelest inclined
We'll form a length'ning file behind,
And dauntless from our forest run
To hear the talks of Jefferson.

Sir Augustus Foster, a member of the British legation, seems to have been equally fascinated by the Indians, for during his stay in Washington they were frequent visitors to his quarters. While the Indians amused themselves eating special foods like oranges and raisins and browsing through his rooms, Foster would take copious notes about their dress and behavior. Wa Pawni Ha, a young Sac chief, was one of his favorite guests. 'He was surprised at seeing a mocking bird in a cage," Foster wrote, "and always expressed his surprise by a laugh in which [he] particularly indulged himself on seeing a little hand organ, that he had listened to for a time with great attention, opened and the work moving within it." Foster also recorded the agents' and interpreters' descriptions of aboriginal life, and he collected a few souvenirs to carry back to England. These included a bow purchased from a Creek warrior, a drawing by Wa Pawni Ha, and several portraits of Indian delegates that Foster had commissioned.[5]

Unfortunately, only a few painters found the early delegates of enough artistic interest to record their likenesses for posterity. One of the first was John Trumbull, the renowned artist of the American Revolution. In 1790 he made striking pencil sketches of several Creek chiefs visiting New York, then the capital city. Trumbull happened to be working on a full-length portrait of President George Washington while the Indians were in New York negotiating a treaty with the newly formed United States. This portrait, in fact, almost cost him the opportunity to draw the Indians. Washington, curious to see what effect his portrait would have on the Indians, directed Trumbull to place it facing the door to the sitting room. Having invited the Indians to dine with him, Washington then brought the Indians to the sitting room, where the effect of seeing another Great Father left them "mute with astonishment." Several of the chiefs rubbed the canvas and generally demonstrated their inability to comprehend how a flat surface could look so much like a real person. "I had been desirous of obtaining portraits of some of the principal men, who possessed a dignity of manner, form, countenance and expression, worthy of Roman senators," Trumbull declared, "but after this I found it impracticable." The Indians considered his art some sort of magic and refused to pose for him, forcing Trumbull to obtain his drawings "by stealth."[6]

The next Indian visitors portrayed by a white artist were members of the Osage delegation of 1804. Described by President Jefferson as "the most gigantic" and "the finest men we have ever seen," the delegates were the first Indians from the Great Plains to visit the East. This may explain why they attracted the attention of the French refugee artist Charles Balthazar Julien Fevret de Saint-Mémin, who supported himself by selling miniature profile portraits that he made with the aid of a mechanical device known as a physionotrace. Saint-Mémin would use the physionotrace to make a full-size profile

Crayon sketch of the chief of the Little Osage drawn by the French refugee artist Charles Balthazar Julien Fevret de Saint-Mémin in July 1804. Made with the aid of a physionotrace, the original drawing is in the custody of the New-York Historical Society.

drawing of his sitter's head. After finishing this drawing in crayon, he used a pantograph to reduce it to a small size for engraving on a copper plate. His charge for the original crayon drawing and twelve impressions was twenty-five dollars for men and thirty-five dollars for women. The crayon drawing without the engraving could be obtained for five dollars. Saint-Mémin, whose advertisements appeared frequently in the *National Intelligencer and Washington Advertiser,* was living in the capital in 1804 when the delegation arrived. Whether the portraits were commissioned or Saint-Mémin chose to do them on his own initiative is unknown. Nevertheless, he executed several fine portraits that are extant today. Five watercolor copies of these portraits were later purchased by Sir Augustus Foster. They remained in the family until 1926, when they were sold at an auction.[7]

Interestingly, a physionotrace was used by the Philadelphia artist and museum proprietor Charles Willson Peale to make miniature silhouettes of another delegation of Plains Indians two years later. The delegation evidently visited Peale's museum in Independence Hall during their visit to Philadelphia. There Peale cut the silhouettes of ten members of the delegation.[8]

The first systematic effort to collect artifacts, portraits, and other related material from Indian visitors did not occur until 1818, when Thomas L. McKenney originated the idea of establishing in Washington an "Archives of the American Indian." For almost fourteen years, from 1816 to 1830, McKenney administered the nation's Indian affairs, serving as superintendent of Indian trade and then as the first head of the Bureau of Indian Affairs. The archives was a project McKenney conceived early in his federal career and then nurtured throughout his years in public office. "I have often regretted," he wrote in 1820, "that no archive exists in which might have been enrolled the progress of things relating to our aborigines." Not only would such an archives be valuable for the administration of Indian affairs, he reasoned, but the accumulated material could be "preserved there for the inspection of the curious, and the information of future generations." McKenney, who was convinced the Indians would soon disappear as a people by assimilation into American society, spent considerable time and money gathering portraits, artifacts, books, and manuscripts relating to Indian life. What he established bore little similarity to a modern archives, however; its holdings were more ethnological than archival in nature. It was, in fact, the first museum in the nation's capital.[9]

The material in the archives came from many sources, including Indians visiting Washington. McKenney was responsible for delegates during their stay, and few left the city without a stop at his office to view the collection. The archives invariably impressed the visitors; some even donated items of personal apparel. McKenney would sometimes attempt to purchase unique objects an Indian owner had failed to offer. Although he was unable to buy Red Jacket's peace medal, tomahawk, and coat—which he probably wanted to complement the chief's portrait that hung in his archives—McKenney did succeed in obtaining two bark canoes from some Passamoquoddy Indians who needed money to get home. The Indians had been hunting dolphins off the Maine coast when they were caught in a storm. A passing ship rescued the Indians and took them to Norfolk, Virginia. From there the Indians went to Washington, where they hoped to get help from the Great Father. The Indians got their money and McKenney got their canoes. At least some of the gifts the president received from visiting Indians also found their way into the archives. For instance, a peace pipe now in the collections of the Smithsonian Institution bears this label in McKenney's hand: "Presented in August 1824 to President James Monroe by Mahaskah, an Ioway Head Chief. T. L. McK."[10]

The most striking feature of the archives was a gallery of Indian portraits that covered the walls of McKenney's small office in the War Department Building. Framed identically and painted on wooden panels measuring approximately seventeen by fourteen inches, the portraits were primarily the work of Charles Bird King, a Washington artist whose studio was a few blocks away on Twelfth Street between E and F streets. King enjoyed an excellent reputation as a painter, and his patrons included such political giants of the nineteenth century as John C. Calhoun, James Monroe, and Henry Clay. His first Indian subjects were members of the impressive Pawnee, Omaha, Kansa, Oto, and Missouri delegation that arrived in the city in November 1821. McKenney commissioned eight portraits. These proved so popular that thereafter McKenney regularly commissioned King to paint portraits of the more prominent members of visiting delegations. King's usual fee was twenty dollars for busts and twenty-seven dollars for full figures. Although the bulk of the commissions came while McKenney was in office, King did some 150 Indian portraits representing twenty tribes over a twenty-year period.[11]

As the gallery grew, it aroused considerable interest. Hezekiah Niles, editor and owner of *Niles' Weekly Register*, informed his readers in June 1826 that "the walls of one of the rooms in the war office are pretty well covered with portraits of distinguished Indians, in their proper costumes." Frances Trollope, the often caustic British traveler, had nothing but praise for the gallery. "The Bureau of Indian Affairs," she noted in her *Domestic Manners of the Americans*, "contains a room of great interest; the walls are entirely covered with original portraits of all the chiefs who, from time to time, have come to negotiate with their great father, as they call the president." The gallery was featured in Jonathan Elliot's 1830 guide to Washington. "But for this gallery," he declared, "our posterity would ask in vain—*'what sort of a looking being was the red man of this country?'* In vain would the inquirers be told to *read* descriptions of him—these never could satisfy. He must be *seen* to be known. Here then is a gift to posterity."[12]

McKenney did not mind the publicity, for he delighted in showing the gallery to visitors. He especially enjoyed telling anecdotes about the various chiefs and warriors, many of whom he knew personally. One visitor who received the full force of his enthusiasm was Nicholas Biddle, the Philadelphia banker. "I remember when I first saw him," Biddle remarked years later, "he was surrounded by uncouth portraits of savages of both sexes, whose merits he explained with as much unction as a Roman Cicerone—how nearly extremes touch when so civilized a gentleman was in contact with so wild & aboriginal a set."[13]

McKenney had reason to be proud, for the portraits were unique. He could boast about having the first portrait by a white artist of an Indian wearing a war bonnet of eagle feathers as well as the first portraits of Plains Indian women, the wives of some of the delegates. Some of the most prominent Indian leaders of the early nineteenth century, such as John Ross, Black Hawk, Keokuk, and Pushmataha, were included in the gallery.

Although a few delegates refused to have their portraits painted, most readily consented. Several even insisted on having copies of their own to take home. The copies, like the originals, were on wood panels, but they were smaller—twelve by ten inches—so the Indians could carry them easily in their luggage. Nevertheless, McKenney claimed, the copies were "just as true and perfect" as the originals.[14]

The gallery grew rapidly until the spring of 1828, when a congressional committee investigating waste in government discovered that McKenney had already spent some three thousand dollars on portraits. Despite the gallery's tremendous historical value, McKenney was publicly ridiculed for squandering public monies. The editor of a Georgetown newspaper offered him "a *petrified Pottawattomie* and a *pickled Kickapoo*

Squaw to adorn the *Indian Bureau.*" A congressman from Kentucky claimed he could not understand why government money should be spent "for the pictures of these wretches. I believe," he wrote, "they are hung up in Mr. McKenney's room at Washington, to gratify the curiosity of strangers."[15]

Criticism of the gallery reached such proportions that McKenney felt compelled to answer the charges publicly. The paintings served a dual purpose, he declared in a letter published in local newspapers. "Apart from the great object of preserving in some form the resemblance of an interesting People . . . it is the *policy* of the thing. Indians are like other people in many respects—and are not less sensible than we are, to marks of respect and attention." All delegations saw the collection, he claimed. "They see this mark of respect to their people, and respect it. Its effects, as is known to me, are, in this view of the subject, highly valuable."[16]

Regrettably, the critics had their way. The use of public monies for delegation portraits practically ceased, although occasional exceptions were made. The Winnebago delegation of 1828 demanded one of these exceptions. The Winnebagos were at first delighted with the gallery because they recognized the portraits of so many neighboring tribesmen. But when told that there was no money to add any Winnebago portraits, the delegates were offended. McKenney sought permission from the secretary of war to have a few of their portraits painted, but his request was ignored. When it appeared that no Winnebago portraits would be added to the gallery, the delegates offered McKenney "their bells, & ornaments, & caps, & . . . war clubs requesting that *these* might hang up here as memorials." The secretary of war was so touched by this gesture that he finally consented to pay for five Winnebago portraits.[17]

The Indians' high regard for the gallery was not exaggerated. A treaty commissioner who visited the Winnebagos a few years later recalled that nothing pleased the chiefs so much "as to tell them that their likenesses were in the War Department, and that their fame was spread through the world." When the Sac chief Black Hawk and a few of his followers were sent east to prison in 1833 following the abortive Black Hawk War, they were shown the gallery, which was still on display in the War Department Building. "They expressed more surprise and pleasure at the portraits," wrote an observer, "than at anything else that was shown them in Washington, recognizing many of them." As late as 1893, Menominee leaders referred to the gallery when requesting permission from the secretary of the interior to send a delegation to Washington. "We are the sons of our Old Chiefs whose pictures are hanging in your great halls," they wrote. "Now again we beg of you to give us the privilege to talk to you and tell you with our own lips what we have to say."[18]

The archives, though important, had an unfortunate history after McKenney's dismissal from office in 1830. Subsequent commissioners lacked McKenney's vision, and the collection of paintings and artifacts endured a period of benign neglect. Perhaps two dozen portraits were added to the gallery over the next twelve years. Most of them were commissioned in 1837 when more than one hundred Indian delegates were in the city as part of the government effort to end the fighting between the Sac and Fox and the eastern Sioux. The last two portraits were added to the gallery in 1842. Both subjects were representatives of relatively obscure tribes. One was John Quinney, the Stockbridge-Munsee preacher, who was in Washington so often in the 1840s that he was almost a resident. The other was Joseph Polis, a Penobscot from Maine. According to the commissioner of Indian affairs, the portrait of Polis was commissioned so that he would be remembered by the people of Washington. "When we look at him," the commissioner wrote, "we will know we are looking at a friend."[19]

The portraits of Quinney and Polis ended that wonderful series. A few months before King received the commission, the gallery and artifacts were transferred from the Bureau of Indian Affairs to the National Institute, a private association originally founded in Washington in 1818 as the Columbian Institute for the Promotion of Art and Science. Drawing its membership primarily from army and naval officers, diplomats, and "professional gentlemen" employed by the federal government, the institute maintained a cabinet of curiosities and a library and sponsored lectures on science and philosophy. In 1840, hoping to become the beneficiary of the strange and marvelous bequest of James Smithson, the British nobleman who had left $500,000 to the United States "to found at Washington an establishment . . . for the increase and diffusion of knowledge," the Columbian Institute changed its name and constitution and broadened its scope. The institute's future seemed assured when, two years later, Congress designated it the official curator of all collections in the arts and sciences in the custody of the federal government and allowed it to house the material in the recently completed Patent Office Building at Eighth and G streets in Washington.[20]

Several months before the institute received official confirmation of its curatorial responsibilities, a three-member committee began visiting government departments in search of collections. One of the first stops was the War Department Building. The secretary of war, probably delighted at the prospect of eliminating the clutter from the crowded quarters of the Bureau of Indian Affairs, readily agreed to transfer McKenney's once-cherished archives to the Patent Office Building. The move was made in June 1841. One of the first to describe the archives in its new setting was David Cooke, a merchant from Philadelphia. "The museum is in the Story above [the Patent Office] in one large room the whole width and breadth of the building," Cooke informed his wife. "Indian implements and curiosities [are] on one side of the room—the other side is similar to the Philadelphia museum—[and] 150 likenesses of Indian warriors are hung around the room."[21]

Despite this auspicious beginning, the National Institute never received the Smithson bequest. Instead, Congress in 1846 chose to establish the Smithsonian Institution, which rapidly became the nation's center for the arts and sciences. The National Institute tried to compete but could not survive without federal financial support and finally disintegrated after almost two decades of struggle. Its collections, untended and disordered, remained in the Patent Office Building to the end.

McKenney's archives was temporarily rescued from oblivion in 1858 when the National Institute formally dissolved and transferred its more important holdings to the Smithsonian Institution. Joseph Henry, first secretary of the Smithsonian, placed the delegation portraits in a second-floor gallery in which another fine collection of American Indian portraits and scenes by the New York artist John Mix Stanley was already on display. The combined exhibit, according to Henry, formed "the most valuable collection in existence of illustrations of the features, costumes, and habits of the aborigines of this country."[22]

The Stanley collection rivaled the War Department gallery in scope and importance. Like Catlin before him, Stanley had been attracted by American Indian life and for ten years traveled extensively in the Far West. He visited forty-three tribes and painted 154 portraits and scenes of everyday life before returning to the East in 1851. He loaned his collection, which he valued at $19,000, to the Smithsonian, hoping that either the institution or Congress would purchase his paintings as the nucleus of a national gallery of art.

Several times over the next ten years he petitioned both houses of Congress and the Smithsonian Board of Regents to buy his collection. With the petitions, he enclosed numerous endorsements, including one from McKenney, then in retirement in New York City. Age had not dimmed his fervor for the Native Americans. "You know," McKenney wrote, "I have seen the Indians in their forest homes, and under every phase of their character. Stanley has immortalized himself by the reflex he has given of this down trodden race." Nothing could be more lifelike, McKenney thought. "The costume is perfect—It is all a reality—truth is the foundation of all." In fact, he continued, "I consider it the last best offering of this sort which will ever come to us from the wilderness home of this people. Their destiny as a race is sealed. They will soon be lost to our sight forever."[23]

Stanley's petitions did arouse some congressional support. In 1853 the Senate Committee on Indian Affairs went so far as to refer one of the petitions to Luke Lea, commissioner of Indian affairs, for his opinion as to "the value, quality and truthfulness of the paintings." The commissioner's reply is touched with irony. Scarcely a decade had passed since McKenney's archives had been transferred to the National Institute, yet evidently no memory of it lingered at the Bureau of Indian Affairs. "As the aboriginal inhabitants of our country are fast disappearing from the face of the Earth," Lea replied, "there seems to be an increasing regret that the Government has not taken more timely and efficient measures for preserving memorials of the race. A National Portrait Gallery of distinguished Indians, permanently located at the seat of Government would certainly be an object of general interest and that interest would continue to increase with the lapse of time." Lea urged the committee to authorize a small sum annually that the bureau could use to commission portraits of prominent Indian visitors to Washington. "Before long," he assured the Senate committee, "a valuable collection could be made that would be highly creditable to the Government."[24]

Despite widespread support, Stanley failed to convince Congress. His efforts to sell the collection to government agencies were equally fruitless. The artist, however, never lost hope that a benefactor would intercede, and so he kept his paintings at the Smithsonian for more than a decade. No doubt the addition of the War Department gallery to the Smithsonian collections buoyed Stanley's belief that the creation of a national gallery of art was inevitable.

Tragically, Stanley's hopes were dashed by the Smithsonian fire of January 24, 1865. To keep warm in an unusually cold winter, a crew of workmen renovating the second-floor exhibit hall had set up a stove, connecting the stovepipe to a chimney they found in a closet. Eight days later the ceiling burst into flames; within minutes the room and its contents were destroyed. The entire wing suffered damage, but fireproof walls saved the building from complete ruin. An investigation later revealed that the stovepipe had not been connected to a chimney but to a ventilator shaft opening onto wooden beams under the slate roof.[25]

The loss was tragic. All but a few of the King and Stanley paintings were destroyed. The fire left Stanley anguished and financially broken, for he never received a penny in compensation. Destiny was kinder to King, since the artist never knew the fate of his gallery; he had died three years earlier, just a few months short of his seventy-seventh birthday.

Even before King had completed his last Indian portrait, however, the camera was making the portrait painter obsolete. As early as 1840, daguerreotypists were visiting Washington to make portrait photographs, and by the end of the decade there were half-a-dozen daguerrean studios along Pennsylvania Avenue competing for the patronage of diplomats and statesmen.[26]

But as in the business of painting the portraits of Indian visitors, quite some time passed before this rapidly changing technology was applied to Indian delegations. The first photograph of an Indian was not even made in the United States. Peter Jones, an ordained Wesleyan Methodist minister of Ojibway-white ancestry, posed in full regalia for David Hill and Robert Adamson of Edinburgh while visiting Great Britain from October 1844 to April 1846. Not only is this the earliest known photograph of a North American Indian; it is also a masterpiece of Victorian portrait photography, taken at a time when photographs of any living subject were still rare.[27]

American photographers were not far behind the Scots. Thomas M. Easterly, a daguerreotypist living in Missouri, photographed several Sac and Fox and Iowa Indians from the Great Nemaha Agency in 1846 or 1847. Among his subjects were Keokuk and No Heart, the protagonists of the tribal congress held in Washington ten years earlier. John Mix Stanley also photographed Indians. In 1853 he worked as an artist for the Pacific Railway Survey, and he took daguerreotype portraits of Assiniboin Indians at Fort Union and of Blackfeet at Fort Benton. Unfortunately, none of Stanley's daguerreotypes is extant.[28]

The earliest known photographs of Indians in Washington were taken at the White House on December 31, 1857. Two versions are known to exist. One shows the Indians, interpreters, and a host of dignitaries clustered in front of the South Portico of the White House. The other shows the same group sitting and standing on an adjoining lawn. The glass plate negatives for these magnificent views, each measuring thirteen by sixteen inches, are today in the custody of the National Archives as a part of the Mathew B. Brady Collection. They were probably commissioned by Charles Mackay, the Scottish songwriter and journalist, who was touring the United States and Canada for the *Illustrated London News*. He later published in that newspaper an illustrated story about the delegations' visit to the White House.[29]

The photographs are remarkable documents in themselves. Four separate delegations are represented: Pawnee, Ponca, Potawatomi, and Sac and Fox. The Pawnees, who had earlier negotiated a treaty with the federal government agreeing to sell most of their landholdings in present-day Nebraska, confirmed that agreement during this visit to Washington. The Poncas were also in the city because the government desired their land; on March 12, 1858, they ceded most of their Nebraska landholdings as well. The Potawatomis and Sac and Fox were unauthorized delegations, and, according to one observer, "somewhat out of favor." The nine Potawatomis, dressed in "shabby European costume," had come to discuss a grievance concerning their annuities. The Sac and Fox delegation was led by Nesouaquoit, whose portrait had been painted twenty years earlier by Charles Bird King. When Andrew Jackson had given Nesouaquoit the peace medal he still proudly wore, the president had told the chief it would be his badge of authority and would make him always welcome in Washington. Nesouaquoit had taken Jackson's words literally. Now, two decades later, his people had demoted him from tribal leadership, and he had come to Washington seeking the Great Father's assistance in the matter.[30]

The ceremony itself, scheduled for noon in the East Room of the White House, was typical of meetings between the Great Father and Indian delegations. A vast throng of congressmen, foreign ministers, and cabinet officers and their ladies had already assembled when the various delegations made their appearance. The Indians formed three sides of a square; the spectators were on the fourth side. President James Buchanan stood in the center of the square and shook hands with each delegate in turn. All the while he wore "that good humored smile which seems so natural to him," one witness recalled. After the introductions, Buchanan made a short speech of welcome and then expressed his willingness to hear what the Indians might have to say. Each delegation spoke in turn of its poverty and need for food and clothes. Buchanan responded with the standard admonition to imitate the white man—be industrious, till the soil, and, above all, cease warlike ways. "I learn," he declared, "that the Pawnees and Poncas now present are deadly enemies. It is my wish, and that of the Great Spirit who implanted it in my breast, that they should be enemies no more; that, in my presence, they should shake hands in token of peace and friendship." After these remarks were interpreted to the silent delegates, Buchanan asked them to shake hands, that the peace between them might be "perpetual." The delegates first shook hands with Buchanan and then with each other. "Will they keep the peace?" someone asked. "I firmly believe they will," Buchanan replied. "A peace ratified in the presence of 'the Great Father' is more than usually sacred."[31] Following this brief ceremony, the entire party except for Buchanan moved outside, where the photographer waited with his cumbersome apparatus.

These Indians were not just photographed as a group. In the following weeks, some sixty delegates from a dozen tribes, including many who appear in the White House views, posed for portrait photographs.

Credit for these portraits probably goes to the studio of James E. McClees, which was operated by Julius Vannerson. McClees, who had operated a daguerrean studio in Philadelphia for several years, opened an art gallery in late 1857 at 308 Pennsylvania Avenue, where he claimed "to produce a better style of Photographs than has hitherto been made in Washington." Although McClees owned the studio, Vannerson conducted the business. Vannerson had operated his own daguerrean studio on Pennsylvania Avenue before joining McClees. According to their advertisement, the partners assured the public that it could obtain at their studio, "not only the best colored, but plain Photographs, Ambrotypes, and Daguerreotypes from Locket to Life Size."[32]

Evidently one of the first projects of the new gallery was the preparation of a collection of Indian photographs, which McClees then offered in one volume "at a reasonable price." The project, he informed his patrons, had been conducted during the winter of 1857–58, when he had assembled an "interesting collection" of portraits "of some of the principal chiefs, Braves, and Councilors of different tribes." McClees thought the series would be of "great value and interest" to "students of our history, as additions to libraries and historical collections." A few copies are scattered in libraries and archives, but little is known of this publication beyond the fact that it became available in late 1858. The six-by-eight-inch portraits include Little Crow, leader of the great Sioux uprising in Minnesota; Hole-in-the-Day of the Chippewas; and Petalesharro of the Pawnees, son of the famous Petalesharro immortalized in oils by King, Neagle, and Morse in 1822.[33]

Perhaps it was this pioneer publication that prompted Joseph Henry, secretary of the Smithsonian Institution, to ask the commissioner of Indian affairs to have Indian delegates photographed as a matter of course. "*Photographic likenesses* of the individuals of the different Indian deputations which from time to time visit Washington," he wrote, "would form a valuable addition to the interesting collection of portraits already possessed by the Government and deposited in the Smithsonian Institution." Henry thought such a collection could best be assembled under the direction of the commissioner. "Nothing," he believed, "would be more agreeable to the Indians themselves who might be furnished with a copy while the portraits would constantly increase in value."[34] The commissioner was not interested. Two years after the fire of 1865, Henry tried again. "This Institution is much interested," he wrote, ". . . [in] the importance of preserving good photographic portraits of the various Indian delegations that visit Washington." Little time remained before the tribes would completely disappear, and then the loss to science would be

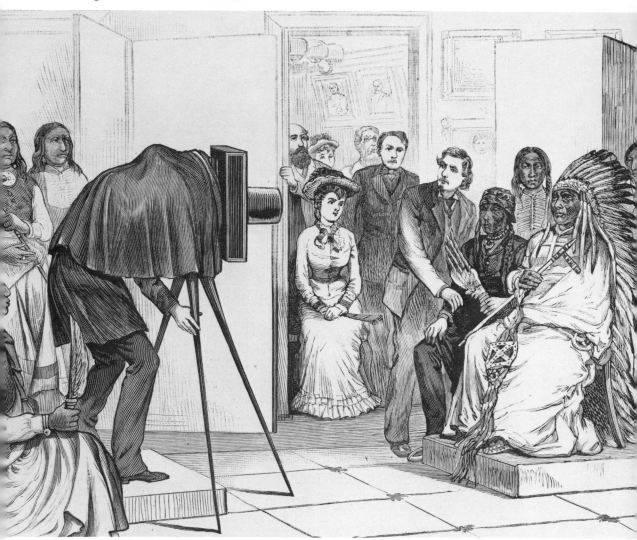

Photographing an Indian delegation, from *Frank Leslie's Illustrated Weekly*, September 10, 1881. According to the accompanying article, the secretary of the interior was so pleased about an accord reached between Ponca and Sioux representatives that he had all the delegates taken to the studio of C. M. Bell, where they were photographed at department expense. "The Indians expressed much gratification at this courtesy," the article noted. "They watched every movement of the operators with great interest, and were profuse in thanks when informed that each one would be given copies of his photograph to take with him to his people."

irretrievable. Henry suggested making facial portraits of individual Indians. The subjects should be bareheaded to show head conformation. Photographs would thus avoid the problem presented by most painted portraits of Indians; artists tended to stress dress and ornaments rather than physiognomy. Henry reminded the commissioner that the bureau, in fact, had once sponsored a collection of Indian portraits. Since fire had destroyed those paintings, the government no longer possessed an official collection of Indian portraits. "The present," therefore, seemed "to be a favorable opportunity to begin anew and to secure at much less cost, a far more authentic and trustworthy collection of likenesses of the principal tribes of the United States." Besides being cheaper than oil portraits, the photographs offered another advantage. The negatives could be preserved and copies furnished at a low cost to anyone who desired them.[35]

The suggestion again fell on deaf ears. The commissioner sent Henry's letter to the secretary of the interior with this snide comment: "As the object of the . . . [Smithsonian] is to diffuse useful knowledge among mankind, does not the bequest of Smithson oblige the Institution to defray this expense?" Henry's letter was not even answered.

Despite apathy in the bureau, photographs of delegates were made. Commercial photographers certainly appreciated the sales appeal offered by unique views of American Indians in native dress. Any number of Washington photographers managed to persuade Indian agents and interpreters—probably for cold cash—to deliver delegations to their studios for picture-taking. The wilder and more savage-looking the Indians, the better the photographers liked it. If the Indians were not suitably dressed, the enterprising camera operators had costumes and weapons on hand to add spice to the photographs. Alexander Gardner, for one, photographed a number of delegations in the decade following the Civil War. Formerly an associate of Mathew Brady, he opened his own gallery on Pennsylvania Avenue in 1863. Among Gardner's delegation photographs are several taken in February 1867 that feature Commissioner of Indian Affairs Lewis V. Bogy and a Sac and Fox delegation led by the younger Keokuk.[36]

Delegation pictures may have been good for business, but they irritated Gardner's wife. She had the unwelcome task of posing the Indians and dressing them from the "smelly" collection of costumes and weapons Gardner kept in his gallery. (By the 1860s Indians often came to Washington wearing a fantastic combination of traditional and European dress entirely unsuitable to the noble savage image the photographers wished to portray.) Furthermore, while Mrs. Gardner and her husband were busy with the adults, the children who sometimes accompanied the delegations helped themselves to whatever struck their fancy.[37]

Surely the task of photographing Indians was not easy. As one government photographer explained in 1877, "The American Indian is extremely superstitious, and every attempt to take his picture is rendered difficult if not entirely frustrated by his deeply-rooted belief that the process places some portion of himself in the power of the white man, and his suspicion that such control may be used to his injury." To complicate matters, the Indians resented being touched or handled in any way, and they would not submit to any inconvenience during the sittings. Needless to say, "much tact and perseverence are required to overcome his superstitious notions, and in many cases, even of the most noted chiefs . . . no portrait can be obtained by any inducement whatever."[38]

The difficulties can be easily imagined. Portrait-making was especially cumbersome and time-consuming in the early days of photography. Exposure time for a picture could take up to twenty minutes depending on the process employed and the available light. To avoid blurring the image, photographers had to use body rests to support the subject's spine and a neck clamp to hold the head rigid. Since few studios had enough apparatus on hand to accommodate a large delegation, neighboring galleries would be scoured for sufficient equipment.[39]

This exchange of clothing and props poses problems for present-day scholars. Delegation photographs have to be examined with a critical eye if judgments are to be made about either the studio or the authenticity of the attire worn by the delegates. Captions for the photographs are equally suspect, especially with respect to the Indian names. It was the rare studio that managed to record correctly the names of the Indians, interpreters, and

Above: Jicarilla Apache delegation at the Corcoran Gallery of Art in Washington, D.C. Photograph taken April 2, 1880. Today this building houses the Renwick Gallery and is part of the Smithsonian Institution. Delegates, left to right: Santiago Largo, Guerito, Augustine Vigil, San Pablo, and Juan Julian. *Below:* Jicarilla Apache delegation at the Corcoran Gallery after changing into citizen's clothing. Photograph taken on the same day as the photograph above. The white men are Alex Read, interpreter, who is standing behind the delegates, and Benjamin Thomas, Indian agent. Delegates, left to right: Guerito, Santiago Largo, Augustine Vigil, San Pablo, and Juan Julian. The clothing was purchased from A. Saks and Company and cost $166.

agents who appeared in the group pictures. The fact that the photographers copied each other's work and then took credit for it compounds the problem. These considerations aside, however, there exists today a superb series of photographs of Indian delegates and delegations dating from 1857 until well into the twentieth century. Many of the original glass-plate negatives are in the custody of the National Anthropological Archives of the Smithsonian Institution, and the National Archives.

Not until the late 1870s did the government become seriously interested in photographing delegations. Even then, the effort was inspired not by officials in the Indian Office but by the corps of energetic and able young scientists working on the post-Civil War federal surveys of the western territories. Although the surveys were primarily geological and geographical in focus, considerable information about Indians living in the areas being surveyed was collected. Many of these young scientists were inspired by the example of John Wesley Powell, the brilliant scholar and one-armed veteran of the Civil War who was in charge of the Rocky Mountain survey. Their scholarly interest in Indians in the capital dates at least from 1874, when Ferdinand V. Hayden, a geologist working for one of the surveys, asked the commissioner of Indian affairs to send delegations visiting Washington "during the coming season" to his office to be photographed.[40]

The surveys were so successful and aroused such popular interest that Congress in 1879 established the U.S. Geological Survey under the Department of the Interior. Congress at the same time transferred responsibility for continuing the ethnographic work of the surveys to the Smithsonian Institution. The secretary of the Smithsonian, now Spencer F. Baird, immediately hired Powell to take charge of this newly imposed responsibility, and the Bureau of American Ethnology (originally the Bureau of Ethnology) was created.

Soon after establishing the BAE, as it was known, Powell addressed the problem of photographing delegates. Indian delegations offered great opportunities for ethnographic study, he informed the secretary of the interior in January 1882. "It is also considered to be important that the photographs of these Indians should be taken." Since this work could be done much more cheaply in Washington than in the field, he urged the secretary to send delegations to the BAE to be photographed, thus enabling the staff to obtain "other ethnographic material." For once a receptive individual was reached. The secretary immediately issued the following directive to agents and other government officers in charge of Indian delegations visiting Washington: "You are hereby instructed to aid Major J. W. Powell, Director of the Bureau of Ethnology, in collecting ethnologic material from the Indians under your charge, and to make arrangements by which their photographs may be taken by the Bureau at such time and in such manner as will not interfere with your duties in connection with the Bureau of Indian Affairs, when and if agreeable to the Indians."[41]

The arrangement was not entirely successful; the Indians, who by this time were not so reluctant to be photographed, did not like going to the BAE. Although the bureau was part of the Smithsonian Institution, its offices until 1910 were in downtown Washington— a considerable distance away from the Mall. The delegates much preferred visiting the Smithsonian museum with its Indian exhibits and other attractions. To keep from being completely thwarted in their scientific endeavors, the staff of the BAE received permission in 1904 to direct the Smithsonian photographer to take pictures of the delegates. The negatives were then transferred to the BAE for classification and filing. At the same time, the BAE hired Andrew John, a Seneca Indian who lived more or less permanently in the capital, to conduct all delegations arriving in Washington to the Smithsonian, where the Indians were photographed and measured and casts were made of their heads. John received five dollars a day for this service. According to the director of the BAE, the arrangement was ideal because John lived at the Beveridge house, "which entertains all delegations and is thus able to make their acquaintance, and to manage them with less difficulty than anyone who might be engaged."[42]

When Andrew John died in 1907, the bureau hired Ben Beveridge, now in his seventies, to continue the service. On March 14, 1908, Ben signed an agreement to secure and conduct Indian delegations to the BAE for photographing. He was to receive a dollar apiece for the first two Indians in a delegation and fifty cents for each additional member. The records, though incomplete, show that Beveridge did receive $17.50 when he signed the agreement for having delivered twenty-five delegates from seven tribes who visited Washington in February and March 1908.[43]

Ben's death two years later ended this unique arrangement, for his children immediately closed the boardinghouse. Fortunately, his son Charles offered to the BAE "a number of Indian photographs" when the family disposed of Ben's personal effects. The head of the bureau was delighted with the offer and insisted his staff get the photographs immediately. "It should be done as soon as possible," he explained, "or I fear they may be thrown away."[44] The transfer of the photographs brought to a close the unusual and colorful association of the Beveridge family with Indian delegations.

Following the establishment of the BAE, the Bureau of Indian Affairs seems to have cooperated more closely with the Smithsonian in the effort to photograph the Native Americans. In 1888, for instance, the commissioner, at the request of the Smithsonian, sent photographs of three Sioux delegations to their respective Indian agents so that the pictures could be properly captioned. Each agent was asked to number and identify the Indians from his delegation and return the photographs to the Smithsonian. The following information, sent by the Cheyenne River agent, is representative of the full and valuable characterization that agents could provide:

No. 1—Spotted Eagle is a Sans Arc Sioux 54 years old—he surrendered in 1881, with Sitting Bull—since the surrender he has been quiet and peaceable.

No. 2—Spotted Elk, is a Minniconjou Sioux, 59 years old, he came in from the hostile camp in 1876 has made but little progress.

No. 3—Swift Bird is a Two Kettle Sioux 56 years old, has always been friendly with the whites.

No. 4—Crow Eagle is a Two Kettle Sioux, 34 years old, has always been friendly with the whites and is classed as a progressive Indian.

No. 5—White Swan, is a Minniconjou Sioux 50 years old, has been peaceable and friendly for many years, and is now quite a successful farmer.

No. 6—Charger, is a Sans Arc Sioux, 55 years old has always been friendly with the whites. He, with Swift Bird of this group, went to the hostile Camp in 1862 or 1863 and rescued seven (7) white persons.

No. 7—Little No Heart is a Blackfoot Sioux, 46 yers old, has always been peaceable and friendly.

No. 8—William Larrabee, is a half-blood is at present Interpreter at Cheyenne River Agency, DT.—he attended school at Hampton Va—is industrious and reliable.

No. 9—Narcisse Narcelle is a half-blood, and is quite successful as a stock raiser.

No. 10—Name is unknown. I believe he is the proprietor of the boarding house where the Indians boarded while in Washington.[45]

Cheyenne River Sioux delegation photographed in October 1888 by T. W. Smillie of the Bureau of American Ethnology. Delegates, front row, left to right: Spotted Eagle, Spotted Elk (Big Foot), Swift Bird, Crow Eagle, White Swan. Middle row, left to right: William Larabee, interpreter; Little No Heart; Charger. Back row: John Wadsworth, a Miami from Indian Territory and not part of the delegation; and Narcisse Narcelle, the agency farmer.

Unfortunately, information about the number and type of photographs taken of the various delegations is almost nonexistent. From the meager records that do exist, it appears that the quantities were substantial. In April 1879, Charles M. Bell, whose studio was at 459–463 Pennsylvania Avenue, photographed for the Interior Department an Umatilla delegation consisting of eleven Indians. He received $58.50 for the following assortment:

Eleven 8-by-10 inch photographs	$1.50 each
Three 11-by-14 inch photographs	4.00 each
Four 14-by-17 inch photographs	5.00 each
Two 17-by-20 inch photographs	5.00 each

The following year the commissioner of Indian affairs authorized the Treasury Department to photograph a Ute delegation under Chief Ouray. The photographer furnished the commissioner with six prints at one dollar each. The commissioner later ordered sixty copies for which he paid sixty dollars. He then ordered five dozen cabinet cards for which he paid three dollars a dozen. The last order, placed June 24, requested half-a-dozen eight-by-ten-inch photographs of the "group, winnemucca & others." The price for these was fifty cents each.[46]

Apparently the Indians themselves received many copies of their photographs. The Cheyenne and Arapaho delegation of 1873, for example, consisted of twenty persons, including the agent and interpreters. The agent bought eight dozen photographs for which he paid four dollars a dozen, or thirty-two dollars. The Crow delegation, which was in Washington at the same time and consisted of nine Indians and the agent, paid forty dollars for photographs. In 1878, the Sioux Chief Big Foot, later to die tragically at Wounded Knee, asked the commissioner to send him a copy of his picture taken in Washington the year before. Red Cloud, a few years later, surprised everyone by asking the commissioner to send him the pictures of two bureau employees whom he had befriended during one of his many trips to Washington. "I would say that the young men referred to whose pictures I want," he wrote in January 1882, "are Mr. Stamca (or Stanna) in the Secretary's office and the one with the black hair and goatee or small whiskers who occupied a desk near yours. I shall be very glad to get their pictures as they are friends of mine."[47]

Not all Indians were so interested in the photographs. Mrs. Beveridge recalled that some of the Indians sold the photographs they received, while others gave them to people they met during their stay in Washington. And if they kept the photographs, the pictures they accumulated while in the city could be quite a burden, especially the oversize prints that were too large to pack in standard valises. These Mary Beveridge shipped to the Indian agents after the delegations left Washington.[48]

Delegations frequently cooperated in other ways with the scientific community. For a number of years after the turn of the twentieth century, the Smithsonian Institution conducted a large-scale project to measure and make head casts of American Indians. This project was largely the work of the renowned physical anthropologist Aleš Hrdlička, who was attempting to document racial variation. Luther Standing Bear, when a student at the Carlisle Indian school, accompanied his father to Washington. During a tour of the Smithsonian, one of the curators requested permission to make a mask of his face. Luther was more than willing, but not the elder Standing Bear. "My father," Luther recalled, "was quite shocked at the idea of my head being covered with plaster of paris to be left on until it hardened; while the idea of my having to breathe through . . . tubes throughout the process was too much for him."[49]

Ethnologist Frances Densmore with Mountain Chief, a Blackfoot Indian, who is listening to a song being played on a phonograph and interpreting it in sign language. The photograph was taken in March 1916 by Harris and Ewing of Washington, D.C.

Linguistic and oral-history projects were also popular. From the days of McKenney, Indian delegations were asked to help with linguistic studies, for nineteenth-century scholars believed they would be able to trace the origins of the American Indian through their languages. McKenney, in fact, assembled quite a collection of Indian vocabularies during his tenure as commissioner of Indian affairs. This work was continued after the creation of the Smithsonian Institution. In December 1863, Joseph Henry asked the commissioner of Indian affairs to send out blank vocabulary forms to superintendents and agents. Powell continued this research while head of the BAE and eventually published a map illustrating the distribution of the different Indian language families in North America.[50]

One of the more unusual projects was conducted by Colonel Garrick Mallery of the U.S. Army. He consulted delegates for his study of American Indian sign language that was published by the Bureau of American Ethnology in 1881. Much of the work for this publication was done in 1880 when, thanks to the opening of the Indian school in nearby Carlisle, Pennsylvania, the government brought more than a dozen delegations to Washington. "Thus," Mallery declared, "the most intelligent of the race from many distant and far separated localities were here in considerable numbers for weeks, and indeed, in some cases, months, and, together with their interpreters and agents, were, by the considerate order of the honorable Secretary of the Interior, placed at the disposal of the Bureau [of Ethnology] for all purposes of gathering ethnologic information." Mallery claimed to have interviewed more than one hundred delegates. Some he worked with individually, others he brought together in groups representing different tribes and different languages, which required them to communicate with each other through signs.[51]

The participation of delegates in scientific and ethnographic studies was evidently so commonplace that the Navajos in 1885 tried to justify a trip to Washington on those grounds. "The Ethnological Bureau," the Navajo agent claimed, "have a desire to get some of them there for the purpose of obtaining some of the legends of the Tribe, and will I believe pay a portion of [the] expenses." The Navajos did not get their trip on this occasion. Nevertheless, BAE personnel recorded the legends, languages, and songs of any number of delegations. The Indian visitors even continued to make contributions to the government collections of ethnographic artifacts. Indeed, many museums at the close of the nineteenth century benefited when Indians, seemingly well on the road to assimilation, discarded the trappings of aboriginal life. One of the proud donors was Nelson Rice, a Pawnee visitor to Washington in 1887, who gave the Smithsonian Institution "a handsome war head-dress."[52]

The Bureau of American Ethnology continued its important work until 1965, when it was absorbed into the Department of Anthropology at the Smithsonian Institution. The songs, legends, photographs, and other ethnographic materials the bureau staff collected are in the National Anthropological Archives at the Smithsonian. There, appropriately, Indian visitors to Washington today use them for their own research to document a way of life that is now past.

XI EPILOGUE: DELEGATIONS IN
THE TWENTIETH CENTURY

The delegation story has no ending, only new chapters. And there have been many since the early days of the nineteenth century. Indians now visit Washington whenever they wish, and for a multitude of reasons. They not only come in greater numbers than ever before, but they also are exceptionally knowledgeable about the workings of government, demonstrating a political sophistication that would have stunned government officials of an earlier era. Indians now participate actively in all levels of Washington political life. They have their own lobbying organization—the National Congress of American Indians; and since 1961, they have been sponsoring their own inaugural ball for each newly installed president.

The participation by Indians in the political life of the United States is, admittedly, a fairly recent development. In part it was a natural result of being made citizens—the last Indians to get the franchise received it in 1924. Increased participation also sprang from the Indians' realization that they could only protect their interests by working with and within the American political system.

The earliest known attempt to involve Indians in the quadrennial presidential inaugural activities came in 1881, when Captain Richard H. Pratt, founder of the Carlisle Indian Industrial School, offered the services of the school band for the James A. Garfield inaugural parade. "I will simply say," he informed the commissioner of Indian affairs, "that I can bring a hundred or a hundred and twenty-five Indian boys uniformed and capable of marching creditably and they can be headed by a brass band composed of themselves and it seems to me a thing quite worth doing." The idea was shelved as being "impracticable."[1]

As a result, despite their well-known regard for the Great Father, Indians had to wait for Theodore Roosevelt's inaugural parade in 1905 for the opportunity to march down Pennsylvania Avenue. Because Roosevelt thought the Indians would add a little color to the presidential pageantry, the Carlisle marching band and several Indian notables were brought to Washington. Besides the six chiefs who led the Carlisle students, there were also two old men from the Yakima reservation—Captain Enias, aged eighty-six, and Thomas Simpson, aged seventy-five—representing the State of Washington. Simpson, it was later discovered, almost rejected the invitation because the men were refused permits to leave the reservation until they agreed to wear citizen's dress. "It broke the old man's heart to have to put on a suit of tight fitting clothes," noted a newspaper reporter, "but by the time he reached Washington, he had become fairly used to them."[2]

One of the Indians featured in the Roosevelt inaugural parade was Chief Hollow Horn Bear of the Brulé Sioux. This prominent and respected leader, who was subsequently honored on the fourteen-cent postage stamp issued in 1922, also participated in Woodrow Wilson's inaugural parade in 1913. He developed pneumonia the following day and died soon after, thus adding his name to the list of tribal leaders who gave their lives paying homage to the Great Father.[3]

Although Indians had received the right to vote in time for the presidential election of 1924, the following election held more meaning for them. For the first time in United States history, someone with Indian blood was one of the contenders, albeit for the vice presidency. This was Charles Curtis—Herbert Hoover's running mate on the Republican ticket—who boasted one-eighth Indian blood through his Kaw grandmother.

The news of the Hoover-Curtis victory electrified the Indian community. The election results had scarcely been tabulated before Indians began clamoring for a role in the inaugural ceremonies. Daniel Pretty Bird of St. Francis, South Dakota, who had been active on behalf of the Republican Party, asked the commissioner of Indian affairs for a seat on the reviewing stand. Alfred C. Smith or Washo-Shay, speaking for all the "Dakota Sioux Republicans," urged the commissioner to ensure that Indians were suitably recognized in the upcoming festivities. "A number of us are personally acquainted with the Vice President," he wrote, and "we are proud to see a genuine American be a Vice President of the United States." Smith recalled that thirty Indians were in the first Wilson inaugural parade, while twenty-three were in the second. "If the democrats were able to recognize Indians on such grand occasions," he declared, "why can't the republicans do the same."[4]

A few Indians wrote directly to Curtis. "We Santee Indians are proud of you," declared Charles Frazier and William Whipple. "Although we have never seen you personally we know that you are part Indian and that you are the best example for the Indians, and that you will do anything in your power to help us Indians." Their first request was for assistance in getting to Washington for the inauguration ceremony. Curtis sent their letter to the commissioner of Indian affairs, who added it to an already bulging file of similar solicitations from Comanches, Otos, Blackfeet, Sioux, Osages, Crows, Pawnees, Cheyennes, and Kaws.[5]

The wishes of the Indian community were finally acknowledged on January 11, 1929, when the Hoover-Curtis Inaugural Committee asked the bureau to arrange for a delegation of Indians to march in the parade. The committee wanted one hundred Indians, but no more than eight could come from any one tribe. All participants were to be "in native costume." Although this requirement flouted more than one hundred years of bureau policy, the commissioner immediately issued a circular urging the various tribes to accept the invitation. His only admonition regarded travel money; Indians who accepted the invitation would have to pay their own expenses.[6]

Neither the commissioner nor the inaugural committee could have anticipated the response from the Indian community—outrage. William Whipple and Charles Frazier, once so anxious to attend, rejected the invitation in blistering language. "Most of our tribe have discarded the War Bonnet and feathers and breech clout for the clothes of the white man," they replied. "We will try and do what the commissioner wants us to do but we will not parade for anybody dressed in native costume." The rejection from the Five Civilized Tribes of Oklahoma was less caustic, but it conveyed the intended message. The tribes could not take advantage of the invitation because they had long since ceased wearing native clothing. They promised, instead, to send a dozen or so representatives to watch the parade.[7]

Most tribes ignored the invitation and chose to honor Curtis with local celebrations. The Mescalero Apaches, for one, held their own inaugural day parade. The agency superintendent sent the commissioner of Indian affairs a snapshot that shows the Mescaleros cheering an honor guard bearing the American flag and a large campaign banner emblazoned with the names of Curtis and Hoover.[8]

The Hoover-Curtis Inaugural Committee eventually got more than enough marchers, but they were by no means representative of the Indian community. Except for a few Sioux in native dress, the marchers were "show" Indians—an all-Indian band with one hundred members under the direction of Chief White Buffalo (Bright Roddy), a prominent Oklahoma Republican, and a troupe of twenty-five Indians under Major Gordon W. Lillie, the popular "Pawnee Bill." Unfortunately, most Washingtonians never knew there had been an Indian boycott. U. S. Grant III, writing on behalf of the Hoover-Curtis Inaugural Committee, thanked the commissioner of Indian affairs for the large Indian turn-out, noting that the vice-president's "Indian descent afforded special opportunity for this interesting and unusual feature in the parade at his inauguration, and the committee is particularly appreciative of the successful way the occasion was taken advantage of." Grant also hoped that "this public participation of representatives of various Indian tribes in an Inaugural Parade . . . [would] prove to have advantageous results in impressing the Indians with the interest taken in them, as well as in the pleasure and interest it added to the occasion for the spectators."[9]

The indignation of the Indian community at the idea of "playing Indian" should not have surprised the commissioner of Indian affairs. After generations of indoctrination, many Indians by the 1920s had finally come to accept white values as their own. In their efforts to emulate life in mainstream America, Indians were cutting their hair, giving up the blanket, and wearing store-bought clothes. Ironically, at the very time the Indians were trying to make this painful transition, white Americans were discovering the romantic West. Now they wanted to see Indians in traditional dress, which they no longer considered a symbol of intransigence. If anything, just the opposite was true. This certainly was evident when Chief Plenty Coups of the Crow tribe participated in the dedication ceremonies at the Tomb of the Unknown Soldier on November 11, 1921.

Although many Indians were not yet citizens of the United States in 1917, thousands volunteered to fight for their country in World War I. Perhaps it was the recognition of this fact by a guilt-ridden government that accounted for Plenty Coups' presence at the dedication ceremonies. Whatever the reason, the choice for the honor was a good one. The Crows were traditional friends of the white man, and they had fought on the side of the United States in many conflicts, including the Sioux wars of the 1870s. Plenty Coups, the last surviving war chief to have earned his rank in the intertribal wars, was seventy years old at the outbreak of World War I and too old to fight, but he urged his young men to volunteer and many did. The aged warrior had earned his right to stand among the world leaders assembled at Arlington Cemetery that blustery November day.

Plenty Coups was not the only Indian to participate in the formal ceremonies. One of the pallbearers was Thomas D. Saunders, a Cheyenne from Oklahoma, who had received the French Croix de Guerre for his exploits in the First World War. But it was Plenty Coups, dressed in full regalia, who captured the attention of the one hundred thousand spectators. Although he was not to speak—that honor had been reserved for President Warren G. Harding—the old war chief could not resist making a few remarks as he laid a magnificent Crow war bonnet and coup stick on the casket. Lifting his arms to the sky and speaking in the Crow tongue in a voice filled with emotion, he said:

I feel it an honor to the red man that he takes part in this great event, because it shows that the thousands of Indians who fought in the great war are appreciated by the white man. I am glad to represent all the Indians of the United States in placing on the grave of this noble warrior this coup stick and war bonnet, every eagle feather of which represents a deed of valor by my race. I hope that the Great Spirit will grant that these noble warriors have not given up their lives in vain and that there will be peace to all men hereafter. This is the Indian's hope and prayer.

This prayer, according to the *New York Times*, "constituted one of the outstanding features of the whole remarkable ceremony."[10]

Plenty Coups not only stole the show, he also helped effect another shift in the delegation story. Indian visitors who wore feathers and buckskins found that they were better able to get the attention of the news media and harried bureaucrats. Before long, "chiefing," as it is known, became an accepted device among visiting delegations. This amazing change is reflected in the experience of the twenty-four Pueblo, Navajo, and Hopi Indians who visited the capital in May 1936. In certain respects, the delegation was a throwback to an earlier era—the Indians not only wore native costumes, but they also danced and sang for the edification of fascinated Washingtonians. But these were the only similarities to early-nineteenth-century delegations. The visit was actually a carefully orchestrated affair designed by John Collier, one of the few truly great men to hold the position of commissioner of Indian affairs, to thwart a potential takeover of Indian land.

For more than twenty years the Indians of the Southwest had been fighting a seemingly endless battle to prevent the alienation of their remaining landholdings. The most serious threat arose in 1921 when Senator H. O. Bursum of New Mexico introduced a bill that would have favored whites in any disputes with Indians over land titles. The following year, Secretary of the Interior Albert B. Fall ruled that "executive order reservations"— reservations established by executive order rather than by treaty or act of Congress— remained public lands and were therefore available to oil and gas interests for exploitation under the General Leasing Act of 1920.[11]

Although these efforts had been defeated, the struggle was not over. According to the Interior Department appropriations bill of 1936, the Pueblos were forbidden to use funds available through the Indian Reorganization Act to buy land adjoining their reservations. At the same time, Congressman John McGroraty of California was pressing for legislation that would end the federal guardianship of Indians, thereby opening their lands to taxation. This would mean, ultimately, the further alienation of tribal land holdings. Since the thrust of these legislative efforts seemed directed at the Indians of the Southwest, Collier, who was attending the All-Pueblo Council meeting held at Santo Domingo Pueblo on April 6, 1936, urged the pueblos to send to Washington a delegation of their most articulate spokesmen to present their plight to the American public and to the Congress. To ensure sufficient attention from the news media, Collier suggested the delegates bring with them samples of their tribal handicrafts and perform a few traditional songs and dances as well. The Interior Department would pay all costs.

Collier's offer both excited and disturbed the council members. Until passage of the Indian Reorganization Act two years earlier, the federal government had consistently tried to eradicate tribalism and traditional culture. Now, a commissioner of Indian affairs was advocating a delegation "play Indian" to protect tribal rights and property. The attitude of the council members to the unusual proposal was expressed best by Martin Vigil of Tesuque Pueblo, who declared: "I am not ashamed to sing." Vigil then explained how, fifteen years earlier, he had gone to Washington as part of a similar delegation opposed to the Bursum bill. The members of that delegation had also performed before various groups in an effort to arouse support for their cause. "I think that is how we brought all American people together to help the Indians," he said. "We did not go traveling about from one city to another like show people. We just did it for the honor of our people." Thanks to Vigil's support, Collier received council endorsement for his plan. He was even authorized to select personally the people who should go. As one member pointed out, Collier knew the leading members of every pueblo, and he knew "who would do the best work."[12]

Armed with council approval, Collier immediately set in motion a media event of major proportions. He arranged for press and radio coverage; he persuaded Paramount Pictures to loan him documentary films on southwestern Indian life and to shoot special footage highlighting some of the land problems unique to the area. The key to obtaining the necessary publicity, of course, was President Franklin D. Roosevelt. Collier sent him a lengthy memorandum outlining the problems of the southwestern Indians and their desire to lay "before Congress and the press the extreme needs of soil and water conservation upon their lands, . . . convincing the American public that they, the Indians, are ready to make and are making big sacrifices." In a covering note to Secretary of the Interior Harold Ickes, who enthusiastically supported his commissioner in this undertaking, Collier explained that his memorandum was written to make Roosevelt realize that the delegation was "worthy" of his attention. "I suggest that it could be made the picturesque and human occasion for a renewed statement having to do with the crisis of our natural resources, particularly our waters and soils."[13]

The commissioner had originally envisioned a rather small group, ten or twelve delegates at most, but this number proved impracticable. Several Pueblos supplemented his group at their own expense. Santo Domingo sent all its tribal officers, while Laguna and Isleta each sent one. Collier himself included several Navajos because that tribe was embroiled in a conflict over a bill to expand their reservation eastward into New Mexico, thereby incorporating about seven thousand tribal members who lived on homestead allotments and competed with white ranchers for grazing rights on public lands.

One delegate questioned Collier's intention to charter a bus to carry the delegation to Washington. "I realize we are going for one purpose like we did in [the] *Bursum Bill*," said Charlie Kie of Old Laguna, who urged the commissioner to charter a railroad coach instead. The delegates would arrive refreshed, and they would be able to rehearse their songs, dances, and speeches along the way. Kie also feared that Collier had not given sufficient thought to the selection of the delegates. He was especially anxious to include Hopi delegates because they had "very beautiful costumes" and were the "best entertainers." Collier assured him his worries were groundless, especially regarding the bus. "Twenty-one Indians came here by bus two years ago and they all liked it," he responded. "The bus will not travel day and night but will make the journey in five days with plenty of rest time."[14]

On May 4, less than a month after Collier had suggested the idea, the delegation left New Mexico for Washington, arriving at a tourist camp in Potomac Park five days later. Aboard the bus were sixteen Pueblo and Navajo delegates. Two additional delegates arrived by train, and four came by automobile. These were joined by two Hopi Indians who were already in Washington as guests of the Smithsonian Institution. Their spokesman was sixty-six-year-old Pablo Abeita of Isleta Pueblo, who was the secretary of the All-Pueblo Council. Abeita, a sprightly man with a refreshing sense of humor, was a veteran delegate who had met every president of the United States since Grover Cleveland's first administration. His first public statement was not very profound, but it made him the darling of the press corps. "Who do the Washington Nationals play today?" he asked. When advised that their foe was the Boston Red Sox, he expressed the hope that the delegation could spend the afternoon at the ball park. Baseball was a popular sport among the Pueblo people, Abeita explained, even though few of them had ever seen a major-league game. "I hope Lefty Grove is pitching today," he declared. When asked if "How" was the proper way to address Indians, he replied: "Perhaps with Indians who don't speak English. We prefer saying 'How do you do?' "[15]

The delegates did more than crack jokes and watch ball games during their week in Washington. On May 14 the delegation met President and Mrs. Roosevelt and then performed before a select audience on the south lawn of the White House. The next day they attended a barbecue at Collier's home in nearby Alexandria, where the guest of honor was the secretary of agriculture. Ickes had also been invited but excused himself, insisting that he had three or four speeches to give in the coming days and had not finished a single one. Nevertheless, the Indians met with him four times during their stay. At a private meeting in his office, he promised to do all in his power to protect and help the Indians of the Southwest. Ickes was also present on the evenings of May 12, 13, and 14, when the delegation entertained a variety of distinguished guests at the Interior Department Auditorium—"mostly Government people, from Congress and from the Departments," according to Collier. The principal speakers on the first night, besides the Indians, were Collier and Ickes; on the second night the director of Emergency Conservation Work was the guest of honor; on the third night the main speaker was the head of the Rural Electrification Administration. The delegation also appeared before the Senate Committee on Indian Affairs, from which they received the usual compliments and promises. The senators assured them that the Navajo Boundary Bill would be passed (it failed), and they promised to remove the objectionable language in the Interior Department appropriations bill at the next hearings. This, amazingly, was done. The delegates enjoyed their finest moment on Saturday evening, May 16, the night before they left for home. At the open-air theater on the grounds of the Washington Monument the delegation delighted an audience of several thousand spectators with speeches and dances.[16]

The delegation, successful though it may have been, did not escape criticism. Congressman McGroraty charged Collier with attempting to manipulate public opinion by using a troupe of show Indians who performed like "trained seals" but who did not reflect the wishes and feelings of the majority of southwestern Indians. Stung by these charges, Collier held a press conference and dismissed McGroraty as a tool of private industry. "Has he no sense at all for facts?" Collier asked. These men were the governors and principal leaders of the Pueblos. None of them were show Indians. They were only hard-working, ordinary men who had come to Washington to protest the "impending breach of faith by Congress, contained in the Interior Department Appropriation Bill."[17]

Because of the criticism, Collier felt obliged to reassure tribal leaders about the accomplishments of the delegation. Collier asked the Navajo superintendent to tell the tribal council that the prospects for passage of the boundary bill had been "decisively" improved by the work of the Navajo delegates, who "conducted themselves with dignity and . . . were effective in every way. Their people ought to be grateful to them, as I am sure they will be." A similar statement went to each of the Pueblo governors. "Among the many Pueblo delegations which have visited Washington through the years," Collier wrote, "I am sure that none ever did better work or gained larger results." He admitted that the Indians had performed a few dances at each of the public meetings, but "these were beautiful and dignified, and . . . added much force to the delegates' plea." Furthermore, the performances "drew to the meetings many important persons who otherwise might not have come."[18]

Even today, delegates who "play Indian" often have the most success in Washington. Robert Pennington, chief of tribal operations at the Bureau of Indian Affairs, has seen this happen time and again. "You get a delegation on the Hill testifying in full regalia and the congressmen behave like a bunch of kids. I often wonder," he said, "why Indians come dressed like us. They should do it differently; they should come in regalia, if they can wear it authentically, because it impresses the congressmen and it attracts the media. I think they are even smart at times to use interpreters."[19]

The independence exercised by today's Indian visitors is another important change in the delegation story. As recently as the 1960s, the Bureau of Indian Affairs was still able to regiment delegation activities. The Office of Tribal Operations, which has responsibility for delegations, required an agenda in advance of a proposed visit. The office made all arrangements for the visit and assigned a staff member to accompany the delegates as they made their round of appointments. This person assisted the Indians in finding their way around Washington and also took notes during the discussions. After the delegation left Washington, the Office of Tribal Operations would send a summary report of the discussions to the tribal council, the area superintendent, and other interested parties. This ensured that everyone with a need to know learned of any commitments or promises, while the tribal governments received verification that their delegates had performed their assigned duties. These reports also served to justify the reimbursement of the delegation's travel expenses.

The Bureau of Indian Affairs still attempts to exercise this coordinating function, but it is almost impossible to get the tribes to cooperate. Visiting delegations now cannot even be counted on to pay a courtesy call at the bureau, much less inform the staff in advance that they are coming to Washington. The reason for this is simple: the bureau is no longer the primary source of tribal financial support. It actually provides only a small percentage of the funds available to the Indian community today. Instead, a host of federal agencies administering poverty, education, health, welfare, and housing programs are now in the business of granting financial assistance to Indians. This decentralized funding sometimes causes waste and confusion as the tribes tend to compete with each other for funds that may not be needed but are taken because of their availability, while the agencies compound the problem by trying to outdo each other in demonstrating their effectiveness in dispensing funds and services to Indians.

The bureau could provide a real service to the Indian community as a coordinator of Indian programs, but neither the tribes nor the granting agencies want that. The Indians enjoy exercising their long-sought freedom from bureau restraints, while the granting agencies would resent oversight of their activities. Thus, as the diminution of the bureau's financial importance to Indians continues, its ability to coordinate the activities of the delegations diminishes accordingly. The trend is not likely to reverse itself. In 1978 the bureau failed in an attempt to reestablish controls over Indian delegations, and staff members now believe it probably will never be able to do so. This places the bureau in an awkward position to say the least. As Pennington points out, the bureau is committed to Indian self-determination, but it also must exercise its role as trustee for the Indian community. "In the long run this fiscal independence will be good for the Indian community, but it sure makes the job of helping Indians more difficult at the present time."[20]

Perhaps the most significant change in the delegation story is the widespread use of attorneys by today's Indian visitors. Where tribes were once prohibited from employing legal counsel when conducting business with the federal government, attorneys are now

Cheyenne River Sioux delegation in front of the White House, by Tom Claymore, 1964. The delegates are, left to right: Alex Chasing Hawk, Felix Benoist, Lloyd LaBeau, Frank Ducheneaux, John Little Cloud, Jack Claymore, and Eddie Claymore (identifications provided by Frank Ducheneaux, Jr.). The painting, which is in the custody of the Tribal Services Branch of the Bureau of Indian Affairs, is oil on illustration board and measures 23¾ by 35½ inches.

an integral part of delegations. There are today many Indian attorneys and Indian law firms. Most of the tribes also retain non-Indian attorneys—"Washington counsels" they are called—who reside in the capital and monitor programs and legislation that affect Indians in general and their clients in particular. As a result, the tribes no longer passively accept adverse decisions or actions. They are quick to bring an issue to litigation for resolution through the courts.

The legal sophistication of the Indians is also reflected in the area of special legislation. Tribes once considered getting a bill introduced in Congress a major accomplishment. Now, they not only get special legislation introduced but also they follow it through the hearing and appropriation process. Most tribes regularly testify at the annual Interior Department appropriation hearings to ensure that their special projects are funded through "add-on" monies to their budgets. Representatives of some one hundred tribes spoke at the 1978 appropriation hearings; if representatives of more than one or two tribes had done so a decade earlier, it would have been unusual.

This new presence does not surprise Frank Ducheneaux, special counsel on Indian affairs to the House of Representatives' Interior and Insular Affairs Committee. "Indians in rough form have achieved the same kind of sophistication in terms of dealing with official Washington as many other groups such as the environmentalists, the National Rifle Association, and the labor unions, but maybe not on that scale." According to Ducheneaux, who is a member of the Cheyenne River Sioux tribe, developing this sophistication has been for Indians a matter of survival. "As a distinct segment of the total population, Indians are day to day affected by what happens on the Hill. They have to know what is happening there and in the executive agencies if they want to survive. And they are beginning to know that more and more."[21]

Modern technology has contributed a great deal to the increased sophistication of the Indian delegates. Because of the telephone, radio, television, and the airplane, Indians are better informed and better able to react when necessary to protect their interests or take advantage of new opportunities. It is not unusual today for a tribal officer to take an early flight to Washington, testify at a government hearing, and be home for supper that evening. Several tribes, most notably the Navajos and Yakimas, own or lease their own aircraft.

Satellite communications portend even more spectacular developments in the delegation story. The first televised conference between Indian and government officials was held in April 1978. Officials at Crow Agency in Montana, the All-Indian Pueblo Council in Albuquerque, New Mexico, and Washington, D.C., participated in a three-day demonstration designed to show the feasibility of tribe-to-tribe, tribe-to-federal-agency, and tribe-to-educational-institution communications. The participants included several United States senators, the governor of Montana, the director of the Indian Health Service, the director of the Office of Indian Education, a special assistant to the vice-president, and an assistant secretary of agriculture. The demonstration proved that time and money can be saved by eliminating or reducing travel between distant points to hold conferences. It also proved that satellite communications could be an important mechanism for developing an informed dialogue between Indian communities and federal, state, and local governments.[22]

Will the development of a satellite communication network bring the delegation story to an end? This does not seem likely as long as Indians obtain so much financial support from the federal government. All too often Indians who try to work through regional or local offices of federal agencies waste their time because important decisions must be referred to Washington anyway. Rather than allow their problems to get lost in a bureaucratic shuffle, the Indians have learned to deal directly with home offices. But there are other reasons as well. Visiting Washington has become almost a rite that a tribal leader must perform to convince his constituents that he is doing his job. As a result, a tribal chairman who insists on bringing a delegation of council members to Washington may have the "hidden agenda" of wishing to ensure his reelection as well as wishing to discuss the important issues he claimed could only be resolved by a personal visit. According to Robert Farring, a tribal relations specialist at the Bureau of Indian Affairs, "The biggest thing Indians get out of coming to Washington is the rapport they establish with the people at the bureau. Certainly it helps us to understand what they need, and what we can do, in our work, to help them." Perhaps there is an important psychological factor as well. "When Indians come here they get to know what Washington

Indian visitors to Washington, July 4, 1976. Photograph by Debra Streuber.

is really like," Pennington points out, "It erases some of the mystique, some of the false impressions that government workers are living the great life. In fact," Pennington chuckled, "they see the crummy offices we work in and they realize their own tribal offices at the tribal agency are better."[23]

The last change in the delegation story is the most ironic. Nowadays Indian delegates frequently deal with Indian bureaucrats. Indians occupy most of the positions in federal agencies concerned with Indian problems and programs. Beginning with Robert L. Bennett during the Lyndon Johnson administration, a person of Indian ancestry has occupied the position of commissioner of Indian affairs. The staff of the bureau itself is largely Indian, and Indians will have complete charge of that agency in the not-too-distant future. Nor is it unusual to find members of Congress who boast of Indian ancestry. Perhaps one day even the Great Father will be an Indian.

NOTES

Abbreviations for sources:

ASP:IA   *American State Papers: Indian Affairs*
BAE   Bureau of American Ethnology
BCIM   Bureau of Catholic Indian Missions Archives, Marquette University
IA LR   Office of Indian Affairs, Letters Received, Record Group 75, National Archives
IA LS   Office of Indian Affairs, Letters Sent, Record Group 75, National Archives
NA   National Archives
NAA   National Anthropological Archives, Smithsonian Institution
PRO/CO   Public Record Office, Colonial Office
RG   Record Group
SW IA LR   Office of the Secretary of War, Letters Received Relating to Indian Affairs, Record Group 75, National Archives
SW IA LS   Office of the Secretary of War, Letters Sent Relating to Indian Affairs, Record Group 75, National Archives
SW LR   Office of the Secretary of War, Letters Received, Record Group 107, National Archives

Preface

1. Black Hawk and Flatmouth quoted in Katherine C. Turner, *Red Men Calling on the Great White Father* (Norman, 1951), p. xiv.
2. Charles Francis Adams, ed., *Memoirs of John Quincy Adams, Comprising Portions of His Diary from 1795 to 1848* (Philadelphia, 1874), 6:273 (cited as Adams, *Diary*).
3. Donald Jackson, ed., *Black Hawk: An Autobiography* (Urbana, 1955), p. 87.
4. The quotation about the buffalo is taken from the "Commentary" by D'Arcy McNickle in Jane F. Smith and Robert M. Kvasnicka, eds., *Indian-White Relations: A Persistent Paradox* (Washington, D.C., 1976), pp. 251–52.

Chapter I: Prologue: Delegations in the Colonial Period

1. John Nelson quoted in Richmond P. Bond, *Queen Anne's American Kings* (New York, 1974), pp. 33, 113.
2. Robert Bennett to Edward Bennett, June 9, 1623, printed in Susan Myra Kingsbury, *Records of the Virginia Company of London* (Washington, D.C., 1935), 4:221.
3. Bond, *Queen Anne's American Kings*, pp. 38–40.
4. Samuel Vetch to Francis Nicholson, Aug. 12, 1709, quoted ibid., p. 29.
5. Ibid., pp. 2, 80.
6. Speech to Queen Anne printed ibid., pp. 94–95.

7. Ibid., pp. 3–4.

8. Ibid., pp. 66–67. Verelst is quoted on page 67.

9. DeFoe is quoted ibid., p. 77.

10. Ibid., p. 55.

11. Richard N. Ellis and Charlie R. Steen, eds., "An Indian Delegation in France," *Journal of the Illinois State Historical Society* 67 (Sept. 1974):385–405.

12. Ibid., pp. 386–87.

13. Ibid., pp. 391–92.

14. Ibid., pp. 401, 402.

15. Ibid., pp. 394, 402.

16. Reuben Gold Thwaites, ed., *The Jesuit Relations and Allied Documents*, vol. 68, *Lower Canada, Crees, Louisiana, 1720–1736* (Cleveland, 1900), p. 215; Seymour Feiler, trans. and ed., *Jean-Bernard Bossu's Travels in the Interior of North America, 1751–1762* (Norman, 1962), pp. 83–84.

17. For a general discussion of Indian visitors to Europe, see Carolyn Thomas Foreman, *Indians Abroad, 1493–1938* (Norman, 1943).

18. Minutes of the Augusta Conference, Nov. 8, 1763, PRO/CO5, vol. 65, folio 53.

19. Foreman, *Indians Abroad*, pp. 83–84; Lords of Trade to Earl of Halifax, Mar. 6, 1765, PRO/CO5, vol. 66, folio 25; Alexander Colden to William Johnson, June 1, 1765, *Collections of the New-York Historical Society for the Year 1923*, vol. 7, *The Letters and Papers of Cadwallader Colden, 1765–1775* (New York, 1923), pp. 38–39.

20. Francis Fauquier to Earl of Egremont, May 1, 1762, PRO/CO5, vol. 1345, folio 1; Samuel Cole Williams, ed., *Lieut. Henry Timberlake's Memoirs, 1756–1765* (Johnson City, 1927), pp. 132, 148, 159 (cited as *Timberlake's Memoirs*); Robert Wood to Mr. Martin, Nov. 3, 1762, PRO/SP Domestic, vol. 44, folio 138, p. 55.

21. *Timberlake's Memoirs*, p. 168.

22. Ibid., p. 171.

23. Lords of Trade to Fauquier, Mar. 1, 1765, PRO/CO5, vol. 1368, pp. 257–58.

24. *Timberlake's Memoirs*, pp. 172–73.

25. Extract of Minutes of the House of Lords, Mar. 6, 1765, PRO/CO5, vol. 66, folio 27, Indian Affairs.

26. *Timberlake's Memoirs*, pp. 132, 133.

27. For a discussion of this aspect of early Indian-white relations, see Wilbur R. Jacobs, *Diplomacy and Indian Gifts: Anglo-French Rivalry Along the Ohio and Northwest Frontiers, 1748–1763* (Palo Alto, 1950). An especially fine treatment of diplomatic gifts presented by the Spanish is found in John C. Ewers, "Symbols of Chiefly Authority in Spanish Louisiana," in John Francis McDermott, ed., *The Spanish in the Mississippi Valley, 1762–1804* (Urbana, 1974), pp. 274–84.

28. Fernando de Leyba to Governor Gálvez, Feb. 5, 1779, quoted in Ewers, "Symbols of Chiefly Authority," p. 276.

29. Minutes of Augusta Conference, Nov. 7, 1763.

30. Don Juan Bautista de Anza quoted in Ewers, "Symbols of Chiefly Authority," pp. 274–75.

31. Ibid., p. 277.

32. Ibid., pp. 278–79.

33. Don Pedro Bautisa Pino quoted ibid., pp. 282–83.

34. Henry Knox to George Washington, July 7, 1789, ASP:IA, 1:54.

Chapter II: Invitation to Washington

1. James Thacher, *A Military Journal During the American Revolutionary War*, 2d ed. (Boston, 1827), pp. 159–60.

2. Iowa chief quoted in William Clark to Secretary of War, May 24, 1811, ASP:IA, 1:800.

3. William Eustis to Clark, June 19, 1812, SW IA LS, vol. C, p. 137.

4. The account of the conference between James Madison and the delegation is found in James Madison Papers, Manuscript Division, Library of Congress, Series 1 (Microfilm Reel 14).

5. "Articles recommended to be delivered to Indian Chiefs and party on a visit to the President of the United States," [Aug. 1812], SW IA LR; *Pittsburgh Gazette*, Sept. 25, 1812.

6. *Niles' Weekly Register*, Mar. 23, 1816, and Jan. 30, 1819; Benjamin O'Fallon to Clark, May 10, 1817, printed in Clarence E. Carter, ed., *The Territorial Papers of the United States*, vol. 15, *The Territory of Louisiana-Missouri, 1815–1821* (Washington, D.C., 1951), p. 264.

7. Thomas L. McKenney to James Barbour, Jan. 24, 1828, IA LS, vol. 4, p. 267.

8. Thomas Jefferson quoted in *National Intelligencer and Washington Advertiser*, Oct. 3, 1804.

9. O'Fallon to John C. Calhoun, Apr. 5, 1821, SW IA LR; Calhoun to O'Fallon, May 22, 1821, SW IA LS, vol. 5, pp. 103–04.

10. O'Fallon to Calhoun, June 23, 1821, SW IA LR; Calhoun to O'Fallon, Aug. 18, 1821, SW IA LS, vol. 5, pp. 148–49. For a detailed account of the O'Fallon delegation, see Herman J. Viola, "Invitation to Washington—A Bid for Peace," *American West* 9 (Jan. 1972): 18–31.

11. *Washington Gazette*, Mar. 4, 1822.

12. "Journal of Colonel Dodge's Expedition from Fort Gibson to the Pawnee Pict Village," printed in *Arkansas Gazette*, Feb. 24, 1835.

13. Ray Allen Billington, *Westward Expansion: A History of the American Frontier*, 4th ed. (New York, 1974), p. 473; Comanches quoted in the expedition journal; the Comanche and Kiowa treaties, dated Aug. 24, 1835, and May, 1837, are printed in Charles J. Kappler, comp. and ed., *Indian Affairs: Laws and Treaties*, vol. 2, *Treaties* (Washington, D.C., 1904), pp. 435–39 and 489–91.

14. *Fourth Annual Report of the Board of Indian Commissioners to the President of the United States* (Washington, D.C., 1872), pp. 5, 125; Commissioner of Indian Affairs to Secretary of the Interior, Apr. 24, 1888, IA LS, vol. 137, Finance, pp. 264–66.

15. For an excellent account of Little Crow's visit to Washington, see Barbara T. Newcombe, "A Portion of the American People," *Minnesota History*, 45 (Fall 1976): 82–96.

16. *New York Daily Tribune*, Sept. 2, 1872. For an account of the Lone Wolf and Satanta delegation, see Herman J. Viola, *Lincoln and the Indians* (Madison, 1976).

17. Black Eagle quoted in Patrick Henry Conger to Commissoner of Indian Affairs, June 15, 1867, IA LR, Yankton Agency (C-264).

18. Nathan Bishop to Felix Brunot, Nov. 23, 1872, printed in *Fourth Annual Report of the Board of Indian Commissioners*, p. 124.

19. John Bigelow, ed., *Works of Benjamin Franklin* (New York, 1904), 10:386–87.

20. Arthur H. DeRosier, Jr., *The Removal of the Choctaw Indians* (Knoxville, 1970), pp. 70–77.

21. William Ward to Calhoun, Aug. 12, 1823, SW LR (W-79); extract of resolutions of Sept. 29, 1823, enclosed with Ward to Calhoun, Oct. 10, 1823, ibid. (W-156); Ward to Calhoun, Feb. 11, 1824, ibid. (W-250); Calhoun to Ward, Jan. 29, 1824, SW IA LS, vol. F, p. 36; Ward to Calhoun, Mar. 12, 1824, IA LR, Choctaw Agency.

22. Henry Conway to Calhoun, May 22, 1824, IA LR, Choctaw Agency; Calhoun to Conway, May 22, 1824, IA LS, vol. 1, p. 79; 4 *Stat.* 35.

23. Ward to Calhoun, May 28, 1824, IA LR, Choctaw Agency; McKenney to Ward, June 24, 1824, IA LS, vol. 1, p. 120.

24. Herman J. Viola, *Thomas L. McKenney: Architect of America's Early Indian Policy, 1816–1830* (Chicago, 1974), pp. 127, 198–99.

25. Pushmataha quoted in Charles Lanham, *Recollections of Curious Characters and Pleasant Places* (Edinburgh, 1881), pp. 211–12.

26. James McDonald to Calhoun, Nov. 16, 1824, Ratified Treaty File, 1801–68, Treaty 124, RG 75, NA.

27. McKenney to Choctaw Delegation, Nov. 16, 1824, IA LS, vol. 1, p. 234; McDonald and David Folsom to Calhoun, Nov. 17, 1824, ASP:IA, 2:551.

28. McKenney to Choctaw Delegation, Nov. 19, 1824, IA LS, vol. 1, p. 236; McDonald and Folsom to Calhoun, Nov. 20, 1824, ASP:IA, 2:551.

29. Choctaw Delegation to Calhoun, Nov. 22, 1824, ASP:IA, 2:551–52.

30. Calhoun to Choctaw Delegation, ibid., p. 552; McKenney to McDonald, Nov. 27, 1824, IA LS, vol. 1, p. 242; McKenney to Choctaw Delegation, ibid., p. 241.

31. Choctaw Delegation to Calhoun, Nov. 30, 1824, ASP:IA, 2:553; Folsom and McDonald to Calhoun, Dec. 1, 1824, Ratified Treaty File, Treaty 124.

32. McKenney to Choctaw Delegation, Dec. 8, 1824, IA LS, vol. 1, p. 258; Calhoun to Choctaw Delegation, Dec. 28, 1824, ibid., p. 274; Calhoun to Choctaw Delegation, Dec. 31, 1824, ASP:IA, 2:553.

33. Choctaw Delegation to Calhoun, Jan. 3, 1825, ASP:IA, 2:553; Calhoun to Choctaw Delegation, Jan. 5, 1825, ibid., pp. 553–54; Choctaw Delegation to Calhoun, Jan. 14, 1825, ibid., p. 554.

34. Expenses of Choctaw Delegation, 1825, IA LR, Choctaw Agency.

35. McKenney to Folsom, Dec. 2, 7, 1824, IA LS, vol. 1, pp. 248, 256; McKenney to McDonald, June 16, 1825, ibid., vol. 2, p. 48

36. McKenney to Joshua Tennison, June 17, 1825, ibid., vol. 2, p. 50.

37. McKenney to Choctaw Chiefs, June 17, 1825, ibid., vol. 2, pp. 48–49.

38. Henry R. Schoolcraft, *Personal Memoirs of a Residence of Thirty Years with the Indian Tribes on the American Frontiers* (Philadelphia, 1851), pp. 198–99.

39. Quoted in William T. Hagan, *The Sac and Fox Indians* (Norman, 1958), p. 215.

40. *Washington National Intelligencer*, Sept. 18, 1837.

41. *Alexandria Gazette*, Oct. 6, 1837.

42. William MacLeod, "About Indian Visits," [1837?], Manuscript Collection, Columbia Historical Society, Washington, D.C.

43. *Washington National Intelligencer*, Oct. 11, 1837.

44. Treaties with the Sioux, Sac and Fox, Winnebago, and Iowa can be found in Kappler, *Treaties*, pp. 493–501.

45. MacLeod, "About Indian Visits."

46. Keokuk quoted in Frederick Webb Hodge, ed., *The Indian Tribes of North America, with Biographical Sketches and Anecdotes of the Principal Chiefs*, by Thomas L. McKenney and James Hall (Edinburgh, 1933), 2:142–43.

47. *Washington Daily National Republican*, Oct. 30, 1873.

48. Commissioner of Indian Affairs to Secretary of the Interior, Dec. 9, 1887, IA LS, vol. 84, Land, p. 466.

49. H. C. Hansbrough to Commissioner of Indian Affairs, Dec. 16, 1899, IA LR, 1899:60261.

50. Newton Edmunds to Commissioner of Indian Affairs, Mar. 17, 1866, IA LR, Yankton Agency (D-170).

51. T. W. Jones to Assistant Adjutant General, Oct. 29, 1887, IA LR, 1887:34062.

52. L. F. Hubbard to Secretary of the Interior, Apr. 19, 1884, IA LR, 1884:7953; William Nicholson to John Q. Smith, Aug. 23, 1877, IA LR, Ponca Agency (C-1212).

53. Petition of Navajo leaders enclosed with William F. M. Arny to Commissioner of Indian Affairs, Jan. 2, 1874, IA LR, New Mexico Superintendency (C-10363).

54. Commissioner of Indian Affairs to Arny, Jan. 26 and Feb. 4, 1874, IA LS, vol. 116, pp. 184–85 and 225–26.

55. Petition of Feb. 11, 1874, enclosed with Arny to Commissioner of Indian Affairs, Feb. 16, 1874, IA LR, New Mexico Superintendency (L-10312).

56. Commissioner of Indian Affairs to Arny, Mar. 11, 1874, IA LS, vol. 116, pp. 429–30.

57. Arny to Commissioner of Indian Affairs, Apr. 8, 1874, IA LR, New Mexico Superintendency (L-10320).

58. Commissioner of Indian Affairs to Arny, Aug. 4, 1874, IA LS, vol. 118, p. 560; Arny to Commissioner of Indian Affairs, Sept. 21, 1874, and Feb. 15, 1875, IA LR, New Mexico Superintendency (L-10359 and L-10932).

59. Thomas Richards to Commissioner of Indian Affairs, Nov. 22, 1898, IA LR, 1898:53621.

60. W. J. Cleveland to Richard H. Pratt, July 23, 1881, IA LR, 1881:13723.

61. John Dougherty to Clark, Feb. 1, 1837, enclosed with Clark to Commissioner of Indian Affairs, Feb. 16, 1837, IA LR, Upper Missouri Agency (C-206).

Chapter III: Unauthorized Delegations

1. Secretary of War to David Henley, Nov. 19, 1800, SW IA LS, vol. A, pp. 1–2; passport dated Nov. 17, 1800, ibid., p. 1.

2. Henry Dearborn to Return J. Meigs, Nov. 20, 1801, ibid., pp. 123–24.

3. Dearborn to Meigs, Nov. 23, 1802, and to Samuel Mitchell, Nov. 27, 1802, ibid., pp. 293–94 and 295–96.

4. Passport dated Nov. 19, 1802, ibid., p. 291.

5. Dearborn to J. W. Brownson, Apr. 19, 1802, ibid., p. 203.

6. Dearborn to Archibald Roane, James Garrard, and George Clinton, Nov. 22, 1802, ibid., pp. 292–93.

7. Circular to Agents, Jan. 14, 1802, ibid., pp. 145–46.

8. James McHenry to Robert G. Harper, Apr. 16, 1800, ASP:IA, 1:645.

9. Edward E. Hill, *The Office of Indian Affairs, 1824–1880: Historical Sketches* (New York, 1974), pp. 1–2.

10. Ibid., pp. 2–3.

11. Secretary of War to Benjamin Hawkins, Nov. 26, 1800, SW IA LS, vol. A, p. 3; Secretary of War to Meigs, July 10, 1801, ibid., pp. 87–89.

12. McKenney to Lewis Cass, Sept. 7, 1824, IA LS, vol. 1, p. 190

13. For a comprehensive treatment of the Indian Intercourse Act of 1834, see F. P. Prucha, *American Indian Policy in the Formative Years: The Indian Intercourse Acts, 1790–1834* (Cambridge, 1962); Elbert Herring to William Clark, July 14, 1834, and to Stevens T. Mason, July 12, 1824, IA LS, vol. 13, pp. 191–92 and 177.

14. Charles E. Mix to R. McClelland, June 18, 1853, Report Books, vol. 7, pp. 262–63, RG 75, NA.

15. T. Hartley Crawford to Thomas H. Harvey, July 22, 1844, IA LS, vol. 35, pp. 359–60.

16. Ibid.

17. Ibid.

18. Crawford to Harvey, July 24, 1844, ibid., p. 363.

19. Crawford to David Agnew, July 24, 1844, ibid., p. 362.

20. Crawford to Harvey, July 26, 1844, ibid., pp. 371–72.

21. Circular to Superintendents and Agents, Oct. 16, 1868, IA LS, vol. 88, pp. 150–52.

22. Albert Wiley to Ely S. Parker, June 1, 1869, IA LR, Sac and Fox Agency (W–295).

23. Wiley to Thomas Murphy, Nov. 24, 1868, enclosed with Murphy to Commissioner of Indian Affairs, Nov. 27, 1868, ibid. (M-2139).

24. Ibid.

25. N. G. Taylor to Secretary of the Interior, Dec. 22, 1868, Report Books, vol. 18, pp. 53–55.

26. Ibid.

27. Wiley to Parker, June 1, 1869, IA LR, Sac and Fox Agency (W–295).

28. Enoch Hoag to Parker, Sept. 3, 1869, ibid. (H-402).

29. *Argument and Brief for the Defendant by James Christian in the Supreme Court of the State of Kansas, January Term, 1870. Albert Wiley vs. Keokuk, On Petition of Error*, pp. 39–40, enclosed with A. C. Farnham to Parker, July 30, 1870, ibid. (H-1305); J. D. Cox to Commissioner of Indian Affairs, Aug. 17, 1870, Letters Sent to Indian Commissioners, vol. 9, pp. 496–97, RG 48, NA.

30. *Annual Report of the Commissioner of Indian Affairs for 1866*, p. 2; Dennis N. Cooley to Edwin Clark, Feb. 21, 1866, IA LS, vol. 79, p. 319.

31. Parker to Agents, Dec. 9, 1869, IA LS, vol. 92, pp. 516–17.

32. *Annual Report of the Commissioner of Indian Affairs for 1872*, p. 99.

33. William M. Leeds to J. F. Cravens, Mar. 13, 1878, IA LS, vol. 138, p. 549.

34. Luther Standing Bear, *My People the Sioux*, edited by E. A. Brininstool (Boston, 1928), p. 133; F. P. Prucha, *American Indian Policy in Crisis: Christian Reformers and the Indian, 1865–1900* (Norman, 1976), pp. 272–74.

35. *Annual Report of the Commissioner of Indian Affairs for 1880*, p. viii.

36. Black Bear to Pratt, July 4, 1881, enclosed with Pratt to Commissioner of Indian Affairs, July 18, 1881, IA LR, 1881:12475.

37. Commissioner of Indian Affairs to Agents, May 6, 1886, IA LS, vol. 122, Finance, p. 356. The circular of 1892 has not been found. Evidence for its issuance comes from several responses to it from concerned Indian agents. See, for instance, George LeRoy Brown to Commissioner of Indian Affairs, May 6, 1892, IA LR, 1892:17656, and Edwin Eells to Commissioner of Indian Affairs, May 3, 1892, IA LR, 1892:17459. The circular by C. N. Bliss is printed in *Annual Report of the Commissioner of Indian Affairs for 1897*, pp. 54–56; it is also found in IA LS, vol. 358, Land, p. 325.

38. W. A. Jones to Robert J. Gamble, Dec. 22, 1899, IA LS, vol. 310, Finance, p. 340; Jones to George Bird Grinnell, Mar. 3, 1900, Letters Sent by the Office of the Commissioner of Indian Affairs, Nov. 1899-Aug, 1900, p. 170.

39. Circular 1480, Oct. 29. 1918; and Circular 1652, Jan. 15, 1921, RG 75, NA.

40. John Collier to Harold Ickes, Apr. 28, 1938, and Ickes to Collier, Apr. 30, 1938, file 13379–1935, General Services 056, Central Files, RG 75, NA.

41. Press Release, May 19, 1938, file 7698–1932, Pine Ridge 056, ibid.

42. Circular 3260, July 21, 1938, RG 75, NA.

43. Order 556, Supplement 1, March 7, 1951, copy in file 9808–1951, General Services 056, Central Files, RG 75, NA.

Chapter IV: Financing the Delegations

1. 2 *Stat.* 83, 85; Secretary of War to Chairman, House Committee on Ways and Means, May 5, 1800, ASP:IA, 1:644.

2. 2 *Stat.* 139–46.

3. 4 *Stat.* 267–68, 519–20.

4. 4 *Stat.* 729–35.

5. 5 *Stat.* 299–301; 9 *Stat.* 40; 5 *Stat.* 323–28, 712; 9 *Stat.* 34–35; 10 *Stat.* 55.

6. 16 *Stat.* 387; 17 *Stat.* 437; 18 *Stat.* 146.

7. 5 *Stat.* 300–01; 9 *Stat.* 572; 8 *Stat.* 161; 26 *Stat.* 989.

8. Daniel Kurtz to John McElvaine, Nov. 21, 1832, IA LS, vol. 9, p. 375.

9. Commissioner of Indian Affairs to Second Auditor, Apr. 11, 1885, IA LS, vol. 112, Finance, pp. 17–19.

10. Second Auditor's Accounts, No. 4686, Alexander McWilliams, 1867, and No. 1721, Amanda F. Beveridge, 1873.

11. Quoted in Schoolcraft, *Personal Memoirs*, p. 319.

12. Augustus Brosius to Commissioner of Indian Affairs, Jan. 31, 1882, IA LR, 1882:2290.

13. Petition enclosed with Second Auditor's Accounts, No. 5916, Sac and Fox, 1882.

14. Second Auditor's Accounts, No. 7302, Samuel W. Beall, 1858.

15. The note is enclosed with Second Auditor's Accounts, No. 8298, Northrup and Chilk, 1859.

16. Commissioner of Indian Affairs to Secretary of the Interior, May 28, 1900, IA LS, vol. 628, Finance, pp. 451–52.

17. Commissioner of Indian Affairs to M. L. Martin, Jan. 18, 1868, IA LS, vol. 85, p. 312.

18. E. H. Bowman to Commissioner of Indian Affairs, July 26, 1882, IA LR, 1882:13897; Commissioner of Indian Affairs to Bowman, July 31, 1882, IA LS, vol. 36, Civilization, p. 227; Bowman to Commissioner of Indian Affairs, Aug. 17, 1882, IA LR, 1882:15630.

19. D. B. Dyer to Commissioner of Indian Affairs, Mar. 18, 1882, IA LR, 1882:5501; Secretary of the Interior to Commissioner of Indian Affairs, Sept. 13, 1899, IA LR, 1899:43691.

20. Commissioner of Indian Affairs to Secretary of the Interior, Feb. 15, 1895, IA LS, vol. 228, Finance, p. 121; Commissioner of Indian Affairs to Secretary of the Interior, May 5, 1899, ibid., vol. 298, pp. 292–93.

21. 10 *Stat.* 56; 9 *Stat.* 587.

22. Timothy Jenkins to Luke Lea, Mar. 23 and 26, 1852, IA LR, New York Agency (F-24 and C-26); Elijah Schenandoah and others to Millard Fillmore, Mar. 30, 1852, ibid. (S-71); Lea to

Schenandoah and others, Apr. 1, 1852, IA LS, vol. 46, p. 2; 10 *Stat.* 15.

23. 33 *Stat.* 280.

24. 48 *Stat.* 362; 49 *Stat.* 176; 51 *Stat.* 528; 53 *Stat.* 765; 50 *Stat.* 564; 55 *Stat.* 327; 56 *Stat.* 528.

25. 64 *Stat.* 595.

26. The most useful guide to early federal fiscal procedures is Robert Mayo, *The Treasury Department and Its Various Fiscal Bureaus, Their Origin, Organization, and Practical Operations, Illustrated* (Washington, D.C., 1847).

27. McKenney to John H. Eaton, Dec. 14, 1829, IA LS, vol. 6, pp. 191–92; McKenney to Deacon Sockbason and Sebatis Neptune, ibid., pp. 192–93.

28. Parker to Cox, Aug. 18, 1870, Report Books, vol. 19, pp. 473–74; Cox to Parker, Oct. 24, 1870, IA LR, Cherokee Agency (I-1265); Francis A. Walker to Columbus Delano, Mar. 15, 1872, Report Books, vol. 21, p. 327; Delano to Walker, March 18, 1872, IA LR, Miscellaneous (I-1265).

29. E. J. Brooks to Second Comptroller, Aug. 13, 1880, enclosed with Second Auditor's Accounts, No. 1749, Auerbach and Brother, 1880.

30. For a readable discussion of the federal accountability process, see Leonard D. White, *The Jeffersonians: A Study in Administrative History, 1801–1829* (New York, 1951), pp. 163–65.

31. Second Auditor's Accounts, No. 2383, Joseph M. Street, 1837.

32. For example, see the form enclosed with Second Auditor's Accounts, No. 4163, Charles Bottineau, 1885.

33. 52 *Stat.* 20.

34. Second Comptroller to William Medill, Feb. 17, 1847, IA LR, Miscellaneous (C-21); Medill to Second Comptroller, Feb. 22, 1847, IA LS, vol. 39, pp. 200–01.

35. Commissioner of Indian Affairs to Second Auditor, n.d., enclosed with Second Auditor's Accounts, No. 1378, I. Hamburger and Sons, 1884. By the turn of the twentieth century, the bureau required Indians to place a thumbprint next to their names on official documents, petitions, and the like. For example, see file 2054-15, General Services 056, Central Files, RG 75, NA.

36. Second Auditor's Accounts, No. 8977, W. W. Denison, 1858.

37. Second Auditor's Accounts, No. 900, Fellows D. Pease, 1874.

38. Second Auditor's Accounts, No. 605, Charles Adams, 1875.

39. Second Auditor's Accounts, No. 725, Auerbach and Brother, 1880.

40. H. R. Clum to Samuel M. Jenney, Aug. 10, 1874, IA LS, vol. 120, pp. 26–27; Oliver O. Howard, *My Life and Experiences Among Our Hostile Indians* (Hartford, 1907), p. 176.

41. Samuel Walker to Felix R. Brunot, June 6, 1873, Letters Sent by the Board of Indian Commissioners, vol. 4, pp. 246–47, RG 75, NA: Walker to Thomas K. Cree, ibid., pp. 250–51.

42. Second Comptroller to Delano, Dec. 15, 1874, IA LR, Miscellaneous (I-1536).

43. Adams to Cree, Dec. 15, 1873; John D. Miles to Cree, Dec. 18, 1873; and Pease to Cree, Dec. 16, 1873, enclosed with Cree to Delano, Feb. 6, 1874, ibid. (I-163).

44. William Vandever to Commissioner of Indian Affairs, Mar. 4, 1874, ibid. (I-1536).

45. Delano to Commissioner of Indian Affairs, Feb. 10, 1874, and Commissioner of Indian Affairs to Vandever, Feb. 11, 1874, enclosed with Vandever to Commissioner of Indian Affairs, ibid.

46. Delano to Commissioner of Indian Affairs, Dec. 19, 1874, ibid.; Commissioner of Indian Affairs to Delano, Dec. 24, 1874, Report Books, vol. 25, pp. 305–06; Delano to Commissioner of Indian Affairs, Dec. 26, 1874, IA LR, Miscellaneous (I-1536); Commissioner of Indian Affairs to Benjamin Beveridge, Jan. 7, 1875, IA LS, vol. 123, p. 75.

47. Henry Wilson to George H. Stuart, Dec. 10, 1873, George H. Stuart Papers, Manuscript Division, Library of Congress; Commissioner of Indian Affairs to W. Wilshire, May 3, 1876, IA LS, vol. 133, p. 99; Alfred J. Works to Commissioner of Indian Affairs, Mar. 10, 1879, IA LR, Miscellaneous (W-578).

48. Adams to Commissioner of Indian Affairs, April 9, 1880, IA LR, Miscellaneous (A-305).

Chapter V: The Indian Dramatis Personae

1. Robert M. Kvasnicka, "From the Wilderness to Washington—and Back Again: The Story of the Chippewa Delegation of 1855," *Kansas Quarterly* 3 (Fall 1971): 63.
2. The incident regarding the Pawnee delegates is discussed in John C. Ewers, " 'Chiefs from the Missouri and Mississippi' and Peale's Silhouettes of 1806," *Smithsonian Journal of History* 1 (Spring 1966): 24.
3. Newspaper clipping, Jan. 10, 1852, vol. 8, BAE Scrapbooks, NAA.
4. The incident regarding Tarecawawaho is described in Hodge, *Indian Tribes of North America*, 2:293–94.
5. *Chicago Herald*, Jan. 29, 1891, Scrapbook, BCIM.
6. Commandant quoted in N. G. Taylor to A. J. Faulk, June 10, 1867, IA LS, vol. 83, pp. 244–45.
7. J. R. Hanson to Faulk, July 6, 1867, enclosed with Faulk to Commissioner of Indian Affairs, July 18, 1867, IA LR, Upper Missouri Agency (D-458).
8. Joseph M. Cataldo to John Mullan, Jan. 10, 1886, BCIM.
9. Viola, "Invitation to Washington," p. 21.
10. Arden R. Smith to Commissioner of Indian Affairs, Dec. 6, 1882, IA LR, 1882:22405; Viola, *Lincoln and the Indians*, p. 6. For a thorough discussion of John Clum's marital escapade, see John Shapard, "A Federally-Funded Wedding and Honeymoon," *Arizona Republic*, July 15, 1979.
11. Taylor to George A. Reynolds, Dec. 11, 1868, IA LS, Vol. 88, pp. 398–99.
12. Red Cloud quoted in V. T. McGillycuddy to Commissioner of Indian Affairs, July 20, 1881, IA LR, 1881:13017.
13. Secretary of the Interior to Commissioner of Indian Affairs, Jan. 23, 1868, enclosed with Second Auditor's Accounts, No. 6352, Baptiste Peoria, 1868. Commissioner of Indian Affairs to A. M. Robinson, Dec. 8, 1858, IA LS, vol. 60, p. 97.
14. Mix to L. E. Webb, May 7, 1868, IA LS, vol. 86, pp. 388–89; Mix to John Jourdan, May 14, 1868, ibid., p. 436; Jourdan to Mix, May 16, 1868, IA LR, New Mexico Superintendency (J-877).
15. J. W. Daniels to J. Q. Smith, Jan. 24, 1876, IA LR, Dakota Superintendency (D-38); E. P. Smith to Richard Joseph, Mar. 20, 1875, IA LS, vol. 123, p. 467.
16. White Ghost and Iron Nation to Commissioner of Indian Affairs, Dec. 11, 1889, IA LR, 1889:35600; Commissioner of Indian Affairs to J. J. Saville, June 1, 1875, IA LS, vol. 124, p. 400.
17. White Ghost to Commissioner of Indian Affairs, Dec. 9, 1889, IA LR, 1889:35328; *New York Daily Tribune*, June 1, 1875.
18. Joshua Given to Pratt, Feb. 8, 1888, Richard H. Pratt Papers, Beinecke Library, Yale University.
19. Transcript of Interview with Sioux Delegation, May 27 and 28, 1875, and undated newspaper clipping, IA LR, Dakota Superintendency (C-727 and C-700).
20. Blackfoot to U. S. Grant, Dec. 5, 1873, enclosed with Cree to Grant, Jan. 7, 1874, IA LR, Montana Superintendency (P-45); Joseph quoted in James M. Hayworth to Commissioner of Indian Affairs, Dec. 24, 1880, IA LR, 1881:715.
21. Pratt to Commissioner of Indian Affairs, Nov. 4, 1884, IA LR, 1884:21179.
22. Herman J. Viola, *The Indian Legacy of Charles Bird King* (Washington, D.C., 1976), p. 32.
23. Viola, *Lincoln and the Indians*, pp. 8–9.
24. Joseph E. Hazard to Commissioner of Indian Affairs, Jan. 30, 1884, IA LR, 1884:2474.
25. Spotted Tail's interview with President Grant is reported in D. C. Poole, *Among the Sioux of Dakota* (New York, 1881), p. 186.
26. Viola, "Invitation to Washington," p. 21.
27. Lawrence Taliaferro to Commissioner of Indian Affairs, [1837], IA LR, St. Peters Agency (T-178-187).
28. Interview between Commissioner of Indian Affairs and Red Cloud, June 5, 1875, IA LR, Dakota Superintendency (C-765).

29. Commissioner of Indian Affairs to M. M. Davis, Jan. 27, 1866, IA LS, vol. 79, p. 202.

30. Thurman Wilkins, *Cherokee Tragedy: The Story of the Ridge Family and the Decimation of a People* (New York, 1970), p. 211. Calvin Colton is also quoted on this page.

31. Calvin Colton, *Tour of the American Lakes, and Among the Indians of the North-West Territory, in 1830* (London, 1833), 2:171–72.

32. For a comprehensive biography of John Ross, see Gary E. Moulton, *John Ross, Cherokee Chief* (Athens, 1978). Information on William P. Adair as a delegate can be found in Thomas M. Holm, "The Cherokee Delegates and the Opposition to the Allotment of Indian Lands" (Master's thesis, University of Oklahoma, 1974), pp. 9–10.

33. John Collier to James H. McGregor, Dec. 31, 1935, file 7698–1932, Pine Ridge Agency 056, Central Files, RG 75, NA.

34. Fred Treon to Commissioner of Indian Affairs, Dec. 14, 1896, IA LR, 1896:47067; Winnebagos to Commissioner of Indian Affairs, Aug. 9, 1881, IA LR, 1881:14477; Cup Paw Hee to Commissioner of Indian Affairs, July 21, 1890, IA LR, 1890:23027.

35. Pah Te and others to [Commissioner of Indian Affairs], Apr. 24, 1856, IA LR, Sac and Fox Agency (P-74). For a typical printed credential, see the one for Overton Love, Jan. 16, 1890, IA LR, 1890:22484.

36. Marion Johnson Mochon, "Stockbridge-Munsee Cultural Adaptations: 'Assimilated Indians,' " *Procedures of the American Philosophical Society* 112 (June 1968): 182–219.

37. Power of Attorney, Second Auditor's Accounts, No. 9783, Albert Miller, 1883; Dennis Turkey and others to Secretary of the Interior, June 1, 1883, ibid.; Albert Miller to Commissioner of Indian Affairs, June 29, 1883, ibid.

38. John A. Wright to Commissioner of Indian Affairs, July 12 and 20, 1883, ibid.

39. Secretary of the Interior to Commissioner of Indian Affairs, Aug. 9, 1883, ibid.

40. Transcript of tribal council meeting of January 27, 1932, enclosed with L. S. Bonnin to Commissioner of Indian Affairs, Feb. 12, 1932, file 926-1931, Cheyenne and Arapaho Agency 056, Central Files, RG 75, NA.

41. Signe Larson, "John W. Quinney: An Episode" (Seminar paper in the author's possession).

42. John W. Quinney diary, John C. Adams Papers, State Historical Society of Wisconsin.

43. Entry for Aug. 3, 1846, ibid.

44. Entry for Aug. 6, 1846, ibid. The act repealing the act of 1843 is 9 *Stat.* 55.

45. Vanessa J. Piala, "John C. Adams: Visitor to Washington, 1876" (Seminar paper in the author's possession).

46. Sara J. Slingerhand to John C. Adams, Apr. 17 and 10, 1888, Adams Papers.

47. Slingerhand to Adams, 1888, ibid.; *Antigo* (Wisconsin) *Journal*, Sept. 28, 1932.

48. Commissioner of Indian Affairs to A. M. Scales, May 9, 1876, IA LS, vol. 130, pp. 208–09.

49. Commissioner of Indian Affairs to James I. Coffey, July 12, 1921, file 16722–1920, General Services 056, Central Files, RG 75; and W. H. Lyons to Commissioner of Indian Affairs, Feb. 18, 1922, file 15011-1922, ibid.

50. William L. Stone, *The Life and Times of Sa-Go-Ye-Wat-Ha, or Red Jacket* (New York, 1841), pp. 363–64.

51. J. H. Leavenworth to Commissioner of Indian Affairs, June 27, 1863, IA LR, Upper Arkansas Agency (L-158 1/2).

52. J. Lee Hall to Commissioner of Indian Affairs, Mar. 29, 1887, IA LR, 1887:9939.

53. Jesse F. Warner to Commissioner of Indian Affairs, Dec. 26, 1886, IA LR, 1886:34577.

54. J. S. Stephan to Commissioner of Indian Affairs, Sept. 7, 1881, printed in *Annual Report of the Commissioner of Indian Affairs for 1881*, p. 60.

55. A. E. Woodson to Commissioner of Indian Affairs, Jan. 26, 1899, IA LR, 1899:5155.

56. Quotation concerning Big White in Roy W. Meyer, *The Village Indians of the Upper Missouri: The Mandans, Hidatsas, and Arikaras* (Lincoln, 1977), p. 45.

57. For a full discussion of the adventures of The Light and his companions, see John C. Ewers, "When the Light Shone in Washington," *Indian Life on the Upper Missouri* (Norman, 1968).

58. Howard, *My Life and Adventures*, p. 178; J. Lee Humfreville, *Twenty Years Among Our Savage Indians* (Hartford, 1897), p. 53; Sitting Bull quoted in Edgar I. Stewart, *Custer's Luck* (Norman, 1955), p. 55.

59. *Annual Report of the Commissioner of Indian Affairs for 1872*, p. 99.

60. Poole, *Among the Sioux of Dakota*, p. 195.

61. *Annual Report of the Board of Indian Commissioners for 1872*, pp. 124–25.

62. Howard, *My Life and Adventures*, p. 183.

63. Young Man Afraid of His Horses quoted in *Baltimore Sun*, Feb. 19, 1891, Scrapbooks, BCIM.

64. Andrew Saltise, Regis, and Pierre Wildshoe to Commissioner of Indian Affairs, Aug. 16, 1887, IA LR, 1887:22425.

Chapter VI: Meeting the Great Father

1. Raymond J. DeMallie, "Touching the Pen: Plains Indian Treaty Councils in Ethnohistorical Perspective," in Frederick C. Luebke, ed., *Ethnicity on the Great Plains* (Lincoln, 1980), pp. 50–51.

2. The information regarding the Cheyenne and Arapaho delegation is found in an unidentified newspaper clipping, Nov. 1851, vol. 8, BAE Scrapbooks, NAA; Hoowaneka quoted in Caleb Atwater, *The Indians of the Northwest* (Columbus, 1850), p. 122; information about Lean Bear is found in Viola, *Lincoln and the Indians*, p. 8; James N. Cusick to [?], Sept. 24, 1845, NA 207, Edward E. Ayer Collection, Newberry Library.

3. Spotted Tail to William J. Pollock, Apr. 16, 1881, IA LR, 1881:8235; Rain in the Face and others to Great Father, July 15, 1881, IA LR, 1881:13419; Sitting Bear, Fighting Bear, and others to Commissioner of Indian Affairs, Feb. 12, 1898, IA LR, 1898:8523.

4. Interview with Henry Old Coyote, Apr. 26, 1978. Transcript in NAA.

5. Interview with Leslie Gay, May 25, 1978. Transcript in NAA.

6. For a complete discussion of the O'Fallon delegation of 1821, see Viola, "Invitation to Washington."

7. Viola, *Thomas L. McKenney*, pp. 159–60.

8. *Washington Daily National Intelligencer*, Dec. 6 and 13, 1828.

9. Entry for Apr. 30, 1861, diary of John Hay, John Hay Papers, Manuscript Division, Library of Congress.

10. Information on the 1863 delegation is found in Viola, *Lincoln and the Indians*.

11. *Washington Gazette*, Jan. 2, 1822.

12. Entry for Jan. 1, 1853, Quinney diary, Adams papers.

13. Interview between Red Cloud delegation and Commissioner of Indian Affairs, June 4, 1875, IA LR, Dakota Superintendency (C-765).

14. For an excellent overview of presentation gifts, see H. Michael Madaus, "Peace and Friendship: Diplomatic Gifts to the Indians," Parts 1–3, *Lore* 22 (Winter 1971, Spring 1972, Summer 1972): 22–42, 68–78, and 107–112.

15. For a comprehensive treatment of peace medals, see F. P. Prucha, *Indian Peace Medals in American History* (Madison, 1971); quote in McKenney to John H. Eaton, Dec. 21, 1829, IA LS, vol. 6, p. 199.

16. Samuel S. Ely to Commissioner of Indian Affairs, July 2, 1878, IA LR, Pawnee Agency (E-181).

17. Prucha, *Indian Peace Medals*.

18. Red Jacket, Polland, and others to Secretary of War, Dec. 13, 1810, SW IA LR; John Tyler to Cherokee Delegation, Sept. 20, 1841, IA LS, vol. 31, pp. 130–32.

19. Viola, *Thomas L. McKenney*, p. 121.

20. Commissioner of Indian Affairs to J. D. Cox, May 20, 1869, Report Books, vol. 18, p. 351.

21. Unidentified newspaper clipping, Sept. 7, 1852, vol. 8, BAE Scrapbooks, NAA.

22. C. F. Hauke to Sylvanus Griswold Morler, Oct. 4, 1913, file 60120-1911, Monuments and Memorials 044, Central Files, RG 75, NA.

23. Cato Sells to J. H. Gallinger, Nov. 17, 1913, ibid.

24. *Washington Daily National Intelligencer*, Dec. 13, 1828.

25. Second Auditor's Accounts, No. 4026, E. Lindsley, 1846; Elbert Herring to Lewis Cass, Feb.

18, 1832, IA LS, vol. 8, p. 118; Madaus, "Peace and Friendship," Part 3, p. 112.

26. McKenney to Little Prince, Feb. 20, 1828, IA LS, vol. 4, pp. 304–05.

27. Cusick to [?], Sept. 24, 1845; *Washington Columbian Fountain*, June 29, 1846.

28. Blackfoot to Grant, Dec. 5, 1873, enclosed with Cree to Grant, Jan. 7, 1874, IA LR, Montana Superintendency (P-45); and Grant to Ute Delegation, Nov. 5, 1873, President's Folder, Letters Received by the Board of Indian Commissioners, RG 75, NA.

29. *Washington Evening Chronicle*, Oct. 4, 1872.

30. Charles Hatton to Commissioner of Indian Affairs, Nov. 24, 1881, IA LR, 1881:20956.

31. *Washington Daily National Intelligencer*, Feb. 16, 1822.

32. Iron Bull quoted in *Washington Evening Star*, Oct. 21, 1873.

33. Andrew Saltise to Grover Cleveland, Nov. 12, 1888, IA LR, 1888:31503.

34. The Klamath visitor and Sarah Winnemucca are quoted in Turner, *Red Men Calling on the Great White Father*, pp. 155, 169.

35. William M. Leeds to J. F. Cravens, Mar. 13, 1878, IA LS, vol. 138, p. 549.

36. C. F. Larrabee to Rudolph Forster, Mar. 12, 1907, Letters Sent by Acting Commissioner C. F. Larrabee, 1905–08, p. 162; RG 75, NA.

37. William Loeb, Jr., to Commissioner of Indian Affairs, Feb. 23, 1903, IA LR, 1903:24646; Roosevelt quoted in *Washington Post*, Mar. 5, 1905.

Chapter VII: Indian Life in the Capital City

1. Howard, *My Life and Experiences*, pp. 173–74; C. E. Vandever to Commissioner of Indian Affairs, Aug. 22, 1890, printed in *Annual Report of the Commissioner of Indian Affairs for 1890*, p. 171.

2. William Howe Downes, "Mr. Dallin's Indian Sculptures," *Scribner's Magazine* 57 (June 1915): 780.

3. John G. Neihardt, *Black Elk Speaks: Being the Life Story of a Holy Man of the Oglala Sioux* (New York, 1932), p. 220; Plenty Coups quoted in Peter Nabokov, ed., *Native American Testimony: An Anthology of Indian and White Relations* (New York, 1978), p 178; Garrick Mallery, "Sign Language Among North American Indians Compared with that Among Other Peoples and Deaf-Mutes," *First Annual Report of the Bureau of Ethnology* (Washington, D.C., 1881), p. 476.

4. Secretary of the Interior to Commissioner of Indian Affairs, Sept. 3, 1877, IA LR, Dakota Superintendency (I-600); C. R. Tuffree to Commissioner of Indian Affairs, Sept. 24 and 25, 1877, ibid. (B-519).

5. J. N. Harlan to D. N. Cooley, Jan. 15, 1866, IA LR, Southern Superintendency (H-13); J. W. Garrett to Cooley, Jan. 18, 1866, ibid. (G-13), enclosed with Garrett to Cooley, March 7, 1866, ibid. (G-35).

6. D. W. Janowitz to Commissioner of Indian Affairs, Aug. 2 and 23, 1881, IA LR, 1881:14920.

7. Poole, *Among the Sioux of Dakota*, pp. 146–47; "Critic," unidentified newspaper clipping, Jan. 29, 1891, Scrapbook, BCIM.

8. "Critic," Jan. 29, 1891.

9. Second Auditor's Accounts, No. 8977, W. W. Dennison, 1858, and No. 900, Fellows D. Pease, 1873; *Washington National Intelligencer*, Oct. 3, 1837.

10. Commissioner of Indian Affairs to Richard Joseph, Nov. 30, 1874, IA LS, vol. 121, pp. 426–27.

11. Second Auditor's Accounts, No. 8977, W. W. Dennison, 1858, and No. 3466, William S. Kelly, 1888.

12. Schoolcraft, *Personal Memoirs*, p. 118; John F. A. Sanford quoted in Ewers, "When the Light Shone in Washington," p. 84.

13. Jonathan E. Fletcher to H. R. Rice, Feb. 19, 1848, enclosed with Second Auditor's Accounts, No. 10893, H. R. Rice, 1850; J. J. Saville to Commissioner of Indian Affairs, enclosed with Second Auditor's Accounts, No. 3487, J. J. Saville, 1877; Commissioner of Indian Affairs to John Burbank, Jan. 15, 1866, IA LS, vol. 79, p. 141.

14. Lawrence Taliaferro to Commissioner of Indian Affairs, [1837], IA LR, St. Peters Agency (T-178-187).

15. Second Auditor's Accounts, No. 1409, A. Saks & Co., 1880; quotation from P. J. Staudenraus, ed., *Mr. Lincoln's Washington: Selections from the Writings of Noah Brooks, Civil War Correspondent* (New York, 1967), pp. 146–47.

16. Standing Bear, *My People, the Sioux*, pp. 69–70.

17. Madaus, "Peace and Friendship," Part 1, p. 39; McKenney to James Barbour, Dec. 24, 1825, IA LS, vol. 2, p. 326.

18. Shaumonekusse quoted in Hodge, *Indian Tribes of North America*, 1:163, n.9.

19. William Welsh to [?] Clark, Sept. 30, 1877, IA LR, Dakota Superintendency (P-441); William J. Pollock to Commissioner of Indian Affairs, March 1, 1880, IA LR, Ponca Agency (P-298); Commissioner of Indian Affairs to Secretary of the Interior, Jan. 10, 1899, IA LS, vol. 292, Finance, p. 103.

20. Second Auditor's Accounts, No. 8870, John D. Miles, 1876; Commissioner of Indian Affairs to Henry W. Bingham and J. W. Daniels, June 9, 1875, IA LS, vol. 125, p. 406; Francis A. Walker to Enoch Hoag, Dec. 27, 1872, IA LS, vol. 109, pp. 196–97; Valentine C. McGillycuddy to Commissioner of Indian Affairs, July 5, 1882, IA LR, 1883:12482.

21. National Park Service, *The Pennsylvania Avenue District in United States History* (Washington, D.C., 1965), pp. 24–26.

22. The author wishes to thank Gary E. Moulton, editor of the John Ross Papers, for providing a copy of the letter from John Ross to his sister, Sarah Stapler, dated Jan. 19, 1866, from which the description of Joy's boardinghouse is taken.

23. *Washington Daily National Intelligencer*, Nov. 21, 1821.

24. See advertisement on the bill from the Indian Queen, enclosed with Second Auditor's Accounts, No. 15854, Henry Harvey, 1832.

25. Benjamin Perley Poore, *Perley's Reminiscences* (Philadelphia, 1886), 1:42–44.

26. McKenney to Gad Humphreys, May 7, 1826, IA LS, vol. 3, p. 62.

27. Barbara T. Newcombe, "A Portion of the American People," p. 88; Maher's advertising statement taken from *Boyd's Washington and Georgetown Directory* (Washington, D.C., 1860), p. 40; Thomas A. Boyd to Commissioner of Indian Affairs, Oct. 25, 1837, IA LR, Miscellaneous (M-234); Comanches quoted in *Arkansas Intelligencer*, Aug. 22, 1846.

28. Benjamin F. Beveridge obituary, *Washington Post*, Mar. 23, 1909.

29. Beveridge quote taken from unidentified newspaper clipping, dated March 18, 1906. The author is indebted to Elizabeth J. Miller of the Columbia Historical Society for bringing this article to his attention.

30. *Washington Chronicle*, May 22, 1875.

31. *Washington Daily Tribune*, undated clipping, IA LR, Dakota Superintendency (C-700).

32. "Report of Interview Between Sioux Delegation and Secretary of the Interior and Commissioner of Indian Affairs," June 5, 1875, ibid. (C-765).

33. Commissioner of Indian Affairs to Secretary of the Interior, Feb. 5, 1878, Report Books, vol. 30, pp. 115–16; Commissioner of Indian Affairs to Beveridge, June 9, 1880, IA LS, vol. 155, pp. 680–81.

34. Commissioner of Indian Affairs to Secretary of the Interior, Jan. 14, 1867, Report Books, vol. 16, p. 78; P. H. Conger, J. R. Hanson, and K. M. Stone to Commissioner of Indian Affairs, Feb. 19, 1867, IA LR, Dakota Superintendency (D-57).

35. *Washington Daily National Intelligencer*, Oct. 3 and 4, 1837.

36. T. K. Cree to Commissioner of Indian Affairs, Oct. 25, 1873, IA LR, Miscellaneous (C-707).

37. R. B. Morrison to Charles Ewing, Dec. 10, 1874, District of Columbia File, BCIM.

38. Cree to Commissioner of Indian Affairs, Oct. 23, 1873; Little Crow quoted in Newcombe, "A Portion of the American People," p. 88.

39. E. W. Duval to Basil Williamson, Mar. 14, 1828, and Samuel S. Hamilton to Barbour, June 30, 1828, enclosed with Second Auditor's Accounts, No. 11815, Basil Williamson, 1828.

40. W. Tharp to Jilson Dove, Feb. 17, 1829, enclosed with Second Auditor's Accounts, No. 12479, R. A. Forsyth, 1829.

41. Commissioner of Indian Affairs to Second Comptroller, Apr. 24, 1880, IA LS, vol. 169, Finance, pp. 676–77; Second Auditor's Accounts, No. 6964, H. S. Ward, 1858; Second Auditor's Accounts, No. 5916, Sac and Fox, 1882.

42. *Washington Daily National Intelligencer,* Nov. 20, 1837; *Washington Union,* Jan. 6, 1858.

43. Temperance Pledge, Apr. 12, 1858, Records of the Northern Superintendency, Accounts—1858, RG 75, NA.

44. Frank P. Hill to Commissioner of Indian Affairs, Jan. 9, 1880, IA LR, Miscellaneous (H-75); H. E. Mullan to Hill, Jan. 9, 1880, enclosed ibid.

45. Commissioner of Indian Affairs to H. W. Andrews, Jan. 10, 1880, vol. 151, pp. 471–72.

46. Williamson to McKenney, May 12, 1830, IA LR, Miscellaneous.

47. McKenney to [Secretary of War], June 5, 1830, enclosed with Second Auditor's Accounts, No. 14198, Basil Williamson, 1830.

48. Mary A. W. Connor to John Bell, Apr. 4, 1841, IA LR, Miscellaneous (C-1380).

49. Amanda F. Beveridge to Commissioner of Indian Affairs, Jan. 23, 1877, IA LR, Dakota Superintendency (B-107).

50. *Washington Globe,* Feb. 10, 1838.

51. Second Auditor's Accounts, No. 6709, T. J. Mesick, 1882.

52. Second Auditor's Accounts, No. 571, Marie Kolb, 1887; Henry L. Dawes to Marie Kolb, May 16, 1888, enclosed ibid.; Second Auditor's Accounts, No. 4011, Nimrod Jarrett Smith, 1888.

53. Commissioner of Indian Affairs to J. P. Kidder, Jan. 22, 1876, IA LS, vol. 131, p. 19; Commissioner of Indian Affairs to A. M. Scales, May 31, 1876, IA LS, vol. 133, pp. 230–32.

54. M. C. Beveridge to Commissioner of Indian Affairs, June 9, 1890, IA LR, 1890: 17614; Commissioner of Indian Affairs to C. R. A. Scobey, Jan. 23, 1899, IA LS, vol. 293, Finance, p. 232. See also Beveridge to Commissioner of Indian Affairs, May 5 and June 23, 1890, IA LR, 1890: 13922 and 19128.

55. Second Auditor to Commissioner of Indian Affairs, Feb. 10, 1903, IA LR, 1903: 9702.

56. Assistant Commissioner of Indian Affairs to New Continental Hotel, Mades Hotel, Vendôme Hotel, New Capitol Hotel, New National Hotel, Feb. 19, 1914, file No. 19053–1914, General Services 056, Central Files, RG 75, NA.

Chapter VIII: Excursions and Diversions

1. Allen R. Jourdan to Commissioner of Indian Affairs, Apr. 12, 1883, IA LR, 1883:6733.

2. Second Auditor's Accounts, No. 2945, Andrew Porter, 1846; Commissioner of Indian Affairs to Vincent Colyer, May 27, 1870, Letters Received by the Board of Indian Commissioners, vol. 1, p. 59, RG 75, NA.

3. C. H. Emerson to O. H. Browning, Jan. 29, 1868, IA LR, Miscellaneous (E-42-52); Mix to Browning, May 9, 1868, enclosed with Browning to Mix, May 14, 1868, ibid. (I-849).

4. Blackfoot quoted in transcript of council with Crow Indians, Oct. 21, 1873, IA LR, Montana Superintendency (I-824); Thomas L. McKenney, *Sketches of a Tour to the Lakes* (Baltimore, 1827), p. 275.

5. W. Fletcher Johnson, *The Red Record of the Sioux: Life of Sitting Bull and History of the Indian War of 1890–91* (Edgewood, 1891), pp. 233–37.

6. For example, see C. F. Larrabee to Rudolph Forster, Mar. 12, 1907, Letters Sent by Acting Commissioner C. F. Larrabee, 1905–08, p. 162, RG 75, NA; Larrabee to James R. Garfield, Mar. 8, 1907, ibid., p. 160.

7. F. E. Leupp to Merrill E. Gates, Dec. 26, 1906, inserted in Letters Sent by the Board of Indian Commissioners, vol. 14, p. 196, RG 75, NA.

8. "Report of the Council Held by the President of the United States and the Visiting Chiefs of the Sioux and Arapahoe Tribes of Indians," Sept. 26, 1877. Typescript enclosed with Secretary of the Bureau of Catholic Indian Missions to Henry Grotegeers, Nov. 27, 1922, BCIM.

9. *Washington National Intelligencer,* Nov. 11 and 14, 1828.

10. *Washington Union,* Jan. 28, 1858.

11. *Second Annual Report of the Board of Indian Commissioners to the Secretary of the Interior . . . for the Year 1870* (Washington, D.C., 1871), p. 39; *Washington News*, Feb. 20, 1858; unidentified newspaper clipping, Dec. 19, 1851, vol. 8, BAE Scrapbooks, NAA.

12. Poole, *Among the Sioux of Dakota*, pp. 177–79; *Washington Union*, Jan. 28, 1858.

13. *National Intelligencer and Washington Advertiser*, Jan. 10, 1806; Poole, *Among the Sioux of Dakota*, p. 179.

14. *Washington Daily Morning Chronicle*, Sept. 24, 1872.

15. *Niles' Weekly Register*, Aug. 1, 1846.

16. Charles Alexander Eastman, *From the Deep Woods to Civilization: Chapters in the Autobiography of an Indian* (Boston, 1916), pp. 162–63.

17. *Washington Evening Star* and *Washington Daily Morning Chronicle*, March 30, 1863; *Washington National Intelligencer*, Oct. 25, 1828.

18. *Washington National Intelligencer*, Oct. 2 and 4, 1837.

19. Entry for Jan. 4, 1858, William Q. Force diary, Manning, Ferguson, Force Papers, University of Washington. The author wishes to thank Carolyn H. Sung of the Library of Congress for bringing this material to his attention.

20. *Washington Daily Morning Chronicle*, Oct. 31, 1873; *Washington Evening Star*, Jan. 31, 1891.

21. Quinney diary, Adams Papers, Wisconsin State Historical Society. The notice about Bushyhead appeared in the *Washington National Intelligencer*, Jan. 6, 1838.

22. Colton, *Tour of the American Lakes*, pp. 208–10.

23. *National Intelligencer and Washington Advertiser*, July 20, 1804.

24. *Washington National Intelligencer*, Mar. 7, 1822; *Philadelphia Franklin Gazette*, Feb. 11, 1822.

25. *Niles' Weekly Register*, Oct. 7, 1837.

26. *Washington Globe*, Feb. 11, 13, and 15, 1836.

27. Commissioner of Indian Affairs to John Dougherty, Nov. 26, 1837, IA LS, vol. 22, p. 560; Commissioner of Indian Affairs to William Broadus Thompson, Apr. 5, 1850, IA LS, vol. 43, p. 116.

28. *Washington Union*, Jan. 28, 1858; J. F. Minniss to Commissioner of Indian Affairs, Aug. 25, 1883, IA LR, 1883:16219.

29. Turner, *Red Men Calling on the Great White Father*, pp. 137–42; J. A. Stephan to Charles Lusk, Sept. 18, 1884, BCIM; Louis Pfaller, " 'Enemies in '76, Friends in '85'—Sitting Bull and Buffalo Bill," *Prologue: The Journal of the National Archives* 1(Fall 1969):22.

30. Samuel G. Colley to P. T. Barnum, Apr. 4, 1863, printed in *New York Times*, Apr. 7, 1863; George S. Bryan, ed., *Struggles and Triumphs: or, The Life of P. T. Barnum, Written by Himself* (New York, 1927), 2:537.

31. *New York Times*, Apr. 11, 1863; *New York World*, Apr. 14, 1863.

32. Viola, *Lincoln and the Indians*, p. 11.

33. Mix to David H. Wheeler, Aug. 16, 1866, IA LS, vol. 81, p. 188; *Annual Report of the Commissioner of Indian Affairs for 1866*, p. 44.

34. Mrs. Mitchell is quoted in Carolyn H. Sung, "Catherine Mitchell's Letters from Washington, 1806–1812," *Quarterly Journal of the Library of Congress* 34 (July 1977):179–80; Turner, *Red Men Calling on the Great White Father*, pp. 148–49.

35. Margaret Bayard Smith, *First Forty Years of Washington Society*, ed. Gaillard Hunt (New York, 1906), p. 245; John Clagett Proctor, *The Sunday Star*, Sept. 26, 1943.

36. Newcombe, "A Portion of the American People," p. 95 n. 43; Turner, *Red Men Calling on the Great White Father*, pp. 152–53.

37. Viola, "Invitation to Washington," p. 30; Proctor, *The Sunday Star*, June 27, 1943.

38. *Washington Daily Chronicle*, Sept. 16, 1872.

39. Ibid.

40. *New York Times*, Aug. 10, 1872.

41. *Washington Union*, Feb. 26, 1858; Newcombe, "A Portion of the American People," p. 88.

42. Interview with Robert Yellowtail by Joseph Medicine Crow, 1973 (transcript in author's

possession); Robert Summers Yellowtail, Sr., "Robert Summers Yellowtail, Sr. at Crow Fair, 1972," *Black Jack* 2 (1973):1–2, 4.

43. Ten Bears quoted in Staudenraus, ed., *Mr. Lincoln's Washington*, p. 147.

44. Viola, *Indian Legacy of Charles Bird King*, pp. 92–107; [?] to Commissioner of Indian Affairs, [Nov. 1837?]. This letter has not been found, but an entry for it is Miscellaneous 266, volume 10, Registers of Letters Received, RG 75, NA.

45. Commissioner of Indian Affairs to Mayors of Baltimore, Boston, New York, and Philadelphia, Nov. 15, 1837, IA LS, vol. 22, p. 530.

46. Samuel A. Eliot to C. A. Harris, Nov. 25, 1837, IA LR, Miscellaneous (E-80); Richard Fletcher to Joel Poinsett, May 30, 1838, ibid. (F-416); Poinsett to Fletcher, June 11, 1838, IA LS, vol. 24, p. 337.

47. Poole, *Among the Sioux of Dakota*, pp. 160–63.

48. Ibid., pp. 169, 191, 197.

49. Ibid., pp. 192, 208.

Chapter IX: Aches and Ailments

1. William Zimmerman to Chan Gurney, Aug. 14, 1940, file No. 7698-1932, Pine Ridge Agency 056, General Services, Central Files, RG 75, NA.

2. Mix to J. B. Blake, Mar. 17, 1859, IA LS, vol. 60, p. 357; Peter Ronan to Commissioner of Indian Affairs, Apr. 2, 1884, IA LR, 1884:6885; Second Auditor's Accounts, No. 1402, William Marmion, 1884.

3. McKenney to Barbour, Dec. 2, 1825, IA LS, vol. 2, p. 276.

4. See for example, McKenney to Pierre Menard, Feb. 19, 1825, ibid., vol. 1, p. 360; and McKenney to Chilly McIntosh, Dec. 10, 1825, ibid., vol. 2, p. 293.

5. Hodge, *The Indian Tribes of North America* 1:287–88; Second Auditor's Accounts, No. 8015, John B. Blake, 1825; McKenney to Calhoun, Aug. 7, 1824, ibid.

6. McKenney to Cyrus Kingsbury, Nov. 5, 1824, IA LS, vol. 1, pp. 220–21; Second Auditor's Accounts, No. 8373, James Dougherty, 1824.

7. Choctaw Delegation to Calhoun, Feb. 20, 1825, Ratified Treaty File, Treaty 124.

8. James Wallace to McKenney, [Mar. 11, 1825], IA LR, Choctaw Agency; Nathanial P. Causin to McKenney, June 21, 1825, ibid.; McKenney to Causin, June 21, 1825, IA LS, vol. 2, pp. 57–58; James McDonald to McKenney, June 22, 1825, IA LR, Choctaw Agency.

9. Elbert Herring to Thomas C. Scott, Feb. 15, 1832, IA LS, vol. 3, p. 111.

10. W. H. Slater and others to Commissioner of Indian Affairs, Oct. 11, 1873, IA LR, Miscellaneous (C-590); H. R. Clum to J. S. Crouse, Oct. 13, 1873, IA LS, vol. 113, p. 381.

11. Crouse to Secretary of the Interior, Dec. 10, 1873, IA LR, Miscellaneous (C-765).

12. Mix to Orville Browning, Jan. 9, 1868, Report Books, vol. 17, p. 82; L. V. Bogy to Alexander McWilliams, Jan. 28, 1867, IA LS, vol. 82, p. 330.

13. Second Auditor's Accounts, No. 4686, Alexander McWilliams, 1867.

14. McWilliams to Bogy, Feb. 13, 1867, IA LR, Miscellaneous (M-91).

15. Second Auditor's Accounts, No. 7251, Alexander McWilliams, 1868.

16. A. G. Boone to H. M. Teller, May 20, 1878, Henry M. Teller Papers, Western History Collection, Denver Public Museum; Commisioner of Indian Affairs to Secretary of the Interior, Feb. 16, 1878, Records of the Office of the Commissioner of Indian Affairs, Letters Sent, Jan.–Nov. 1878, pp. 25–26.

17. Second Auditor's Accounts, No. 4914, Richard Fields, 1847, and No. 653, Sundry Persons, 1887.

18. A. F. Beveridge per James Lee to John Q. Smith, Feb. 21, 1876, IA LR, Oregon Superintendency (B-275).

19. Second Auditor's Accounts, No. 4322, Luther Webb, 1866.

20. *Statement of disbursements for contingent and miscellaneous purposes for the Indian service, &c.*, House Executive Document 71, 40 Congress, 2 session, serial 1332, p. 206.

21. Ewers, "Chiefs from the Missouri and Mississippi," pp. 13–14.

22. Ibid., p. 15.

23. President's Talk to the Arikara Nation, 1806, SW LS IA, vol. B, p. 200.

24. Joshua Pilcher to William Clark, Feb. 5, 1838, enclosed with Clark to Commissioner of Indian Affairs, Feb. 6, 1838, IA LR, Upper Missouri Agency (C-558); Mix to R. M. Smith, June 18, 1866, IA LS, vol. 80, pp. 406–07; Mix to McWilliams, Jan. 14, 1868, ibid., vol. 85, p. 283.

25. *Washington Union*, Jan. 28 and Mar. 31, 1858; Second Auditor's Accounts, No. 8977, William Dennison, 1858.

26. R. David Edmunds, " 'Nothing Has Been Effected': The Vincennes Treaty of 1792," *Indiana Magazine of History* 74(March 1978):32.

27. H. B. Denman to Commissioner of Indian Affairs, June 15, 1867, enclosing S. D. Hinsman to Denman, May 31, 1867, IA LR, St. Peters Agency (D-359).

28. C. Bush to Commissioner of Indian Affairs, Oct. 24, 1837, IA LR, Upper Missouri Agency (B-339).

29. Fellows D. Pease to Commissioner of Indian Affairs, Nov. 1, 1873, IA LR, Montana Superintendency (P-459); Blackfoot to Grant, Dec. 5, 1873, enclosed with Cree to Grant, Jan. 7, 1874, IA LR, Montana Superintendency (P-45).

30. *Washington National Intelligencer*, July 17, 1824.

31. Samuel Flagg Bemis, *John Quincy Adams and the Union* (New York, 1956), pp. 80–81.

32. Adams, *Diary*, 7:61–62, 106.

33. See for example, Poole, *Among the Sioux of Dakota*, p. 147.

34. Clark to Secretary of War, Sept. 16 and 17, 1812, SW LR, RG 107, NA; Hiram Martin Chittenden, *A History of the American Fur Trade of the Far West* (Palo Alto, 1954), 1:119–24; Finis E. Downing, "With the Ute Peace Delegation of 1863, Across the Plains and at Conejos," *Colorado Magazine* 22(Sept. 1945):199–200.

35. LeRoy R. Hafen, *Broken Hand: The Life of Thomas Fitzpatrick, Mountain Man, Guide, and Indian Agent* (Denver, 1973), p. 305; J. B. Bassett to Commissioner of Indian Affairs, Apr. 22, 1867, IA LR, Chippewa Agency (B-221).

36. Clipping from *Washington Chronicle*, n. d., submitted with bill for advertisement, June 12, 1867, IA LR, Miscellaneous (C-267).

37. J. R. Brown and Benjamin Thompson to Commissioner of Indian Affairs, Mar. 19, 1867, IA LR, St. Peters Agency (T-59); Commissioner of Indian Affairs to Brown, Apr. 24, 1867, IA LS, vol. 83, pp. 19–20; *Monument to Scarlet Crow*, Senate Report 140, 64 Congress, 1 session, serial 6897, vol. 1, p. 1.

38. Moulton, *John Ross, Cherokee Chief*, p. 22.

39. Woodworth Clum, *Apache Agent: The Story of John P. Clum* (Boston, 1936), p. 187.

40. Quinney diary, June 13, 1846, Adams Papers; *Washington National Intelligencer*, Feb. 4, 1868.

41. *Washington Union*, Mar. 31, 1858; *Washington Weekly Star*, Apr. 3, 1858.

42. *Washington Chronicle*, Apr. 8, 1863; *Washington Star*, Apr. 6, 1863.

43. Hodge, *The Indian Tribes of North America* 1:70.

44. Turner, *Red Men Calling on the Great White Father*, p. 143.

45. *Washington, City and Capital* (Washington, D.C., 1937), p. 613.

46. Ibid., p. 614.

47. Moulton, *John Ross, Cherokee Chief*, pp. 195–96; Senate Report 440, 61 Cong., 2 session, serial 5589, vol. C, p. 1.

48. Undated newspaper clipping, Scrapbooks, BCIM.

49. Typescript of page from the diary of W. C. Larwill, MS 4434-a Historical, NAA.

Chapter X: Indian Delegations and the Arts and Sciences

1. James Fenimore Cooper, *Notions of the Americans, Picked Up by a Travelling Bachelor* (Philadelphia, 1828), 2:381, 382; John C. Ewers, "The Emergence of the Plains Indian as the Symbol of the North American Indian," *Annual Report of the Smithsonian Institution . . . 1964* (Washington, D.C., 1965), p. 533.

2. Dorothy Wollon, ed., "Sir Augustus J. Foster and 'The Wild Natives of the Woods,' 1805–1807," *William and Mary Quarterly*, 3d series, 9 (1952): 208.

3. Samuel Mitchell to Catherine Mitchell, Feb. 10 and 19, 1806, Samuel Latham Mitchell Papers, Museum of the City of New York. The author is indebted to Carolyn H. Sung, who brought the Mitchell papers to his attention and who kindly loaned him electrostatic copies of the correspondence between Mr. and Mrs. Mitchell.

4. Mitchell to his wife, Jan. 5, 1806, ibid. See also Ewers, "Chiefs from the Missouri and Mississippi," pp. 15, 18.

5. Wollon, "Sir Augustus J. Foster," pp. 194, 207, 211–14.

6. John Trumbull, *Autobiography, Reminiscences and Letters of John Trumbull, From 1756 to 1841* (New York, 1841), pp. 164–65.

7. Luke Vincent Lockwood, "The St. Memin Indian Portraits," *New-York Historical Society Quarterly Bulletin* 12 (Apr. 1928):3–6.

8. The story of the Peale silhouettes is in Ewers, "Chiefs from the Missouri and Mississippi."

9. McKenney to T. Lewis, Nov. 22, 1820, Office of Indian Trade, Letters Sent, vol. F, p. 81, RG 75, NA. For a comprehensive account of the archives, see Chapter 13, "The Indian Office Museum," in Viola, *Thomas L. McKenney*, pp. 237–50.

10. Viola, *Thomas L. McKenney*, p. 240.

11. For a comprehensive account of the War Department gallery, see Viola, *Indian Legacy of Charles Bird King*.

12. *Niles' Weekly Register*, June 10, 1826; Frances Trollope, *Domestic Manners of the Americans* (London, 1832), 1:314–15; Jonathan Elliot, *Historical Sketches of the Ten Mile Square Forming the District of Columbia* (Washington, D.C., 1830), pp. 167–68.

13. Nicholas Biddle to Daniel Webster, Mar. 2, 1841, SW LR (M-1841).

14. McKenney to John Ridge, Dec. 14, 1825, IA LS, vol. 2, p. 309. Information about the copies is meager. Only one is known to be extant, in the custody of the Wilmette Historical Commission, Wilmette, Illinois. This is a portrait of the Creek delegate Coosa Tustennuggee and was painted by George Cooke, a Washington artist who may have been studying under King at the time.

15. *Metropolitan and Georgetown Commercial Gazette*, Jan. 6, 1827; "Address of Thomas R. Moore to His Constituents," June 27, 1828, printed in the *Louisville Public Advertiser*, July 19, 1828.

16. *Alexandria Gazette*, May 22, 1828, and *Washington National Intelligencer*, May 21, 1828.

17. McKenney to Peter B. Porter, Nov. 3, 1828, IA LS, Vol. 5, p. 169; McKenney to Porter, Dec. 9, 1828, IA LR, Miscellaneous.

18. Atwater, *The Indians of the Northwest*, p. 119; Thomas Donaldson, *The George Catlin Indian Gallery in the U.S. National Museum (Smithsonian Institution) with Memoir and Statistics* (Washington, D.C., 1887), p. 795; Achenamy Oshkosh to the Secretary of the Interior, May 10, 1893, IA LR, 1893:17859.

19. T. Hartley Crawford to the First and Second Chiefs of the Penobscot Tribe of Indians, Apr. 15, 1842, IA LS, vol. 32, p. 109.

20. Viola, *Indian Legacy of Charles Bird King*, p. 113.

21. J. J. Abert, Francis Markoe, and A. O. Dayton to John Bell, June 18, 1841, IA LR, Miscellaneous (N-110); David Cooke to Mary Cooke, June 20, 1842, printed in Thomas Forsythe Nelson, "An Old Letter: Some Forgotten History of the City and the Man—Washington," *Records of the Columbia Historical Society* 14(1911):42–43.

22. *Annual Report of the Board of Regents of the Smithsonian Institution . . . 1858* (Washington, D.C., 1859), pp. 41–42.

23. McKenney to [John Mix Stanley], Mar. 20, 1857, copy enclosed with "Memorial of John M. Stanley praying Congress to purchase his gallery of Indian paintings now deposited in the Smithsonian Institution," Committee of the Library, SEN34A-H10, RG 46, NA.

24. Luke Lea to W. R. Sebastian, Jan. 22, 1853, Report Books, vol. 7, pp. 205–06.

25. *Annual Report of the Board of Regents of the Smithsonian Institution . . . 1865* (Washington, D.C., 1866), pp. 15–16.

26. Josephine Cobb, "Mathew B. Brady's Photographic Gallery in Washington," *Records of the Columbia Historical Society* 53–54(1959):34–36.

27. William C. Sturtevant, "The Earliest Photograph of a North American Indian," entry 372 in R. M. Weatherford, *Catalog 20—Americana* (Columbus, Ohio, 1978), p. 34.

28. John C. Ewers, "Thomas M. Easterly's Pioneer Daguerreotypes of Plains Indians," *Bulletin of the Missouri Historical Society* 24 (July 1968):330–32.

29. "Transatlantic Sketches—Interview of Indians with the 'Great Father,'" *Illustrated London News*, Feb. 13, 1858.

30. Ibid.; Secretary of the Interior to Mix, Mar. 5, 1858, IA LR, Great Nemaha Agency (I-776).

31. *Illustrated London News*, Feb. 13, 1858.

32. *Boyd's Washington and Georgetown Directory, 1858* (Washington, D.C., 1858), p. xxv.

33. Promotional letter of J. E. McClees, [1858?], MS76-112, NAA.

34. Joseph Henry to John W. Denver, Feb. 2, 1859, IA LR, Miscellaneous (H-1368).

35. Henry to Lewis V. Bogy, Feb. 20, 1867, ibid. (H-70).

36. Josephine Cobb, "Alexander Gardner," *Image: Journal of Photography and Motion Pictures of the George Eastman House* (June 1958), p. 133.

37. Ibid., p. 134.

38. Ferdinand V. Hayden, "Prefatory Note," in W. H. Jackson, *Descriptive Catalogue of Photographs of North American Indians* (Washington, D.C., 1877), pp. iii–iv.

39. Cobb, "Brady's Photographic Gallery," pp. 44–45.

40. Hayden to E. P. Smith, Oct. 26, 1875, IA LR, Miscellaneous (H-1456).

41. John Wesley Powell to the Secretary of the Interior, Jan. 24, 1882, BAE Letters Sent, vol. 9, pp. 475–77, NAA; S. J. Kirkwood to Indian Agents, Jan. 27, 1882, Letters Sent, Indian Division, Miscellaneous, vol. 29, p. 52, RG 48, NA.

42. W. H. Holmes to Richard Rathbun, Jan. 15, 1904, BAE Letters Sent, vol. 44, pp. 178–79, NAA; Rathbun to Holmes, Feb. 6, 1904, BAE Letters Received from the Secretary of the Smithsonian Institution, NAA.

43. Benjamin Beveridge to Holmes, Mar. 14, 1908, BAE Letters Received and Sent, NAA.

44. F. W. Hodge to Charles Beveridge, Jan. 11, 1911, ibid.; Mrs. Charles Beveridge to Hodge, Jan. 16, 1911, ibid.; Hodge to James O. Dorsey, Feb. 28, 1911, ibid. These letters are all in the Mrs. Charles Beveridge folder.

45. Charles E. McChesney to Commissioner of Indian Affairs, Dec. 24, 1888, IA LR, 1889:5622. See also James McLaughlin to Commissioner of Indian Affairs, Dec. 17, 1888, IA LR, 1889:5630, and W. W. Anderson to Commissioner of Indian Affairs, Dec. 24, 1888, IA LR, 1888:31830.

46. Second Auditor's Accounts, No. 9009, C. M. Bell, 1879; E. J. Brooks to Secretary of the Interior, June 23, 1879, Report Books, vol. 34, p. 383; Commissioner of Indian Affairs to Supervising Architect of the Treasury Department, Apr. 29, 1880, IA LS, vol. 169, Finance, p. 692; Second Auditor's Accounts, No. 1824, Treasury Department, 1880.

47. Red Cloud to Commissioner of Indian Affairs, Jan. 31, 1882, IA LR, 1882:2474.

48. Mary C. Beveridge to Commissioner of Indian Affairs, Nov. 20, 1891, IA LR, 1891:41619; Frank D. Lewis to Mary C. Beveridge, Oct. 5, 1891, IA LR, 1891:36652.

49. Standing Bear, *My People the Sioux*, p. 169.

50. Viola, *Thomas L. McKenney*, pp. 242–45; Commissioner of Indian Affairs to Joseph Henry, May 2, 1864, IA LS, vol. 74, p. 54.

51. Mallery, "Sign Language Among North American Indians," p. 399.

52. John H. Bowman to Commissioner of Indian Affairs, Sept. 5, 1885, IA LR, 1885:21976; Commissioner of Indian Affairs to Bowman, Oct. 2, 1885, IA LS, vol. 70, Land, p. 365; Nelson Rice to G. Brown Goode, Feb. 28, 1888, IA LR, 1888:7111; Commissioner of Indian Affairs to Rice, Mar. 31, 1888, IA LS, vol. 86, Land, p. 497.

Chapter XI: Epilogue: Delegations in the Twentieth Century

1. Pratt to Commissioner of Indian Affairs, Jan. 13, 1881, IA LR, 1881:757.

2. *Washington Post*, Mar. 3, 1905.

3. Frederick J. Dockstader, *Great American Indians: Profiles in Life and Leadership* (New York, 1977), pp. 111–13.

4. John Old Chief to Commissioner of Indian Affairs, Nov. 26, 1928, file 57545-1928, General Services 056, Central files, RG 75, NA; Alfred C. Smith to Hoover-Curtis Inaugural Committee, Jan. 26, 1929, ibid.

5. Charles Frazier and William Whipple to Charles Curtis, Dec. 12, 1928, ibid.

6. Anton Stephen to Commissioner of Indian Affairs, Jan. 11, 1929, ibid.; Circular 2537, "Inaugural Parade," Jan. 18, 1929, ibid.

7. Whipple to Commissioner of Indian Affairs, Feb. 9, 1929, ibid.; Ellis to Commissioner of Indian Affairs, Feb. 19, 1929, ibid.

8. O. M. Boggess to Commissioner of Indian Affairs, Mar. 13, 1929, ibid.

9. A. R. Snyder to Commissioner of Indian Affairs, Feb. 20, 1929, ibid.; Commissioner of Indian Affairs to J. J. Fitzgerald, Feb. 20, 1929, ibid.; U. S. Grant III to Commissioner of Indian Affairs, Mar. 13, 1929, ibid.

10. For a complete discussion of this interesting story, see John C. Ewers, "A Crow Chief's Tribute to the Unknown Soldier," *American West* 8 (Nov. 1971): 30–35; the prayer is printed on pages 34–35.

11. Wilcomb E. Washburn, *The Indian in America* (New York, 1975), pp. 252–53.

12. Minutes of All-Pueblo Council Meeting, Apr. 6, 1936, John Collier Papers, RG 75, NA.

13. John Collier to Harold Ickes, Apr. 17, 1936, ibid.

14. Charles Kie to Collier, Apr. 17, 1936, and Collier to Kie, Apr. 23, 1936, ibid.

15. Pablo Abeita quoted in *Washington Evening Star*, May 9, 1936.

16. Collier to Pueblo Governors, May 22, 1936, Collier Papers.

17. Transcript of interview with Associated Press, May 15, 1936, ibid.

18. Collier to E. S. Fryer, May 27, 1936, ibid.; Collier to Pueblo Governors, May 22, 1936, ibid.

19. Robert Pennington to author, Apr. 21, 1978. Transcript of interview in author's possession.

20. Interview with members of tribal services staff, Bureau of Indian Affairs, Mar. 5, 1980.

21. Frank Ducheneaux to author, May 11, 1978. Transcript of interview in author's possession.

22. For a summary report of this experiment, see *American Indian Telecommunications Satellite Demonstration Project* (May 1979), a pamphlet prepared by the Lyndon B. Johnson Space Center and available from the National Aeronautics and Space Administration, Washington, D.C.

23. Interview with staff of the Branch of Tribal Services, Bureau of Indian Affairs, Apr. 21, 1978. Transcript in author's possession.

BIBLIOGRAPHY

Records in the National Archives

Record Group 46. Records of the United States Senate.
  Petitions and Memorials, Resolutions of State Legislatures, and Related Documents.
Record Group 48. Records of the Office of the Secretary of the Interior.
  Letters Sent.
  Letters Received.
Record Group 75. Records of the Bureau of Indian Affairs.
  Records of the Board of Indian Commissioners.
    Letters Received, 1869–99.
    Letters Sent, 1870–91.
  Records of the Bureau of Indian Affairs.
    Letters Received, 1824–1907.
    Letters Sent, 1824–1907.
    Report Books, 1838–85.
    Central Classified Files, 1907–60.
    Ratified Treaty File, 1801–68.
    Unratified Treaty File, 1821–69.
    Register of Indians Visiting the Bureau, 1914–17.
  Records of the Office of Indian Trade.
    Letters Sent, 1807–30.
  Records of the Office of the Commissioner of Indian Affairs.
    John Collier Papers.
  Records of the Office of the Secretary of War Relating to Indian Affairs.
    Letters Received, 1800–23.
    Letters Sent, 1800–24.
Record Group 107. Records of the Office of the Secretary of War.
  Letters Received, 1812.
Record Group 217. Records of the United States General Accounting Office.
  Second Auditor's Accounts, 1816–1909.

Records in the Public Record Office of Great Britain

  Colonial Papers, General Series (C.O. 1).
  Colonial Papers, America and West Indies (C.O. 5).

Records in the National Anthropological Archives, Smithsonian Institution

  Records of the Bureau of American Ethnology.
    Letters Received.

Letters Sent.
Numbered Manuscripts.
Photographs.
Scrapbooks of Newspaper Clippings.

Manuscript Collections

John C. Adams Papers. State Historical Society of Wisconsin.
Edward E. Ayer Collection. The Newberry Library.
Bureau of Catholic Indian Missions Archives. Marquette University.
John Hay Papers. Manuscript Division, Library of Congress.
James Madison Papers. Manuscript Division, Library of Congress.
Manning, Ferguson, Force Papers. University of Washington.
Samuel Latham Mitchell Papers. Museum of the City of New York.
Richard H. Pratt Papers. Beinecke Library, Yale University.
George H. Stuart Papers. Manuscript Division, Library of Congress.
Henry M. Teller Papers. Western History Collection, Denver Public Museum.

Published Government Sources

American State Papers: Indian Affairs. 2 vols. Washington, D.C., 1832–34.
Annual Report of the Board of Regents of the Smithsonian Institution . . . 1858. Washington,
D.C., 1859.
Annual Report of the Board of Regents of the Smithsonian Institution . . . 1865. Washington,
D.C., 1866.
Board of Indian Commissioners. *Annual Reports.*
Second Annual Report. Washington, D.C., 1870.
Fourth Annual Report. Washington, D.C., 1872.
Carter, Clarence E., comp. and ed. *The Territorial Papers of the United States.* 26 vols.
Washington, D.C., 1934–62.
Commissioner of Indian Affairs. *Annual Reports.*
1866. House Executive Document 1. 39 Congress, 2 session, serial 1284.
1872. House Executive Document 1, part 5. 42 Congress, 3 session, serial 1560.
1880. House Executive Document 1, part 5. 46 Congress, 3 session, serial 1959.
1881. House Executive Document 1, part 5, volume 2. 47 Congress, 1 session, serial 2018.
1890. House Executive Document 1, part 5, volume 2. 51 Congress, 2 session, serial 2841.
1897. House Document 5. 55 Congress, 2 session, serial 3641.
Funeral and Transportation Expenses of Certain Bois Fort Indians. Senate Report 440, 61
Congress, 2 session, serial 5589.
Kappler, Charles J., comp. and ed. *Indian Affairs: Laws and Treaties.* 2 vols. Washington, D.C.,
1904.
Lyndon B. Johnson Space Center. *American Indian Telecommunications Satellite Demonstration
Project: Summary Report.* Houston, National Aeronautics and Space Administration, 1979.
Mallery, Garrick. "Sign Language Among North American Indians Compared with that Among
Other Peoples and Deaf-Mutes." *First Annual Report of the Bureau of Ethnology to the Secretary
of the Smithsonian Institution, 1879–80.* Washington, D.C., 1881.
Mayo, Robert. *The Treasury Department and Its Various Fiscal Bureaus, Their Origin, Organi-
zation, and Practical Operations, Illustrated: Being a Supplement to the Synopsis of Treasury
Instructions for the Administration of the Revenue Laws Affecting the Commercial and Revenue
System of the United States.* 2 vols., Washington, D.C., 1847.
Monument to Scarlet Crow. Senate Report 140, 64 Congress, 1 session, serial 6897.
National Park Service. *The Pennsylvania Avenue District in United States History: A Report on
the National Significance of Pennsylvania Avenue and Historically Related Environs, Washington,
D.C.* Washington, D.C.: Department of the Interior, 1965.

Statement of disbursements for contingent and miscellaneous purposes for the Indian service, &c.. **221**
House Executive Document 71, 40 Congress, 2 session, serial 5589.
United States Statutes at Large.

Newspapers

Alexandria Gazette
Antigo Journal (Wisconsin)
Arkansas Gazette
Columbian Fountain (Washington, D.C.)
Illustrated London News
Louisville Public Advertiser
Metropolitan and Georgetown Commercial Gazette
National Intelligencer and Washington Advertiser
New York Times
New York Tribune
New York World
Niles' Weekly Register
Philadelphia Franklin Gazette
Pittsburgh Gazette
Washington Chronicle
Washington Daily Morning Chronicle
Washington Daily National Intelligencer
Washington Evening Star
Washington Gazette
Washington Globe
Washington National Republican
Washington Post
Washington Union
Washington Weekly Star

Contemporary Published Works

Adams, Charles Francis, ed. *Memoirs of John Quincy Adams, Comprising Portions of His Diary from 1795 to 1848.* 12 vols. Philadelphia, 1874.

Atwater, Caleb. *The Indians of the Northwest, Their Manners, Customs, &c. &c. or Remarks Made on a Tour to Prairie du Chien and Thence to Washington City in 1829.* Columbus, Ohio, 1850.

Barnum, P. T. *Struggles and Triumphs: or, The Life of P. T. Barnum, Written By Himself.* Edited by George S. Bryan. 2 vols. New York, 1927.

Bigelow, John, comp. and ed. *The Works of Benjamin Franklin, Including the Private as Well as the Official and Scientific Correspondence Together with the Unmutilated and Correct Version of the Autobiography.* 12 vols. New York and London, 1904.

Boyd, William H., comp. *Boyd's Washington and Georgetown Directory, Containing a Business Directory of Washington, Georgetown, and Alexandria, Congressional and Department Directory, and an Appendix of Much Useful Information.* Washington, D.C., 1860.

Collections of the New-York Historical Society for the Year 1923. Vol. 7, *The Letters and Papers of Cadwallader Colden, 1765–1775.* New York, 1922.

Colton, Calvin. *Tour of the American Lakes, and Among the Indians of the North-West Territory, in 1830: Disclosing the Character and Prospects of the Indian Race.* 2 vols. London, 1833.

Cooper, James Fenimore. *Notions of the Americans, Picked Up By a Travelling Bachelor.* 2 vols. Philadelphia, 1828.

Downes, William Howe. "Mr. Dallin's Indian Sculptures." *Scribner's Magazine* 57 (June 1915):779–82.

Eastman, Charles A. *From the Deep Woods to Civilization: Chapters in the Autobiography of an Indian.* Boston, 1916.

Elliot, Jonathan. *Historical Sketches of the Ten Miles Square Forming the District of Columbia; with a Picture of Washington, Describing Objects of General Interest or Curiosity at the Metropolis of the Union.* Washington, D.C., 1830.

Ellis, Richard N., and Charlie R. Steen, eds. "An Indian Delegation in France, 1725." *Journal of the Illinois State Historical Society* 67 (Sept. 1974):385–405. Translation of a French report.

Feiler, Seymour, trans. and ed. *Jean-Bernard Bossu's Travels in the Interior of North America, 1751–1762.* Norman, 1962.

Hayden, Ferdinand V. "Prefatory Note." *Descriptive Catalogue of Photographs of North American Indians* by W. H. Jackson, Miscellaneous Publications, No. 9. Washington, D.C., 1877.

Howard, Oliver O. *My Life and Experiences Among Our Hostile Indians, a Record of Personal Observations, Adventures, and Campaigns Among the Indians of the Great West with some Account of Their Life, Habits, Traits, Religion, Ceremonies, Dress, Savage Instincts, and Customs in Peace and War.* Hartford, Conn., 1907.

Humfreville, J. Lee. *Twenty Years Among Our Savage Indians.* Hartford, Conn., 1897.

Jackson, Donald, ed. *Black Hawk (Ma-Ka-Tai-Me-She-Kia-Kiak): An Autobiography.* Urbana, 1955.

Kingsbury, Susan Myra, ed. *The Records of the Virginia Company of London.* 4 vols. Washington, D.C., 1935.

Lanman, Charles. *Recollections of Curious Characters and Pleasant Places.* Edinburgh, 1881.

McKenney, Thomas L. *Sketches of a Tour to the Lakes, of the Character and Customs of the Chippeway Indians, and of Incidents Connected with the Treaty of Fond Du Lac.* Baltimore, 1827.

———, and James Hall. *The Indian Tribes of North America with Biographical Sketches and Anecdotes of the Principal Chiefs.* Edited by Frederick Webb Hodge. 3 vols. Edinburgh, 1933.

Nabokov, Peter, ed. *Native American Testimony: An Anthology of Indian and White Relations, First Encounter to Dispossession.* New York, 1978.

Neihardt, John G. *Black Elk Speaks: Being the Life Story of a Holy Man of the Oglala Sioux as Told to John G. Neihardt.* New York, 1932.

Nelson, Thomas Forsythe. "An Old Letter: Some Forgotten History of the City and the Man—Washington." *Records of the Columbia Historical Society* 14 (Washington, D.C., 1911):25–48.

Poole, D. C. *Among the Sioux of Dakota: Eighteen Months Experience as an Indian Agent.* New York, 1881.

Poore, Benjamin Perley. *Perley's Reminiscences.* 2 vols. Philadelphia, 1886.

Schoolcraft, Henry R. *Personal Memoirs of a Residence of Thirty Years with the Indian Tribes on the American Frontier: with Brief Notices of Passing Events, Facts, and Opinions, A. D. 1812 to A. D. 1842.* Philadelphia, 1851.

Smith, Margaret Bayard. *The First Forty Years of Washington Society.* Edited by Gaillard Hunt. New York, 1906.

Standing Bear, Luther. *My People the Sioux.* Edited by E. A. Brininstool. Boston and New York, 1928.

Thacher, James. *A Military Journal During the American Revolutionary War, from 1775 to 1783; Describing Interesting Events and Transactions of this Period; with Numerous Facts and Anecdotes, from the Original Manuscript.* 2d edition. Boston, 1827.

Thwaites, Reuben Gold, ed. *The Jesuit Relations and Allied Documents: Travels and Explorations of the Jesuit Missionaries in New France, 1610–1791.* 73 vols. Cleveland, 1896–1901.

Trollope, Frances. *Domestic Manners of the Americans.* 2 vols. London, 1832.

Trumbull, John. *Autobiography, Reminiscences and Letters of John Trumbull, From 1756 to 1841.* New York, 1841.

Williams, Samuel Cole, ed. *Lieut. Henry Timberlake's Memoirs, 1756–1765.* Johnson City, Tenn., 1927. Originally published as *The Memoirs of Lieut. Henry Timberlake, (Who accompanied the Three Cherokee Indians to England in the Year 1762) Containing Whatever he observed remarkable, or worthy of public Notice, during his Travels to and from that Nation;*

wherein the Country, Government, Genius, and Customs of the Inhabitants, are authentically described. Also the Principal Occurrences during their Residence in London. London, 1765.

Wollon, Dorothy, ed. "Sir Augustus J. Foster and 'The Wild Natives of the Woods,' 1805–1807." *William and Mary Quarterly*, 3d series 9 (Apr. 1952):191–214.

Yellowtail, Robert Summers, Sr. "Robert Summers Yellowtail, Sr. at Crow Fair, 1972." *Black Jack* 2 (Albuquerque, 1973).

Secondary Works

Bemis, Samuel Flagg. *John Quincy Adams and the Union.* New York, 1956.

Billington, Ray Allen. *Westward Expansion: A History of the American Frontier.* 4th edition. New York, 1974.

Bond, Richmond P. *Queen Anne's American Kings.* New York, 1974.

Chittenden, Hiram Martin. *The American Fur Trade of the Far West.* 3 vols. New York, 1902. Reprint, Palo Alto, 1954.

Clum, Woodworth. *Apache Agent: The Story of John P. Clum.* Boston, 1936.

Cobb, Josephine. "Alexander Gardner." *Image: Journal of Photography and Motion Pictures of the George Eastman House* 7 (June 1958):124–36.

————. "Mathew Brady's Photographic Gallery in Washington." *Records of the Columbia Historical Society* 53–54 (Washington, D.C., 1959):28–69.

DeMallie, Raymond J. "Touching the Pen: Plains Indian Treaty Councils in Ethnohistorical Perspective." *Ethnicity on the Great Plains.* Edited by Frederick C. Luebke. Lincoln, 1980.

DeRosier, Arthur H., Jr. *The Removal of the Choctaw Indians.* Knoxville, 1970.

Dockstader, Frederick J. *Great American Indians: Profiles in Life and Leadership.* New York, 1977.

Donaldson, Thomas. *The George Catlin Indian Gallery in the U.S. National Museum (Smithsonian Institution), with Memoir and Statistics.* Washington, D.C., 1887.

Downing, Finis E. "With the Ute Peace Delegation of 1863, Across the Plains and at Conjeos." *Colorado Magazine* 22 (Sept. 1945):193–205.

Edmunds, R. David. " 'Nothing Has Been Effected': The Vincennes Treaty of 1792." *Indiana Magazine of History* 74 (Mar. 1978):23–35.

Ewers, John C. " 'Chiefs from the Missouri and Mississippi' and Peale's Silhouettes of 1806." *Smithsonian Journal of History* 1 (Spring 1966):1–26.

————. "A Crow Chief's Tribute to the Unknown Soldier." *The American West* 8 (Nov. 1971):30–35.

————. "The Emergence of the Plains Indian as the Symbol of the North American Indian." *Annual Report of the Board of Regents of the Smithsonian Institution . . . 1964.* Washington, D.C., 1965, pp. 531–44.

————. "Symbols of Chiefly Authority in Spanish Louisiana." *The Spanish in the Mississippi Valley, 1762–1804.* Edited by John Francis McDermott. Urbana, 1974.

————. "Thomas M. Easterly's Pioneer Daguerreotypes of Plains Indians." *Bulletin of the Missouri Historical Society* 24 (July 1968):329–339.

————. "When the Light Shone in Washington." *Montana, the Magazine of Western History* 6 (Oct. 1956):2–11. Reprinted in John C. Ewers, *Indian Life on the Upper Missouri.* Norman, 1968, pp. 75–90.

Foreman, Carolyn Thomas. *Indians Abroad, 1493–1938.* Norman, 1943.

Hafen, LeRoy R. *Broken Hand: The Life of Thomas Fitzpatrick, Mountain Man, Guide, and Indian Agent.* Revised edition. Denver, 1973.

Hagan, William T. *The Sac and Fox Indians.* Norman, 1958.

Hill, Edward E. *The Office of Indian Affairs, 1824–1880: Historical Sketches.* New York, 1974.

Holm, Thomas M. "The Cherokee Delegates and the Opposition to the Allotment of Indian Lands." Master's thesis, University of Oklahoma, 1974.

Jacobs, Wilbur R. *Diplomacy and Indian Gifts: Anglo-French Rivalry Along the Ohio and Northwest Frontiers, 1748–1763.* Palo Alto, 1950.

224

Johnson, W. Fletcher. *The Red Record of the Sioux: Life of Sitting Bull and History of the Indian War of 1890–91*. Philadelphia, 1891.

Kvasnicka, Robert M. "From the Wilderness to Washington—and Back Again: The Story of the Chippewa Delegation of 1855." *Kansas Quarterly* 3 (Fall 1971):56–63.

Lockwood, Luke Vincent. "The St. Memin Indian Portraits." *New-York Historical Society Quarterly Bulletin* 12 (Apr. 1928):3–26.

Madaus, H. Michael. "Peace and Friendship: Diplomatic Gifts to the Indians." *Lore* 22 (Winter 1971, Spring, Summer 1972):33–42, 68–78, 106–112.

Meyer, Roy W. *The Village Indians of the Upper Missouri: The Mandans, Hidatsas, and Arikaras*. Lincoln, 1977.

Mochon, Marion Johnson. "Stockbridge-Munsee Cultural Adaptations: 'Assimilated Indians.' " *Proceedings of the American Philosophical Society* 112 (June 1968):182–219.

Moulton, Gary E. *John Ross, Cherokee Chief*. Athens, 1978.

Newcombe, Barbara T. " 'A Portion of the American People': The Sioux Sign a Treaty in Washington in 1858." *Minnesota History* 45 (Fall 1976):82–96.

Pfaller, Louis. " 'Enemies in '76, Friends in '85'—Sitting Bull and Buffalo Bill." *Prologue: The Journal of the National Archives* 1 (Fall 1969):16–31.

Prucha, Francis Paul. *American Indian Policy in Crisis: Christian Reformers and the Indian, 1865–1900*. Norman, 1976.

———. *Indian Peace Medals in American History*. Madison, 1971.

———. *American Indian Policy in the Formative Years: The Indian Trade and Intercourse Acts, 1790–1834*. Cambridge, Mass. 1962.

Shapard, John, "A Federally-Funded Wedding and Honeymoon." *Arizona Republic* (July 15, 1979).

Smith, Jane F., and Robert M. Kvasnicka, eds. *Indian-White Relations: A Persistent Paradox*. Washington, D.C., 1976.

Staudenraus, P. J., ed. *Mr. Lincoln's Washington: Selections from the Writings of Noah Brooks, Civil War Correspondent*. New York, 1967.

Stewart, Edgar I. *Custer's Luck*. Norman, 1955.

Stone, William L. *The Life and Times of Sa-Go-Ye-Wat-Ha, or Red Jacket*. New York, 1841.

Sturtevant, William C. "The Earliest Photograph of a North American Indian." *Catalog 20—Americana* by R. M. Weatherford. Columbus, Ohio, 1978.

Sung, Carolyn Hoover. "Catherine Mitchill's Letters from Washington, 1806–1812." *Quarterly Journal of the Library of Congress* 34 (July 1977):171–89.

Turner, Katherine C. *Red Men Calling on the Great White Father*. Norman, 1951.

Viola, Herman J. *The Indian Legacy of Charles Bird King*. Washington, D.C. 1976.

———. "Invitation to Washington—a Bid for Peace." *American West* 9 (Jan. 1972):18–31.

———. *Lincoln and the Indians*. Historical Bulletin 31. Madison: Lincoln Fellowship of Wisconsin, 1976.

———. *Thomas L. McKenney: Architect of America's Early Indian Policy, 1816–1830*. Chicago, 1974.

Washburn, Wilcomb E. *The Indian in America*. New York, 1975.

White, Leonard D. *The Jeffersonians: A Study in Administrative History, 1801–1829*. New York, 1951.

Wilkins, Thurman. *Cherokee Tragedy: The Story of the Ridge Family and the Decimation of a People*. New York, 1970.

Interviews

Interview with Robert Yellowtail of the Crow Tribe conducted in 1973 by Joseph Medicine Crow, Tribal Historian. Transcript in author's possession.

Interview with Robert Pennington, John "Bud" Shapard, Arlene Brown, Robert M. Farring, Jr., Dennis Petersen, and Mitchell L. Bush, Jr., Branch of Tribal Services, Bureau of Indian Affairs, April 21, 1978.

Interview with Henry Old Coyote, Senate Staff, Select Committee on Indian Affairs, April 26, 1978.

Interview with Frank Ducheneaux, Jr., Special Counsel on Indian Affairs, House of Representatives Interior and Insular Affairs Committee, May 11, 1978.

Interview with Leslie M. Gay, Branch of Tribal Services, Bureau of Indian Affairs, May 25, 1978.

Interview with Robert Pennington, Michael Smith, Evelyn Pickett, James Thomas, Robert Farring, Jr., and Chizu Toda, Branch of Tribal Serivices, Bureau of Indian Affairs, March 5, 1980.

Seminar Papers

Papers prepared for graduate seminar, "Research Seminar in the Use of Archival Resources," Department of Library Science, Catholic University, directed by the author. Typescripts in the author's possession.

Clarke, Devereux. "The Red Man's Grand Tour: The Pawnee Delegation of 1858." 1975.

Elliot, Joanne. "A Picturesque Touch of Color: Theodore Roosevelt and the Delegation of 1905." 1975.

Griffiths, Kent R. "And High Unconquered Pride: The Black Hawk Delegation of 1833." 1975.

Hartman, Elizabeth Elaine. "In the Wrong Place at the Wrong Time: The Cherokee Treaty for Peace, 1866." 1975.

Heller, Rebecca A. "The Long Path to the Great Father: The Delegation of 1812." 1975.

Larson, Signe. "John W. Quinney: An Episode." 1977.

MacKnight, Robert L. "The Texas Indian Visit to Washington, D.C., 1846." 1975.

Moon, Calista. "With Their Consent: The Ponca Delegation of 1877." 1975.

Newcombe, Barbara T. "A Portion of the American People: The Santee Sioux Delegation of 1858." 1975.

Piala, Vanessa J. "John C. Adams: Visitor to Washington, 1876." 1977.

Stokes, Erika E. "Long Road to the Treaty Ground: The Ute Delegation of 1863." 1975.

INDEX

This book was produced by the Smithsonian Institution Press, Washington, D.C.
Printed by Braun Brumfield, Inc.
Set in VIP Electra by Monotype Composition Co., Inc.
The text paper is 60 pound Warren's "66"
with Holliston Roxite "C" linen finish cover
and 80 pound Natural Endleaf endpapers.
Designed by Stephen Kraft.